# DC★SUPER FRIENDS

## HEAD OF THE CLASS

**SHOLLY FISCH**
Writer

**J. BONE**
Original Series Covers

**TRAVIS LA** RIANO
Letterers

**HEROIC AGE**
Colors

Rachel Gluckstern Editor-Original Series
Bob Harras Group Editor-Collected Editions
Anton Kawasaki Editor
Robbin Brosterman Design Director-Books

DC COMICS

Diane Nelson President
Dan DiDio and Jim Lee Co-Publishers
Geoff Johns Chief Creative Officer
Patrick Caldon EVP-Finance and Administration
John Rood EVP-Sales, Marketing and Business Development
Amy Genkins SVP-Business and Legal Affairs
Steve Rotterdam SVP-Sales and Marketing
John Cunningham VP-Marketing
Terri Cunningham VP-Managing Editor
Alison Gill VP-Manufacturing
David Hyde VP-Publicity
Sue Pohja VP-Book Trade Sales
Alysse Soll VP-Advertising and Custom Publishing
Bob Wayne VP-Sales
Mark Chiarello Art Director

SUPER FRIENDS: HEAD OF THE CLASS



DC Comics, 1700 Broadway, New York, NY 10019
A Warner Bros. Entertainment Company
Printed by Quad/Graphics, Dubuque, IA, USA 11/3/10. First Printing.
ISBN: 978-1-4012-2912-2

SUSTAINABLE FORESTRY INITIATIVE
Certified Chain of Custody
Promoting Sustainable Forest Management

Fiber used in this product line meets the sourcing requirements of the SFI program.
www.sfiprogram.org PWC-SFICOC-260

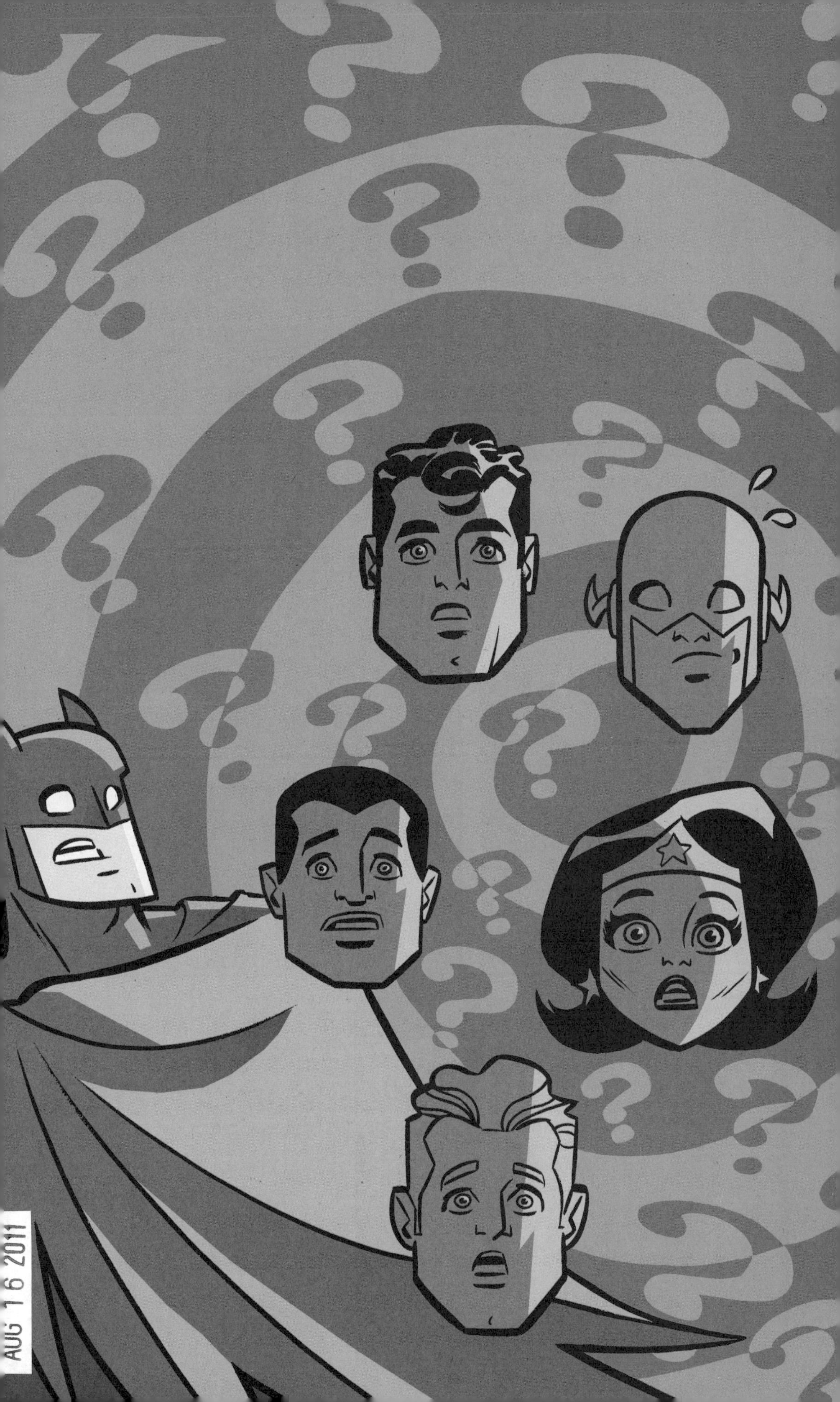

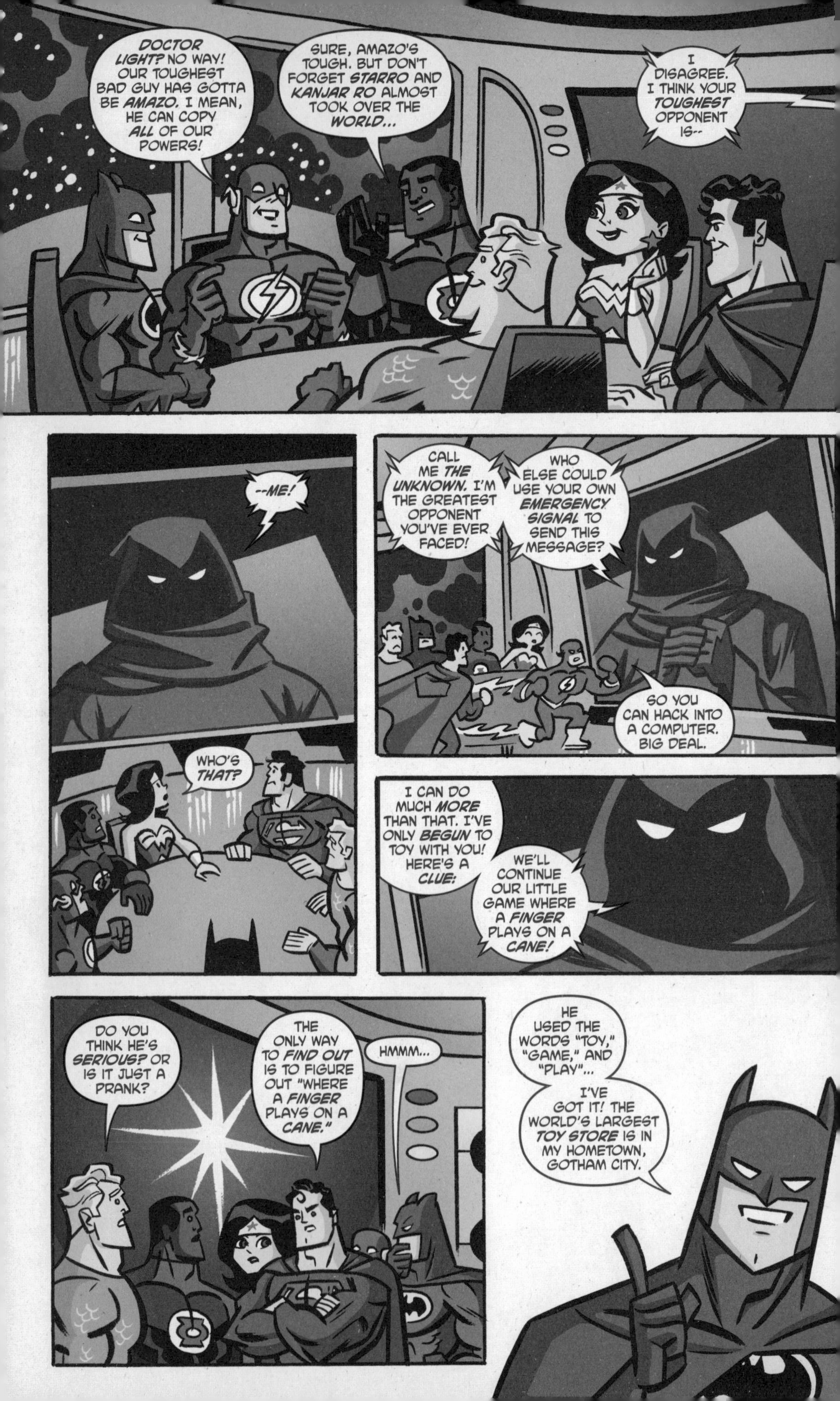
DOCTOR LIGHT? NO WAY! OUR TOUGHEST BAD GUY HAS GOTTA BE AMAZO. I MEAN, HE CAN COPY ALL OF OUR POWERS!
SURE, AMAZO'S TOUGH. BUT DON'T FORGET STARRO AND KANJAR RO ALMOST TOOK OVER THE WORLD...
I DISAGREE. I THINK YOUR TOUGHEST OPPONENT IS--
--ME!
CALL ME THE UNKNOWN. I'M THE GREATEST OPPONENT YOU'VE EVER FACED!
WHO ELSE COULD USE YOUR OWN EMERGENCY SIGNAL TO SEND THIS MESSAGE?
SO YOU CAN HACK INTO A COMPUTER. BIG DEAL.
WHO'S THAT?
I CAN DO MUCH MORE THAN THAT. I'VE ONLY BEGUN TO TOY WITH YOU! HERE'S A CLUE:
WE'LL CONTINUE OUR LITTLE GAME WHERE A FINGER PLAYS ON A CANE!
DO YOU THINK HE'S SERIOUS? OR IS IT JUST A PRANK?
THE ONLY WAY TO FIND OUT IS TO FIGURE OUT "WHERE A FINGER PLAYS ON A CANE."
HMMM...
HE USED THE WORDS "TOY," "GAME," AND "PLAY"...
I'VE GOT IT! THE WORLD'S LARGEST TOY STORE IS IN MY HOMETOWN, GOTHAM CITY.

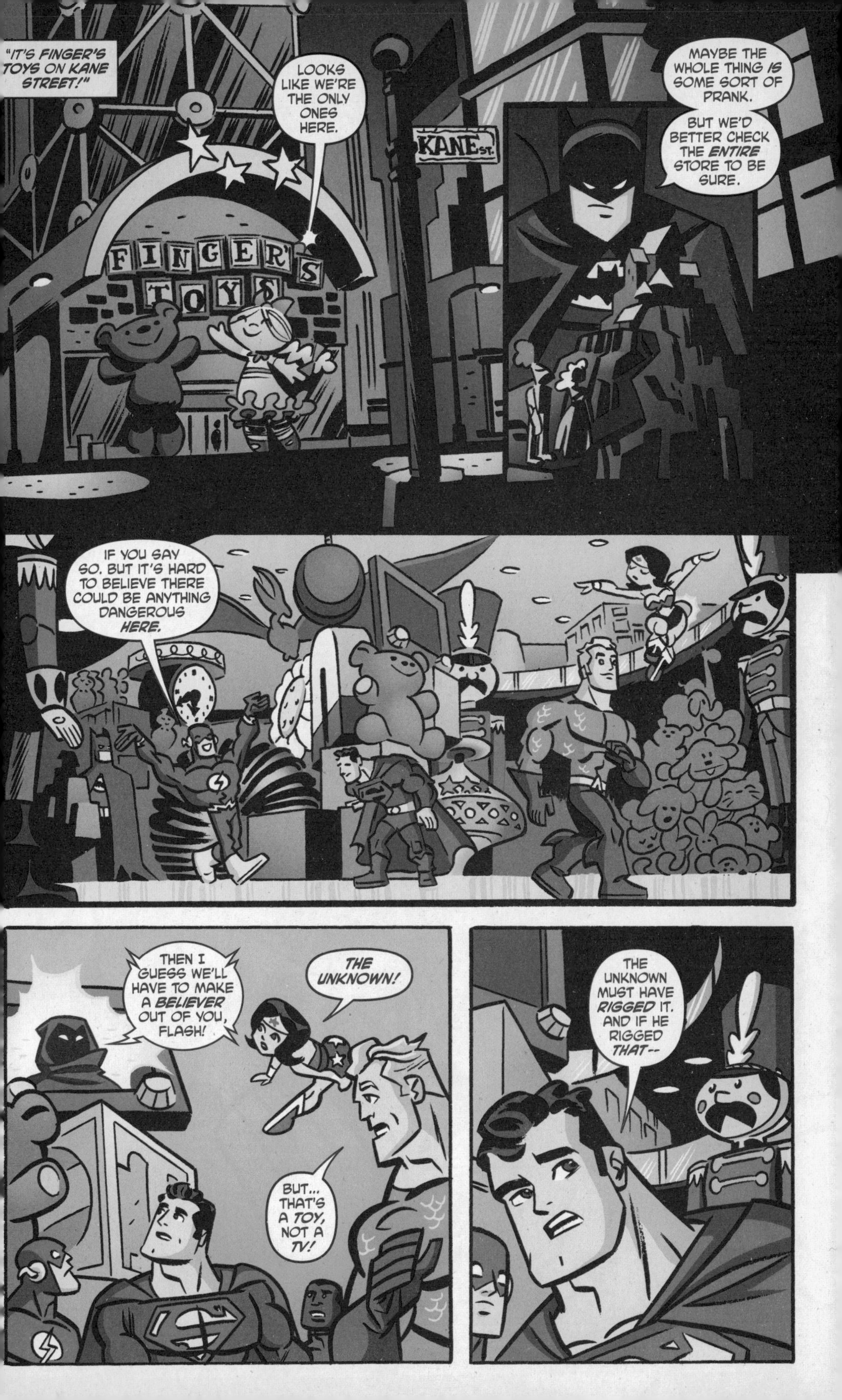
"IT'S FINGER'S TOYS ON KANE STREET!"
LOOKS LIKE WE'RE THE ONLY ONES HERE.
FINGER'S TOYS
KANE ST.
MAYBE THE WHOLE THING IS SOME SORT OF PRANK.
BUT WE'D BETTER CHECK THE ENTIRE STORE TO BE SURE.
IF YOU SAY SO. BUT IT'S HARD TO BELIEVE THERE COULD BE ANYTHING DANGEROUS HERE.
THEN I GUESS WE'LL HAVE TO MAKE A BELIEVER OUT OF YOU, FLASH!
THE UNKNOWN!
BUT... THAT'S A TOY, NOT A TV!
THE UNKNOWN MUST HAVE RIGGED IT. AND IF HE RIGGED THAT--

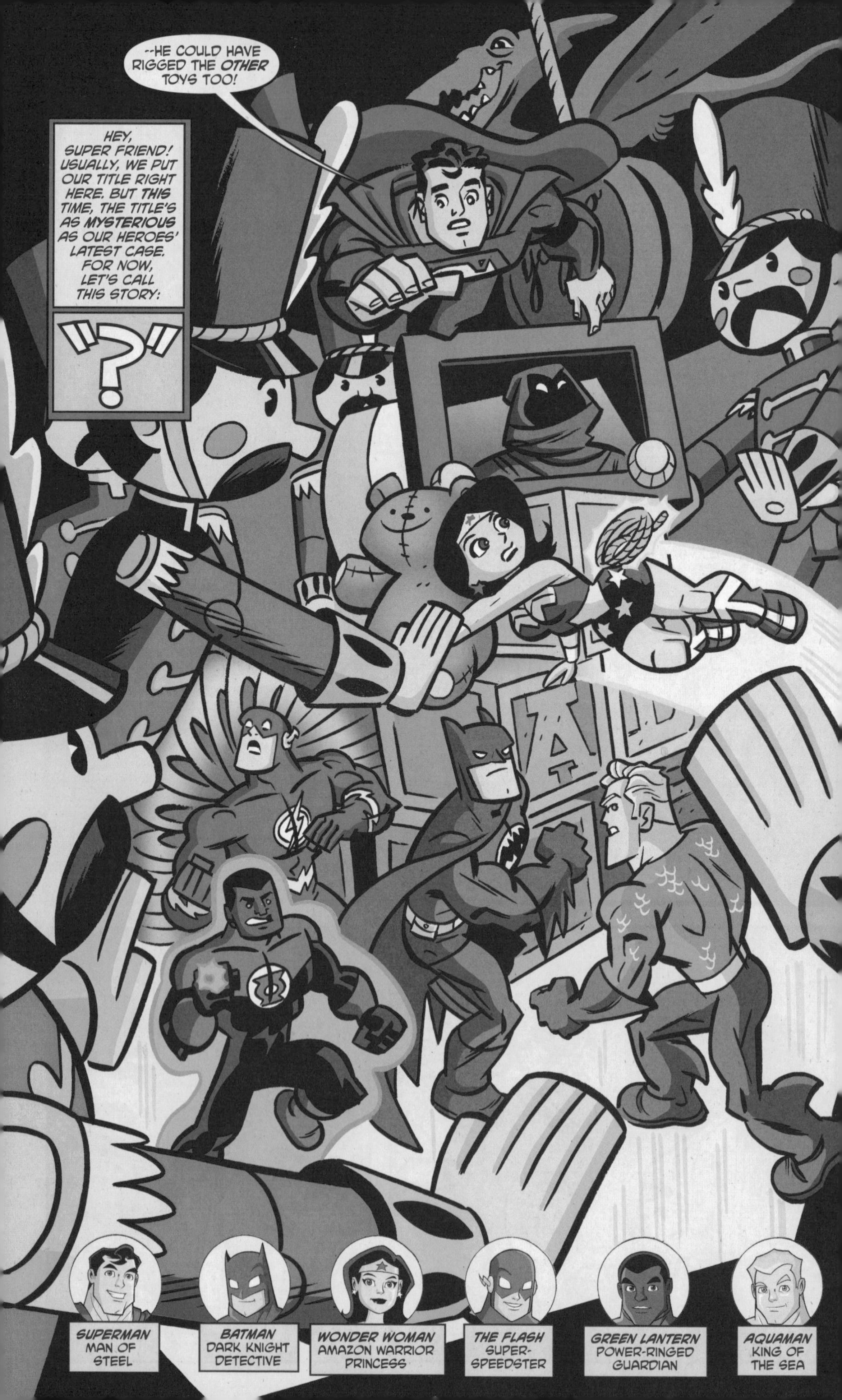
--HE COULD HAVE RIGGED THE OTHER TOYS TOO!
HEY, SUPER FRIEND! USUALLY, WE PUT OUR TITLE RIGHT HERE. BUT THIS TIME, THE TITLE'S AS MYSTERIOUS AS OUR HEROES' LATEST CASE. FOR NOW, LET'S CALL THIS STORY:
"?"
SUPERMAN MAN OF STEEL
BATMAN DARK KNIGHT DETECTIVE
WONDER WOMAN AMAZON WARRIOR PRINCESS
THE FLASH SUPER-SPEEDSTER
GREEN LANTERN POWER-RINGED GUARDIAN
AQUAMAN KING OF THE SEA

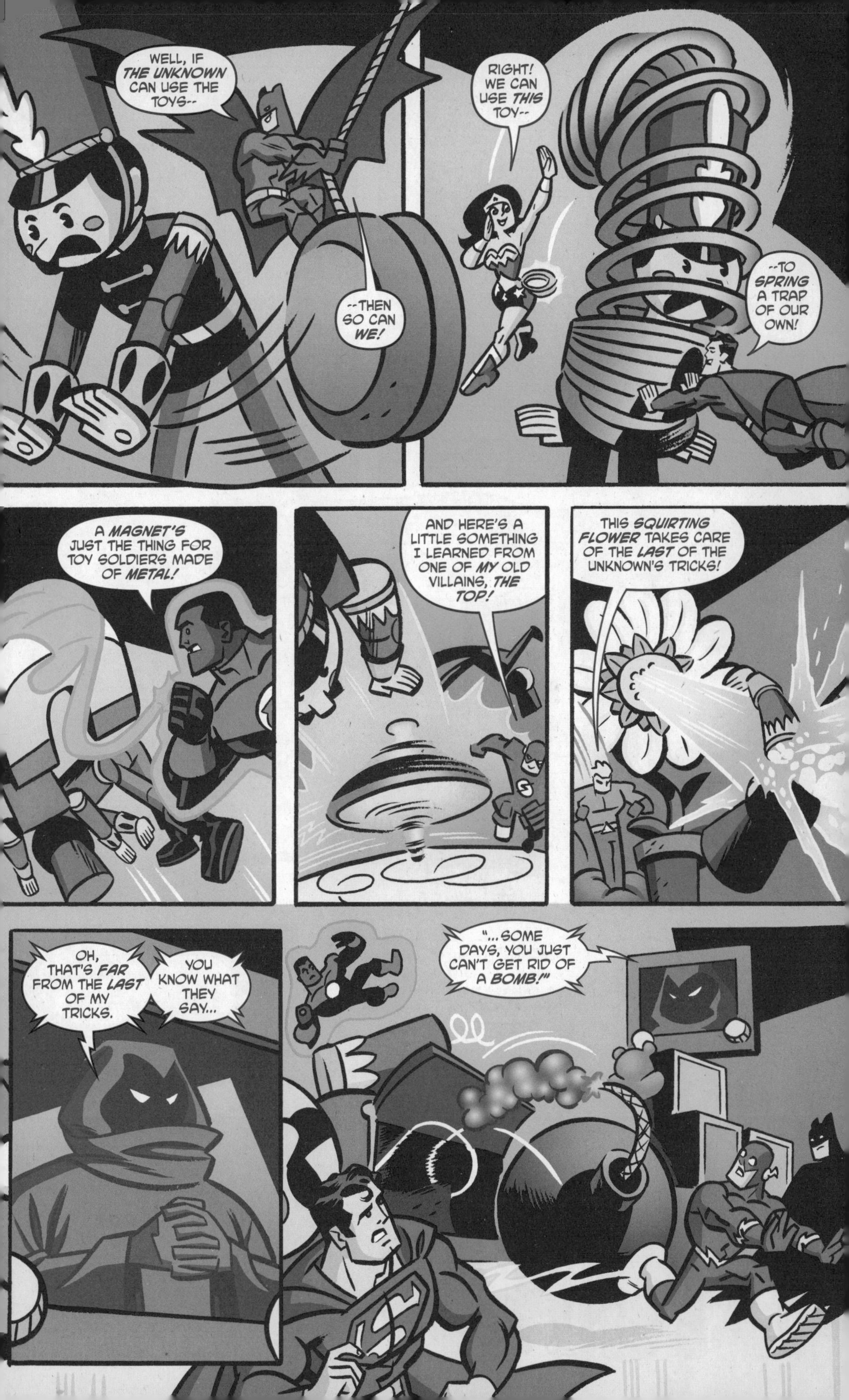
WELL, IF THE UNKNOWN CAN USE THE TOYS--
--THEN SO CAN WE!
RIGHT! WE CAN USE THIS TOY--
--TO SPRING A TRAP OF OUR OWN!
A MAGNET'S JUST THE THING FOR TOY SOLDIERS MADE OF METAL!
AND HERE'S A LITTLE SOMETHING I LEARNED FROM ONE OF MY OLD VILLAINS, THE TOP!
THIS SQUIRTING FLOWER TAKES CARE OF THE LAST OF THE UNKNOWN'S TRICKS!
OH, THAT'S FAR FROM THE LAST OF MY TRICKS.
YOU KNOW WHAT THEY SAY...
"...SOME DAYS, YOU JUST CAN'T GET RID OF A BOMB!"

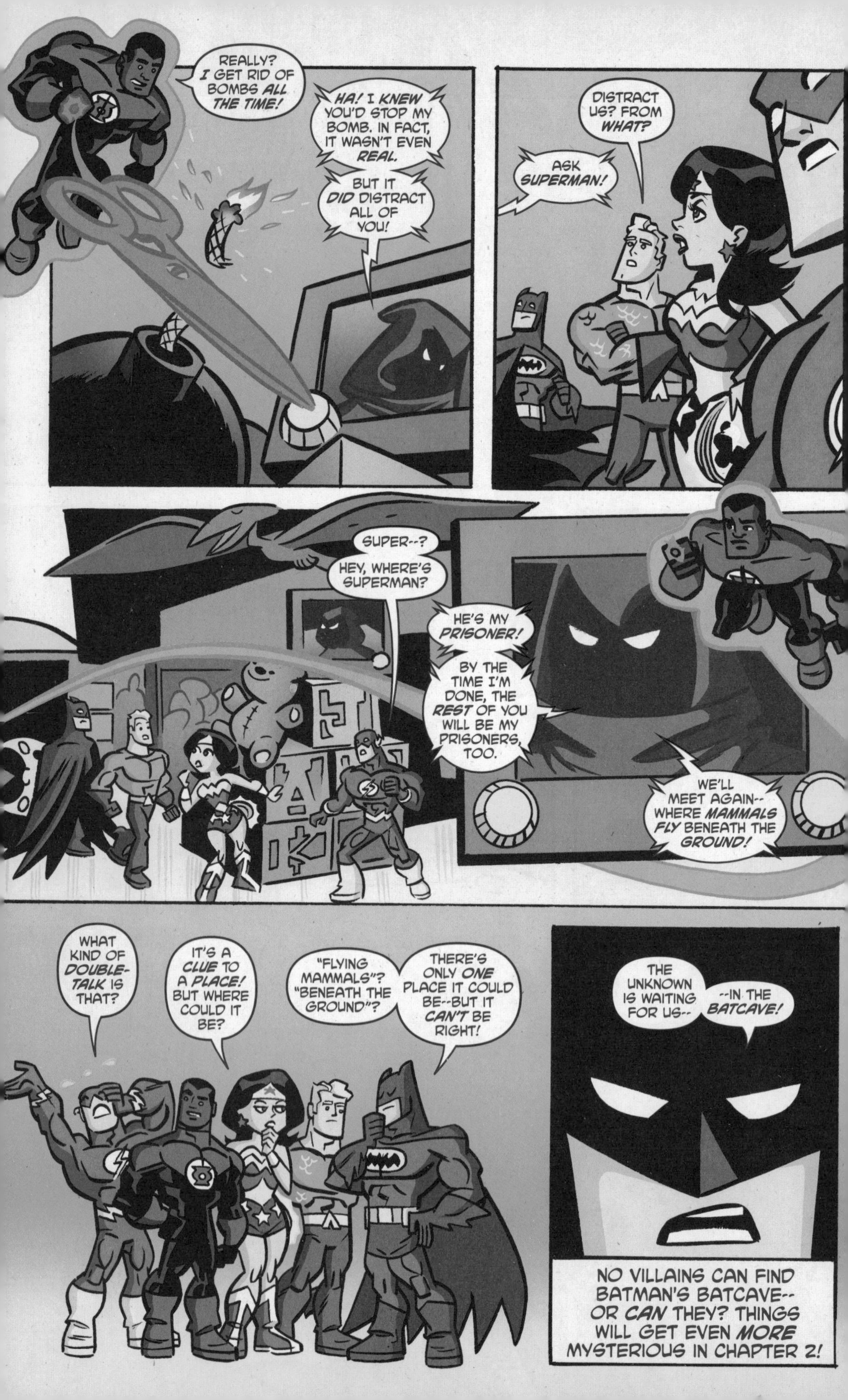
REALLY? I GET RID OF BOMBS ALL THE TIME!
HA! I KNEW YOU'D STOP MY BOMB. IN FACT, IT WASN'T EVEN REAL.
BUT IT DID DISTRACT ALL OF YOU!
DISTRACT US? FROM WHAT?
ASK SUPERMAN!
SUPER--?
HEY, WHERE'S SUPERMAN?
HE'S MY PRISONER!
BY THE TIME I'M DONE, THE REST OF YOU WILL BE MY PRISONERS, TOO.
WE'LL MEET AGAIN-- WHERE MAMMALS FLY BENEATH THE GROUND!
WHAT KIND OF DOUBLE-TALK IS THAT?
IT'S A CLUE TO A PLACE! BUT WHERE COULD IT BE?
"FLYING MAMMALS"? "BENEATH THE GROUND"?
THERE'S ONLY ONE PLACE IT COULD BE--BUT IT CAN'T BE RIGHT!
THE UNKNOWN IS WAITING FOR US--
--IN THE BATCAVE!
NO VILLAINS CAN FIND BATMAN'S BATCAVE-- OR CAN THEY? THINGS WILL GET EVEN MORE MYSTERIOUS IN CHAPTER 2!

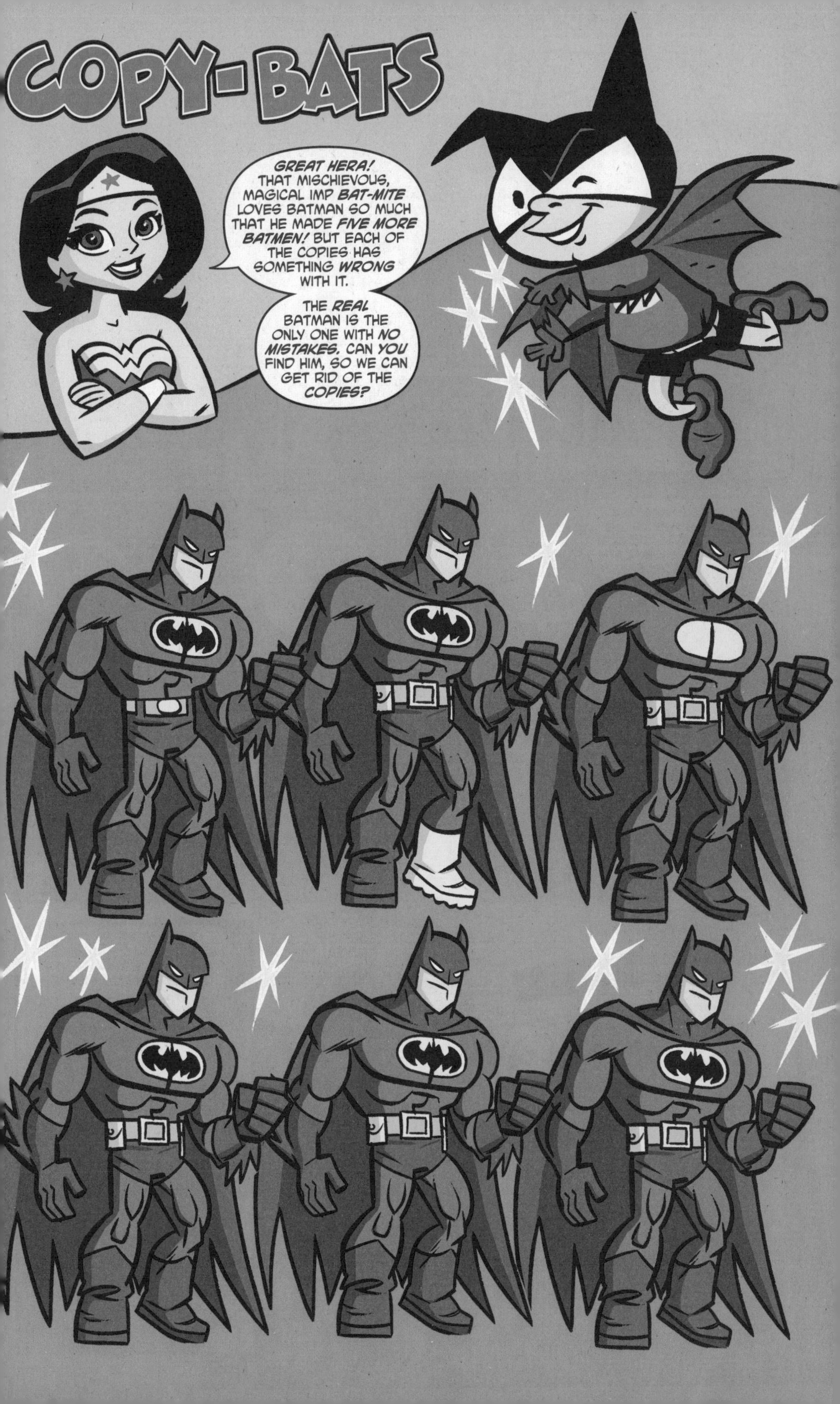
COPY-BATS
GREAT HERA! THAT MISCHIEVOUS, MAGICAL IMP BAT-MITE LOVES BATMAN SO MUCH THAT HE MADE FIVE MORE BATMEN! BUT EACH OF THE COPIES HAS SOMETHING WRONG WITH IT.
THE REAL BATMAN IS THE ONLY ONE WITH NO MISTAKES. CAN YOU FIND HIM, SO WE CAN GET RID OF THE COPIES?

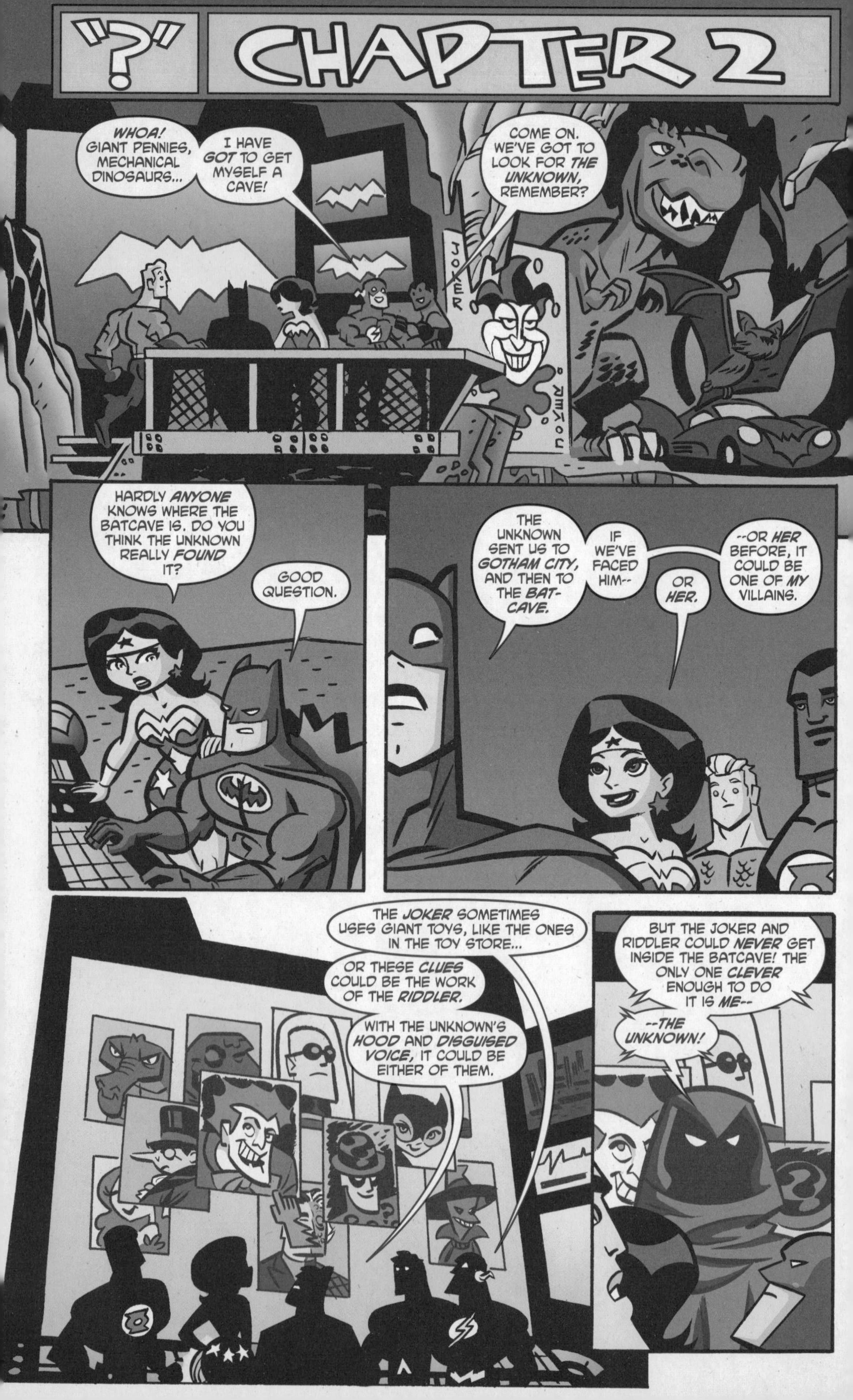
"?" CHAPTER 2
WHOA! GIANT PENNIES, MECHANICAL DINOSAURS...
I HAVE GOT TO GET MYSELF A CAVE!
COME ON. WE'VE GOT TO LOOK FOR THE UNKNOWN, REMEMBER?
JOKER
HARDLY ANYONE KNOWS WHERE THE BATCAVE IS. DO YOU THINK THE UNKNOWN REALLY FOUND IT?
GOOD QUESTION.
THE UNKNOWN SENT US TO GOTHAM CITY, AND THEN TO THE BAT-CAVE.
IF WE'VE FACED HIM--
OR HER.
--OR HER BEFORE, IT COULD BE ONE OF MY VILLAINS.
THE JOKER SOMETIMES USES GIANT TOYS, LIKE THE ONES IN THE TOY STORE...
OR THESE CLUES COULD BE THE WORK OF THE RIDDLER.
WITH THE UNKNOWN'S HOOD AND DISGUISED VOICE, IT COULD BE EITHER OF THEM.
BUT THE JOKER AND RIDDLER COULD NEVER GET INSIDE THE BATCAVE! THE ONLY ONE CLEVER ENOUGH TO DO IT IS ME--
--THE UNKNOWN!

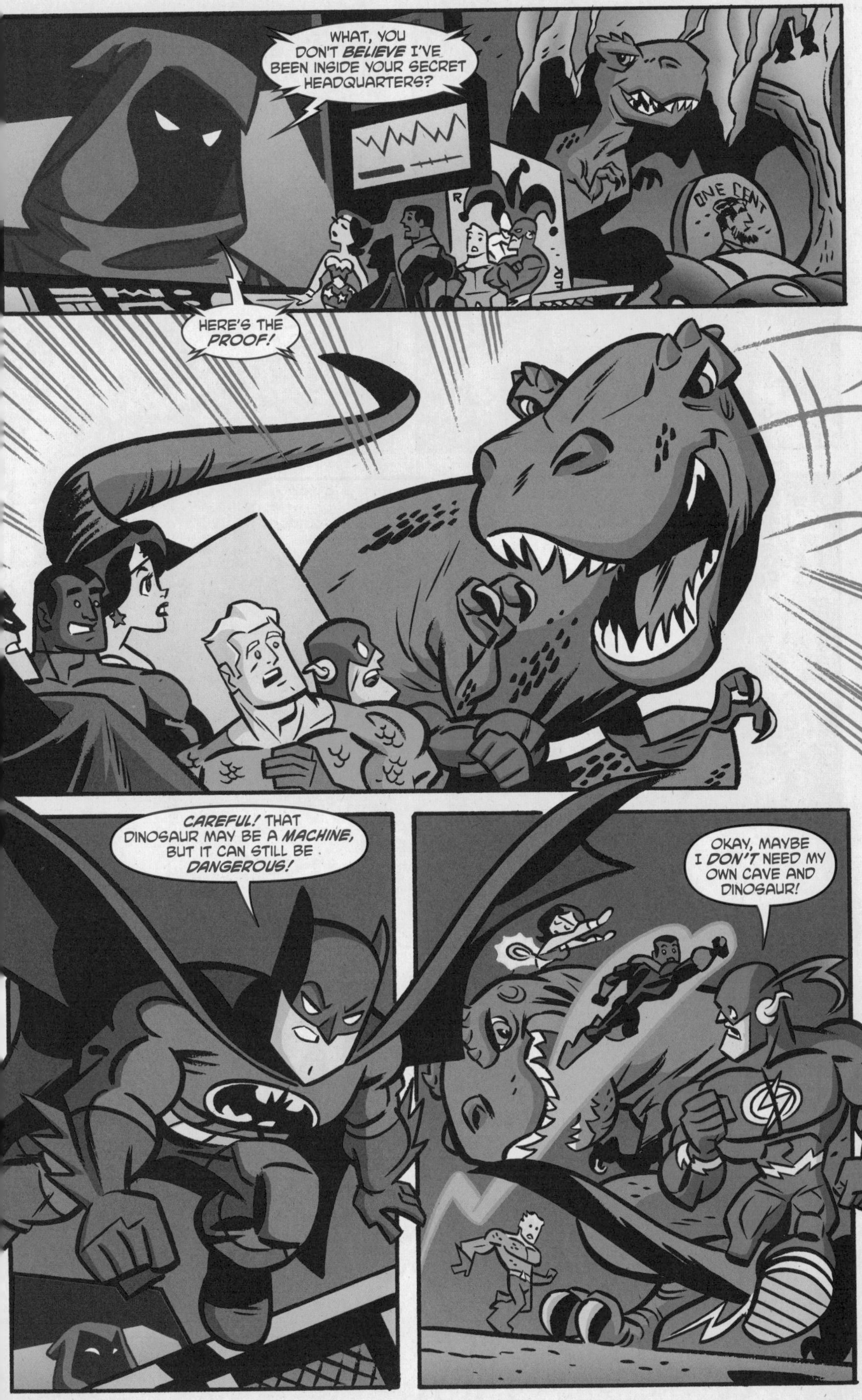
WHAT, YOU DON'T *BELIEVE* I'VE BEEN INSIDE YOUR SECRET HEADQUARTERS?
ONE CENT
HERE'S THE *PROOF!*
*CAREFUL!* THAT DINOSAUR MAY BE A *MACHINE,* BUT IT CAN STILL BE *DANGEROUS!*
OKAY, MAYBE I *DON'T* NEED MY OWN CAVE AND DINOSAUR!

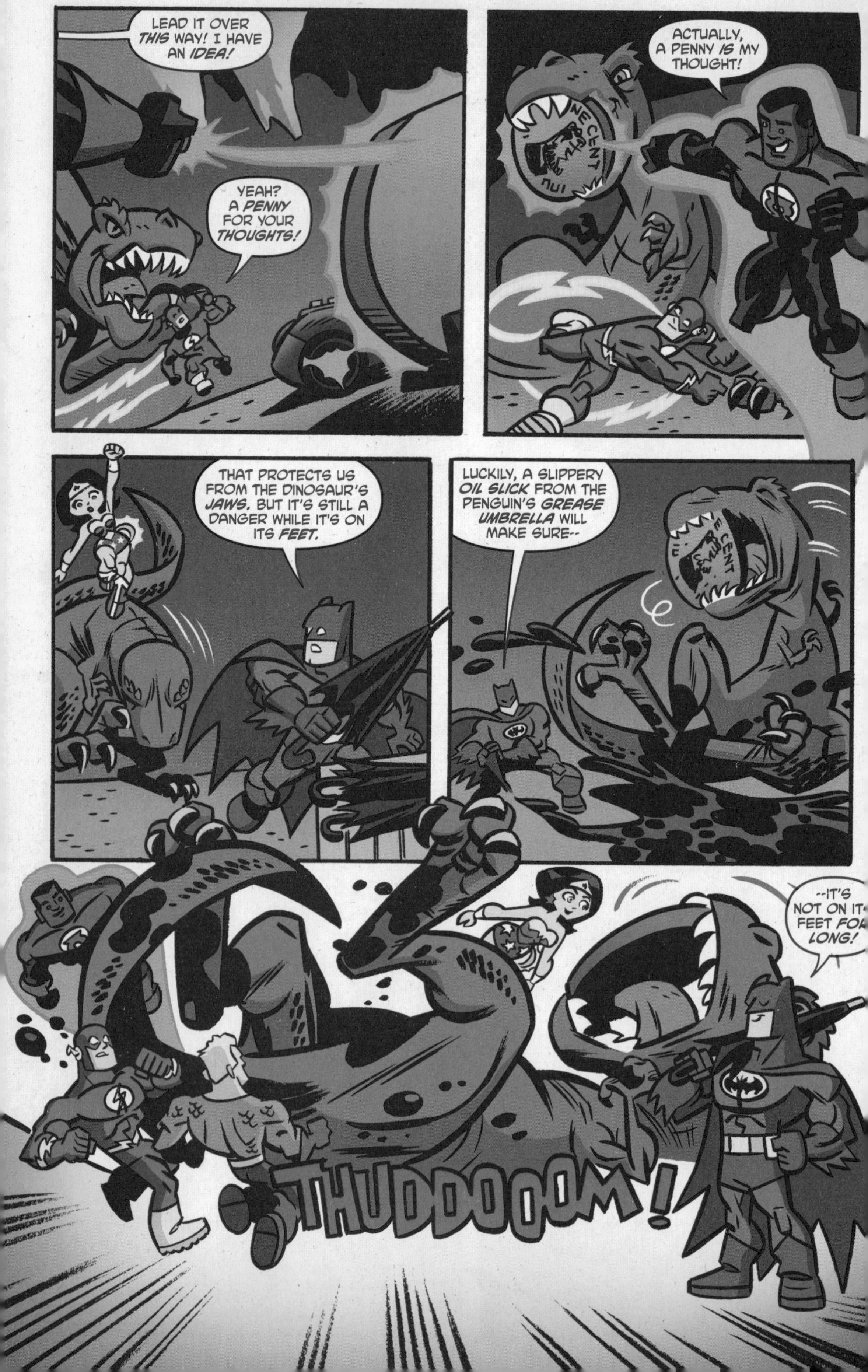

LEAD IT OVER THIS WAY! I HAVE AN IDEA!
YEAH? A PENNY FOR YOUR THOUGHTS!
ACTUALLY, A PENNY IS MY THOUGHT!
THAT PROTECTS US FROM THE DINOSAUR'S JAWS. BUT IT'S STILL A DANGER WHILE IT'S ON ITS FEET.
LUCKILY, A SLIPPERY OIL SLICK FROM THE PENGUIN'S GREASE UMBRELLA WILL MAKE SURE--
--IT'S NOT ON IT FEET FO LONG!
THUDOOOOM!

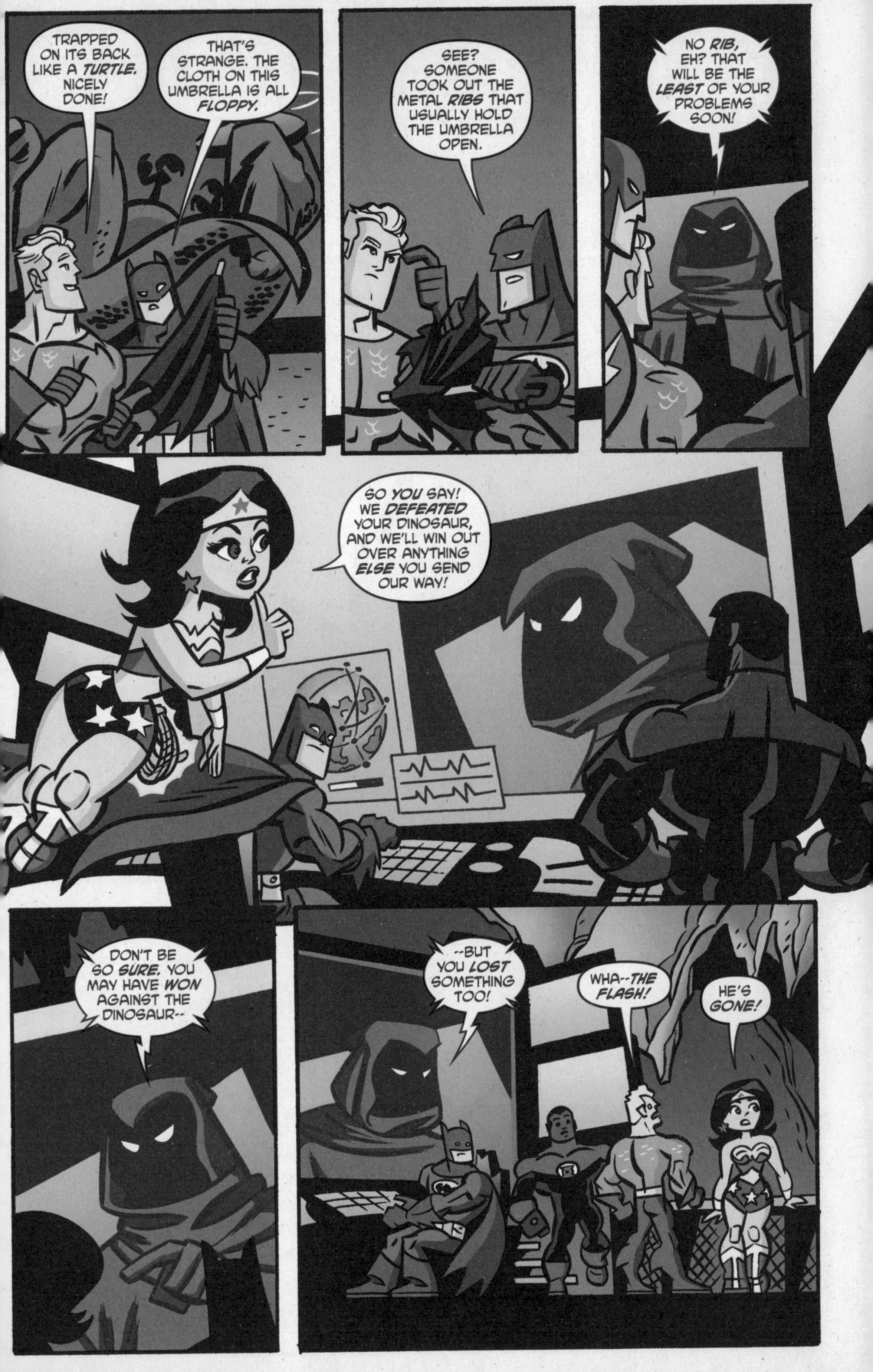
TRAPPED ON ITS BACK LIKE A *TURTLE.* NICELY DONE!
THAT'S STRANGE. THE CLOTH ON THIS UMBRELLA IS ALL *FLOPPY.*
SEE? SOMEONE TOOK OUT THE METAL *RIBS* THAT USUALLY HOLD THE UMBRELLA OPEN.
NO *RIB,* EH? THAT WILL BE THE *LEAST* OF YOUR PROBLEMS SOON!
SO *YOU* SAY! WE *DEFEATED* YOUR DINOSAUR, AND WE'LL WIN OUT OVER ANYTHING *ELSE* YOU SEND OUR WAY!
DON'T BE SO *SURE.* YOU MAY HAVE *WON* AGAINST THE DINOSAUR--
--BUT YOU *LOST* SOMETHING TOO!
WHA--*THE FLASH!*
HE'S *GONE!*

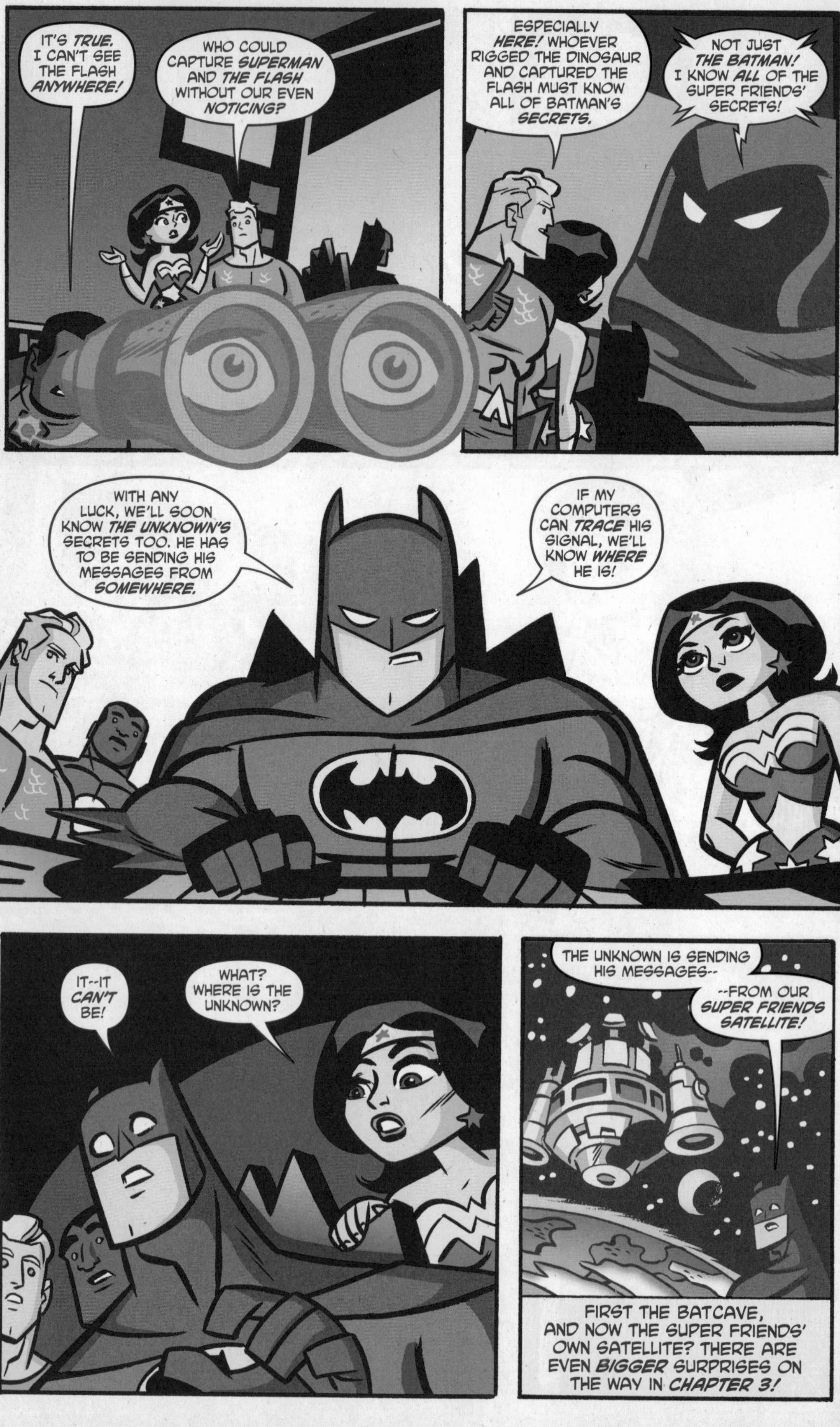
IT'S TRUE. I CAN'T SEE THE FLASH ANYWHERE!
WHO COULD CAPTURE SUPERMAN AND THE FLASH WITHOUT OUR EVEN NOTICING?
ESPECIALLY HERE! WHOEVER RIGGED THE DINOSAUR AND CAPTURED THE FLASH MUST KNOW ALL OF BATMAN'S SECRETS.
NOT JUST THE BATMAN! I KNOW ALL OF THE SUPER FRIENDS' SECRETS!
WITH ANY LUCK, WE'LL SOON KNOW THE UNKNOWN'S SECRETS TOO. HE HAS TO BE SENDING HIS MESSAGES FROM SOMEWHERE.
IF MY COMPUTERS CAN TRACE HIS SIGNAL, WE'LL KNOW WHERE HE IS!
IT--IT CAN'T BE!
WHAT? WHERE IS THE UNKNOWN?
THE UNKNOWN IS SENDING HIS MESSAGES--
--FROM OUR SUPER FRIENDS SATELLITE!
FIRST THE BATCAVE, AND NOW THE SUPER FRIENDS' OWN SATELLITE? THERE ARE EVEN BIGGER SURPRISES ON THE WAY IN CHAPTER 3!

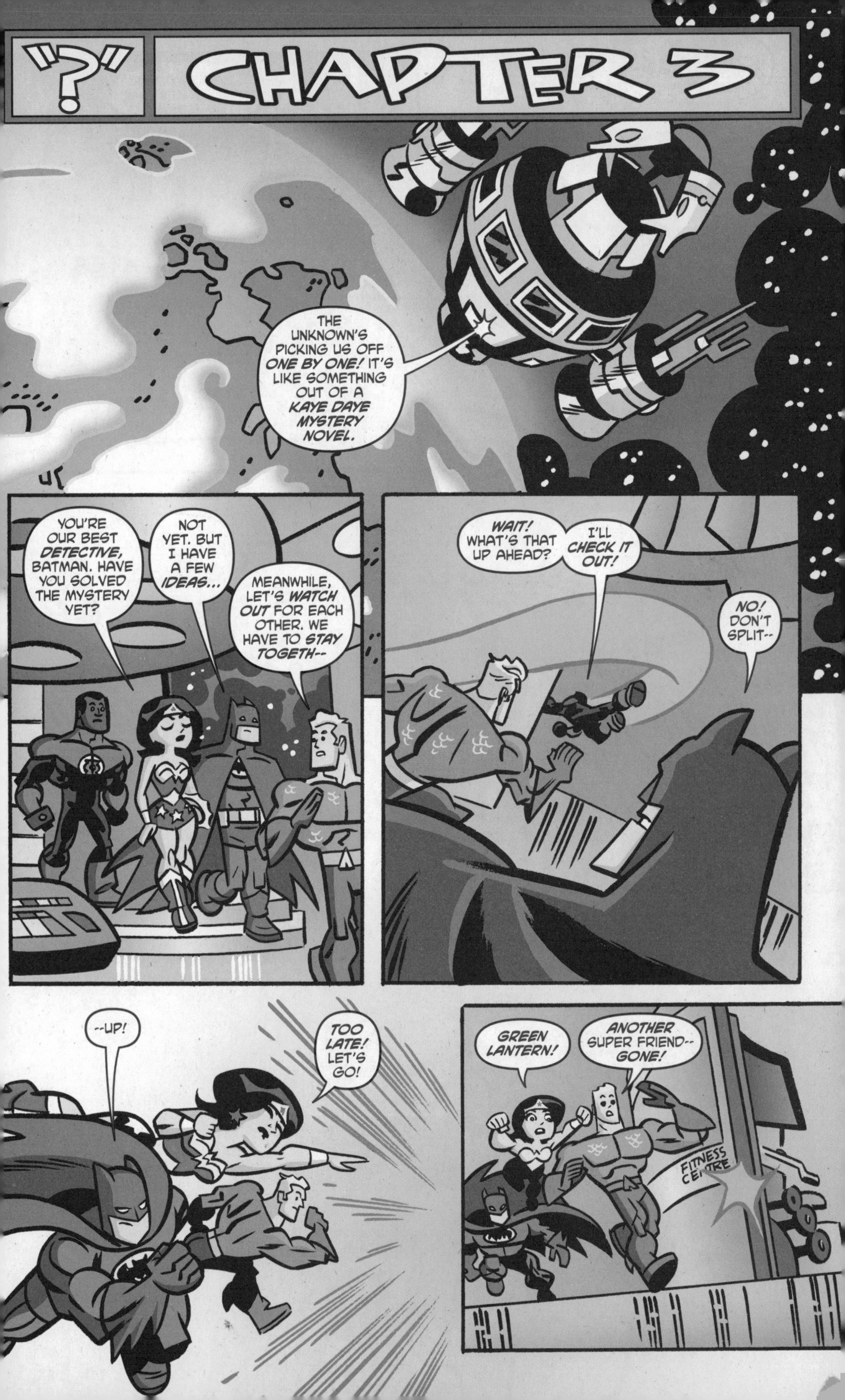
"?"
CHAPTER 3
THE UNKNOWN'S PICKING US OFF ONE BY ONE! IT'S LIKE SOMETHING OUT OF A KAYE DAYE MYSTERY NOVEL.
YOU'RE OUR BEST DETECTIVE, BATMAN. HAVE YOU SOLVED THE MYSTERY YET?
NOT YET. BUT I HAVE A FEW IDEAS...
MEANWHILE, LET'S WATCH OUT FOR EACH OTHER. WE HAVE TO STAY TOGETH--
WAIT! WHAT'S THAT UP AHEAD?
I'LL CHECK IT OUT!
NO! DON'T SPLIT--
--UP!
TOO LATE! LET'S GO!
GREEN LANTERN!
ANOTHER SUPER FRIEND-- GONE!
FITNESS CENTRE

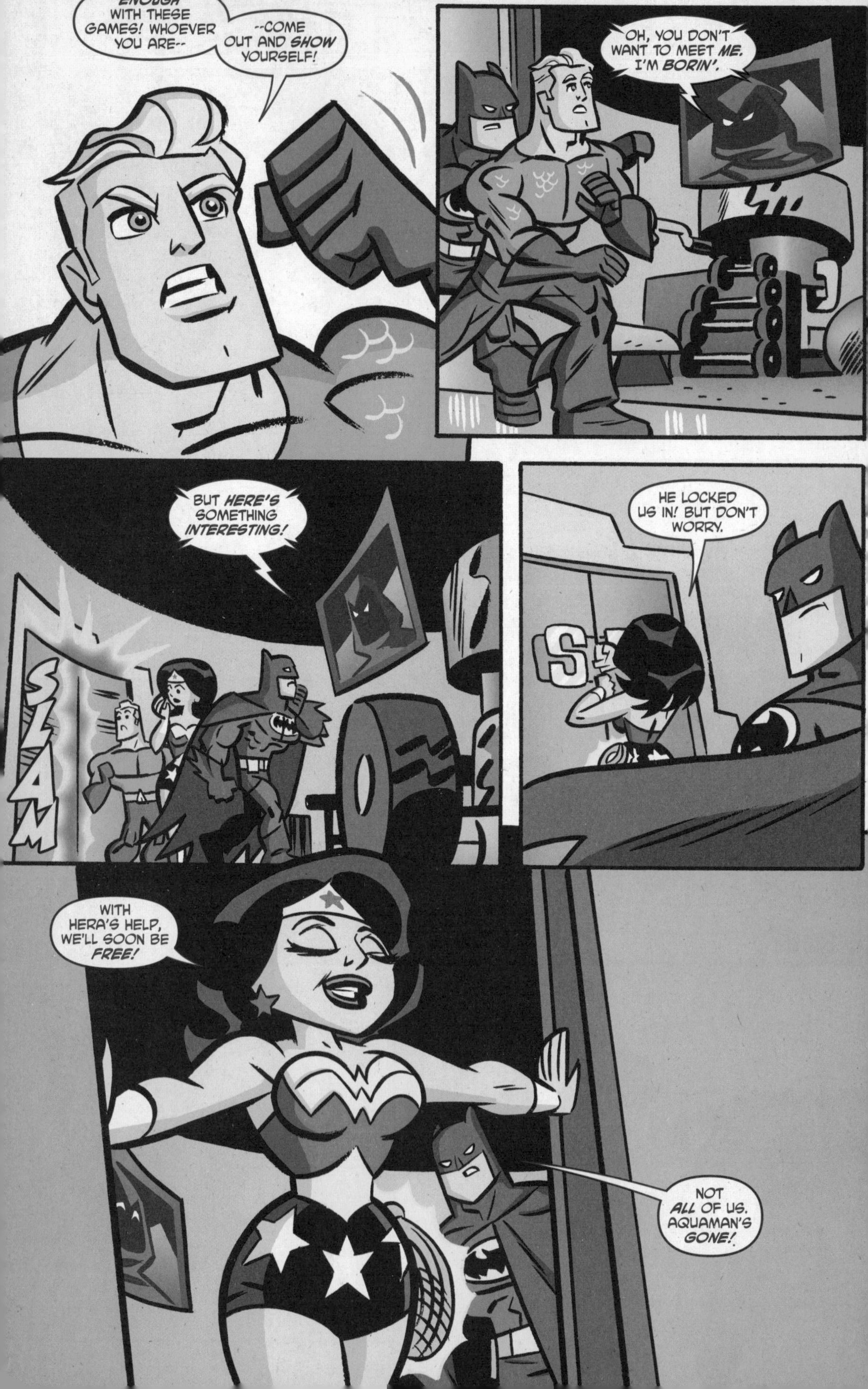
ENOUGH WITH THESE GAMES! WHOEVER YOU ARE--
--COME OUT AND SHOW YOURSELF!
OH, YOU DON'T WANT TO MEET ME. I'M BORIN'.
BUT HERE'S SOMETHING INTERESTING!
SLAM
HE LOCKED US IN! BUT DON'T WORRY.
WITH HERA'S HELP, WE'LL SOON BE FREE!
NOT ALL OF US. AQUAMAN'S GONE!

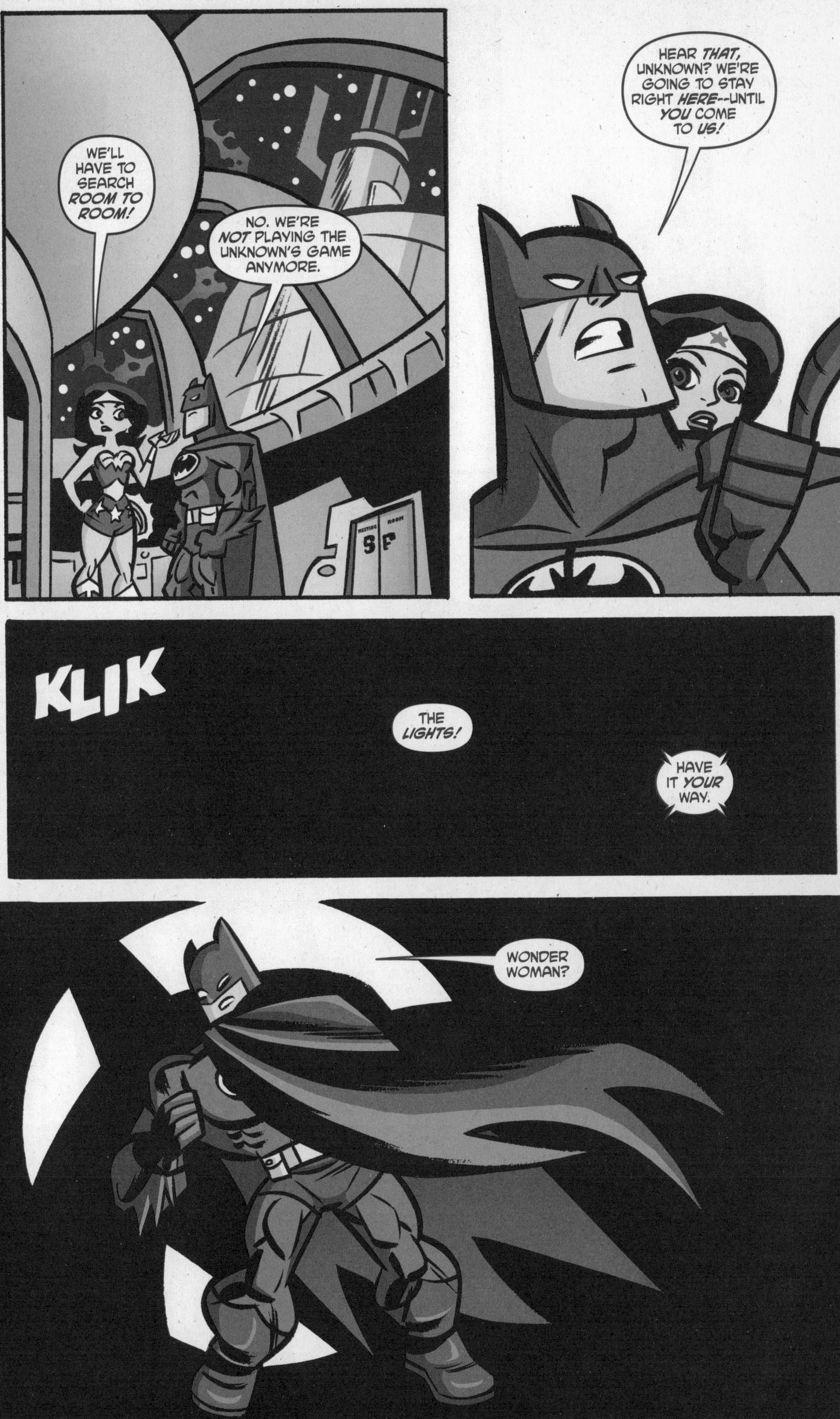
WE'LL HAVE TO SEARCH ROOM TO ROOM!
NO. WE'RE NOT PLAYING THE UNKNOWN'S GAME ANYMORE.
MEETING ROOM
5F
HEAR THAT, UNKNOWN? WE'RE GOING TO STAY RIGHT HERE--UNTIL YOU COME TO US!
KLIK
THE LIGHTS!
HAVE IT YOUR WAY.
WONDER WOMAN?

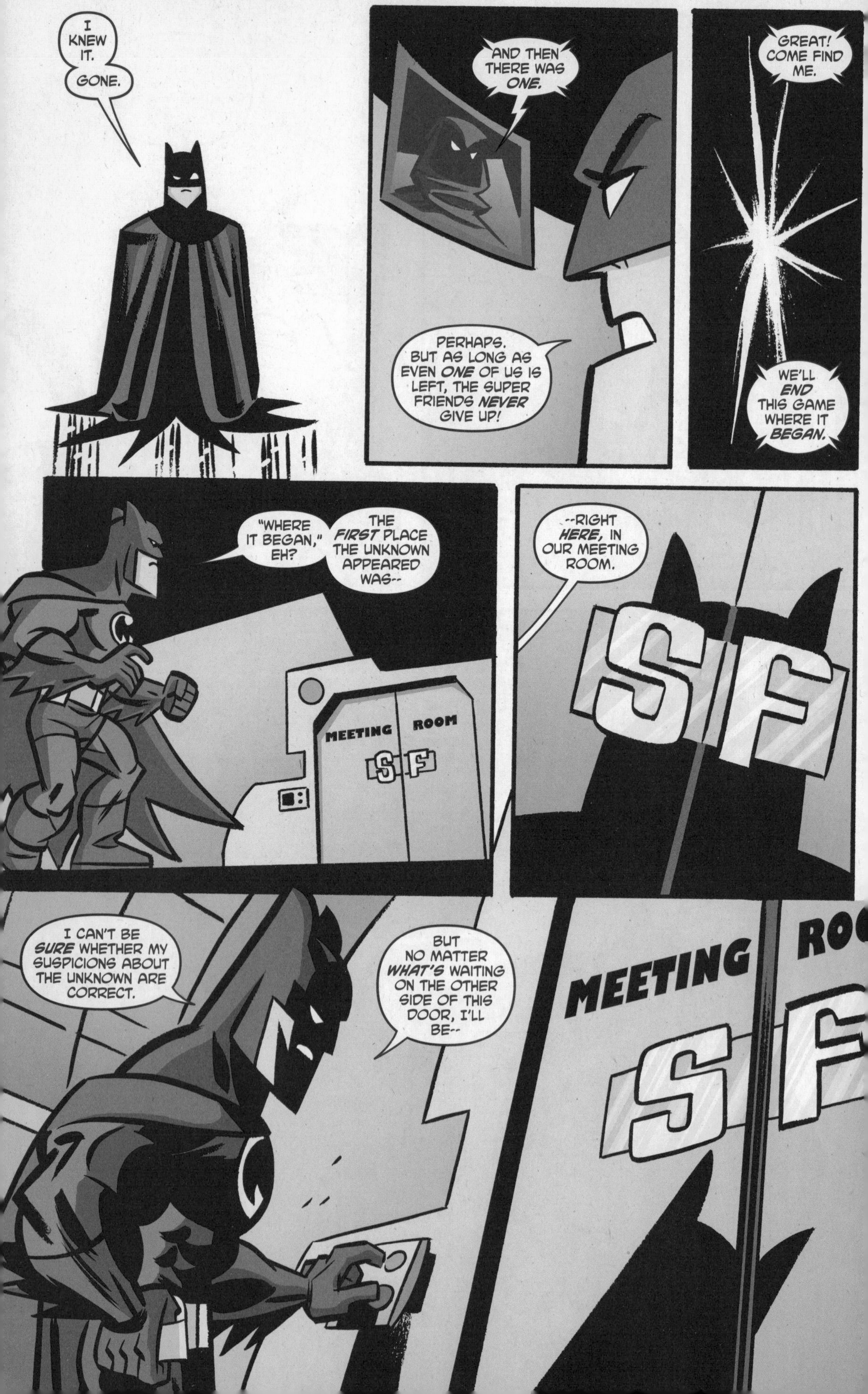
I KNEW IT.
GONE.
AND THEN THERE WAS ONE.
PERHAPS. BUT AS LONG AS EVEN ONE OF US IS LEFT, THE SUPER FRIENDS NEVER GIVE UP!
GREAT! COME FIND ME.
WE'LL END THIS GAME WHERE IT BEGAN.
"WHERE IT BEGAN," EH?
THE FIRST PLACE THE UNKNOWN APPEARED WAS--
MEETING ROOM
SF
--RIGHT HERE, IN OUR MEETING ROOM.
SF
I CAN'T BE SURE WHETHER MY SUSPICIONS ABOUT THE UNKNOWN ARE CORRECT.
BUT NO MATTER WHAT'S WAITING ON THE OTHER SIDE OF THIS DOOR, I'LL BE--
MEETING
SF

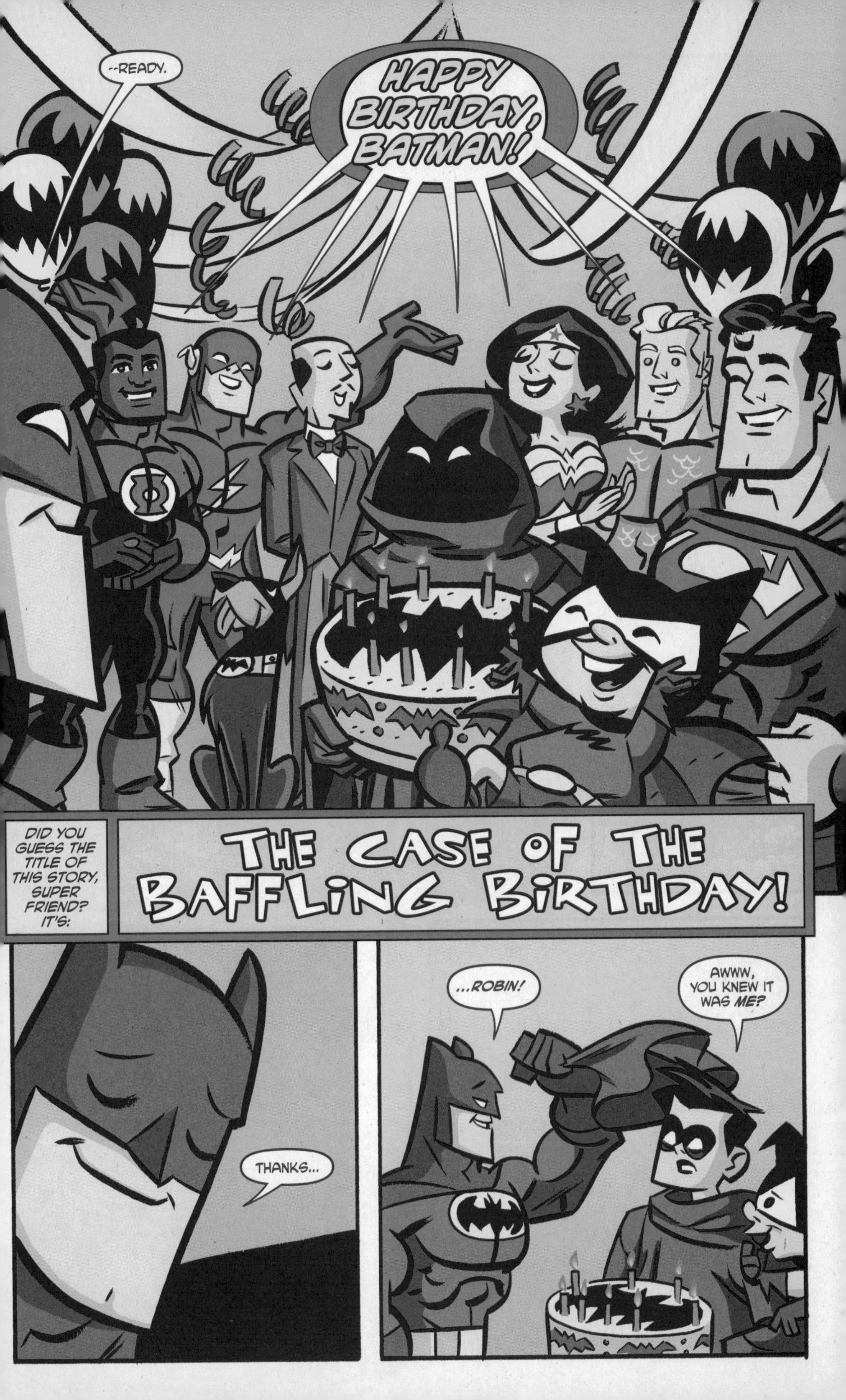
--READY.
HAPPY BIRTHDAY, BATMAN!
DID YOU GUESS THE TITLE OF THIS STORY, SUPER FRIEND? IT'S:
THE CASE OF THE BAFFLING BIRTHDAY!
THANKS...
...ROBIN!
AWWW, YOU KNEW IT WAS ME?

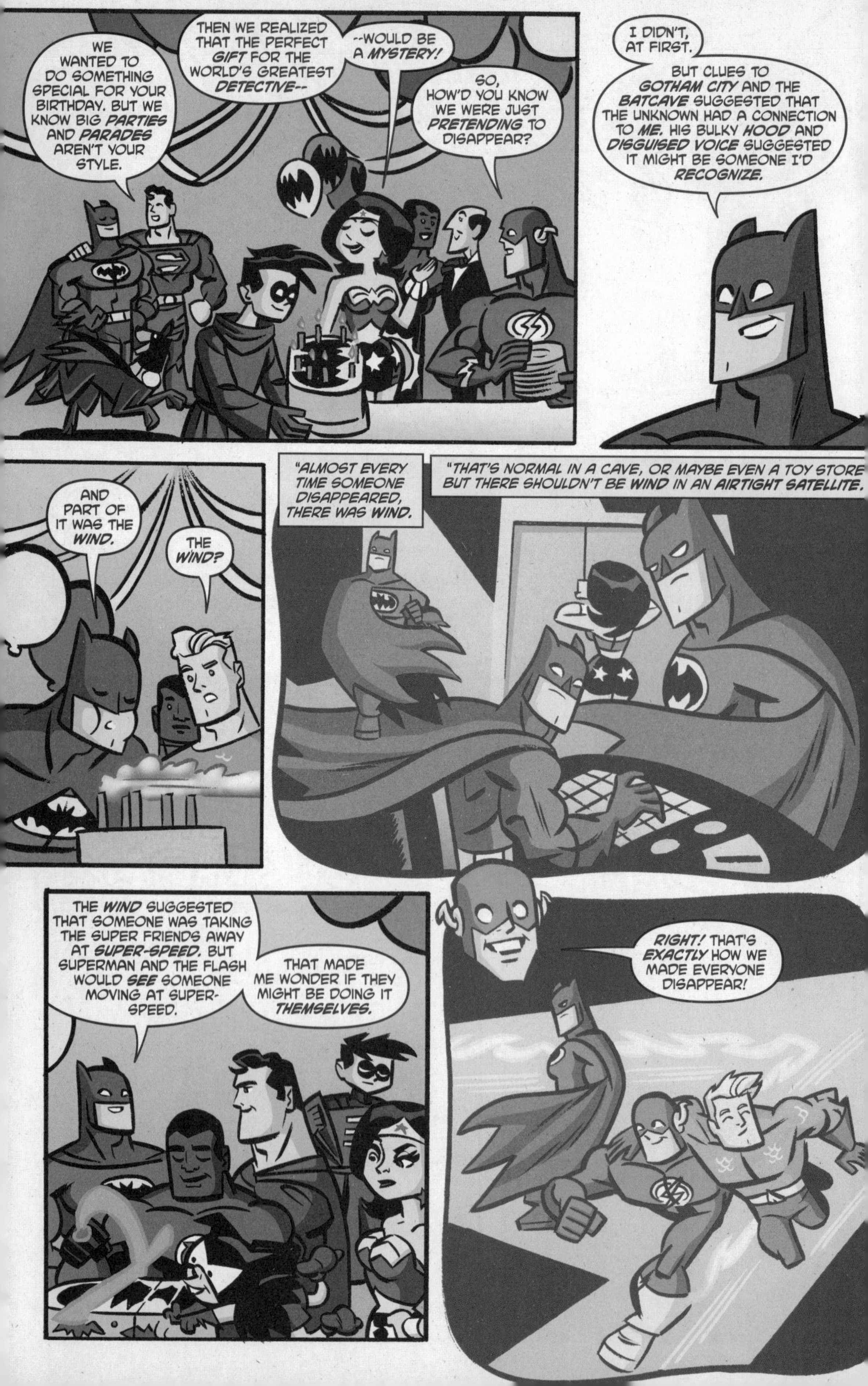

WE WANTED TO DO SOMETHING SPECIAL FOR YOUR BIRTHDAY. BUT WE KNOW BIG PARTIES AND PARADES AREN'T YOUR STYLE.
THEN WE REALIZED THAT THE PERFECT GIFT FOR THE WORLD'S GREATEST DETECTIVE--
--WOULD BE A MYSTERY!
SO, HOW'D YOU KNOW WE WERE JUST PRETENDING TO DISAPPEAR?
I DIDN'T, AT FIRST.
BUT CLUES TO GOTHAM CITY AND THE BATCAVE SUGGESTED THAT THE UNKNOWN HAD A CONNECTION TO ME. HIS BULKY HOOD AND DISGUISED VOICE SUGGESTED IT MIGHT BE SOMEONE I'D RECOGNIZE.
AND PART OF IT WAS THE WIND.
THE WIND?
"ALMOST EVERY TIME SOMEONE DISAPPEARED, THERE WAS WIND.
"THAT'S NORMAL IN A CAVE, OR MAYBE EVEN A TOY STORE BUT THERE SHOULDN'T BE WIND IN AN AIRTIGHT SATELLITE.
THE WIND SUGGESTED THAT SOMEONE WAS TAKING THE SUPER FRIENDS AWAY AT SUPER-SPEED. BUT SUPERMAN AND THE FLASH WOULD SEE SOMEONE MOVING AT SUPER-SPEED.
THAT MADE ME WONDER IF THEY MIGHT BE DOING IT THEMSELVES.
RIGHT! THAT'S EXACTLY HOW WE MADE EVERYONE DISAPPEAR!

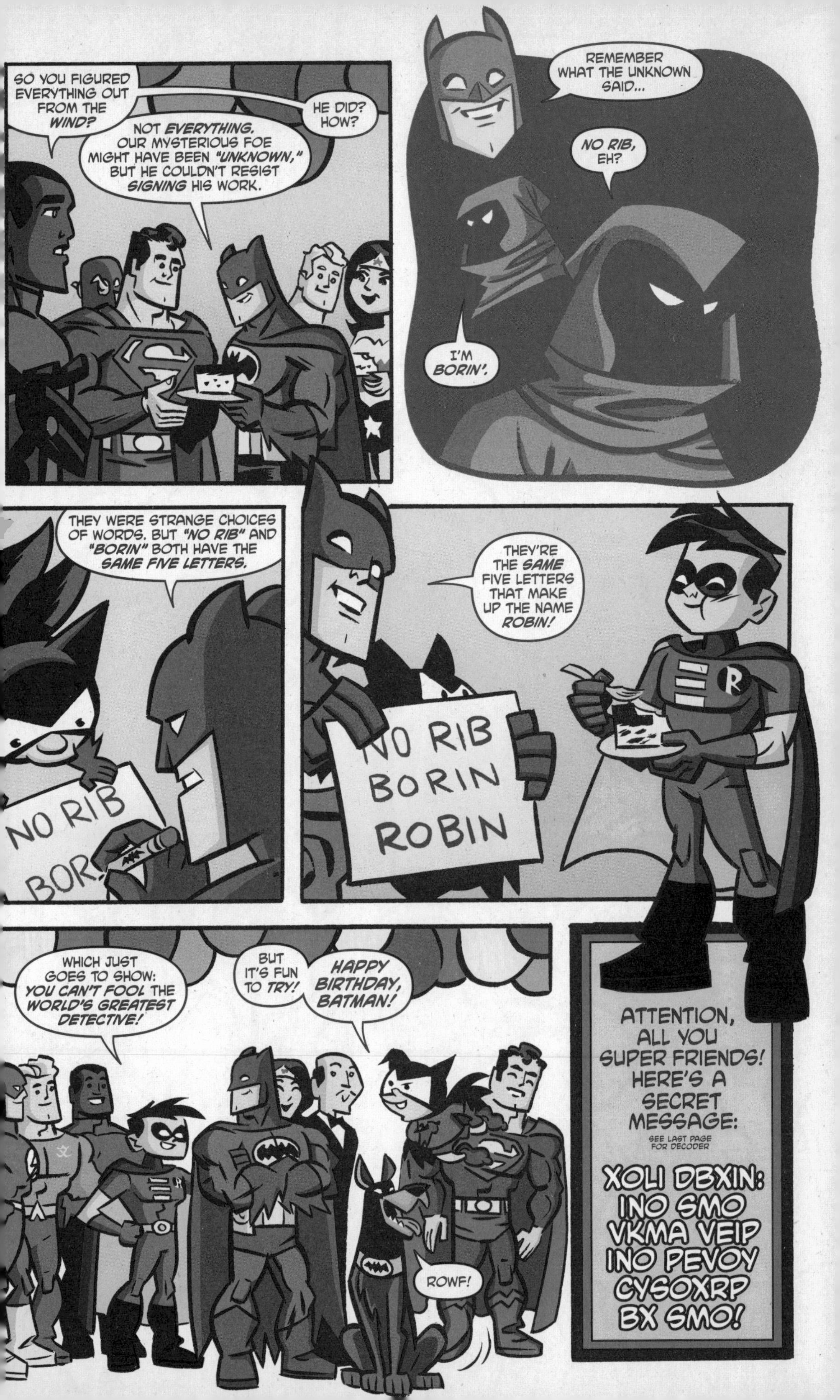

SO YOU FIGURED EVERYTHING OUT FROM THE *WIND?*
HE DID? HOW?
NOT *EVERYTHING.* OUR MYSTERIOUS FOE MIGHT HAVE BEEN *"UNKNOWN,"* BUT HE COULDN'T RESIST *SIGNING* HIS WORK.
REMEMBER WHAT THE UNKNOWN SAID...
*NO RIB,* EH?
I'M *BORIN'.*
THEY WERE STRANGE CHOICES OF WORDS. BUT *"NO RIB"* AND *"BORIN"* BOTH HAVE THE *SAME FIVE LETTERS.*
NO RIB
BOR
THEY'RE THE *SAME* FIVE LETTERS THAT MAKE UP THE NAME *ROBIN!*
NO RIB
BORIN
ROBIN
WHICH JUST GOES TO SHOW: *YOU CAN'T FOOL* THE *WORLD'S GREATEST DETECTIVE!*
BUT IT'S FUN TO *TRY!*
*HAPPY BIRTHDAY, BATMAN!*
ROWF!
ATTENTION, ALL YOU SUPER FRIENDS! HERE'S A SECRET MESSAGE:
SEE LAST PAGE FOR DECODER
XOLI DBXIN: INO SMO VKMA VEIP INO PEVOY CYSOXRP BX SMO!

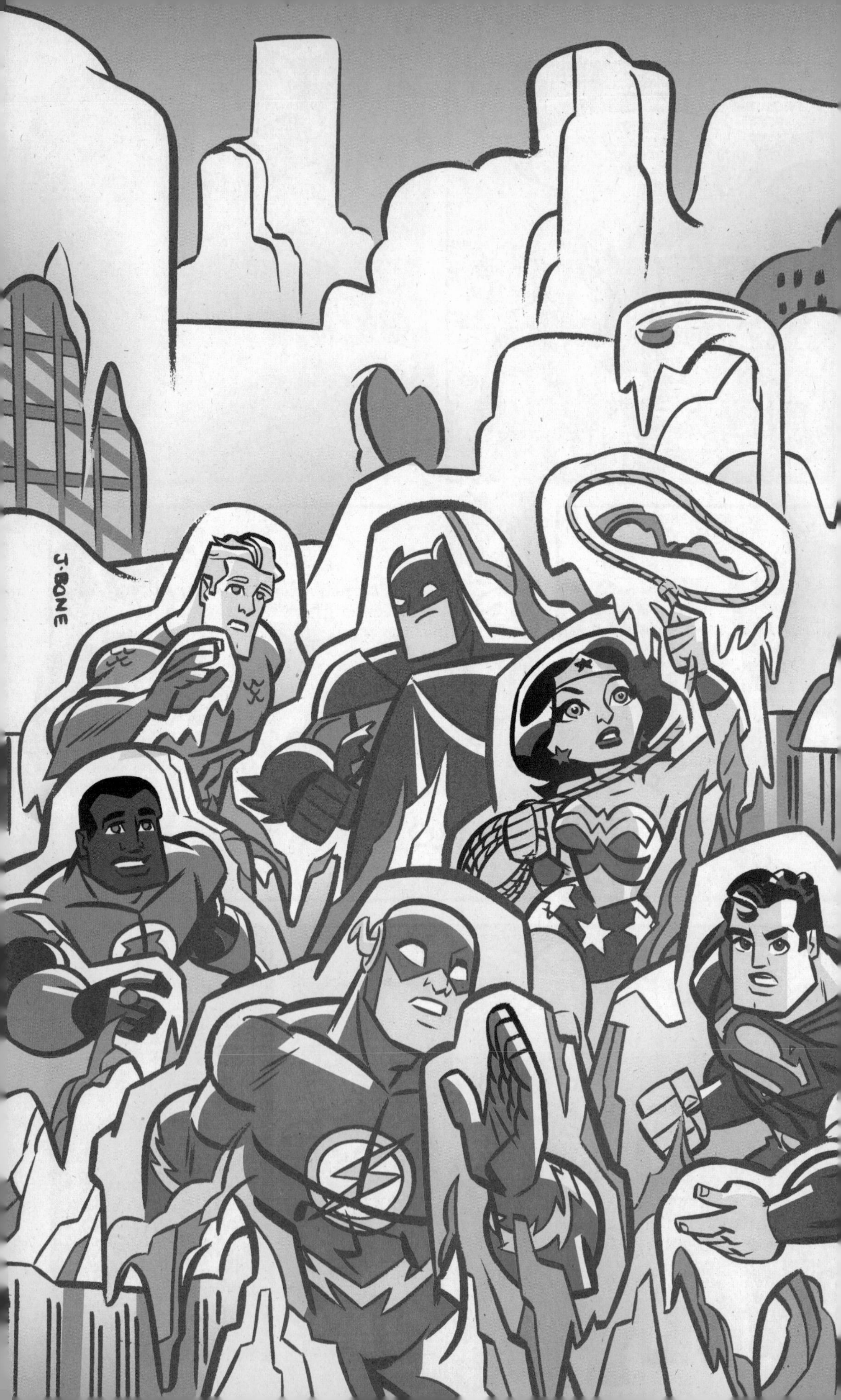
J·BONE

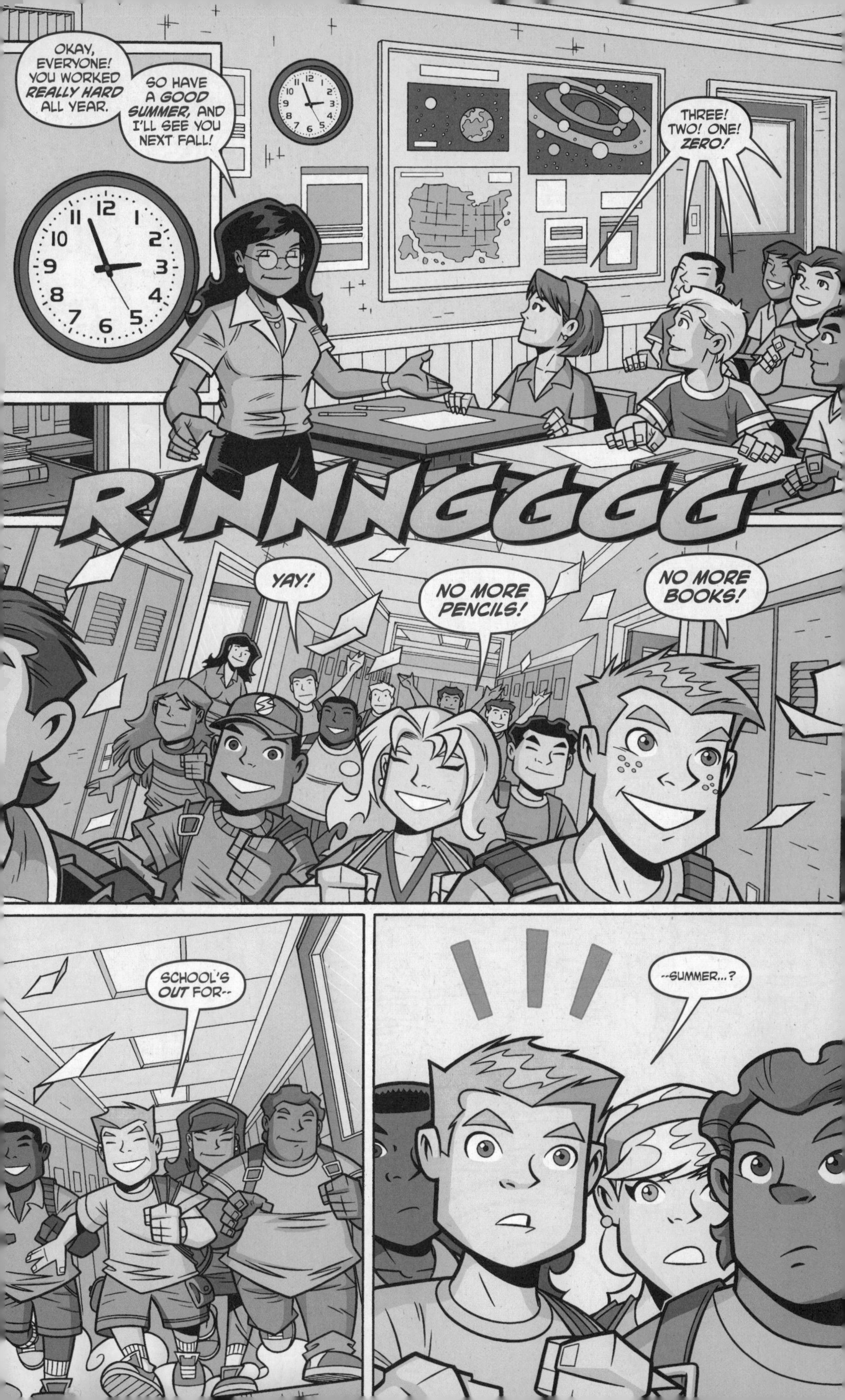
OKAY, EVERYONE! YOU WORKED REALLY HARD ALL YEAR.
SO HAVE A GOOD SUMMER, AND I'LL SEE YOU NEXT FALL!
THREE! TWO! ONE! ZERO!
RINNNGGGG
YAY!
NO MORE PENCILS!
NO MORE BOOKS!
SCHOOL'S OUT FOR--
--SUMMER...?

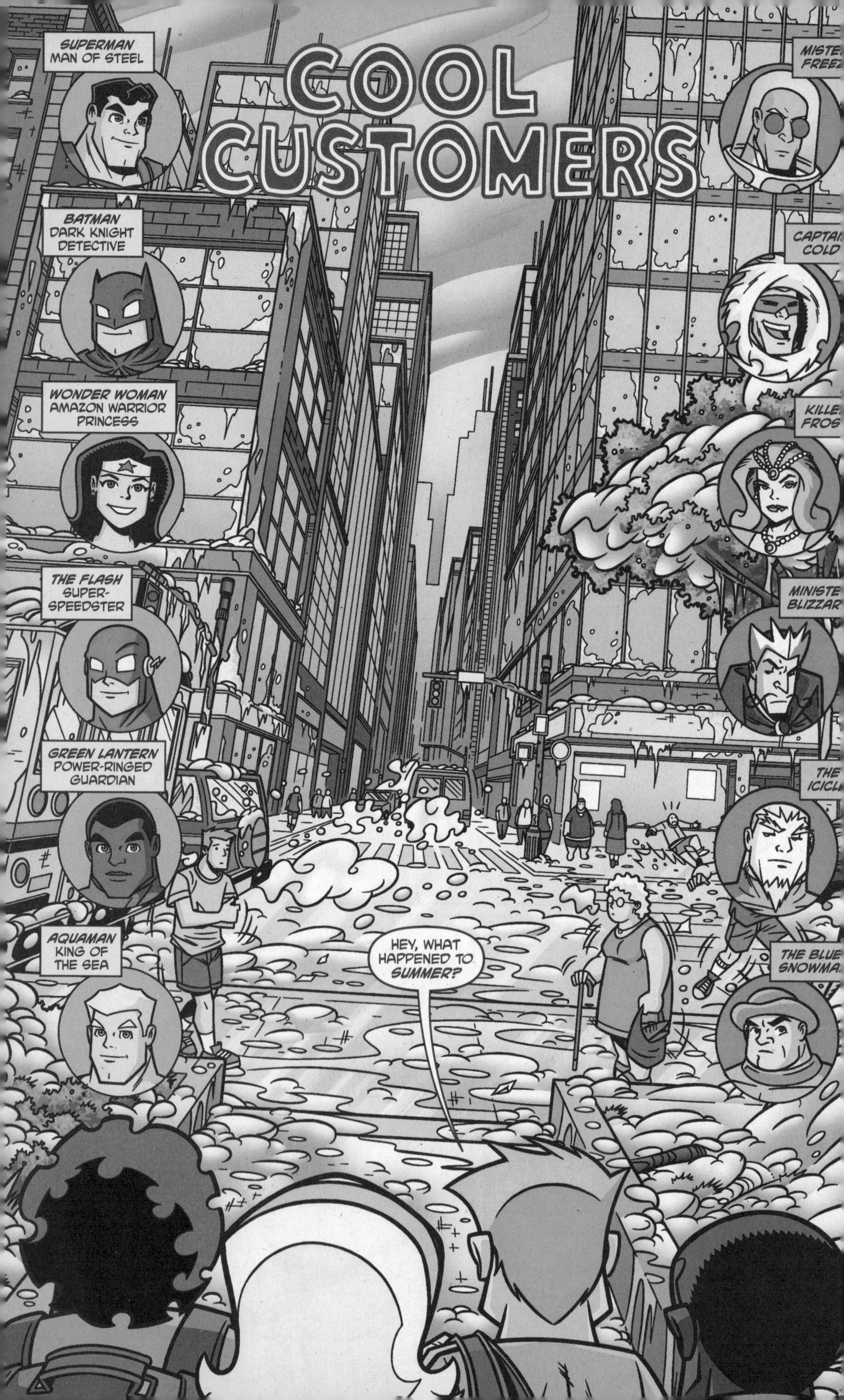
COOL CUSTOMERS
SUPERMAN MAN OF STEEL
BATMAN DARK KNIGHT DETECTIVE
WONDER WOMAN AMAZON WARRIOR PRINCESS
THE FLASH SUPER-SPEEDSTER
GREEN LANTERN POWER-RINGED GUARDIAN
AQUAMAN KING OF THE SEA
MISTE FREEZ
CAPTAI COLD
KILLE FROS
MINISTE BLIZZAR
THE ICICL
THE BLUE SNOWMA
HEY, WHAT HAPPENED TO SUMMER?

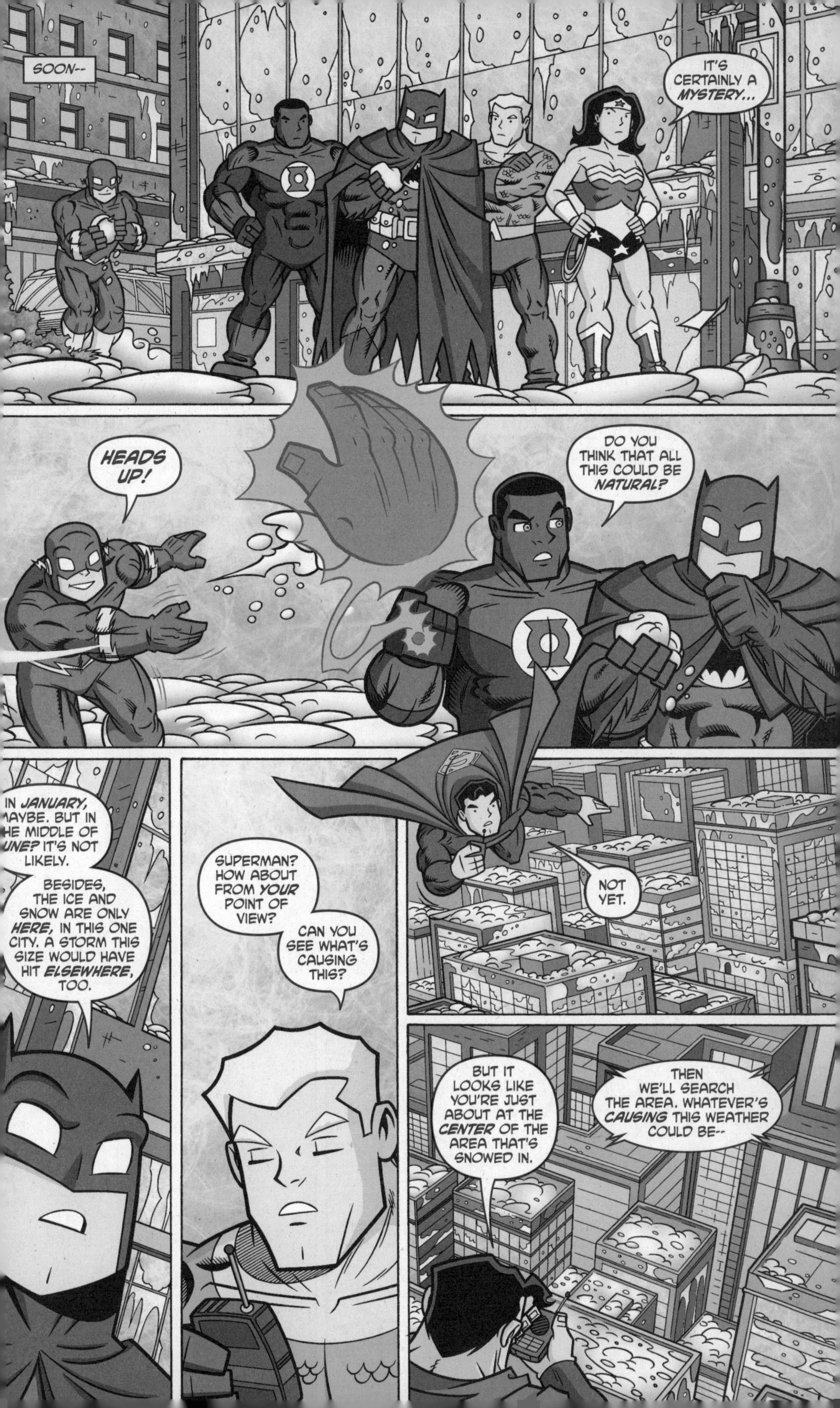

SOON--
IT'S CERTAINLY A *MYSTERY...*
*HEADS UP!*
DO YOU THINK THAT ALL THIS COULD BE *NATURAL?*
IN *JANUARY,* MAYBE. BUT IN HE MIDDLE OF UNE? IT'S NOT LIKELY.
BESIDES, THE ICE AND SNOW ARE ONLY *HERE,* IN THIS ONE CITY. A STORM THIS SIZE WOULD HAVE HIT *ELSEWHERE,* TOO.
SUPERMAN? HOW ABOUT FROM *YOUR* POINT OF VIEW?
CAN YOU SEE WHAT'S CAUSING THIS?
NOT YET.
BUT IT LOOKS LIKE YOU'RE JUST ABOUT AT THE *CENTER* OF THE AREA THAT'S SNOWED IN.
THEN WE'LL SEARCH THE AREA. WHATEVER'S *CAUSING* THIS WEATHER COULD BE--

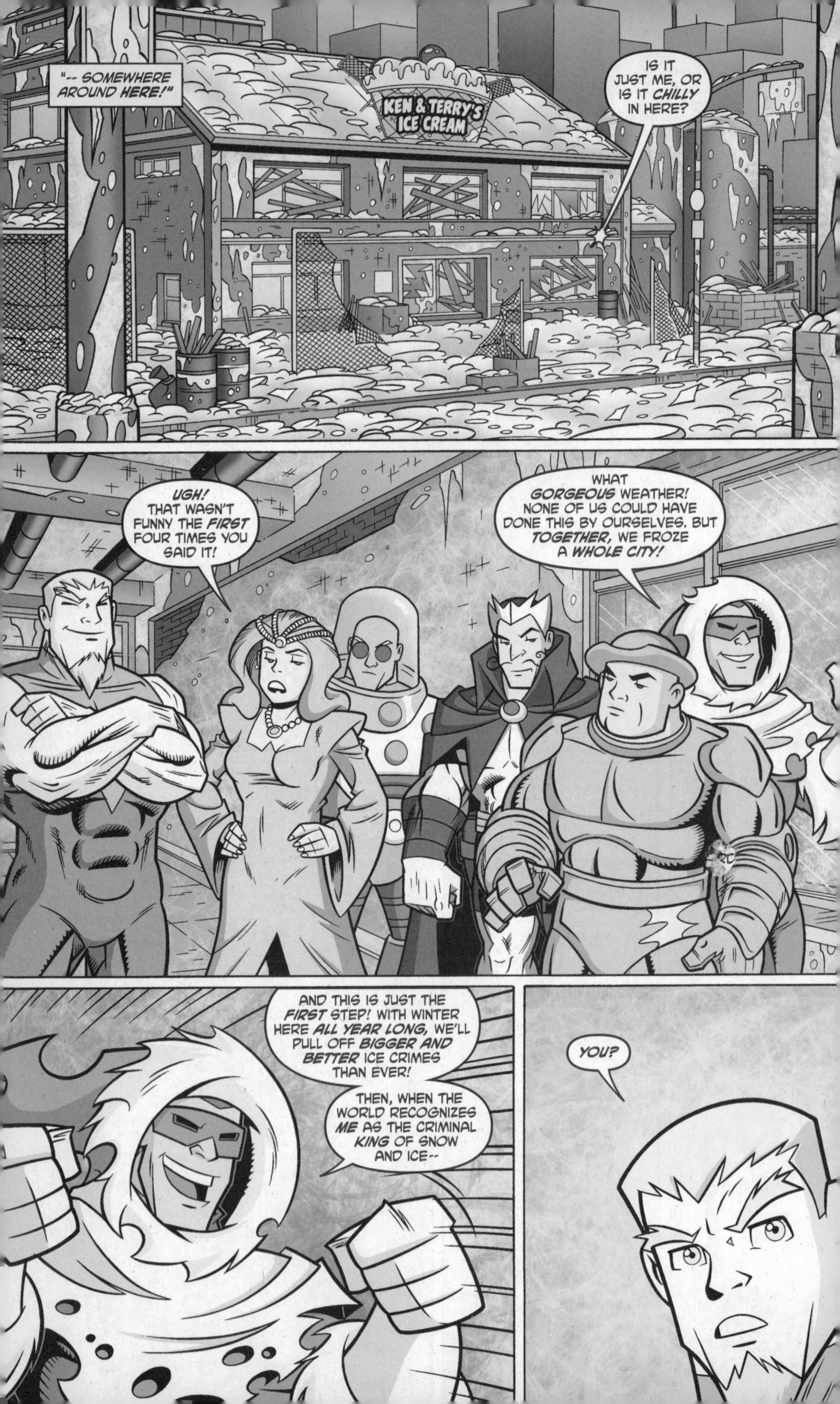
"-- SOMEWHERE AROUND HERE!"
KEN & TERRY'S ICE CREAM
IS IT JUST ME, OR IS IT CHILLY IN HERE?
UGH! THAT WASN'T FUNNY THE FIRST FOUR TIMES YOU SAID IT!
WHAT GORGEOUS WEATHER! NONE OF US COULD HAVE DONE THIS BY OURSELVES. BUT TOGETHER, WE FROZE A WHOLE CITY!
AND THIS IS JUST THE FIRST STEP! WITH WINTER HERE ALL YEAR LONG, WE'LL PULL OFF BIGGER AND BETTER ICE CRIMES THAN EVER!
THEN, WHEN THE WORLD RECOGNIZES ME AS THE CRIMINAL KING OF SNOW AND ICE--
YOU?

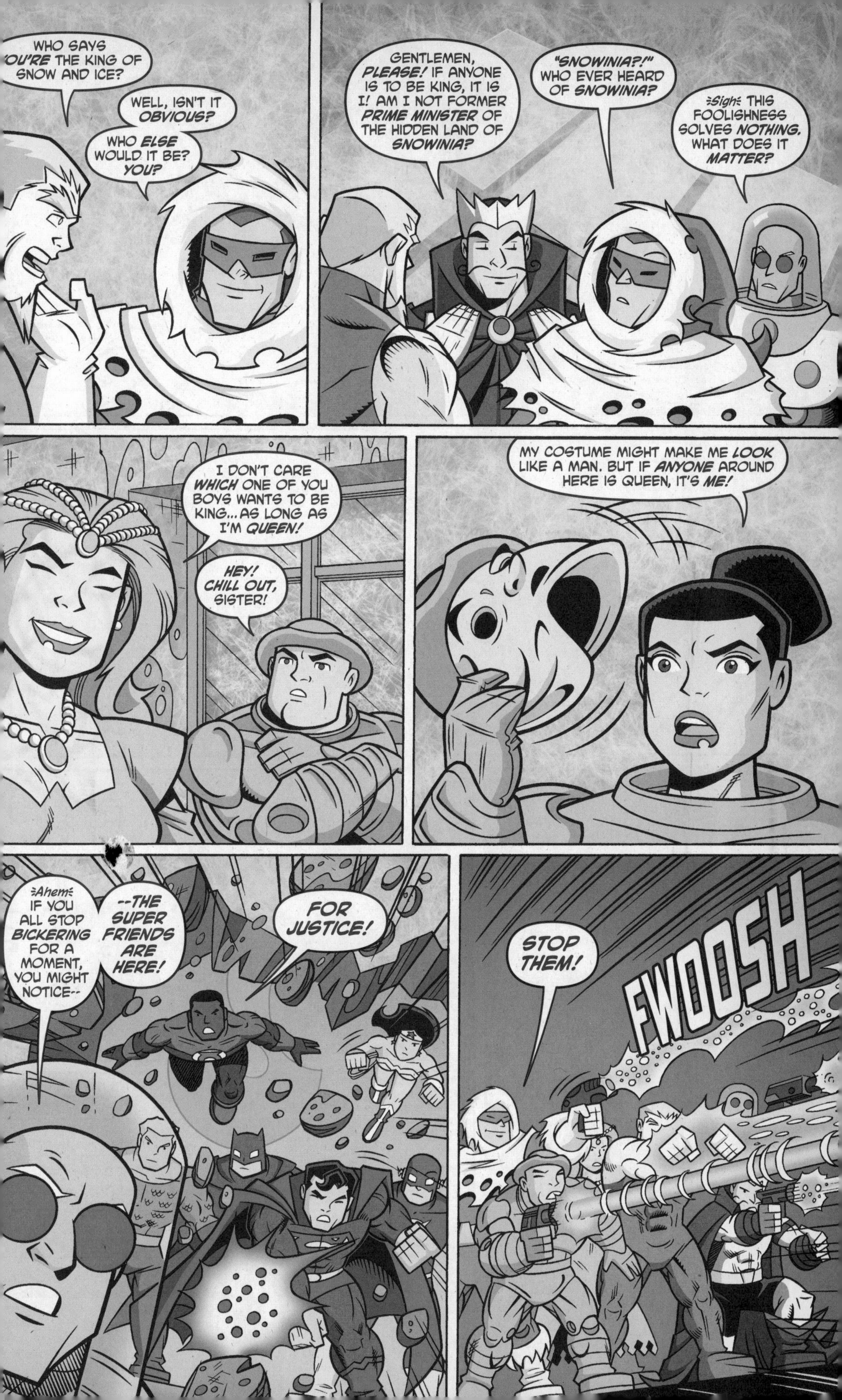

WHO SAYS YOU'RE THE KING OF SNOW AND ICE?
WELL, ISN'T IT OBVIOUS?
WHO ELSE WOULD IT BE? YOU?
GENTLEMEN, PLEASE! IF ANYONE IS TO BE KING, IT IS I! AM I NOT FORMER PRIME MINISTER OF THE HIDDEN LAND OF SNOWINIA?
"SNOWINIA?!" WHO EVER HEARD OF SNOWINIA?
Sigh THIS FOOLISHNESS SOLVES NOTHING. WHAT DOES IT MATTER?
I DON'T CARE WHICH ONE OF YOU BOYS WANTS TO BE KING...AS LONG AS I'M QUEEN!
HEY! CHILL OUT, SISTER!
MY COSTUME MIGHT MAKE ME LOOK LIKE A MAN. BUT IF ANYONE AROUND HERE IS QUEEN, IT'S ME!
Ahem IF YOU ALL STOP BICKERING FOR A MOMENT, YOU MIGHT NOTICE--
--THE SUPER FRIENDS ARE HERE!
FOR JUSTICE!
STOP THEM!
FWOOSH

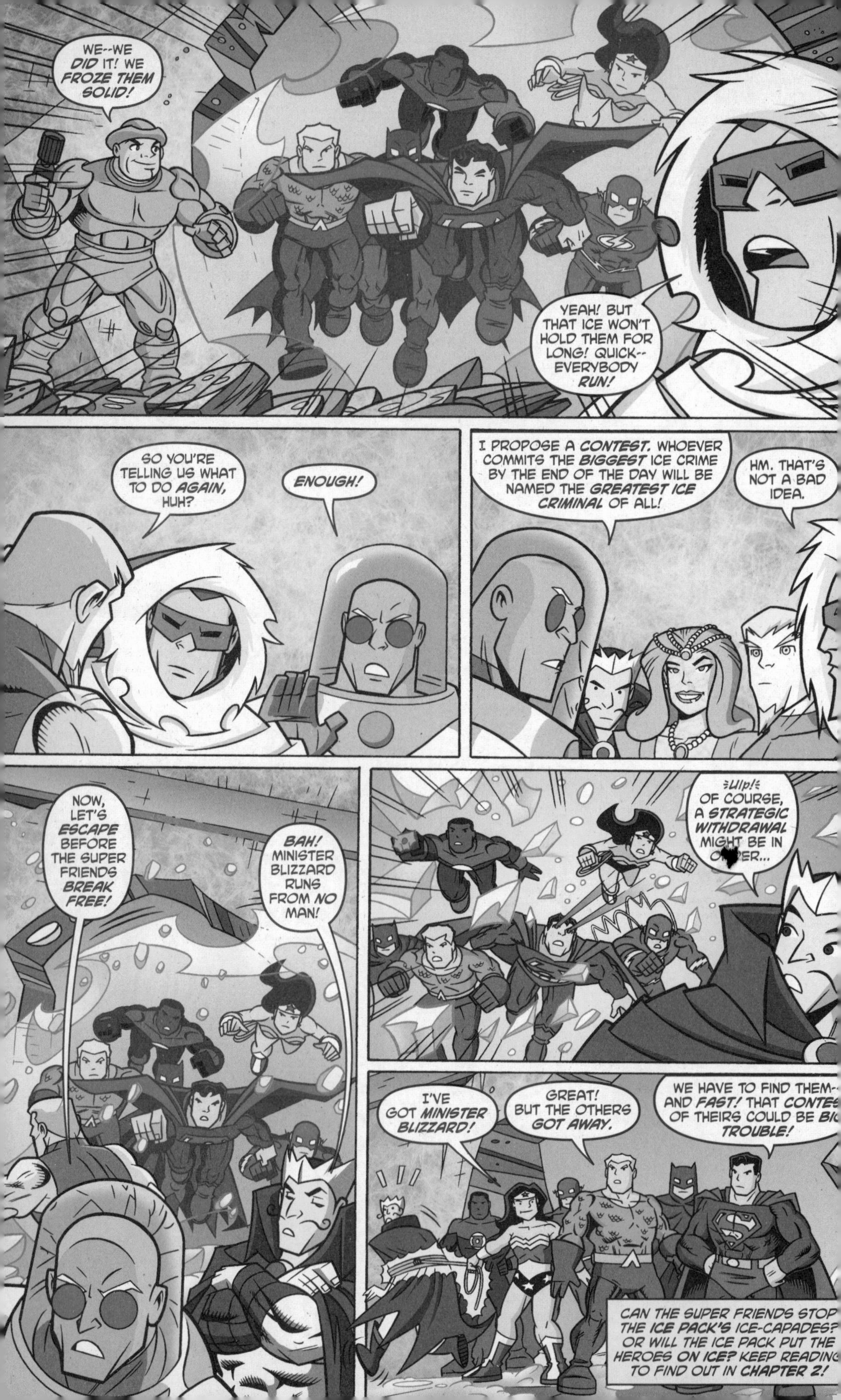
WE--WE DID IT! WE FROZE THEM SOLID!
YEAH! BUT THAT ICE WON'T HOLD THEM FOR LONG! QUICK-- EVERYBODY RUN!
SO YOU'RE TELLING US WHAT TO DO AGAIN, HUH?
ENOUGH!
I PROPOSE A CONTEST. WHOEVER COMMITS THE BIGGEST ICE CRIME BY THE END OF THE DAY WILL BE NAMED THE GREATEST ICE CRIMINAL OF ALL!
HM. THAT'S NOT A BAD IDEA.
NOW, LET'S ESCAPE BEFORE THE SUPER FRIENDS BREAK FREE!
BAH! MINISTER BLIZZARD RUNS FROM NO MAN!
ULP! OF COURSE, A STRATEGIC WITHDRAWAL MIGHT BE IN ORDER...
I'VE GOT MINISTER BLIZZARD!
GREAT! BUT THE OTHERS GOT AWAY.
WE HAVE TO FIND THEM-- AND FAST! THAT CONTES OF THEIRS COULD BE BI TROUBLE!
CAN THE SUPER FRIENDS STOP THE ICE PACK'S ICE-CAPADES? OR WILL THE ICE PACK PUT THE HEROES ON ICE? KEEP READING TO FIND OUT IN CHAPTER 2!

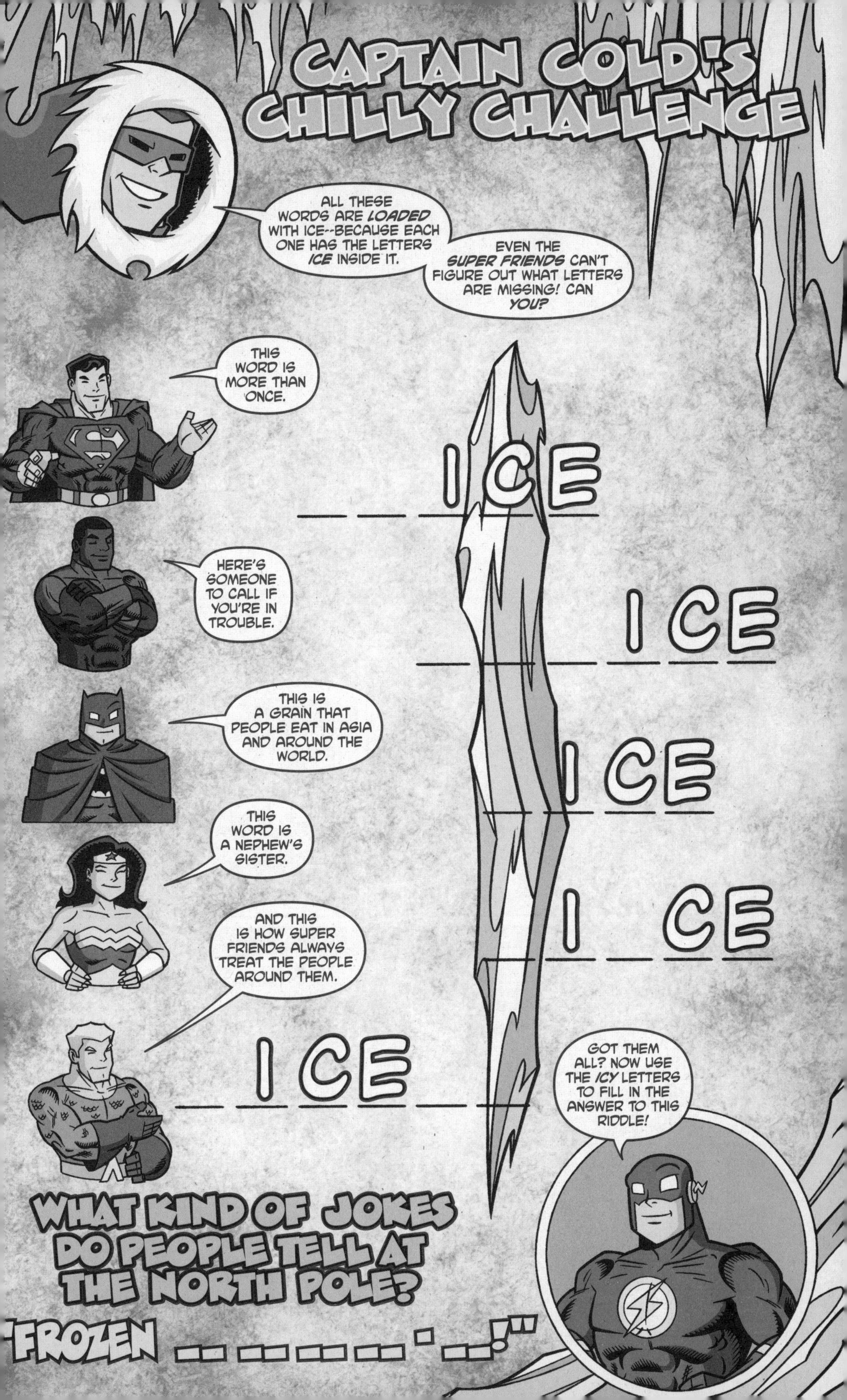

CAPTAIN COLD'S CHILLY CHALLENGE
ALL THESE WORDS ARE *LOADED* WITH ICE--BECAUSE EACH ONE HAS THE LETTERS *ICE* INSIDE IT.
EVEN THE *SUPER FRIENDS* CAN'T FIGURE OUT WHAT LETTERS ARE MISSING! CAN *YOU*?
THIS WORD IS MORE THAN ONCE.
ICE
HERE'S SOMEONE TO CALL IF YOU'RE IN TROUBLE.
ICE
THIS IS A GRAIN THAT PEOPLE EAT IN ASIA AND AROUND THE WORLD.
ICE
THIS WORD IS A NEPHEW'S SISTER.
I CE
AND THIS IS HOW SUPER FRIENDS ALWAYS TREAT THE PEOPLE AROUND THEM.
ICE
GOT THEM ALL? NOW USE THE *ICY* LETTERS TO FILL IN THE ANSWER TO THIS RIDDLE!
WHAT KIND OF JOKES DO PEOPLE TELL AT THE NORTH POLE?
"FROZEN _ _ _ _ _ _ ' _!"

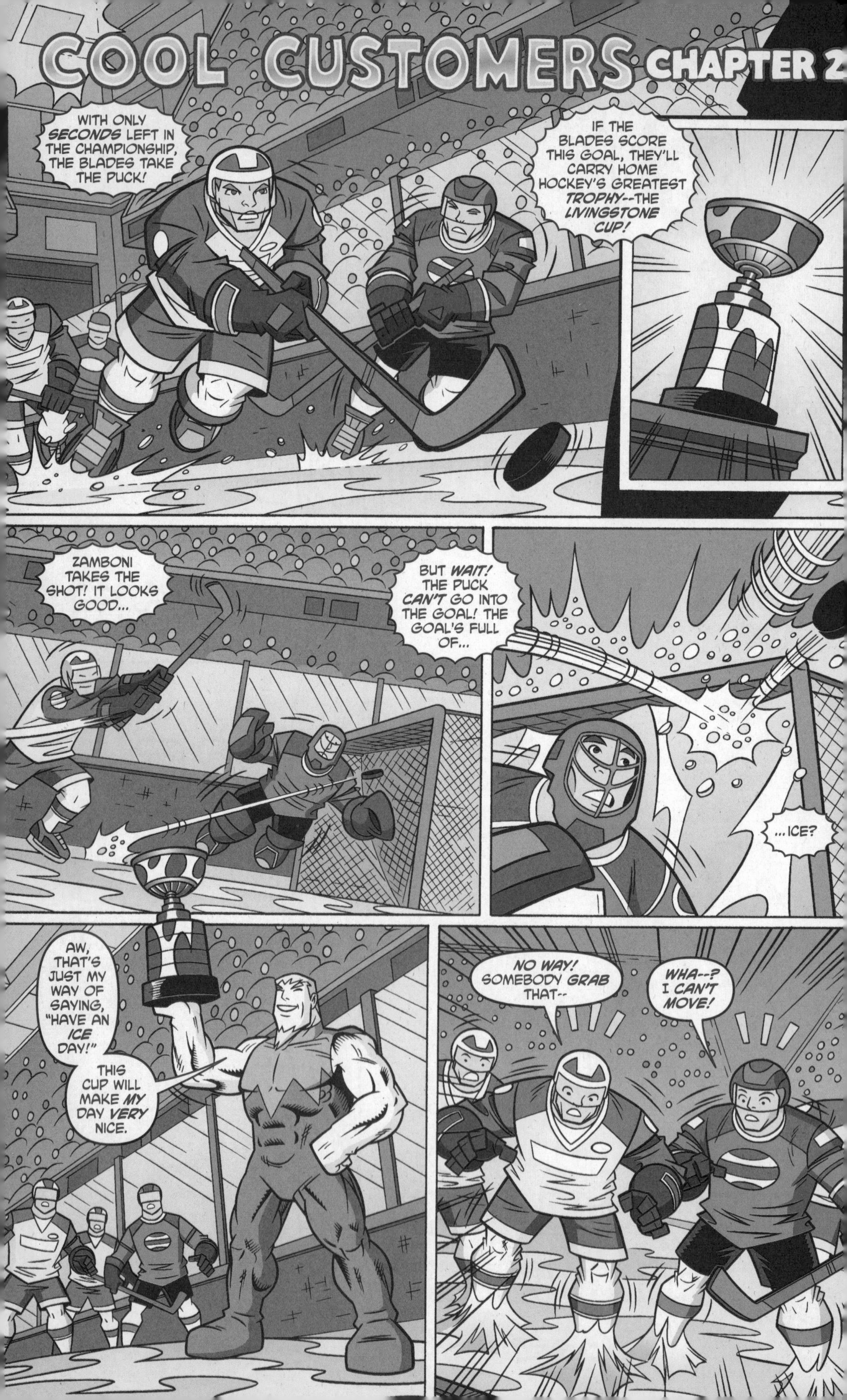
COOL CUSTOMERS CHAPTER 2
WITH ONLY SECONDS LEFT IN THE CHAMPIONSHIP, THE BLADES TAKE THE PUCK!
IF THE BLADES SCORE THIS GOAL, THEY'LL CARRY HOME HOCKEY'S GREATEST TROPHY--THE LIVINGSTONE CUP!
ZAMBONI TAKES THE SHOT! IT LOOKS GOOD...
BUT WAIT! THE PUCK CAN'T GO INTO THE GOAL! THE GOAL'S FULL OF...
...ICE?
AW, THAT'S JUST MY WAY OF SAYING, "HAVE AN ICE DAY!"
THIS CUP WILL MAKE MY DAY VERY NICE.
NO WAY! SOMEBODY GRAB THAT--
WHA--? I CAN'T MOVE!

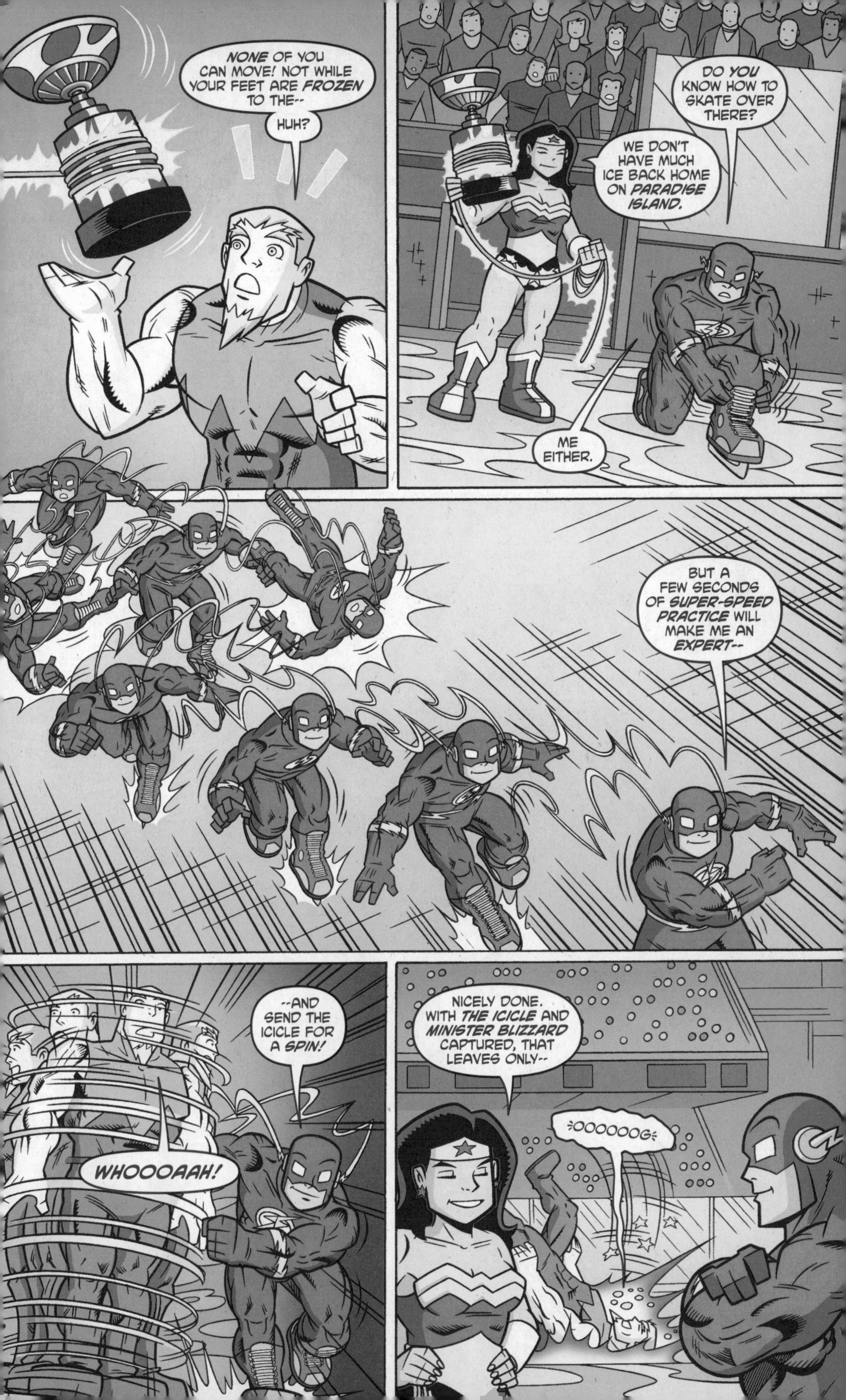
NONE OF YOU CAN MOVE! NOT WHILE YOUR FEET ARE FROZEN TO THE--
HUH?
DO YOU KNOW HOW TO SKATE OVER THERE?
WE DON'T HAVE MUCH ICE BACK HOME ON PARADISE ISLAND.
ME EITHER.
BUT A FEW SECONDS OF SUPER-SPEED PRACTICE WILL MAKE ME AN EXPERT--
--AND SEND THE ICICLE FOR A SPIN!
WHOOOAAH!
NICELY DONE. WITH THE ICICLE AND MINISTER BLIZZARD CAPTURED, THAT LEAVES ONLY--
OOOOOOG

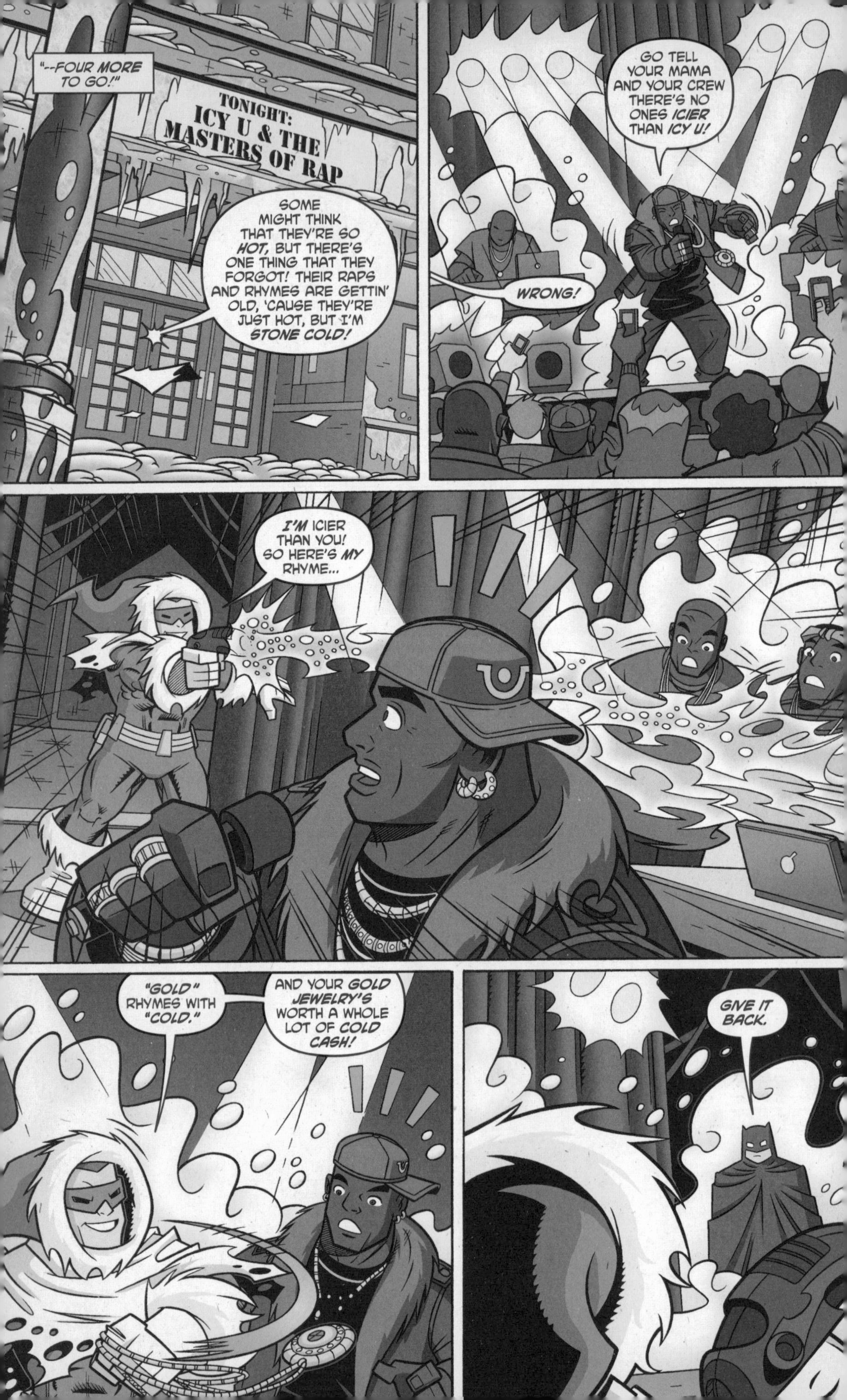
"--FOUR MORE TO GO!"
TONIGHT: ICY U & THE MASTERS OF RAP
SOME MIGHT THINK THAT THEY'RE SO HOT, BUT THERE'S ONE THING THAT THEY FORGOT! THEIR RAPS AND RHYMES ARE GETTIN' OLD, 'CAUSE THEY'RE JUST HOT, BUT I'M STONE COLD!
GO TELL YOUR MAMA AND YOUR CREW THERE'S NO ONES ICIER THAN ICY U!
WRONG!
I'M ICIER THAN YOU! SO HERE'S MY RHYME...
"GOLD" RHYMES WITH "COLD."
AND YOUR GOLD JEWELRY'S WORTH A WHOLE LOT OF COLD CASH!
GIVE IT BACK.

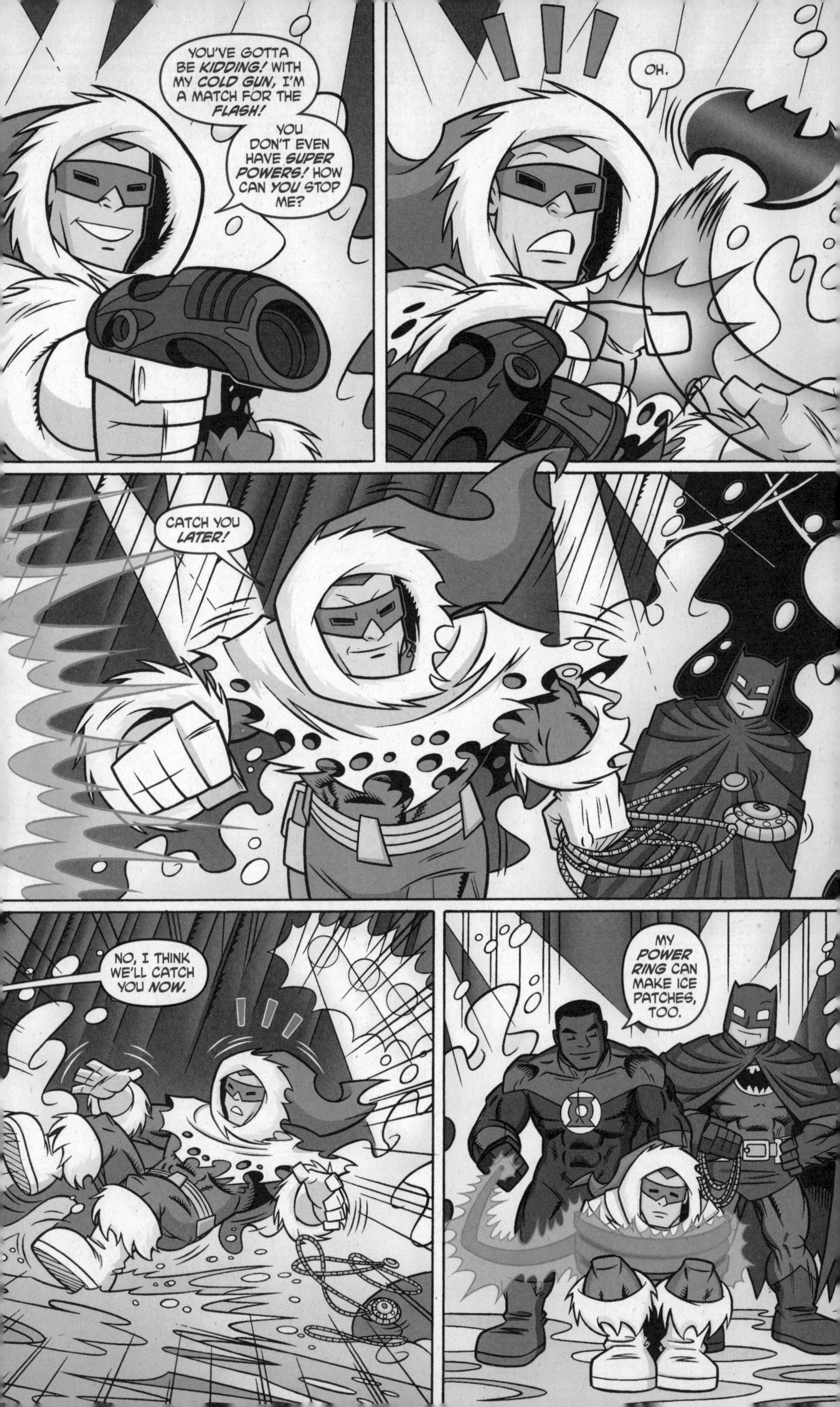
YOU'VE GOTTA BE KIDDING! WITH MY COLD GUN, I'M A MATCH FOR THE FLASH!
YOU DON'T EVEN HAVE SUPER POWERS! HOW CAN YOU STOP ME?
OH.
CATCH YOU LATER!
NO, I THINK WE'LL CATCH YOU NOW.
MY POWER RING CAN MAKE ICE PATCHES, TOO.

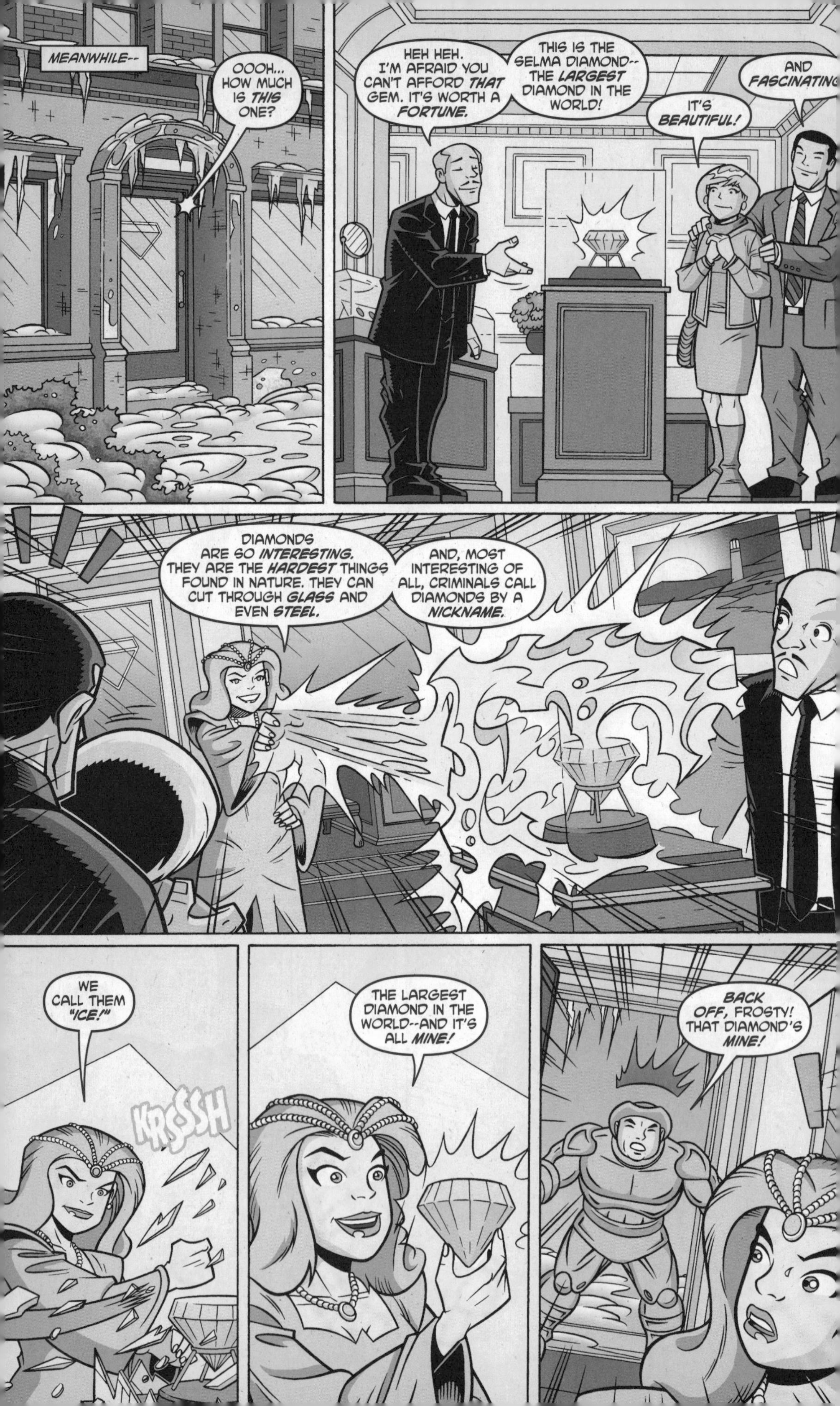
MEANWHILE--
OOOH... HOW MUCH IS THIS ONE?
HEH HEH. I'M AFRAID YOU CAN'T AFFORD THAT GEM. IT'S WORTH A FORTUNE.
THIS IS THE SELMA DIAMOND-- THE LARGEST DIAMOND IN THE WORLD!
IT'S BEAUTIFUL!
AND FASCINATING
DIAMONDS ARE SO INTERESTING. THEY ARE THE HARDEST THINGS FOUND IN NATURE. THEY CAN CUT THROUGH GLASS AND EVEN STEEL.
AND, MOST INTERESTING OF ALL, CRIMINALS CALL DIAMONDS BY A NICKNAME.
WE CALL THEM "ICE!"
KRSSSH
THE LARGEST DIAMOND IN THE WORLD--AND IT'S ALL MINE!
BACK OFF, FROSTY! THAT DIAMOND'S MINE!

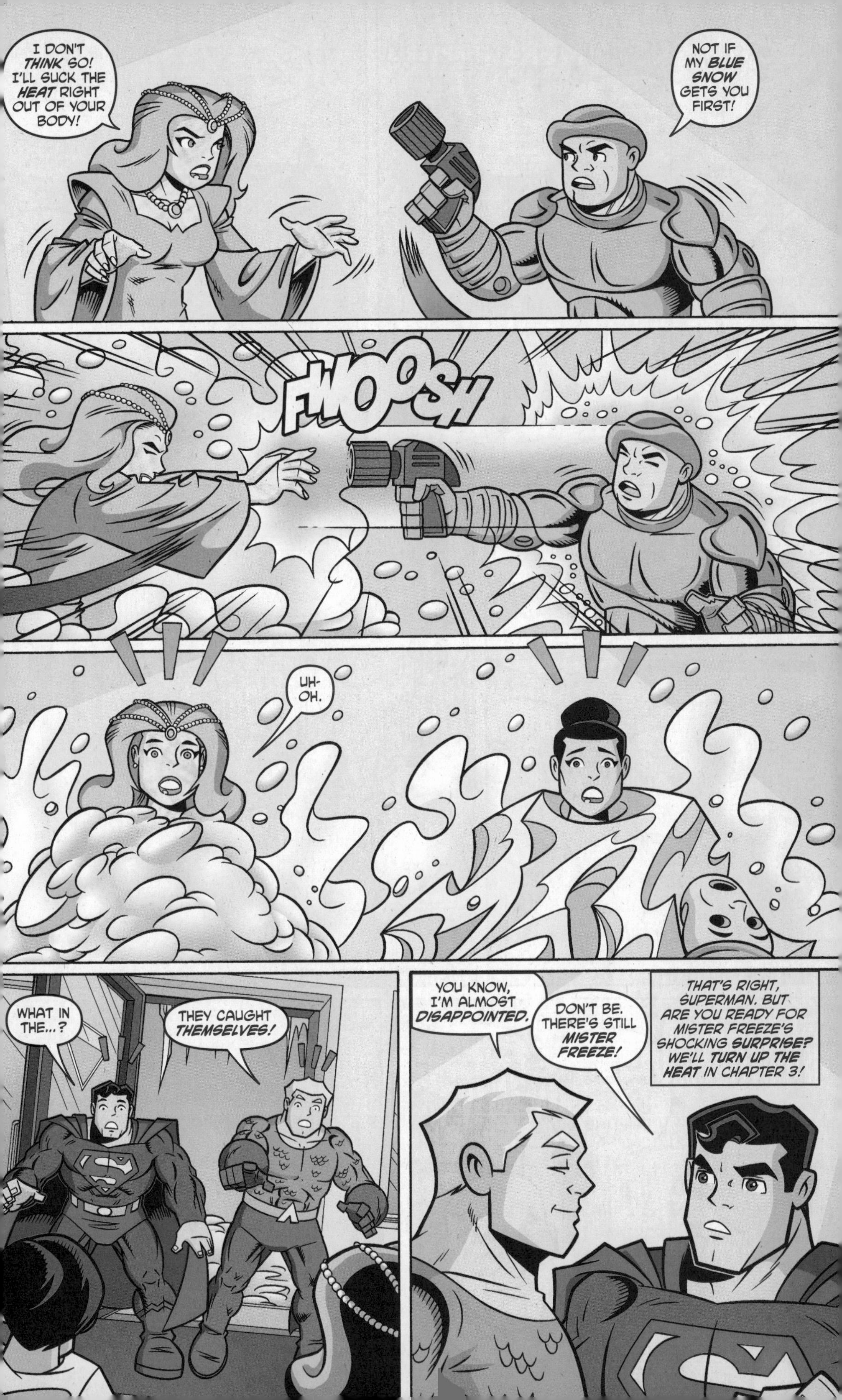

I DON'T THINK SO! I'LL SUCK THE HEAT RIGHT OUT OF YOUR BODY!
NOT IF MY BLUE SNOW GETS YOU FIRST!
FWOOSH
UH-OH.
WHAT IN THE...?
THEY CAUGHT THEMSELVES!
YOU KNOW, I'M ALMOST DISAPPOINTED.
DON'T BE. THERE'S STILL MISTER FREEZE!
THAT'S RIGHT, SUPERMAN. BUT ARE YOU READY FOR MISTER FREEZE'S SHOCKING SURPRISE? WE'LL TURN UP THE HEAT IN CHAPTER 3!

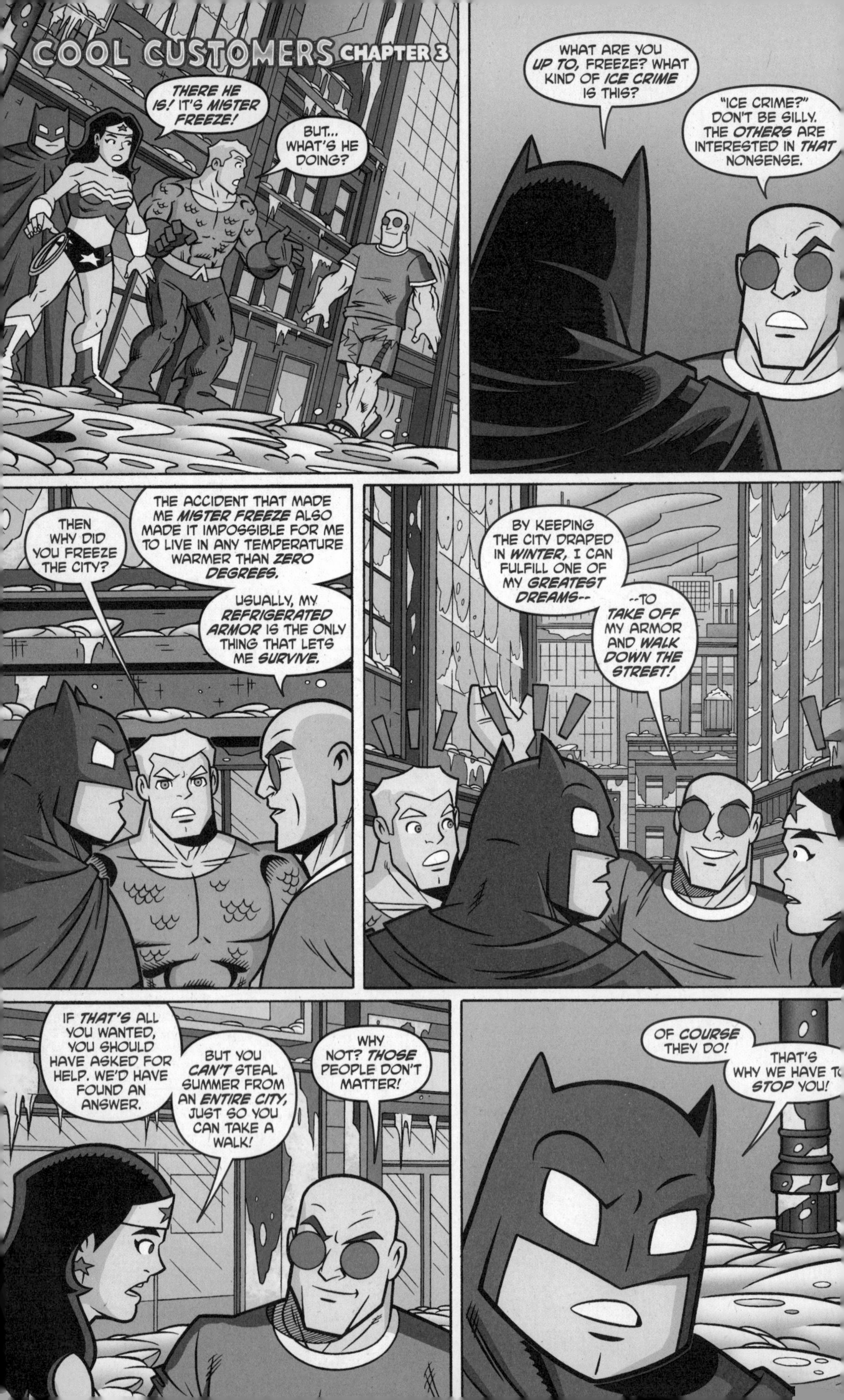
COOL CUSTOMERS CHAPTER 3
THERE HE IS! IT'S MISTER FREEZE!
BUT... WHAT'S HE DOING?
WHAT ARE YOU UP TO, FREEZE? WHAT KIND OF ICE CRIME IS THIS?
"ICE CRIME?" DON'T BE SILLY. THE OTHERS ARE INTERESTED IN THAT NONSENSE.
THEN WHY DID YOU FREEZE THE CITY?
THE ACCIDENT THAT MADE ME MISTER FREEZE ALSO MADE IT IMPOSSIBLE FOR ME TO LIVE IN ANY TEMPERATURE WARMER THAN ZERO DEGREES.
USUALLY, MY REFRIGERATED ARMOR IS THE ONLY THING THAT LETS ME SURVIVE.
BY KEEPING THE CITY DRAPED IN WINTER, I CAN FULFILL ONE OF MY GREATEST DREAMS--
--TO TAKE OFF MY ARMOR AND WALK DOWN THE STREET!
IF THAT'S ALL YOU WANTED, YOU SHOULD HAVE ASKED FOR HELP. WE'D HAVE FOUND AN ANSWER.
BUT YOU CAN'T STEAL SUMMER FROM AN ENTIRE CITY, JUST SO YOU CAN TAKE A WALK!
WHY NOT? THOSE PEOPLE DON'T MATTER!
OF COURSE THEY DO!
THAT'S WHY WE HAVE TO STOP YOU!

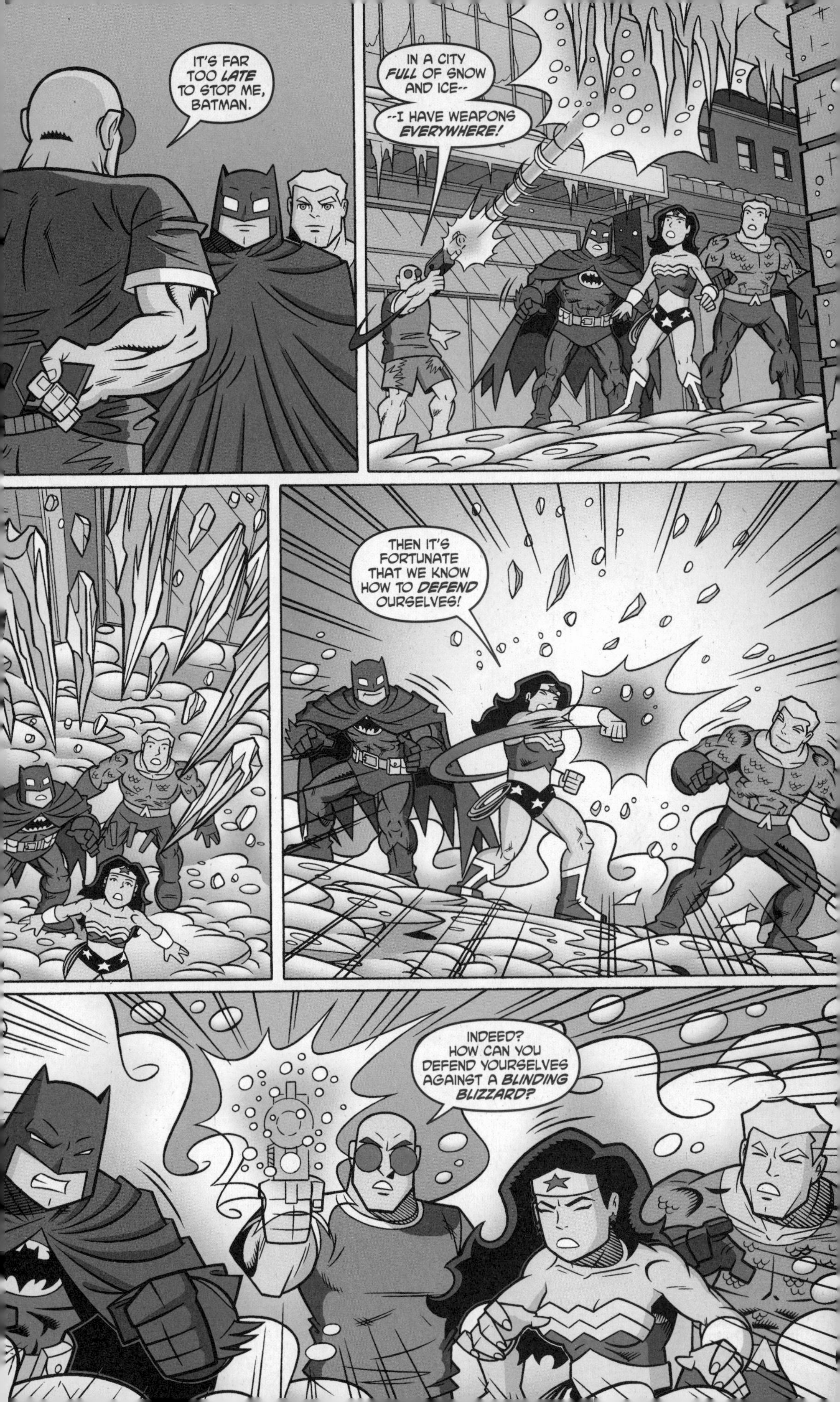
IT'S FAR TOO LATE TO STOP ME, BATMAN.
IN A CITY FULL OF SNOW AND ICE--
--I HAVE WEAPONS EVERYWHERE!
THEN IT'S FORTUNATE THAT WE KNOW HOW TO DEFEND OURSELVES!
INDEED? HOW CAN YOU DEFEND YOURSELVES AGAINST A BLINDING BLIZZARD?

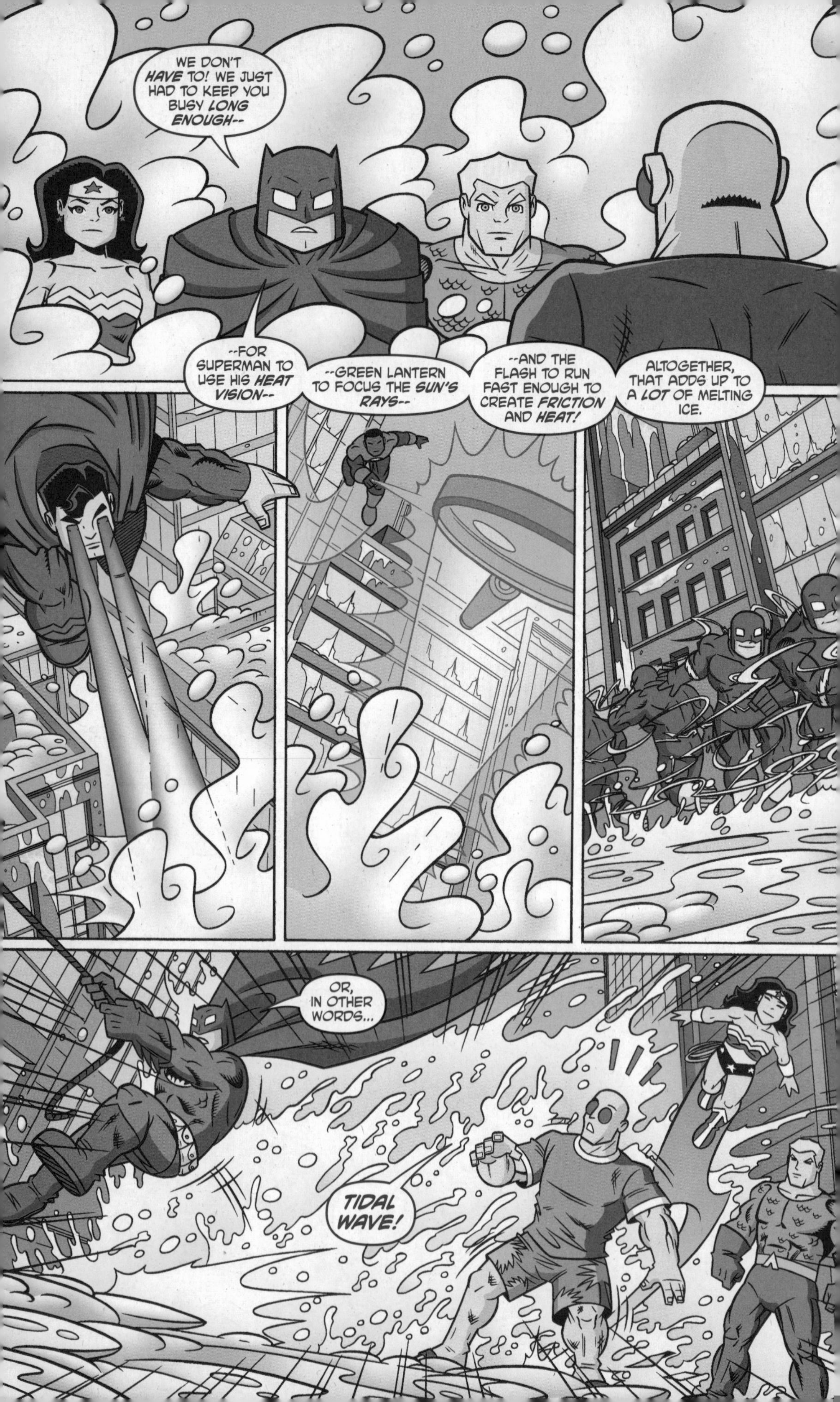

WE DON'T HAVE TO! WE JUST HAD TO KEEP YOU BUSY LONG ENOUGH--
--FOR SUPERMAN TO USE HIS HEAT VISION--
--GREEN LANTERN TO FOCUS THE SUN'S RAYS--
--AND THE FLASH TO RUN FAST ENOUGH TO CREATE FRICTION AND HEAT!
ALTOGETHER, THAT ADDS UP TO A LOT OF MELTING ICE.
OR, IN OTHER WORDS...
TIDAL WAVE!

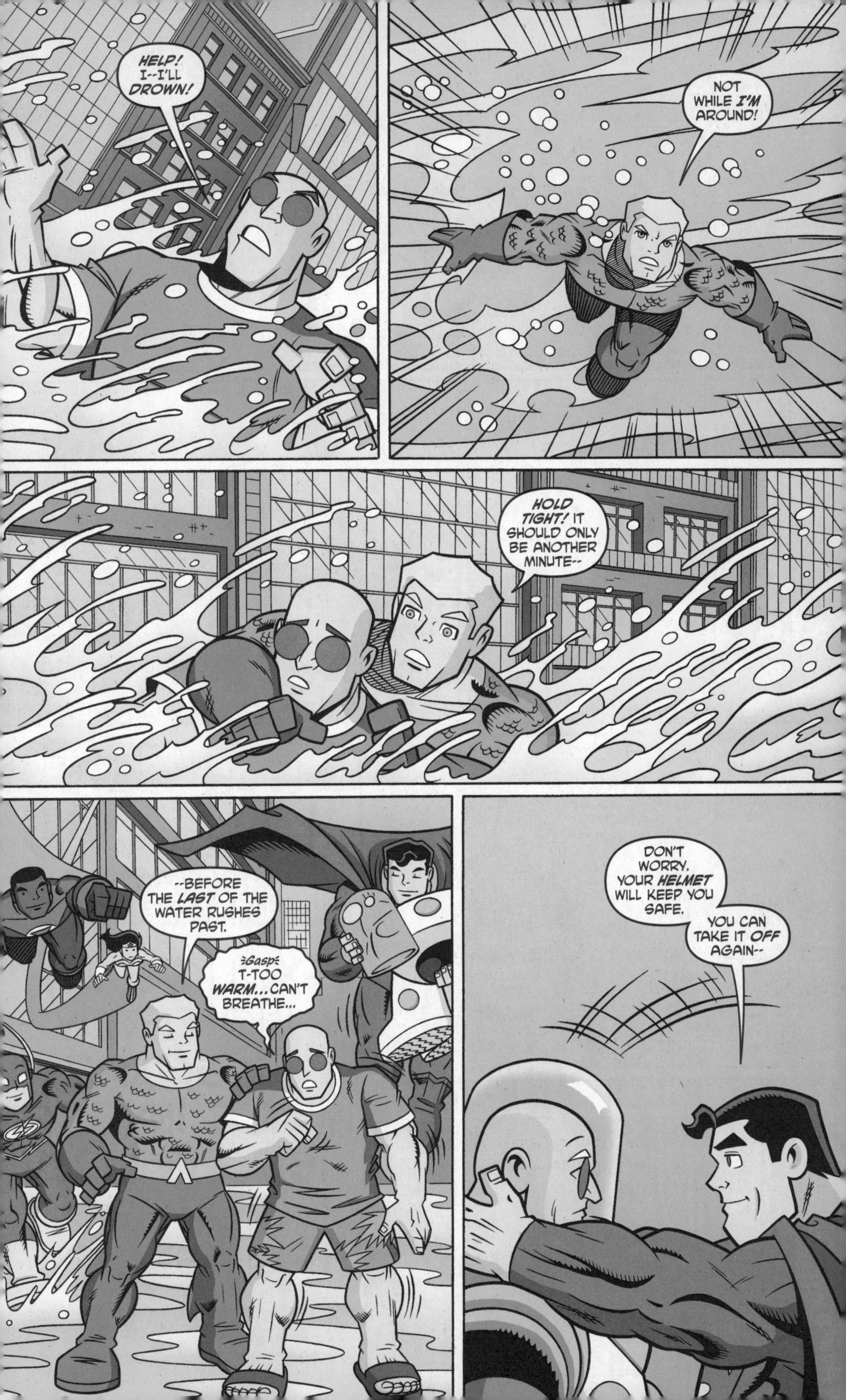
HELP! I--I'LL DROWN!
NOT WHILE I'M AROUND!
HOLD TIGHT! IT SHOULD ONLY BE ANOTHER MINUTE--
--BEFORE THE LAST OF THE WATER RUSHES PAST.
Gasp T-TOO WARM... CAN'T BREATHE...
DON'T WORRY. YOUR HELMET WILL KEEP YOU SAFE.
YOU CAN TAKE IT OFF AGAIN--

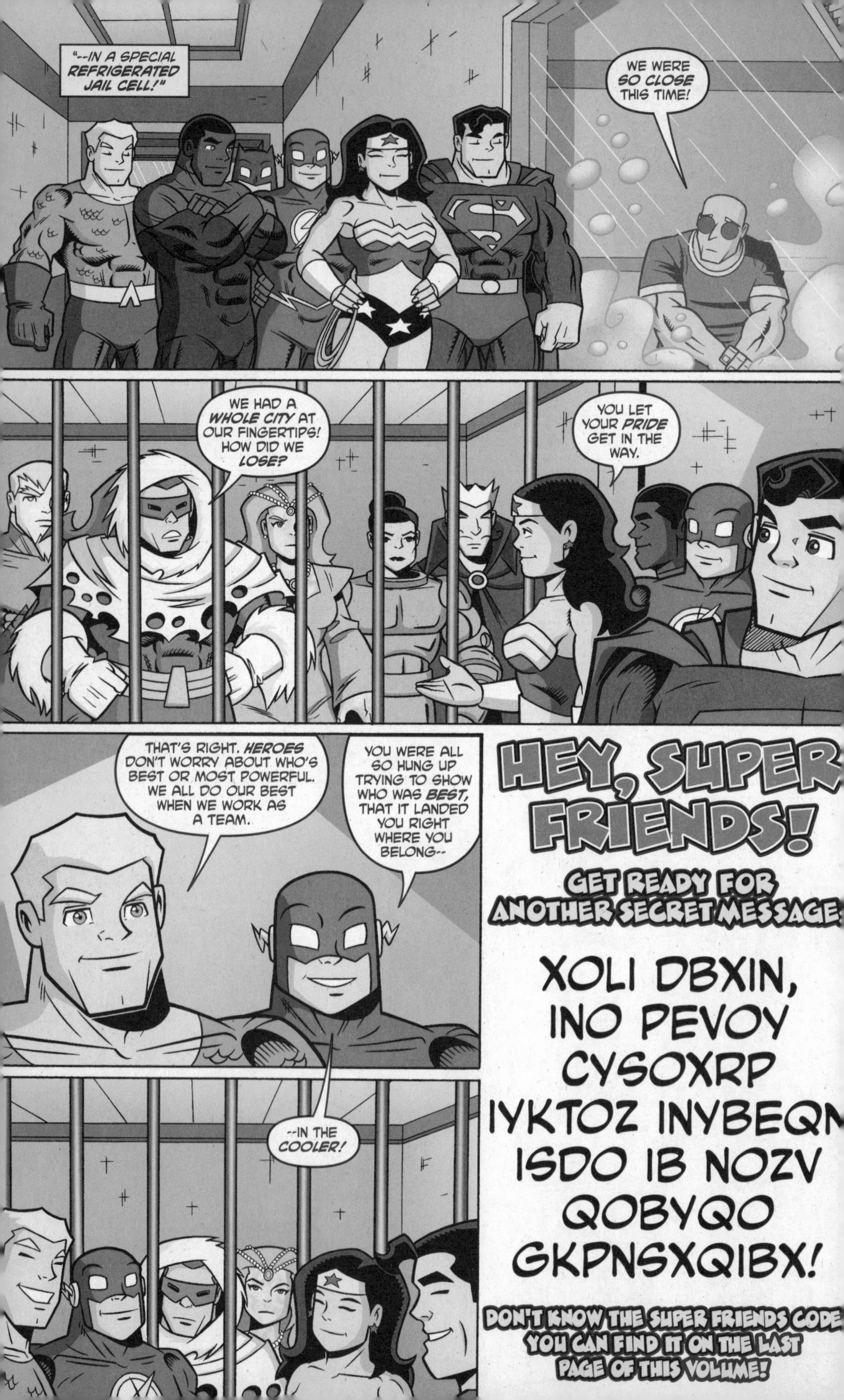
"--IN A SPECIAL REFRIGERATED JAIL CELL!"
WE WERE SO CLOSE THIS TIME!
WE HAD A WHOLE CITY AT OUR FINGERTIPS! HOW DID WE LOSE?
YOU LET YOUR PRIDE GET IN THE WAY.
THAT'S RIGHT. HEROES DON'T WORRY ABOUT WHO'S BEST OR MOST POWERFUL. WE ALL DO OUR BEST WHEN WE WORK AS A TEAM.
YOU WERE ALL SO HUNG UP TRYING TO SHOW WHO WAS BEST, THAT IT LANDED YOU RIGHT WHERE YOU BELONG--
--IN THE COOLER!
HEY, SUPER FRIENDS!
GET READY FOR ANOTHER SECRET MESSAGE
XOLI DBXIN,
INO PEVOY
CYSOXRP
IYKTOZ INYBEQ
ISDO IB NOZV
QOBYQO
GKPNSXQIBX!
DON'T KNOW THE SUPER FRIENDS CODE? YOU CAN FIND IT ON THE LAST PAGE OF THIS VOLUME!

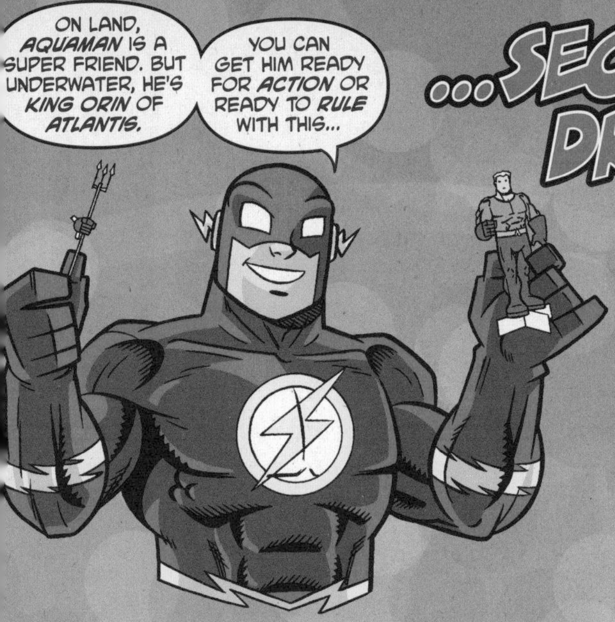
ON LAND, *AQUAMAN* IS A SUPER FRIEND. BUT UNDERWATER, HE'S *KING ORIN* OF *ATLANTIS.*
YOU CAN GET HIM READY FOR *ACTION* OR READY TO *RULE* WITH THIS...

# ...SECRET IDENTITY DRESS-UP KIT

## INSTRUCTIONS:

1.) CUT OUT FIGURE AND STAND.

2.) PASTE THE FIGURE AND STAND ONTO CARDBOARD. TRIM THE CARDBOARD TO FIT.

3.) CUT THE DOTTED SLOTS IN BOTTOM OF THE FIGURE AND THE BASE. SLIDE ONE SLOT INTO THE OTHER, TO ATTACH THE FIGURE TO THE BASE.

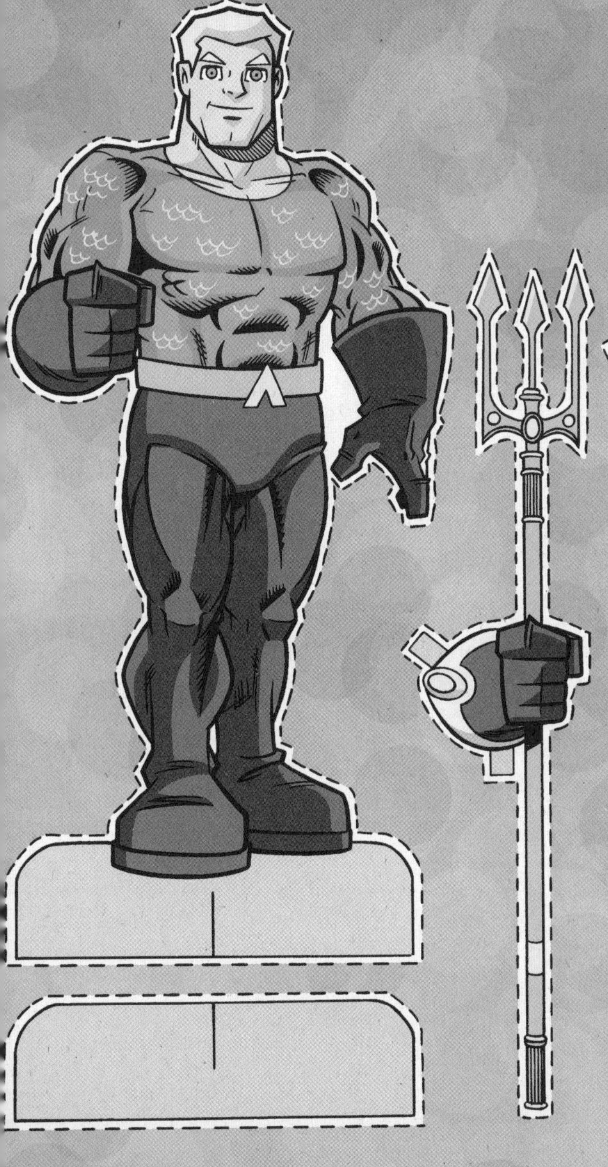

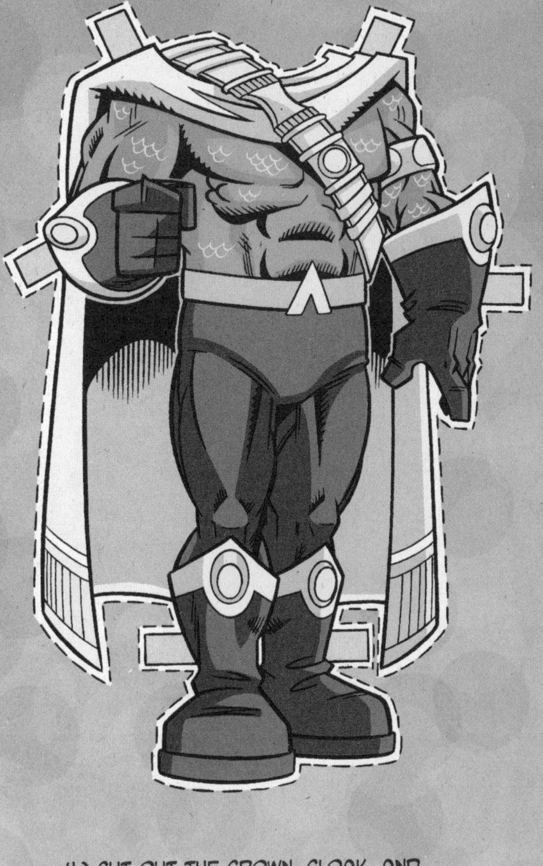

4.) CUT OUT THE CROWN, CLOAK, AND TRIDENT. KEEP THEIR TABS ATTACHED.

5.) FOLD OVER THE TABS ON THE PIECES. USE THEM TO ATTACH THE PIECES TO THE FIGURE.

6.) ***ANCHORS AWEIGH!***

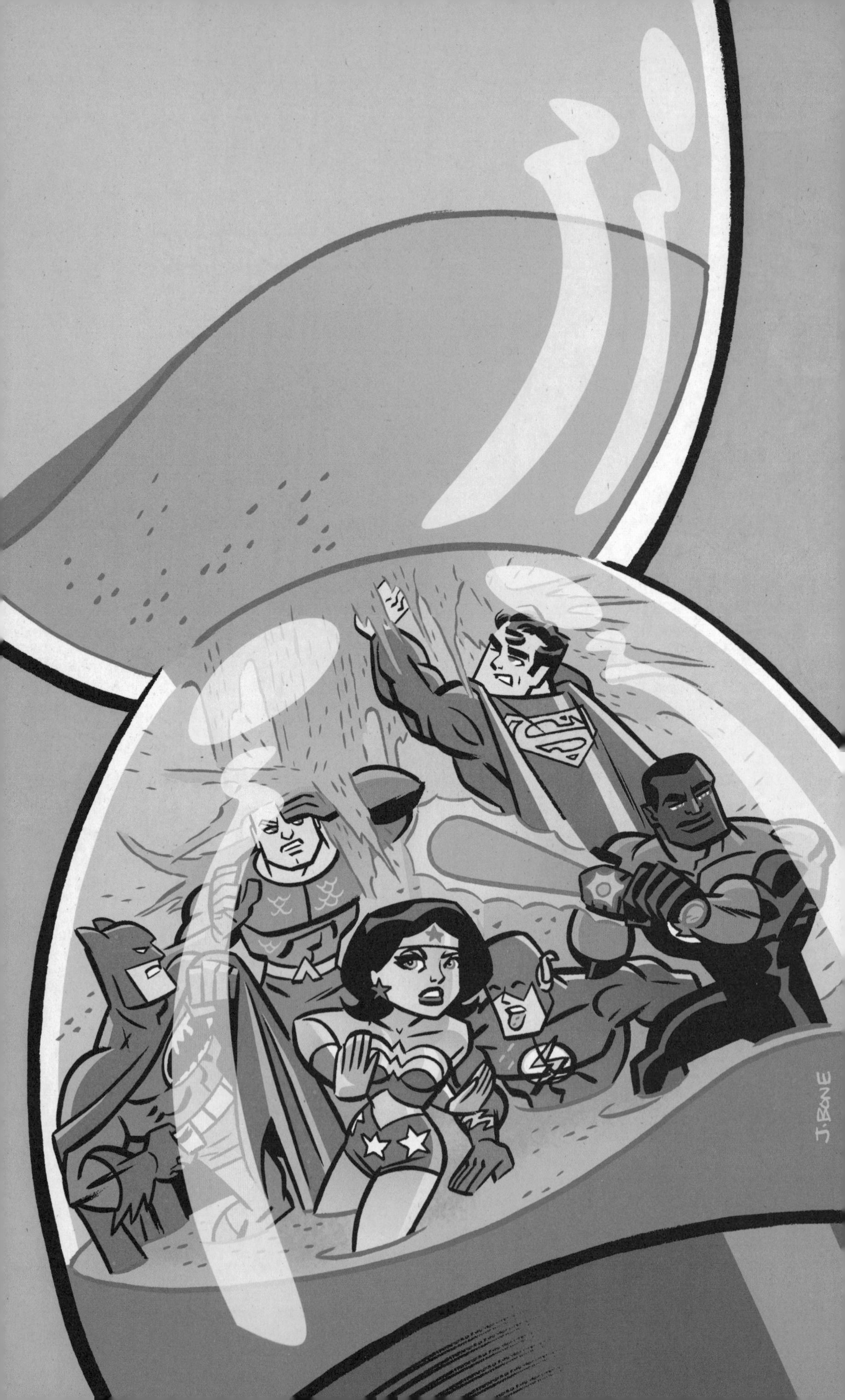
J.BONE

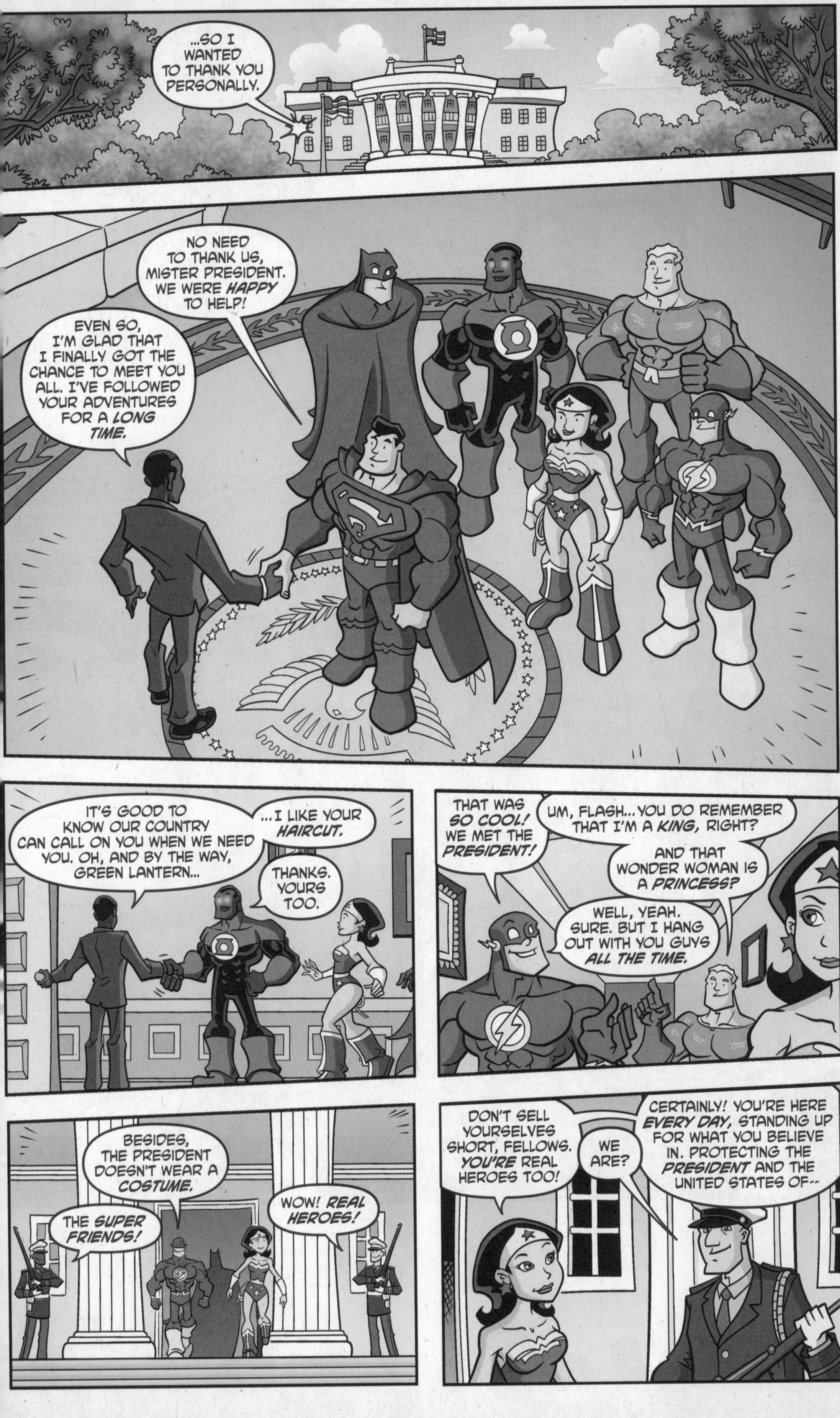
...SO I WANTED TO THANK YOU PERSONALLY.
NO NEED TO THANK US, MISTER PRESIDENT. WE WERE HAPPY TO HELP!
EVEN SO, I'M GLAD THAT I FINALLY GOT THE CHANCE TO MEET YOU ALL. I'VE FOLLOWED YOUR ADVENTURES FOR A LONG TIME.
IT'S GOOD TO KNOW OUR COUNTRY CAN CALL ON YOU WHEN WE NEED YOU. OH, AND BY THE WAY, GREEN LANTERN...
...I LIKE YOUR HAIRCUT.
THANKS. YOURS TOO.
THAT WAS SO COOL! WE MET THE PRESIDENT!
UM, FLASH... YOU DO REMEMBER THAT I'M A KING, RIGHT?
AND THAT WONDER WOMAN IS A PRINCESS?
WELL, YEAH. SURE. BUT I HANG OUT WITH YOU GUYS ALL THE TIME.
BESIDES, THE PRESIDENT DOESN'T WEAR A COSTUME.
THE SUPER FRIENDS!
WOW! REAL HEROES!
DON'T SELL YOURSELVES SHORT, FELLOWS. YOU'RE REAL HEROES TOO!
WE ARE?
CERTAINLY! YOU'RE HERE EVERY DAY, STANDING UP FOR WHAT YOU BELIEVE IN. PROTECTING THE PRESIDENT AND THE UNITED STATES OF--

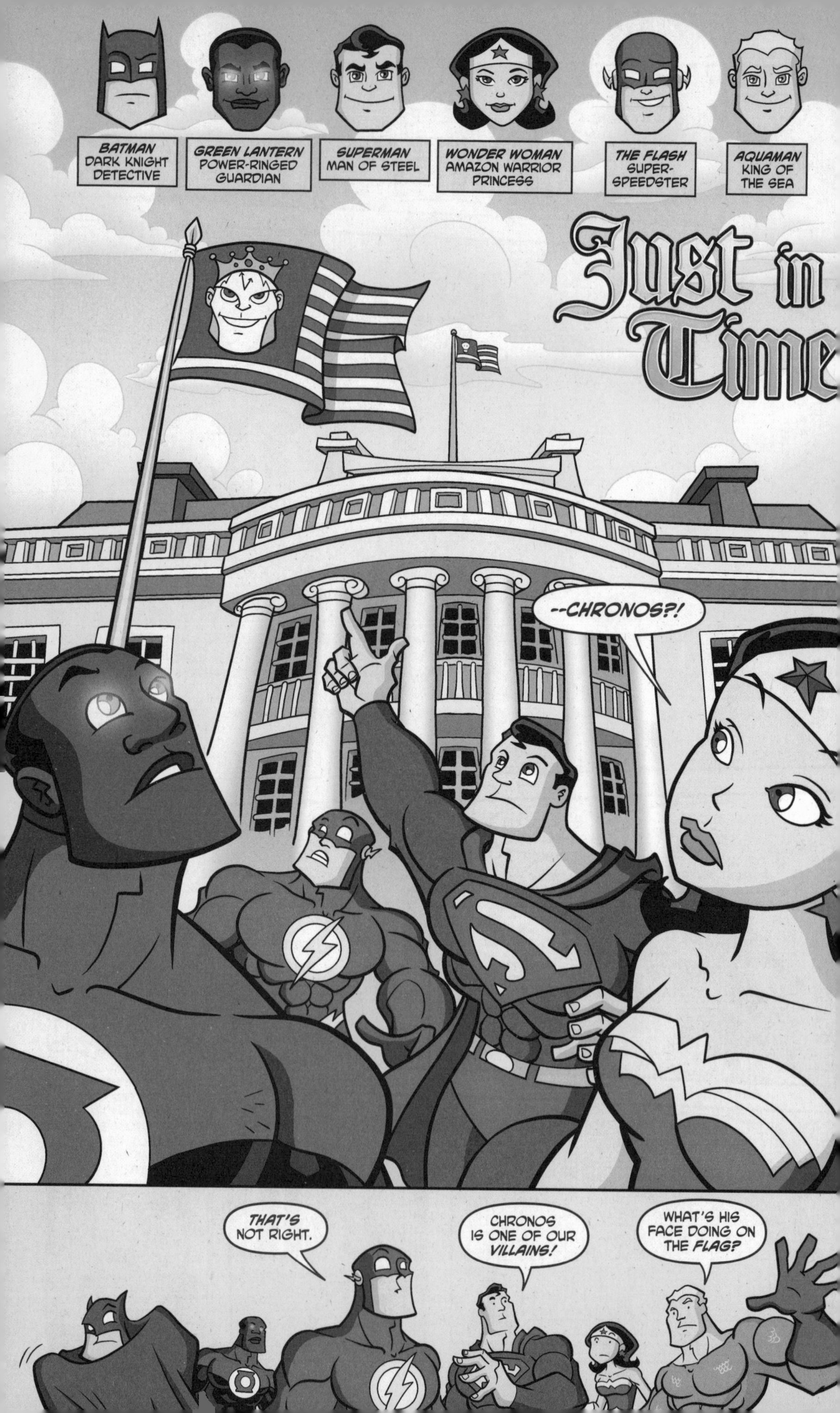

BATMAN DARK KNIGHT DETECTIVE
GREEN LANTERN POWER-RINGED GUARDIAN
SUPERMAN MAN OF STEEL
WONDER WOMAN AMAZON WARRIOR PRINCESS
THE FLASH SUPER-SPEEDSTER
AQUAMAN KING OF THE SEA
Just in Time
--CHRONOS?!
THAT'S NOT RIGHT.
CHRONOS IS ONE OF OUR VILLAINS!
WHAT'S HIS FACE DOING ON THE FLAG?

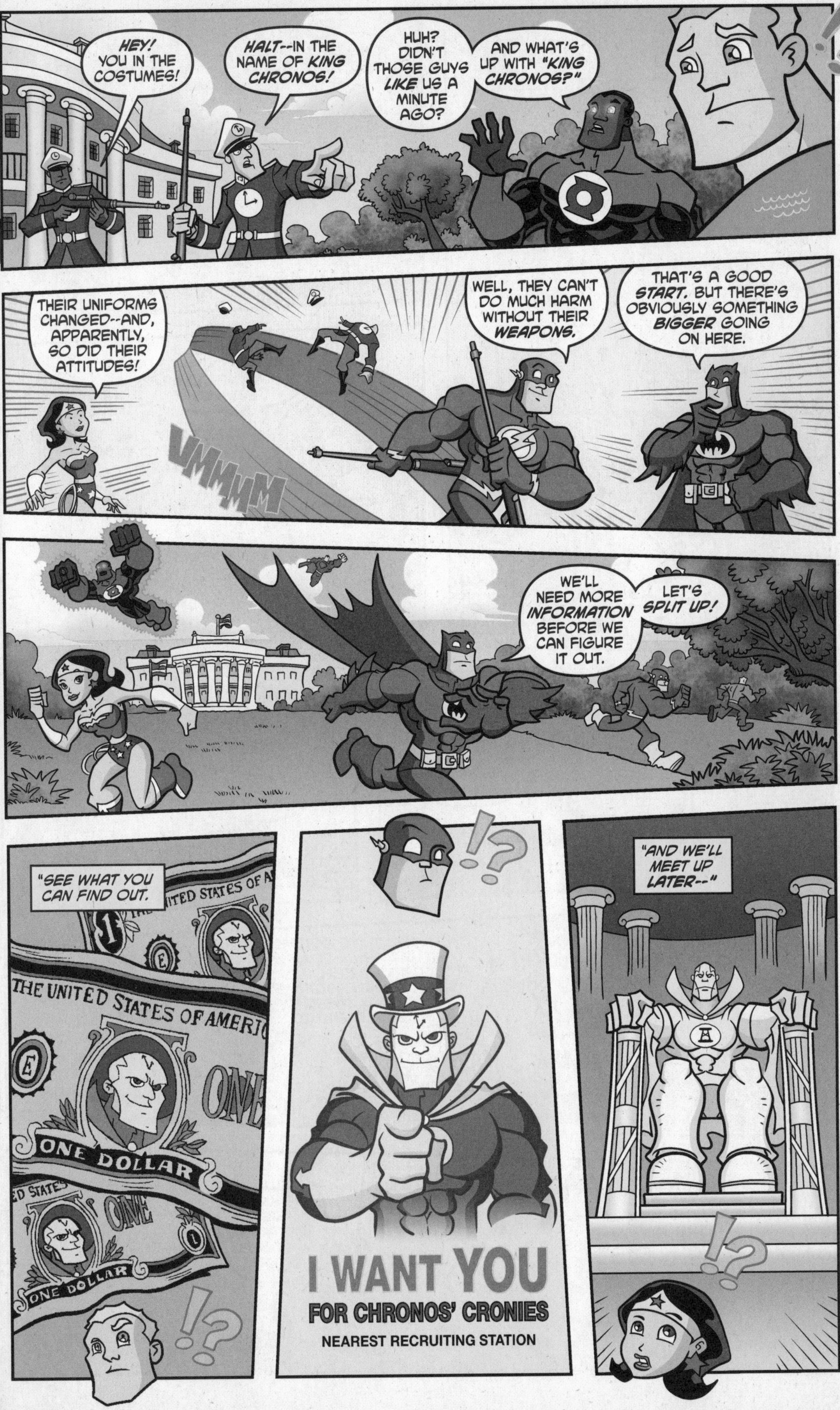

HEY! YOU IN THE COSTUMES!
HALT--IN THE NAME OF KING CHRONOS!
HUH? DIDN'T THOSE GUYS LIKE US A MINUTE AGO?
AND WHAT'S UP WITH "KING CHRONOS?"
!?
THEIR UNIFORMS CHANGED--AND, APPARENTLY, SO DID THEIR ATTITUDES!
VMMMM
WELL, THEY CAN'T DO MUCH HARM WITHOUT THEIR WEAPONS.
THAT'S A GOOD START. BUT THERE'S OBVIOUSLY SOMETHING BIGGER GOING ON HERE.
WE'LL NEED MORE INFORMATION BEFORE WE CAN FIGURE IT OUT.
LET'S SPLIT UP!
"SEE WHAT YOU CAN FIND OUT.
THE UNITED STATES OF AMERIC
ONE
ONE DOLLAR
!?
!?
I WANT YOU
FOR CHRONOS' CRONIES
NEAREST RECRUITING STATION
"AND WE'LL MEET UP LATER--"
!?

"--AT THE *WASHINGTON MONUMENT!*"

*THIS* IS THE *WASHINGTON MONUMENT?* I DON'T REMEMBER IT LOOKING LIKE *THIS...*

#1

IT NEVER *USED* TO.

YEAH, BUT THAT'S WHEN IT WAS STILL THE *WASHINGTON MONUMENT.* IT'S THE *CHRONOS MONUMENT* NOW!

CHRONOS IS SUDDENLY THE KING OF THE WHOLE *COUNTRY!* BUT...*HOW?*

HE'S A *MASTER OF TIME.* HE MUST HAVE *CHANGED* HISTORY--

--TO MAKE HIMSELF *RULER OF AMERICA!*

CLICK!

THEN I'M AFRAID WE HAVE A *PROBLEM.* AMERICA IS MORE THAN *TWO HUNDRED YEARS* OLD!

HOW CAN WE EVER FIND THE *EXACT DATE* WHEN CHRONOS CHANGED THINGS?

JULY 2, 1776.

!?

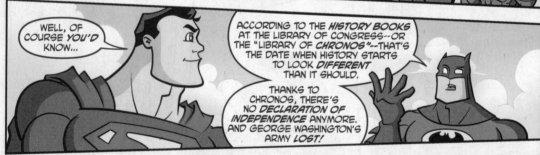

WELL, OF COURSE *YOU'D* KNOW...

ACCORDING TO THE *HISTORY BOOKS* AT THE *LIBRARY OF CONGRESS*--OR THE "LIBRARY OF *CHRONOS"*--THAT'S THE DATE WHEN HISTORY STARTS TO LOOK *DIFFERENT* THAN IT SHOULD.

THANKS TO CHRONOS, THERE'S NO *DECLARATION OF INDEPENDENCE* ANYMORE. AND GEORGE WASHINGTON'S ARMY *LOST!*

THEN ALL WE HAVE TO DO IS FIND A WAY TO *TRAVEL THROUGH TIME, STOP CHRONOS,* AND *FIX HISTORY.*

HEY, *NO SWEAT!*

WELL... WE KNOW WHERE TO FIND A *TIME MACHINE,* ANYWAY--

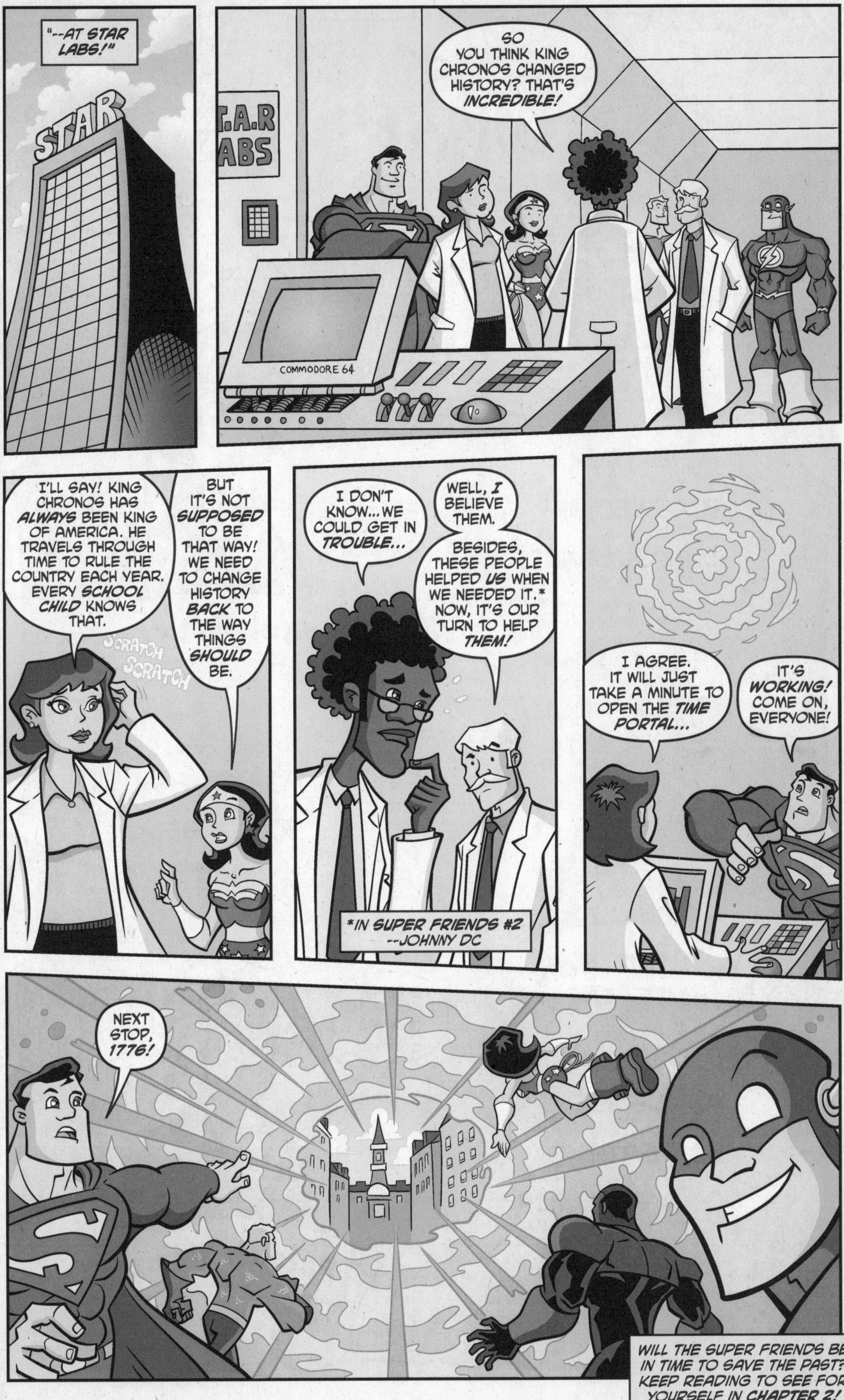

"--AT STAR LABS!"
STAR
S.T.A.R LABS
SO YOU THINK KING CHRONOS CHANGED HISTORY? THAT'S *INCREDIBLE!*
COMMODORE 64
I'LL SAY! KING CHRONOS HAS *ALWAYS* BEEN KING OF AMERICA. HE TRAVELS THROUGH TIME TO RULE THE COUNTRY EACH YEAR. EVERY *SCHOOL CHILD* KNOWS THAT.
SCRATCH SCRATCH
BUT IT'S NOT *SUPPOSED* TO BE THAT WAY! WE NEED TO CHANGE HISTORY *BACK* TO THE WAY THINGS *SHOULD* BE.
I DON'T KNOW... WE COULD GET IN *TROUBLE...*
WELL, *I* BELIEVE THEM.
BESIDES, THESE PEOPLE HELPED *US* WHEN WE NEEDED IT.* NOW, IT'S OUR TURN TO HELP *THEM!*
*IN *SUPER FRIENDS #2* --JOHNNY DC
I AGREE. IT WILL JUST TAKE A MINUTE TO OPEN THE *TIME PORTAL...*
IT'S *WORKING!* COME ON, EVERYONE!
NEXT STOP, *1776!*
WILL THE SUPER FRIENDS BE IN TIME TO SAVE THE PAST? KEEP READING TO SEE FOR YOURSELF IN *CHAPTER 2!*

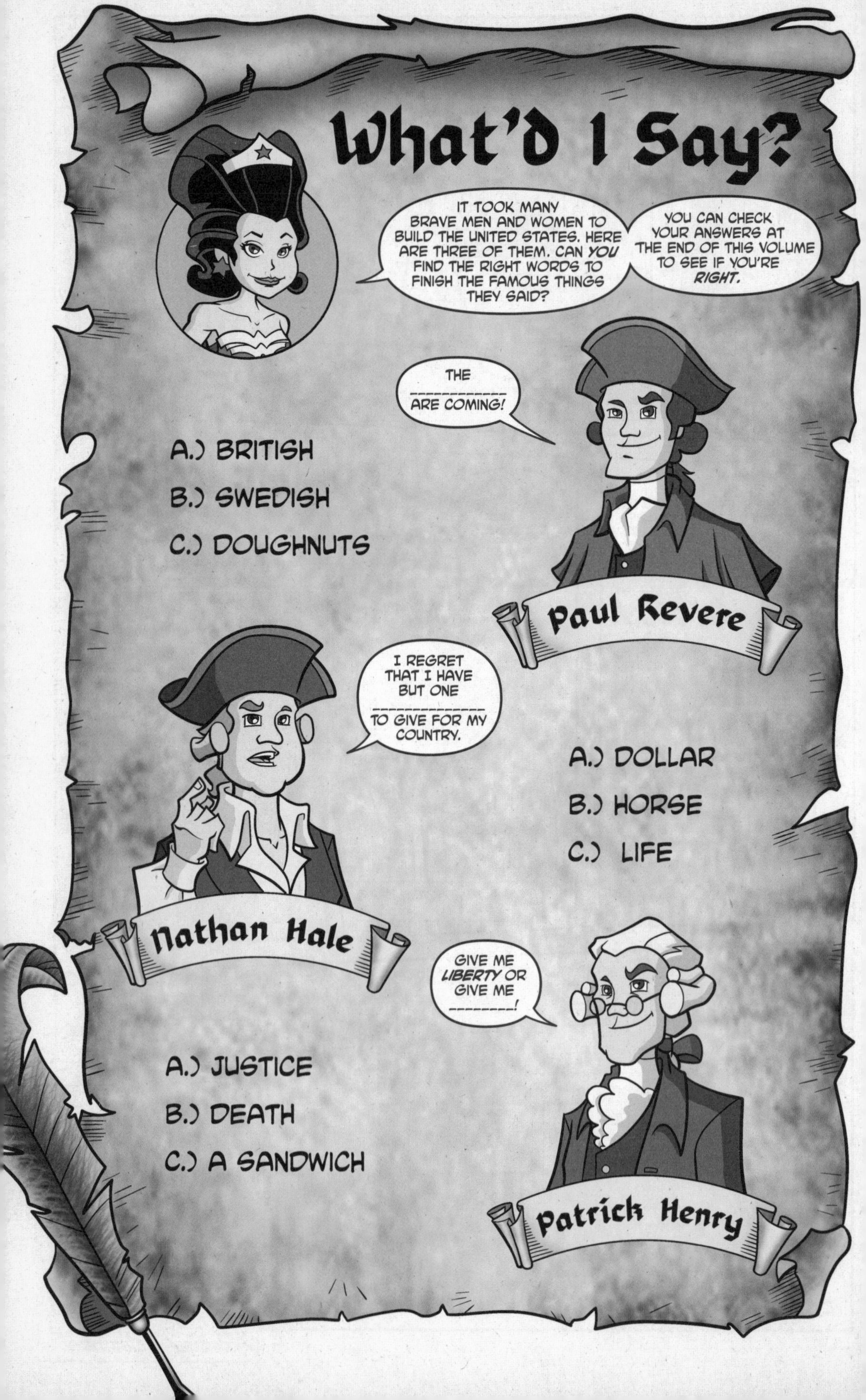
What'd I Say?
IT TOOK MANY BRAVE MEN AND WOMEN TO BUILD THE UNITED STATES. HERE ARE THREE OF THEM. CAN *YOU* FIND THE RIGHT WORDS TO FINISH THE FAMOUS THINGS THEY SAID?
YOU CAN CHECK YOUR ANSWERS AT THE END OF THIS VOLUME TO SEE IF YOU'RE *RIGHT.*
THE ____________ ARE COMING!
A.) BRITISH
B.) SWEDISH
C.) DOUGHNUTS
Paul Revere
I REGRET THAT I HAVE BUT ONE ____________ TO GIVE FOR MY COUNTRY.
A.) DOLLAR
B.) HORSE
C.) LIFE
Nathan Hale
GIVE ME *LIBERTY* OR GIVE ME _________!
A.) JUSTICE
B.) DEATH
C.) A SANDWICH
Patrick Henry

# Just in Time Chapter

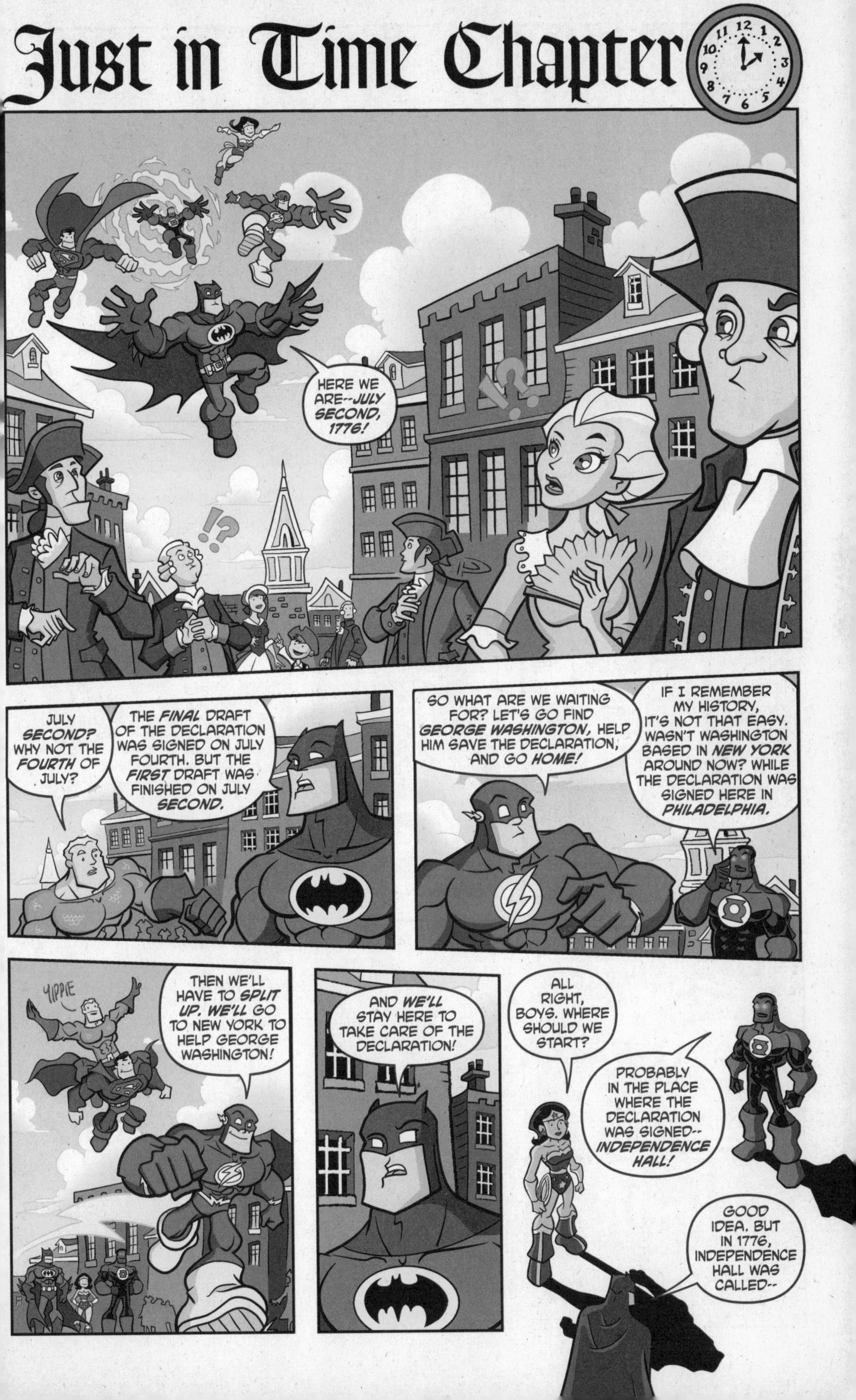

11 12 1 2 3 4 5 6 7 8 9 10
HERE WE ARE--JULY SECOND, 1776!
!?
!?
JULY SECOND? WHY NOT THE FOURTH OF JULY?
THE FINAL DRAFT OF THE DECLARATION WAS SIGNED ON JULY FOURTH. BUT THE FIRST DRAFT WAS FINISHED ON JULY SECOND.
SO WHAT ARE WE WAITING FOR? LET'S GO FIND GEORGE WASHINGTON, HELP HIM SAVE THE DECLARATION, AND GO HOME!
IF I REMEMBER MY HISTORY, IT'S NOT THAT EASY. WASN'T WASHINGTON BASED IN NEW YORK AROUND NOW? WHILE THE DECLARATION WAS SIGNED HERE IN PHILADELPHIA.
YIPPIE
THEN WE'LL HAVE TO SPLIT UP. WE'LL GO TO NEW YORK TO HELP GEORGE WASHINGTON!
AND WE'LL STAY HERE TO TAKE CARE OF THE DECLARATION!
ALL RIGHT, BOYS. WHERE SHOULD WE START?
PROBABLY IN THE PLACE WHERE THE DECLARATION WAS SIGNED--INDEPENDENCE HALL!
GOOD IDEA. BUT IN 1776, INDEPENDENCE HALL WAS CALLED--

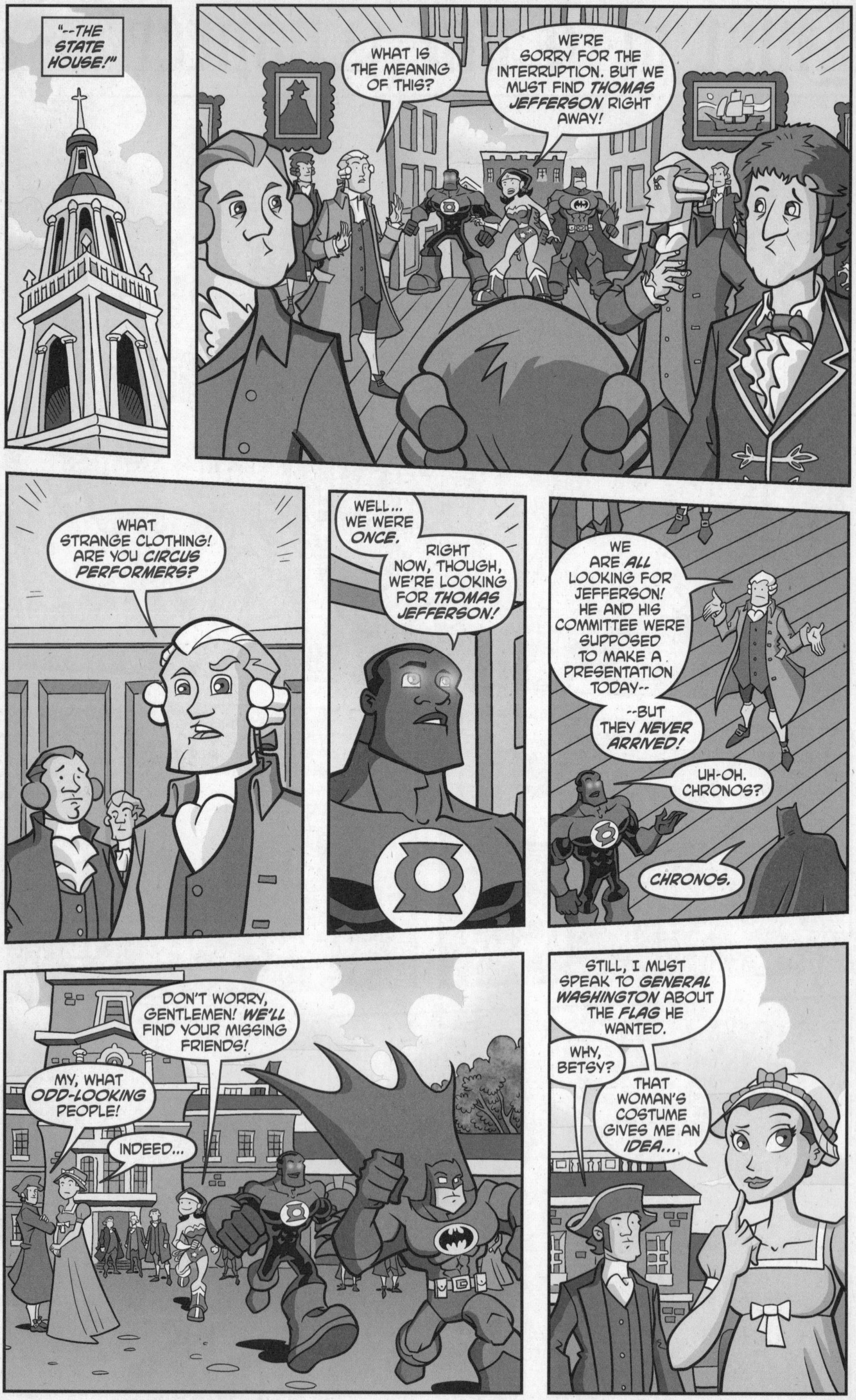
"--THE STATE HOUSE!"
WHAT IS THE MEANING OF THIS?
WE'RE SORRY FOR THE INTERRUPTION. BUT WE MUST FIND THOMAS JEFFERSON RIGHT AWAY!
WHAT STRANGE CLOTHING! ARE YOU CIRCUS PERFORMERS?
WELL... WE WERE ONCE.
RIGHT NOW, THOUGH, WE'RE LOOKING FOR THOMAS JEFFERSON!
WE ARE ALL LOOKING FOR JEFFERSON! HE AND HIS COMMITTEE WERE SUPPOSED TO MAKE A PRESENTATION TODAY--
--BUT THEY NEVER ARRIVED!
UH-OH. CHRONOS?
CHRONOS.
DON'T WORRY, GENTLEMEN! WE'LL FIND YOUR MISSING FRIENDS!
MY, WHAT ODD-LOOKING PEOPLE!
INDEED...
STILL, I MUST SPEAK TO GENERAL WASHINGTON ABOUT THE FLAG HE WANTED.
WHY, BETSY?
THAT WOMAN'S COSTUME GIVES ME AN IDEA...

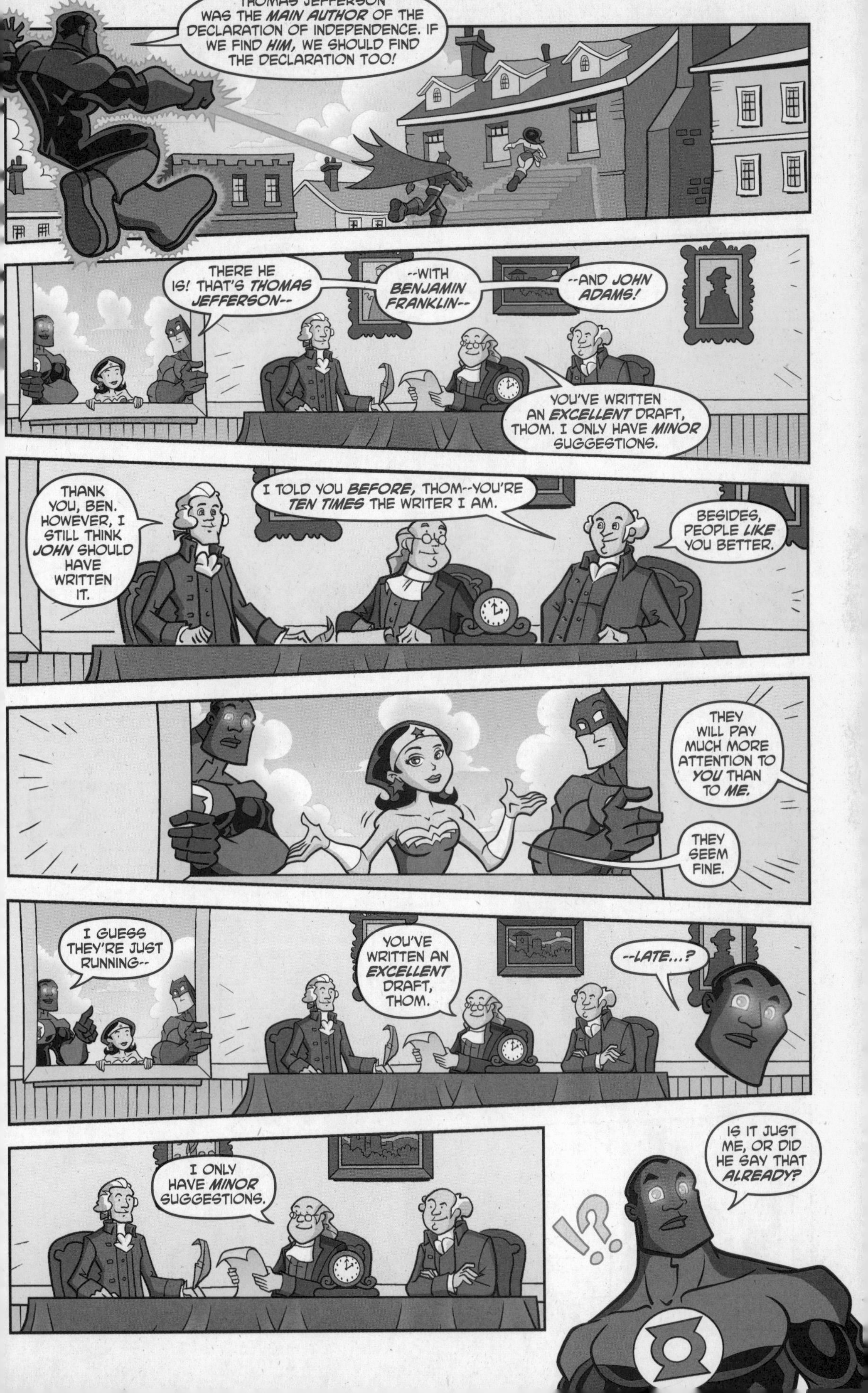
THOMAS JEFFERSON WAS THE MAIN AUTHOR OF THE DECLARATION OF INDEPENDENCE. IF WE FIND HIM, WE SHOULD FIND THE DECLARATION TOO!
THERE HE IS! THAT'S THOMAS JEFFERSON--
--WITH BENJAMIN FRANKLIN--
--AND JOHN ADAMS!
YOU'VE WRITTEN AN EXCELLENT DRAFT, THOM. I ONLY HAVE MINOR SUGGESTIONS.
THANK YOU, BEN. HOWEVER, I STILL THINK JOHN SHOULD HAVE WRITTEN IT.
I TOLD YOU BEFORE, THOM--YOU'RE TEN TIMES THE WRITER I AM.
BESIDES, PEOPLE LIKE YOU BETTER.
THEY WILL PAY MUCH MORE ATTENTION TO YOU THAN TO ME.
THEY SEEM FINE.
I GUESS THEY'RE JUST RUNNING--
YOU'VE WRITTEN AN EXCELLENT DRAFT, THOM.
--LATE...?
I ONLY HAVE MINOR SUGGESTIONS.
IS IT JUST ME, OR DID HE SAY THAT ALREADY?
!?

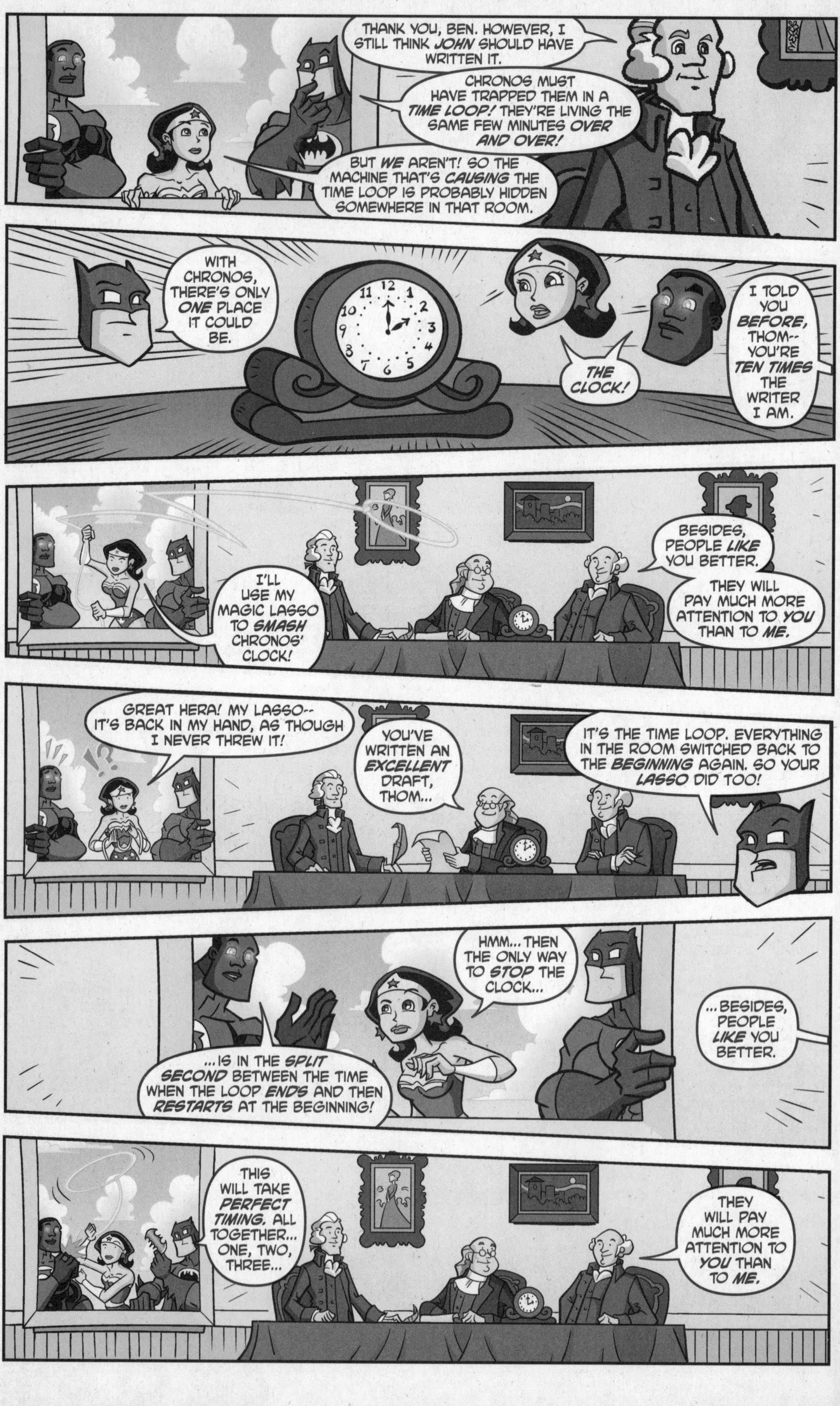
THANK YOU, BEN. HOWEVER, I STILL THINK JOHN SHOULD HAVE WRITTEN IT.
CHRONOS MUST HAVE TRAPPED THEM IN A TIME LOOP! THEY'RE LIVING THE SAME FEW MINUTES OVER AND OVER!
BUT WE AREN'T! SO THE MACHINE THAT'S CAUSING THE TIME LOOP IS PROBABLY HIDDEN SOMEWHERE IN THAT ROOM.
WITH CHRONOS, THERE'S ONLY ONE PLACE IT COULD BE.
THE CLOCK!
I TOLD YOU BEFORE, THOM-- YOU'RE TEN TIMES THE WRITER I AM.
I'LL USE MY MAGIC LASSO TO SMASH CHRONOS' CLOCK!
BESIDES, PEOPLE LIKE YOU BETTER.
THEY WILL PAY MUCH MORE ATTENTION TO YOU THAN TO ME.
!?
GREAT HERA! MY LASSO-- IT'S BACK IN MY HAND, AS THOUGH I NEVER THREW IT!
YOU'VE WRITTEN AN EXCELLENT DRAFT, THOM...
IT'S THE TIME LOOP. EVERYTHING IN THE ROOM SWITCHED BACK TO THE BEGINNING AGAIN. SO YOUR LASSO DID TOO!
HMM... THEN THE ONLY WAY TO STOP THE CLOCK...
...IS IN THE SPLIT SECOND BETWEEN THE TIME WHEN THE LOOP ENDS AND THEN RESTARTS AT THE BEGINNING!
...BESIDES, PEOPLE LIKE YOU BETTER.
THIS WILL TAKE PERFECT TIMING. ALL TOGETHER... ONE, TWO, THREE...
THEY WILL PAY MUCH MORE ATTENTION TO YOU THAN TO ME.

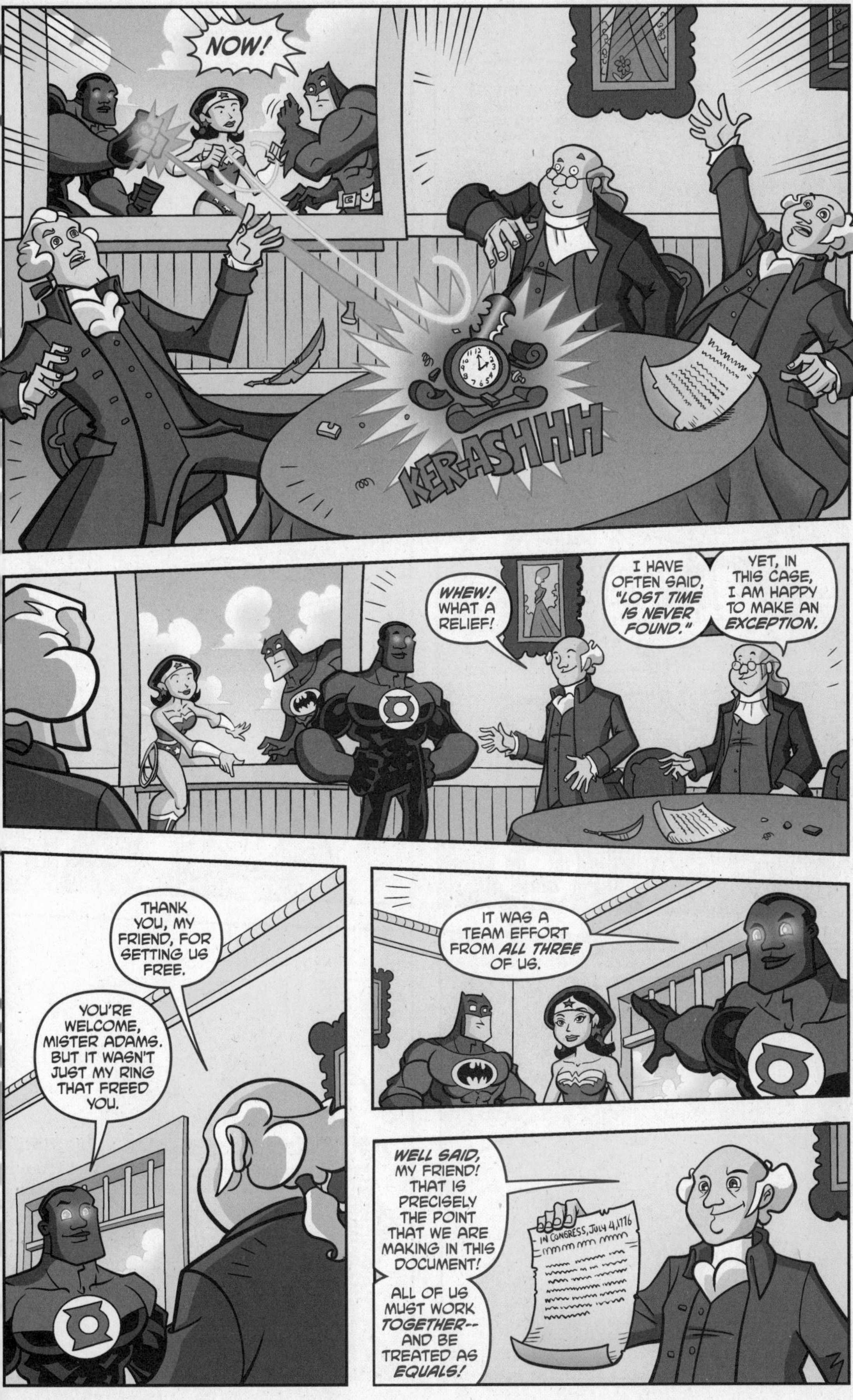
NOW!
KER-ASHHH
WHEW! WHAT A RELIEF!
I HAVE OFTEN SAID, "LOST TIME IS NEVER FOUND."
YET, IN THIS CASE, I AM HAPPY TO MAKE AN EXCEPTION.
THANK YOU, MY FRIEND, FOR SETTING US FREE.
YOU'RE WELCOME, MISTER ADAMS. BUT IT WASN'T JUST MY RING THAT FREED YOU.
IT WAS A TEAM EFFORT FROM ALL THREE OF US.
WELL SAID, MY FRIEND! THAT IS PRECISELY THE POINT THAT WE ARE MAKING IN THIS DOCUMENT!
ALL OF US MUST WORK TOGETHER-- AND BE TREATED AS EQUALS!
IN CONGRESS, JULY 4, 1776

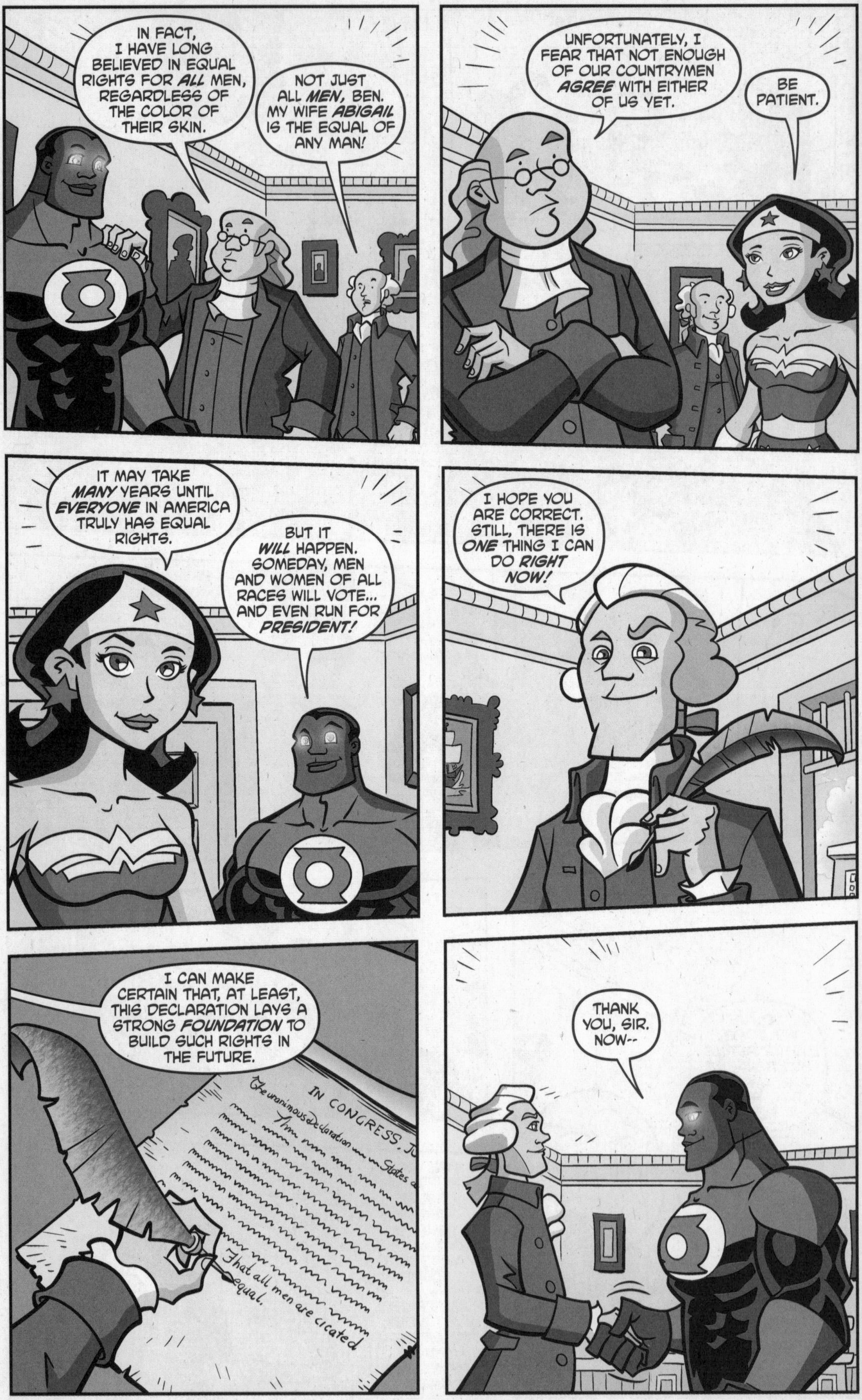
IN FACT, I HAVE LONG BELIEVED IN EQUAL RIGHTS FOR ALL MEN, REGARDLESS OF THE COLOR OF THEIR SKIN.
NOT JUST ALL MEN, BEN. MY WIFE ABIGAIL IS THE EQUAL OF ANY MAN!
UNFORTUNATELY, I FEAR THAT NOT ENOUGH OF OUR COUNTRYMEN AGREE WITH EITHER OF US YET.
BE PATIENT.
IT MAY TAKE MANY YEARS UNTIL EVERYONE IN AMERICA TRULY HAS EQUAL RIGHTS.
BUT IT WILL HAPPEN. SOMEDAY, MEN AND WOMEN OF ALL RACES WILL VOTE... AND EVEN RUN FOR PRESIDENT!
I HOPE YOU ARE CORRECT. STILL, THERE IS ONE THING I CAN DO RIGHT NOW!
I CAN MAKE CERTAIN THAT, AT LEAST, THIS DECLARATION LAYS A STRONG FOUNDATION TO BUILD SUCH RIGHTS IN THE FUTURE.
IN CONGRESS,
The unanimous Declaration
That all men are created equal.
THANK YOU, SIR. NOW--

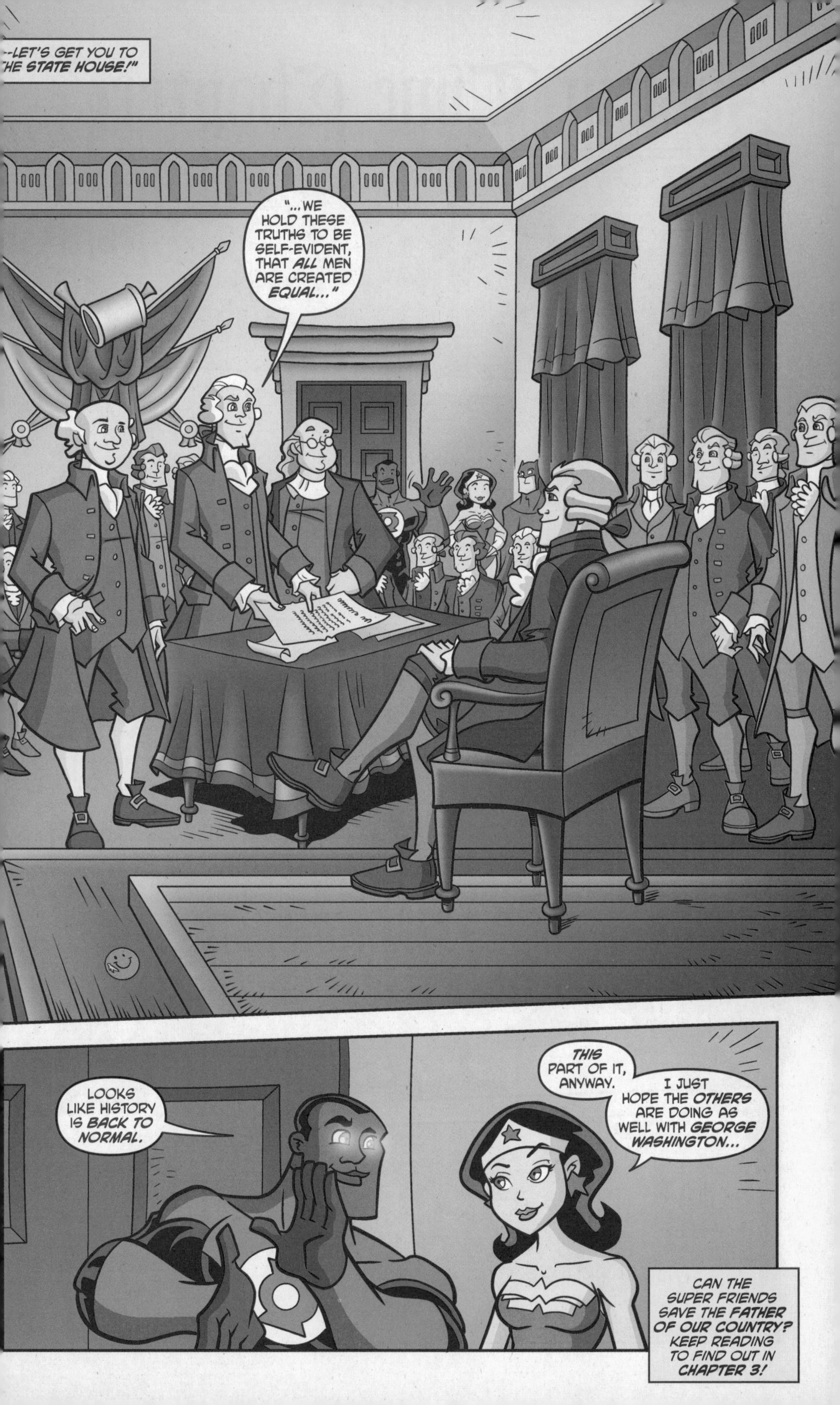
--LET'S GET YOU TO THE STATE HOUSE!"
"...WE HOLD THESE TRUTHS TO BE SELF-EVIDENT, THAT ALL MEN ARE CREATED EQUAL..."
LOOKS LIKE HISTORY IS BACK TO NORMAL.
THIS PART OF IT, ANYWAY.
I JUST HOPE THE OTHERS ARE DOING AS WELL WITH GEORGE WASHINGTON...
CAN THE SUPER FRIENDS SAVE THE FATHER OF OUR COUNTRY? KEEP READING TO FIND OUT IN CHAPTER 3!

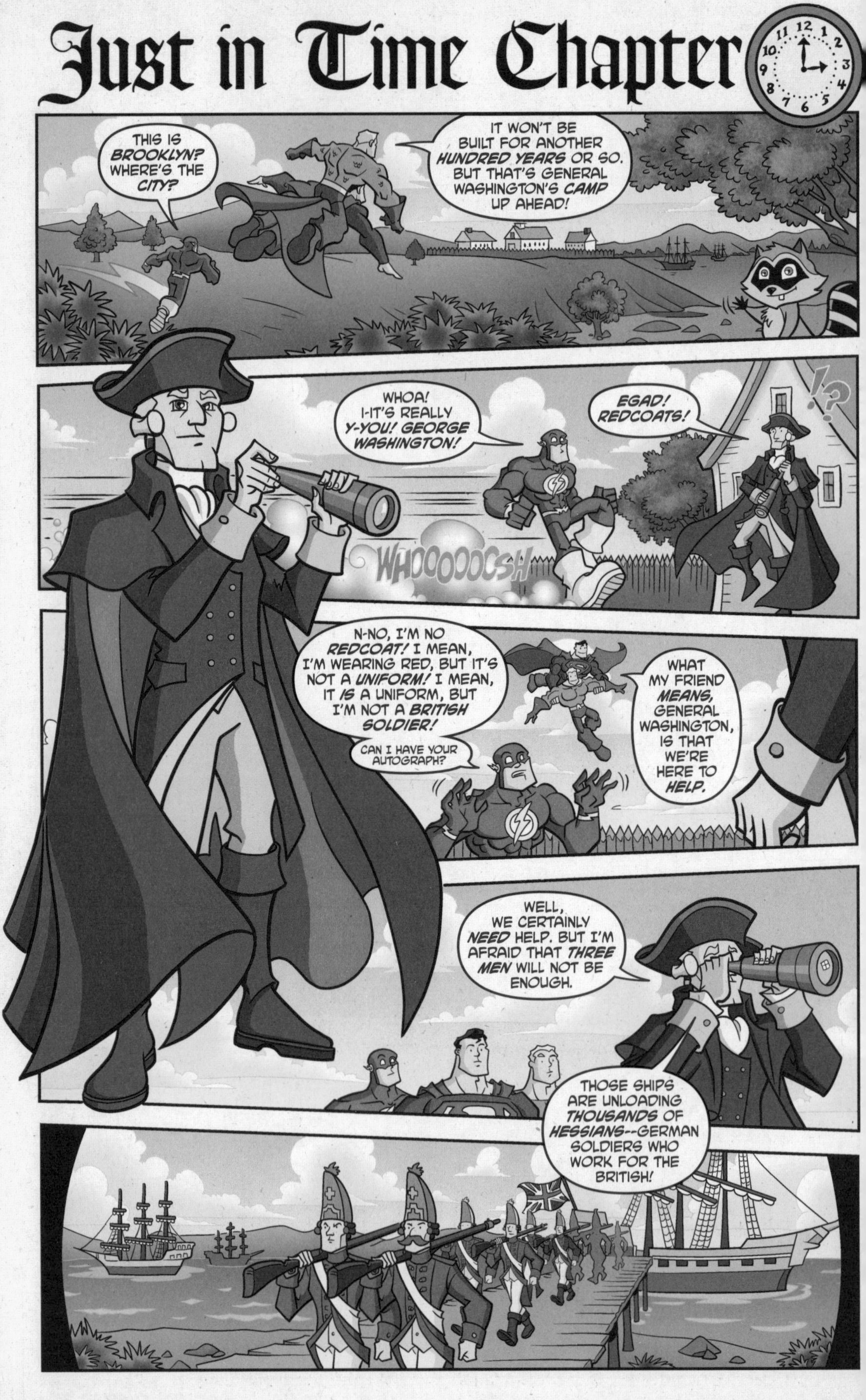
Just in Time Chapter
THIS IS BROOKLYN? WHERE'S THE CITY?
IT WON'T BE BUILT FOR ANOTHER HUNDRED YEARS OR SO. BUT THAT'S GENERAL WASHINGTON'S CAMP UP AHEAD!
WHOA! I-IT'S REALLY Y-YOU! GEORGE WASHINGTON!
EGAD! REDCOATS!
!?
WHOOOOOOCSH
N-NO, I'M NO REDCOAT! I MEAN, I'M WEARING RED, BUT IT'S NOT A UNIFORM! I MEAN, IT IS A UNIFORM, BUT I'M NOT A BRITISH SOLDIER!
CAN I HAVE YOUR AUTOGRAPH?
WHAT MY FRIEND MEANS, GENERAL WASHINGTON, IS THAT WE'RE HERE TO HELP.
WELL, WE CERTAINLY NEED HELP. BUT I'M AFRAID THAT THREE MEN WILL NOT BE ENOUGH.
THOSE SHIPS ARE UNLOADING THOUSANDS OF HESSIANS--GERMAN SOLDIERS WHO WORK FOR THE BRITISH!

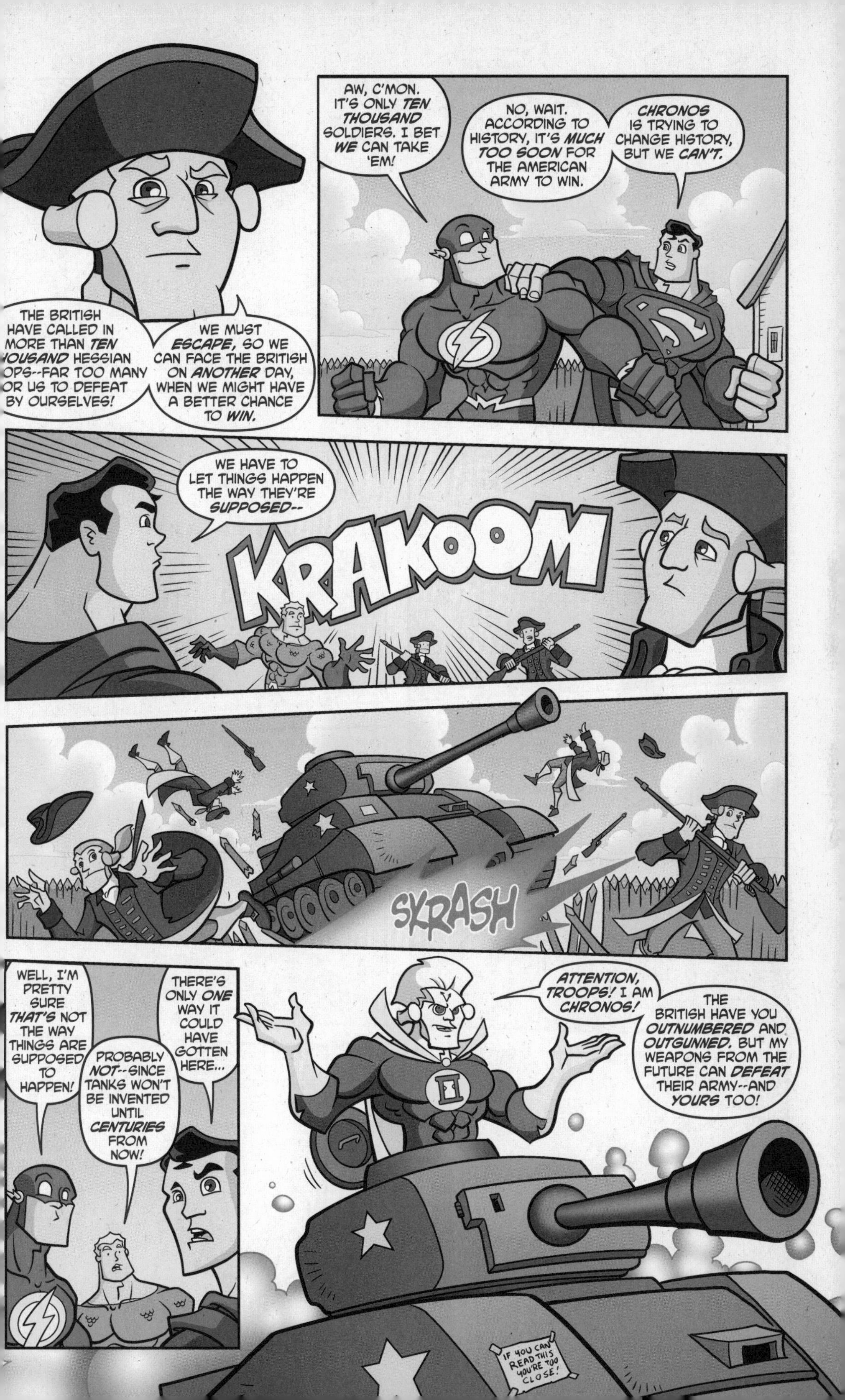
THE BRITISH HAVE CALLED IN MORE THAN TEN THOUSAND HESSIAN TROOPS--FAR TOO MANY FOR US TO DEFEAT BY OURSELVES!
WE MUST ESCAPE, SO WE CAN FACE THE BRITISH ON ANOTHER DAY, WHEN WE MIGHT HAVE A BETTER CHANCE TO WIN.
AW, C'MON. IT'S ONLY TEN THOUSAND SOLDIERS. I BET WE CAN TAKE 'EM!
NO, WAIT. ACCORDING TO HISTORY, IT'S MUCH TOO SOON FOR THE AMERICAN ARMY TO WIN.
CHRONOS IS TRYING TO CHANGE HISTORY, BUT WE CAN'T.
WE HAVE TO LET THINGS HAPPEN THE WAY THEY'RE SUPPOSED--
KRAKOOM
SKRASH
WELL, I'M PRETTY SURE THAT'S NOT THE WAY THINGS ARE SUPPOSED TO HAPPEN!
PROBABLY NOT--SINCE TANKS WON'T BE INVENTED UNTIL CENTURIES FROM NOW!
THERE'S ONLY ONE WAY IT COULD HAVE GOTTEN HERE...
ATTENTION, TROOPS! I AM CHRONOS!
THE BRITISH HAVE YOU OUTNUMBERED AND OUTGUNNED. BUT MY WEAPONS FROM THE FUTURE CAN DEFEAT THEIR ARMY--AND YOURS TOO!
IF YOU CAN READ THIS YOU'RE TOO CLOSE!

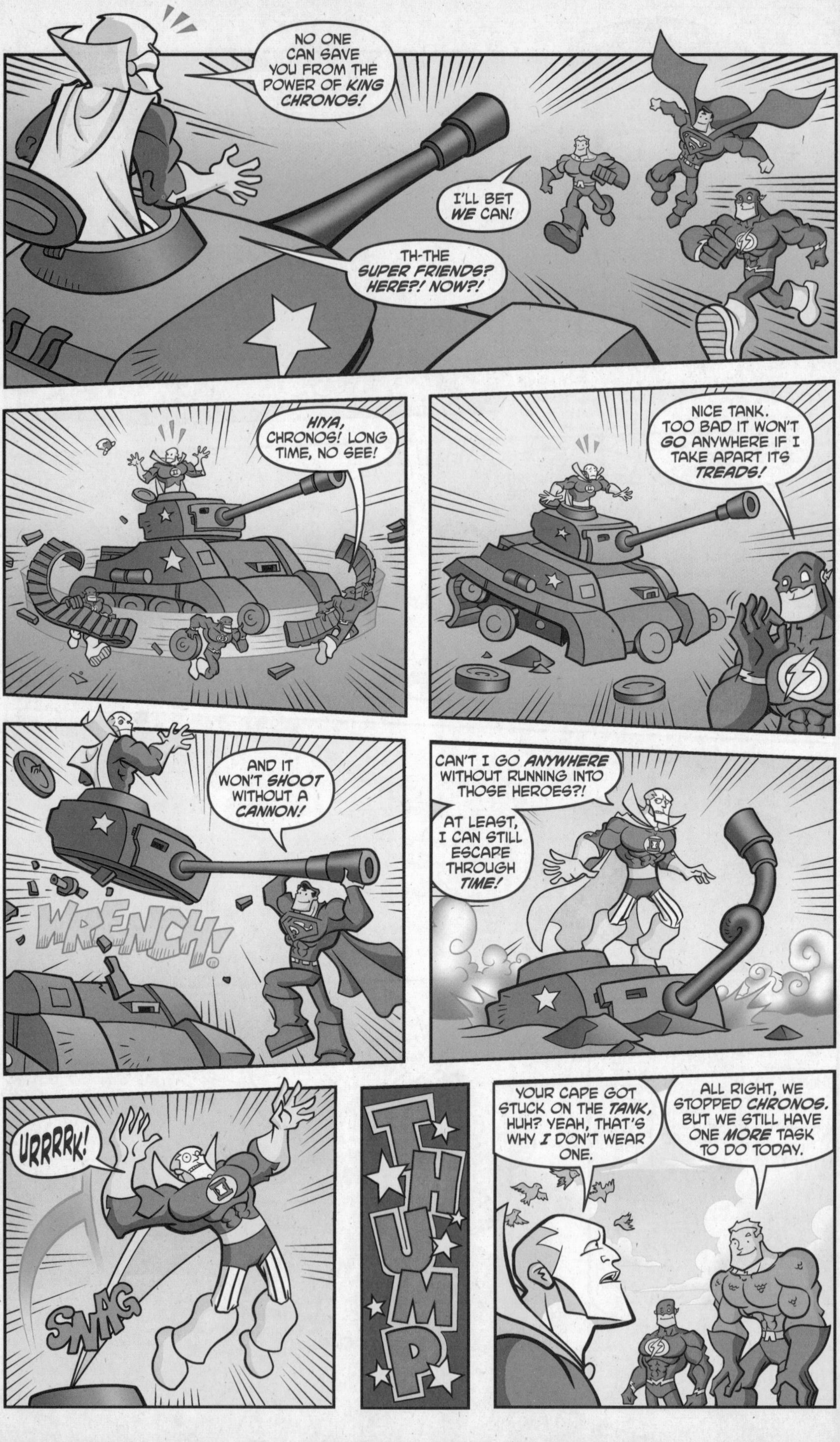
NO ONE CAN SAVE YOU FROM THE POWER OF KING CHRONOS!
I'LL BET WE CAN!
TH-THE SUPER FRIENDS? HERE?! NOW?!
HIYA, CHRONOS! LONG TIME, NO SEE!
NICE TANK. TOO BAD IT WON'T GO ANYWHERE IF I TAKE APART ITS TREADS!
AND IT WON'T SHOOT WITHOUT A CANNON!
WRENCH!
CAN'T I GO ANYWHERE WITHOUT RUNNING INTO THOSE HEROES?!
AT LEAST, I CAN STILL ESCAPE THROUGH TIME!
URRRRK!
SNAG
THUMP
YOUR CAPE GOT STUCK ON THE TANK, HUH? YEAH, THAT'S WHY I DON'T WEAR ONE.
ALL RIGHT, WE STOPPED CHRONOS. BUT WE STILL HAVE ONE MORE TASK TO DO TODAY.

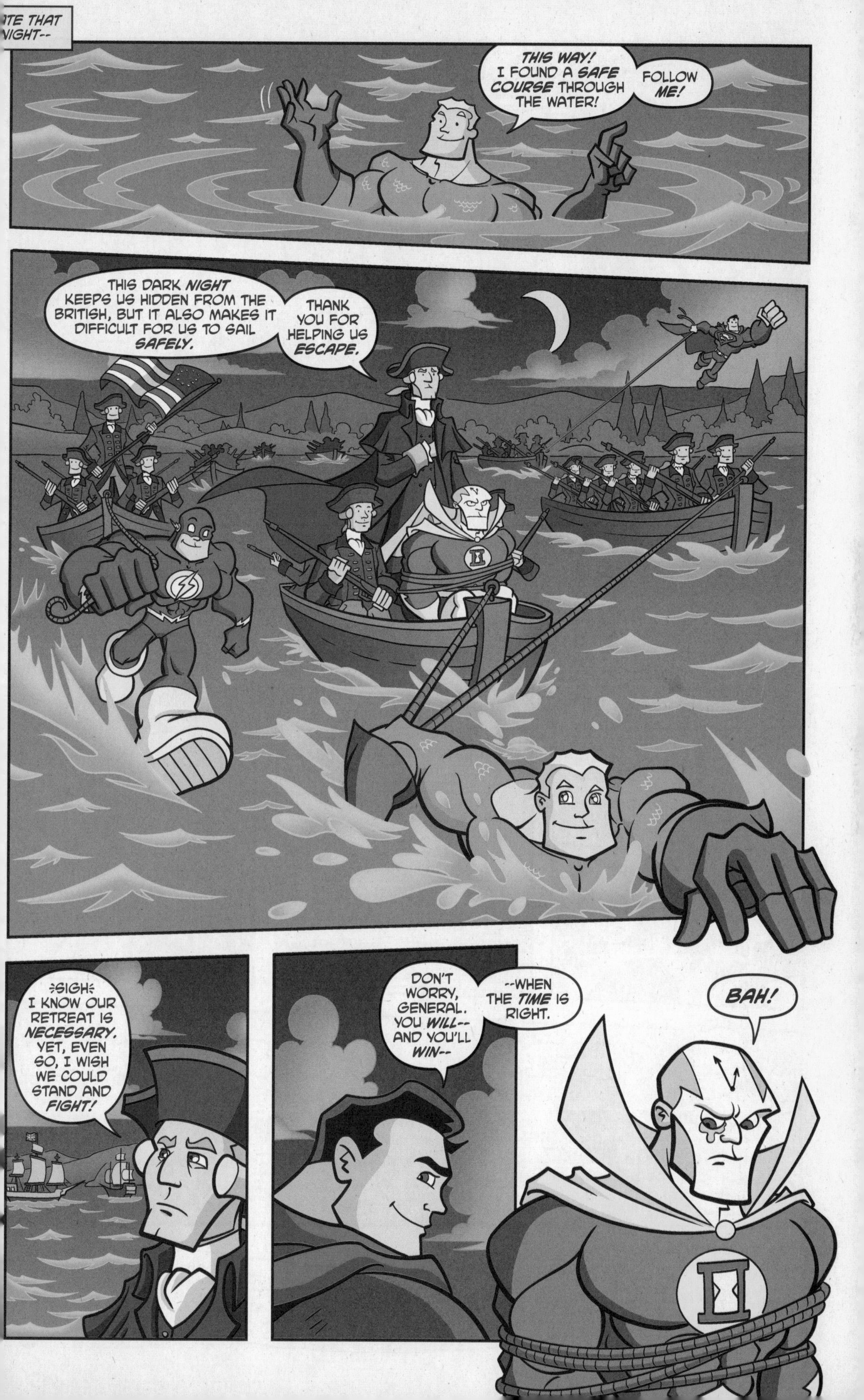

TE THAT NIGHT--
THIS WAY! I FOUND A SAFE COURSE THROUGH THE WATER!
FOLLOW ME!
THIS DARK NIGHT KEEPS US HIDDEN FROM THE BRITISH, BUT IT ALSO MAKES IT DIFFICULT FOR US TO SAIL SAFELY.
THANK YOU FOR HELPING US ESCAPE.
*SIGH* I KNOW OUR RETREAT IS NECESSARY. YET, EVEN SO, I WISH WE COULD STAND AND FIGHT!
DON'T WORRY, GENERAL. YOU WILL-- AND YOU'LL WIN--
--WHEN THE TIME IS RIGHT.
BAH!

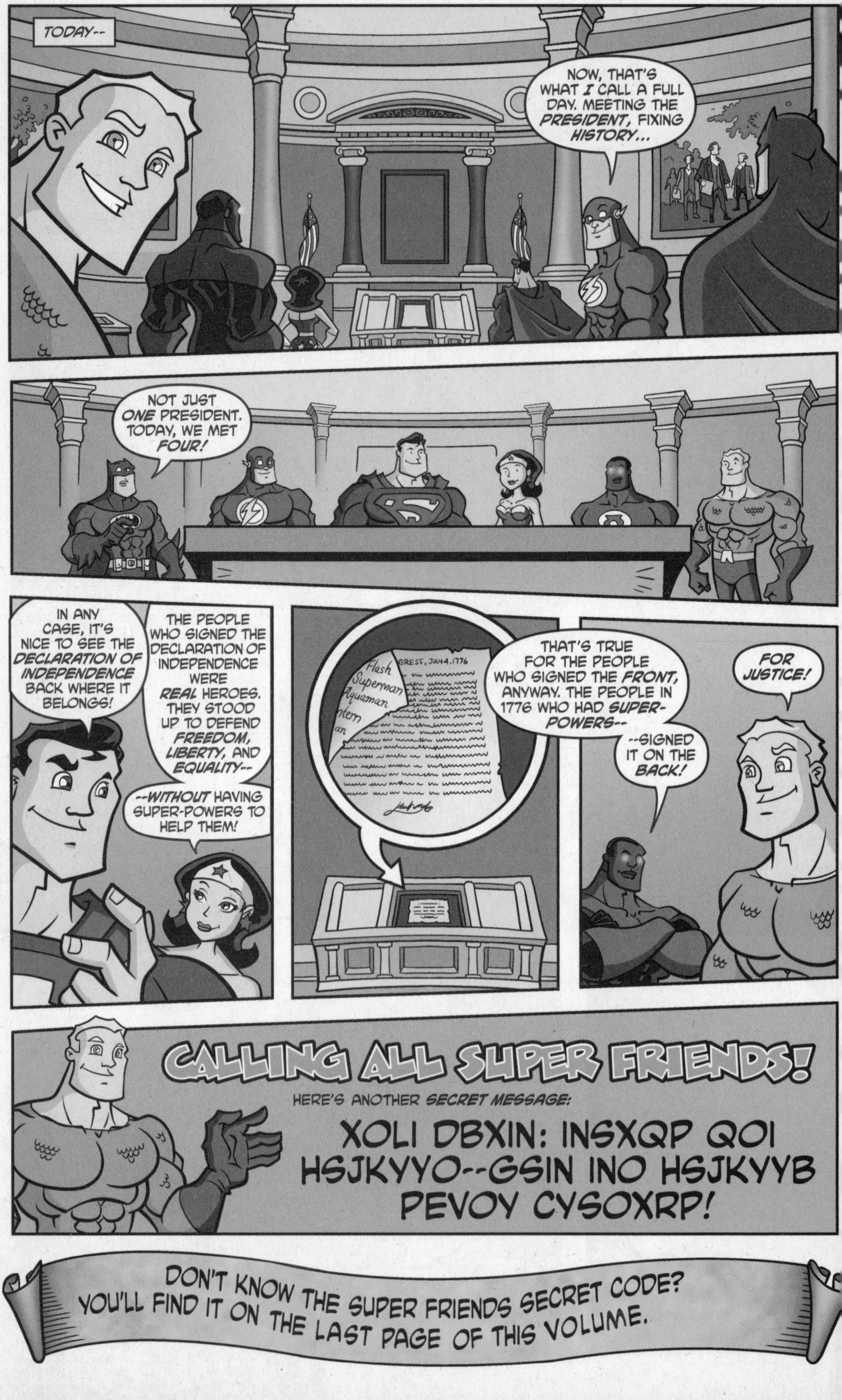
TODAY--
NOW, THAT'S WHAT I CALL A FULL DAY. MEETING THE PRESIDENT, FIXING HISTORY...
NOT JUST ONE PRESIDENT. TODAY, WE MET FOUR!
IN ANY CASE, IT'S NICE TO SEE THE DECLARATION OF INDEPENDENCE BACK WHERE IT BELONGS!
THE PEOPLE WHO SIGNED THE DECLARATION OF INDEPENDENCE WERE REAL HEROES. THEY STOOD UP TO DEFEND FREEDOM, LIBERTY, AND EQUALITY--
--WITHOUT HAVING SUPER-POWERS TO HELP THEM!
GRESS, JULY 4, 1776
Flash
Superman
Aquaman
THAT'S TRUE FOR THE PEOPLE WHO SIGNED THE FRONT, ANYWAY. THE PEOPLE IN 1776 WHO HAD SUPER-POWERS--
--SIGNED IT ON THE BACK!
FOR JUSTICE!
CALLING ALL SUPER FRIENDS!
HERE'S ANOTHER SECRET MESSAGE:
XOLI DBXIN: INSXQP QOI HSJKYYO--GSIN INO HSJKYYB PEVOY CYSOXRP!
DON'T KNOW THE SUPER FRIENDS SECRET CODE? YOU'LL FIND IT ON THE LAST PAGE OF THIS VOLUME.

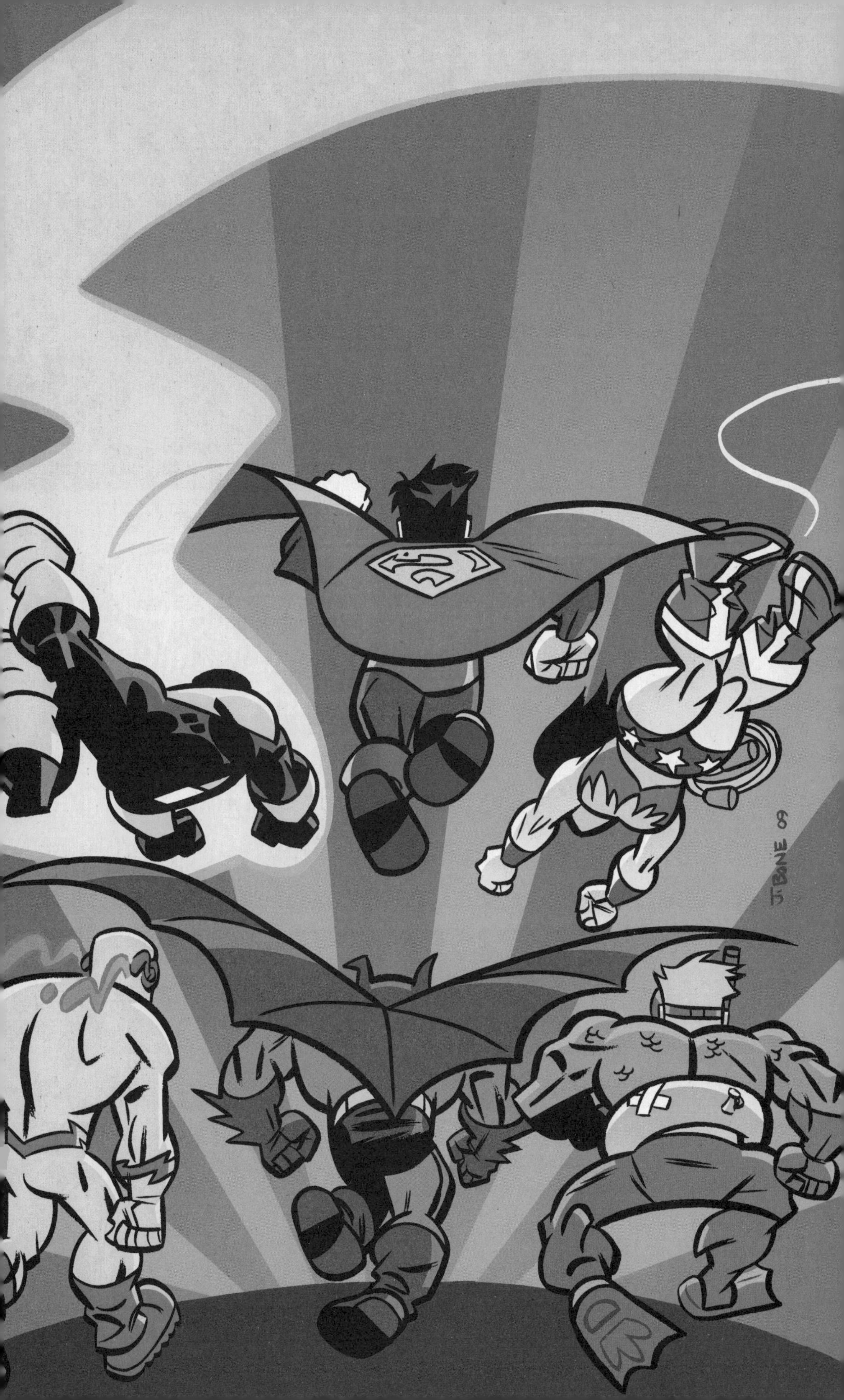
J.BONE

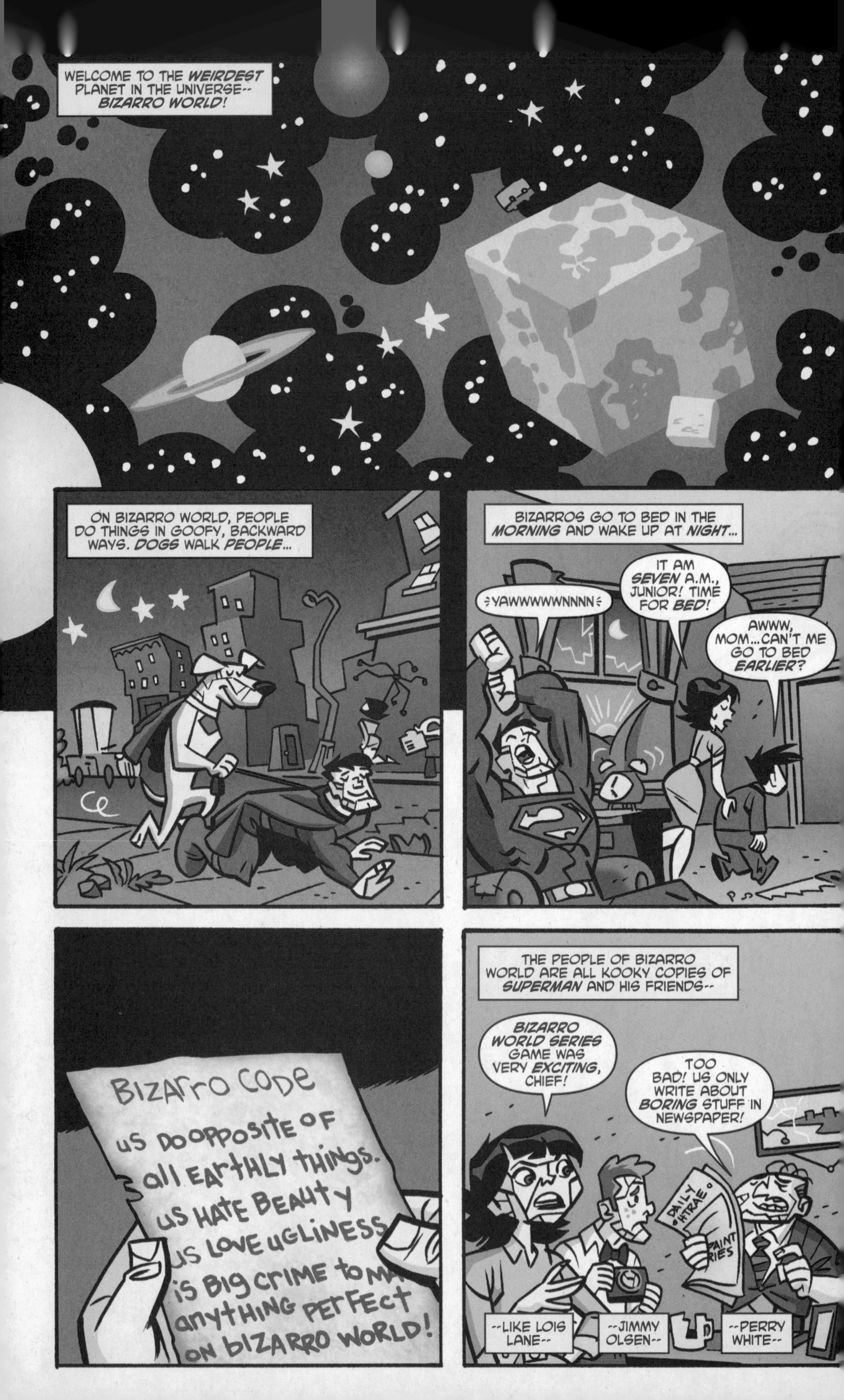
WELCOME TO THE WEIRDEST PLANET IN THE UNIVERSE-- BIZARRO WORLD!
ON BIZARRO WORLD, PEOPLE DO THINGS IN GOOFY, BACKWARD WAYS. DOGS WALK PEOPLE...
BIZARROS GO TO BED IN THE MORNING AND WAKE UP AT NIGHT...
YAWWWWWNNNN
IT AM SEVEN A.M., JUNIOR! TIME FOR BED!
AWWW, MOM...CAN'T ME GO TO BED EARLIER?
Bizarro Code
us Do opposite of all earthly things.
us hate Beauty
us love ugliness
is Big crime to ma anything perfect on bizarro world!
THE PEOPLE OF BIZARRO WORLD ARE ALL KOOKY COPIES OF SUPERMAN AND HIS FRIENDS--
BIZARRO WORLD SERIES GAME WAS VERY EXCITING, CHIEF!
TOO BAD! US ONLY WRITE ABOUT BORING STUFF IN NEWSPAPER!
DAILY PLANET
--LIKE LOIS LANE--
--JIMMY OLSEN--
--PERRY WHITE--

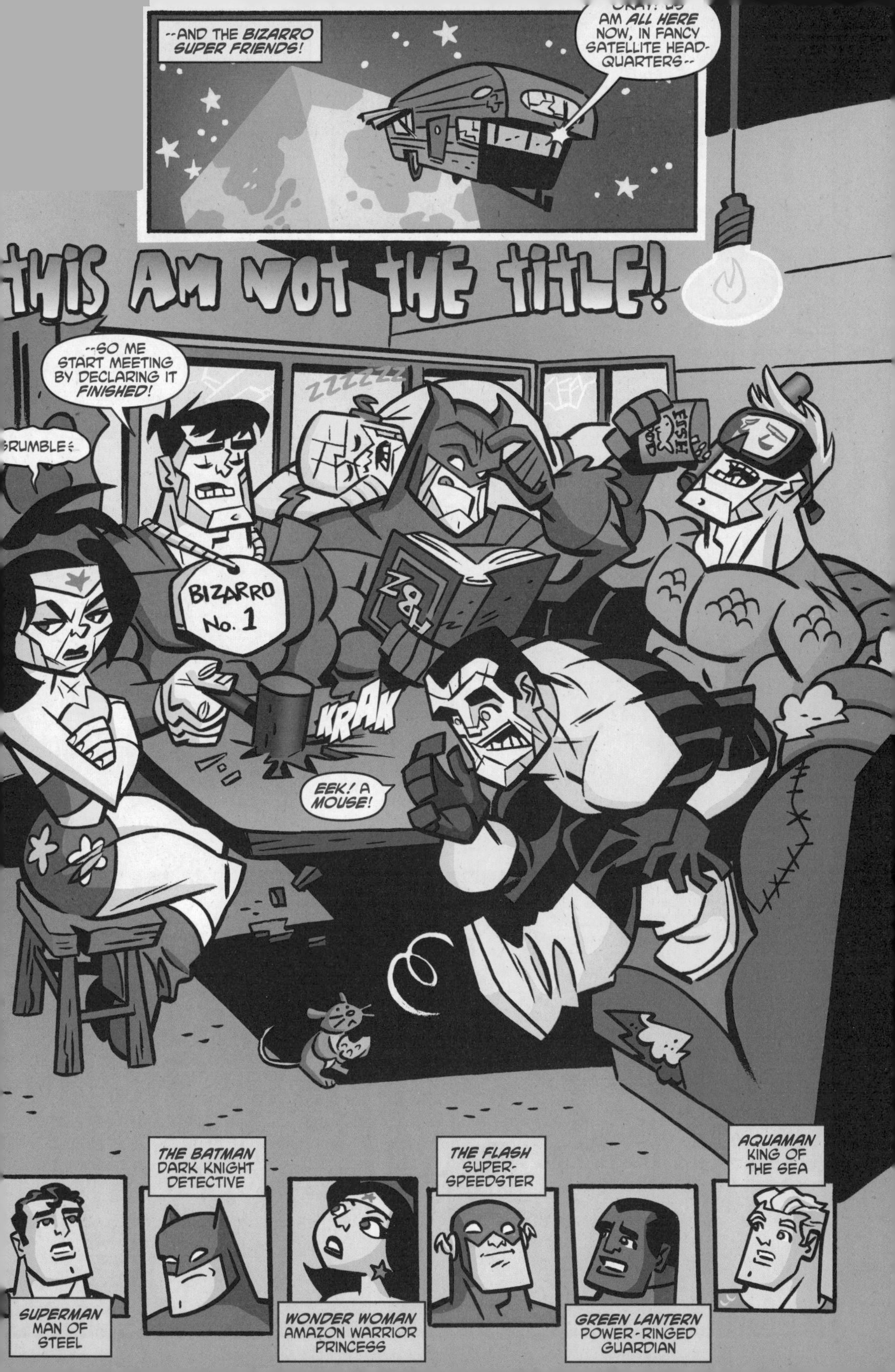
--AND THE BIZARRO SUPER FRIENDS!
OKAY! US AM ALL HERE NOW, IN FANCY SATELLITE HEAD-QUARTERS--
THIS AM NOT THE TITLE!
--SO ME START MEETING BY DECLARING IT FINISHED!
GRUMBLE
ZZZZZZ
BIZARRO No. 1
FISH
KRAK
EEK! A MOUSE!
SUPERMAN MAN OF STEEL
THE BATMAN DARK KNIGHT DETECTIVE
WONDER WOMAN AMAZON WARRIOR PRINCESS
THE FLASH SUPER-SPEEDSTER
GREEN LANTERN POWER-RINGED GUARDIAN
AQUAMAN KING OF THE SEA

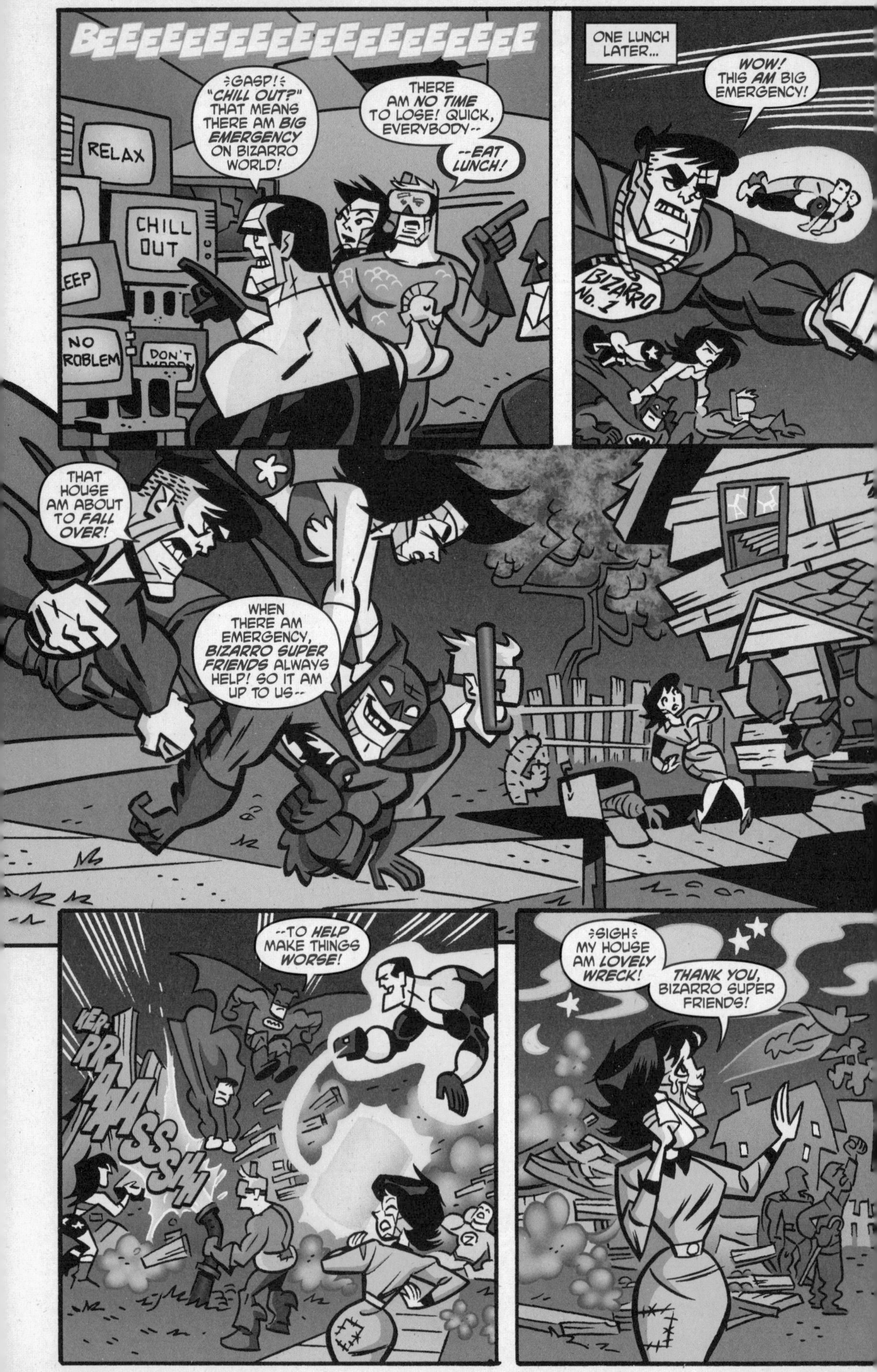
BEEEEEEEEEEEEEEEEEEEEE
RELAX
CHILL OUT
LEEP
NO
ROBLEM
DON'T
≈GASP!≈ "CHILL OUT?" THAT MEANS THERE AM BIG EMERGENCY ON BIZARRO WORLD!
THERE AM NO TIME TO LOSE! QUICK, EVERYBODY--
--EAT LUNCH!
ONE LUNCH LATER...
WOW! THIS AM BIG EMERGENCY!
BIZARRO No. 1
THAT HOUSE AM ABOUT TO FALL OVER!
WHEN THERE AM EMERGENCY, BIZARRO SUPER FRIENDS ALWAYS HELP! SO IT AM UP TO US--
--TO HELP MAKE THINGS WORSE!
KER-RRAAASSSHH
≈SIGH≈ MY HOUSE AM LOVELY WRECK!
THANK YOU, BIZARRO SUPER FRIENDS!

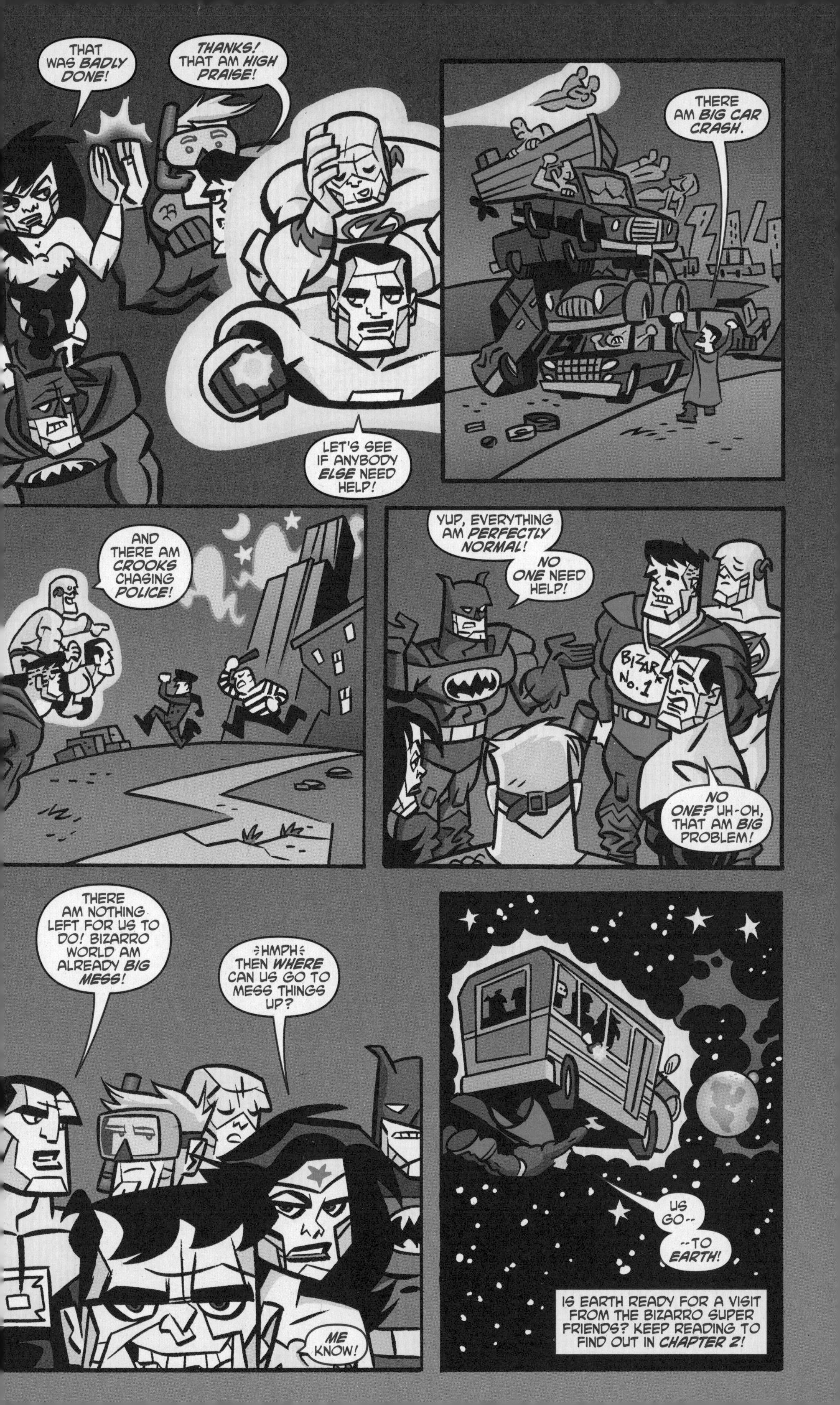

THAT WAS BADLY DONE!
THANKS! THAT AM HIGH PRAISE!
LET'S SEE IF ANYBODY ELSE NEED HELP!
THERE AM BIG CAR CRASH.
AND THERE AM CROOKS CHASING POLICE!
YUP, EVERYTHING AM PERFECTLY NORMAL!
NO ONE NEED HELP!
BIZARRO No. 1
NO ONE? UH-OH, THAT AM BIG PROBLEM!
THERE AM NOTHING LEFT FOR US TO DO! BIZARRO WORLD AM ALREADY BIG MESS!
HMPH THEN WHERE CAN US GO TO MESS THINGS UP?
ME KNOW!
US GO--
--TO EARTH!
IS EARTH READY FOR A VISIT FROM THE BIZARRO SUPER FRIENDS? KEEP READING TO FIND OUT IN CHAPTER 2!

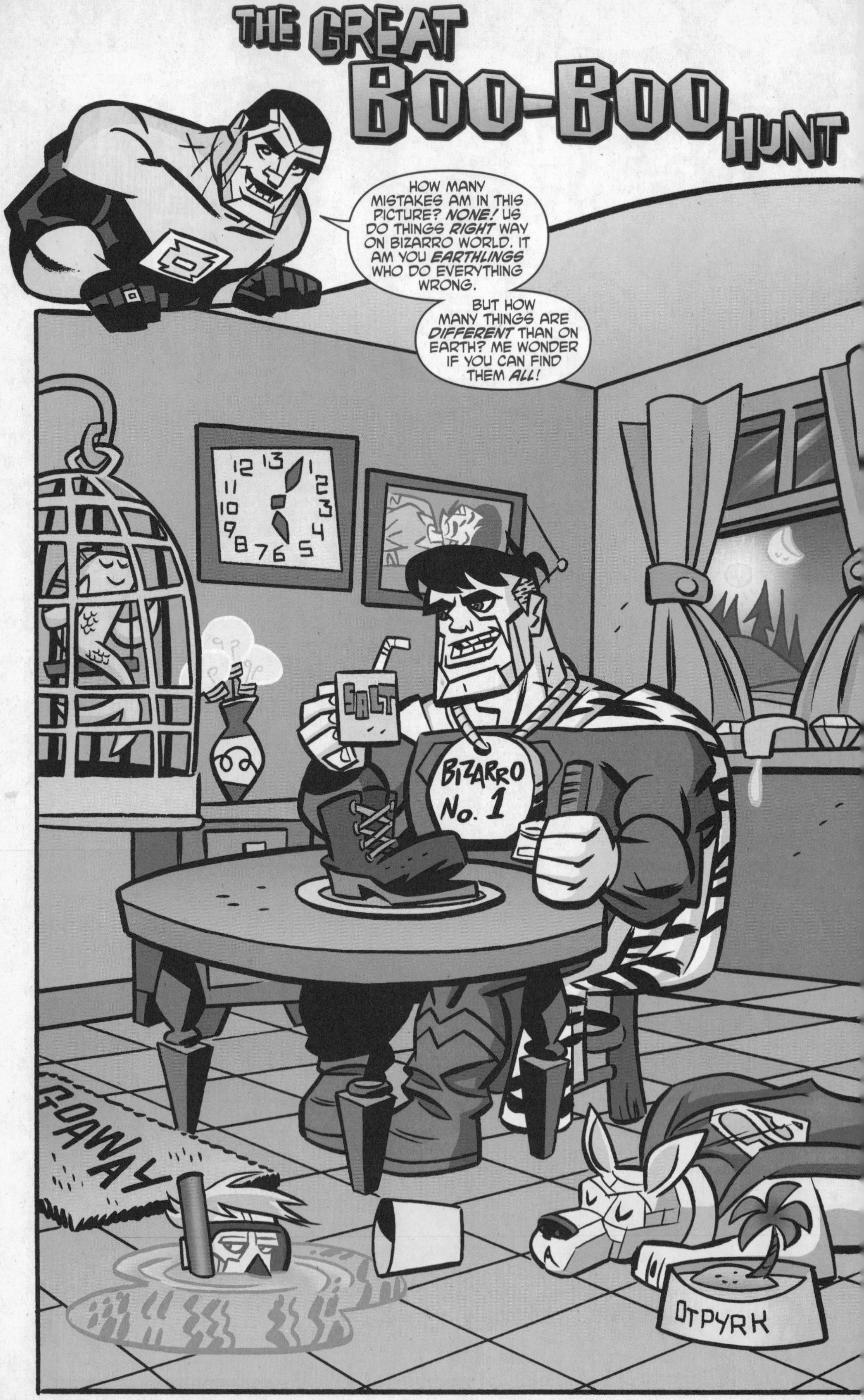
THE GREAT BOO-BOO HUNT
HOW MANY MISTAKES AM IN THIS PICTURE? NONE! US DO THINGS RIGHT WAY ON BIZARRO WORLD. IT AM YOU EARTHLINGS WHO DO EVERYTHING WRONG.
BUT HOW MANY THINGS ARE DIFFERENT THAN ON EARTH? ME WONDER IF YOU CAN FIND THEM ALL!
BIZARRO No. 1
GOAWAY
OTPYRK

# THIS AM NOT THE TITLE! CHAPTER 2

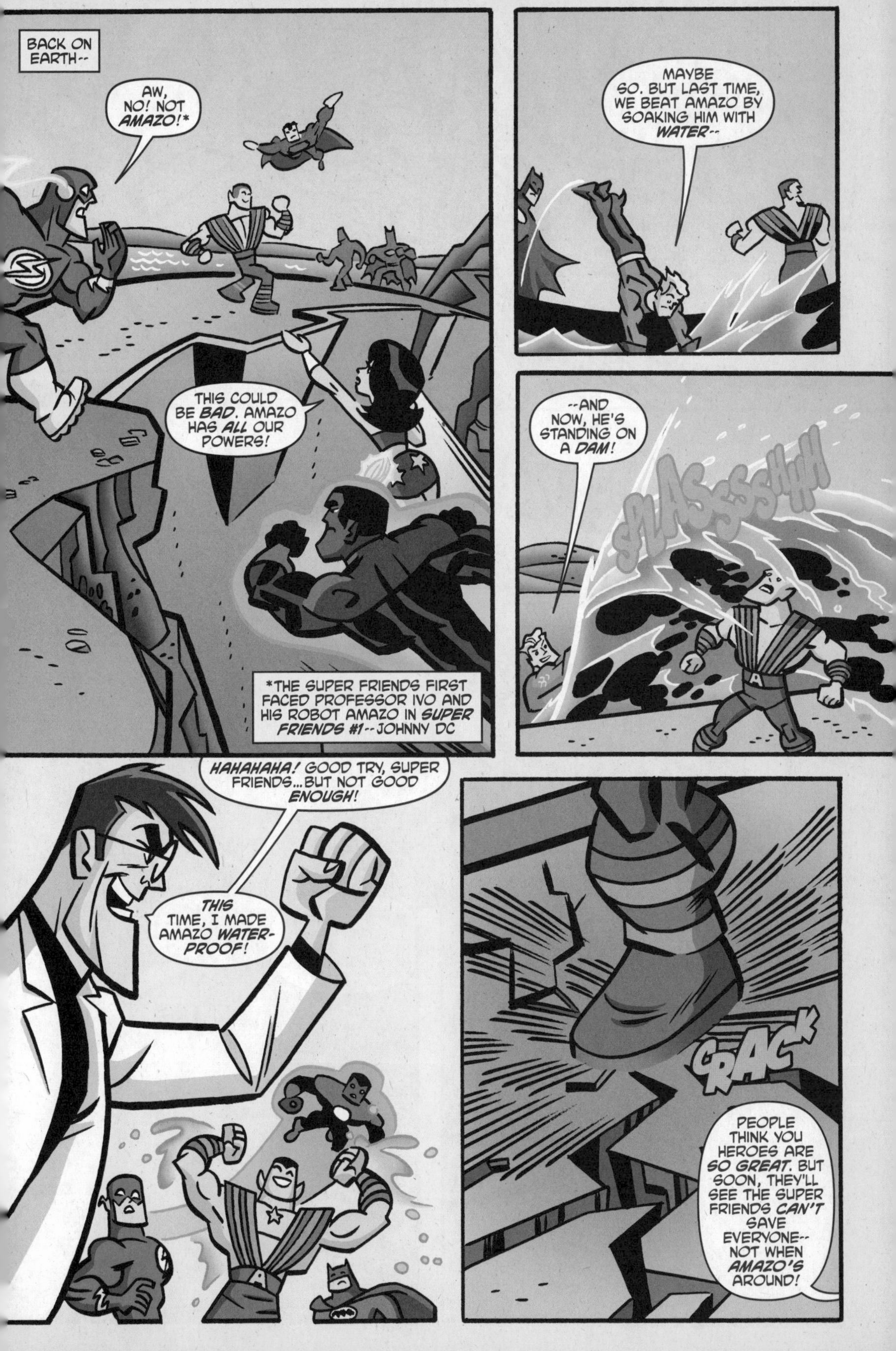

BACK ON EARTH--
AW, NO! NOT AMAZO!*
THIS COULD BE BAD. AMAZO HAS ALL OUR POWERS!
*THE SUPER FRIENDS FIRST FACED PROFESSOR IVO AND HIS ROBOT AMAZO IN SUPER FRIENDS #1--JOHNNY DC
MAYBE SO. BUT LAST TIME, WE BEAT AMAZO BY SOAKING HIM WITH WATER--
--AND NOW, HE'S STANDING ON A DAM!
SPLASSSSHHH
HAHAHAHA! GOOD TRY, SUPER FRIENDS...BUT NOT GOOD ENOUGH!
THIS TIME, I MADE AMAZO WATER-PROOF!
CRACK
PEOPLE THINK YOU HEROES ARE SO GREAT. BUT SOON, THEY'LL SEE THE SUPER FRIENDS CAN'T SAVE EVERYONE-- NOT WHEN AMAZO'S AROUND!

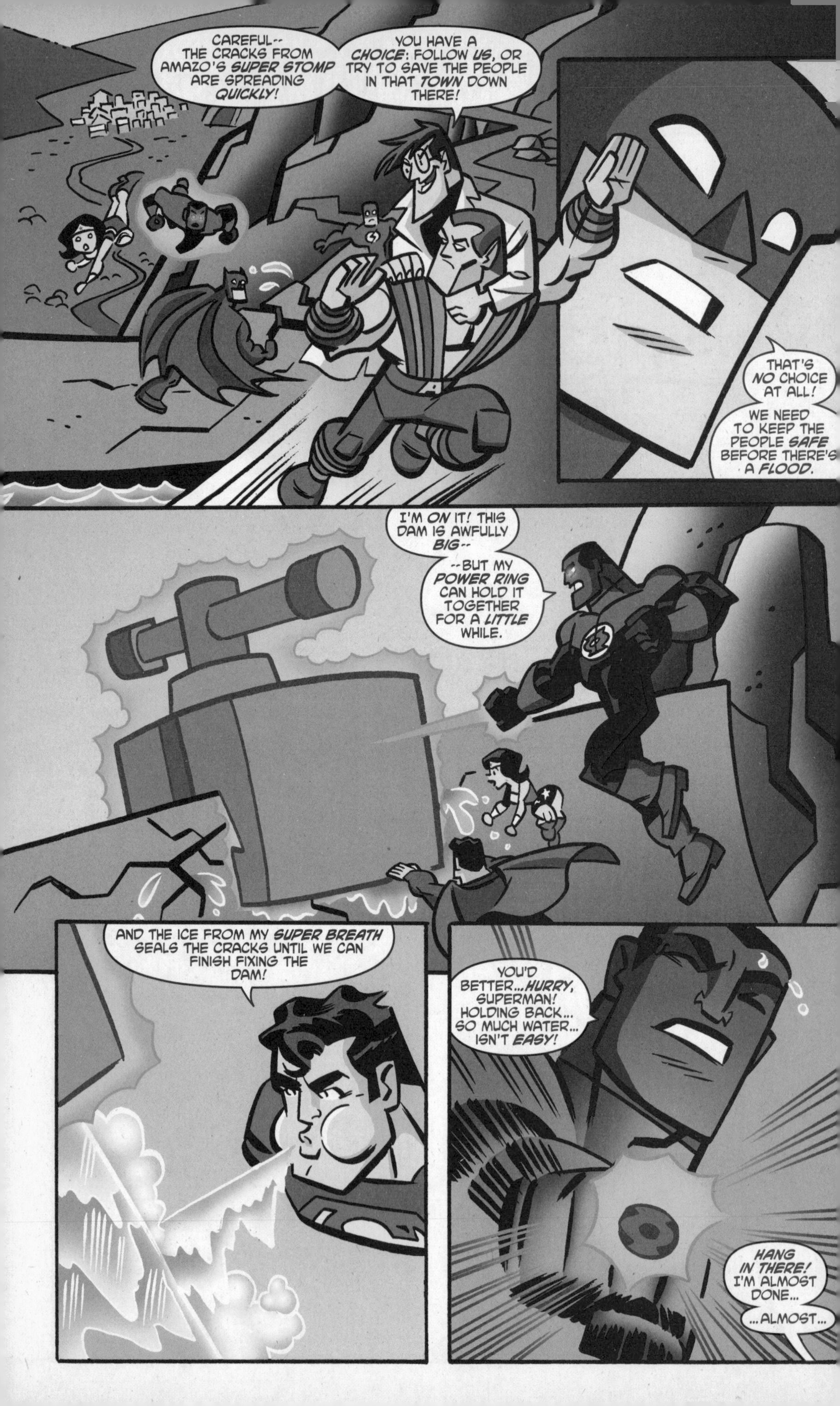

CAREFUL-- THE CRACKS FROM AMAZO'S SUPER STOMP ARE SPREADING QUICKLY!
YOU HAVE A CHOICE: FOLLOW US, OR TRY TO SAVE THE PEOPLE IN THAT TOWN DOWN THERE!
THAT'S NO CHOICE AT ALL!
WE NEED TO KEEP THE PEOPLE SAFE BEFORE THERE'S A FLOOD.
I'M ON IT! THIS DAM IS AWFULLY BIG--
--BUT MY POWER RING CAN HOLD IT TOGETHER FOR A LITTLE WHILE.
AND THE ICE FROM MY SUPER BREATH SEALS THE CRACKS UNTIL WE CAN FINISH FIXING THE DAM!
YOU'D BETTER...HURRY, SUPERMAN! HOLDING BACK... SO MUCH WATER... ISN'T EASY!
HANG IN THERE! I'M ALMOST DONE...
...ALMOST...

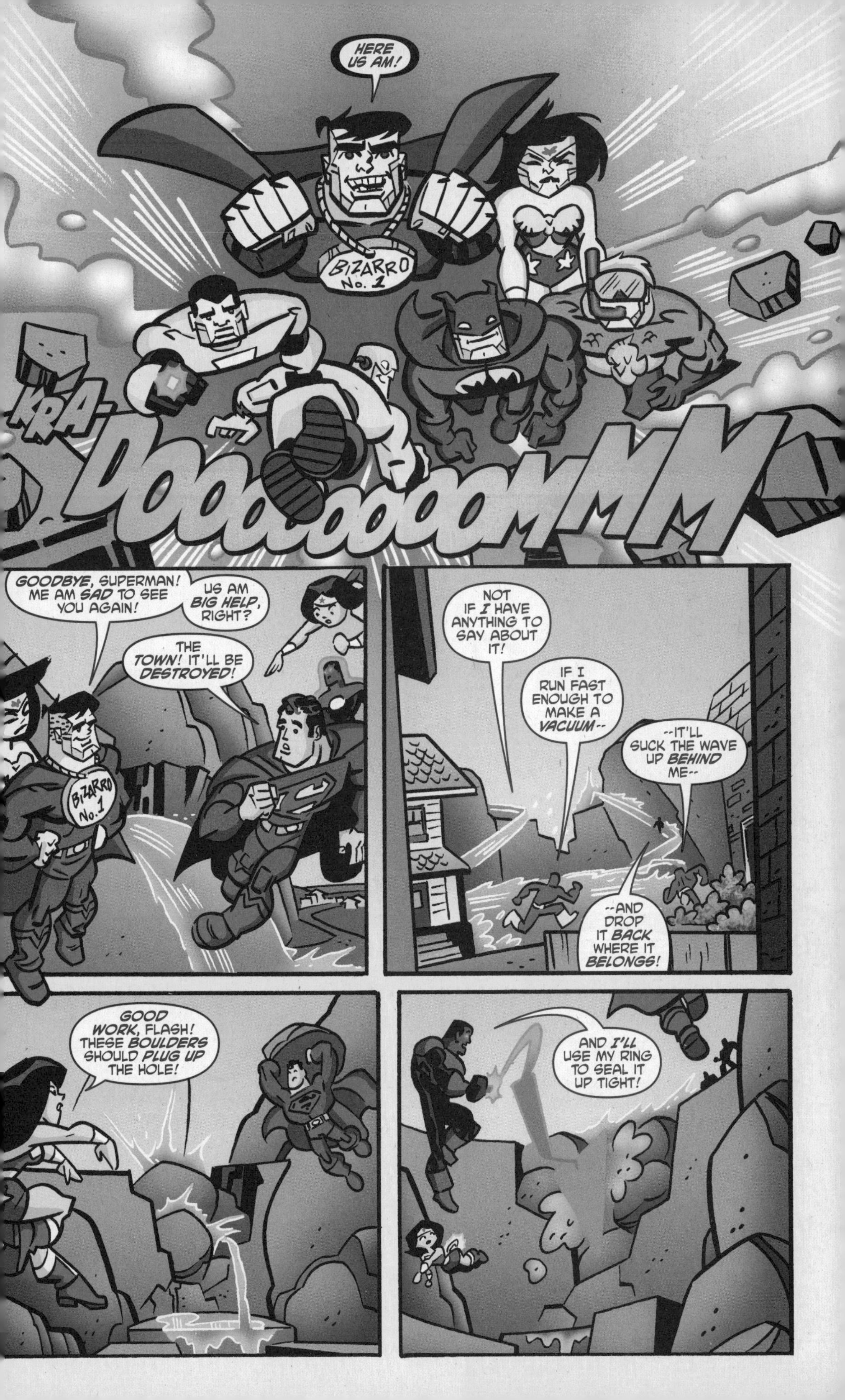
HERE US AM!
KRA-DOOOOOOOOMMM
GOODBYE, SUPERMAN! ME AM SAD TO SEE YOU AGAIN!
US AM BIG HELP, RIGHT?
THE TOWN! IT'LL BE DESTROYED!
NOT IF I HAVE ANYTHING TO SAY ABOUT IT!
IF I RUN FAST ENOUGH TO MAKE A VACUUM--
--IT'LL SUCK THE WAVE UP BEHIND ME--
--AND DROP IT BACK WHERE IT BELONGS!
GOOD WORK, FLASH! THESE BOULDERS SHOULD PLUG UP THE HOLE!
AND I'LL USE MY RING TO SEAL IT UP TIGHT!

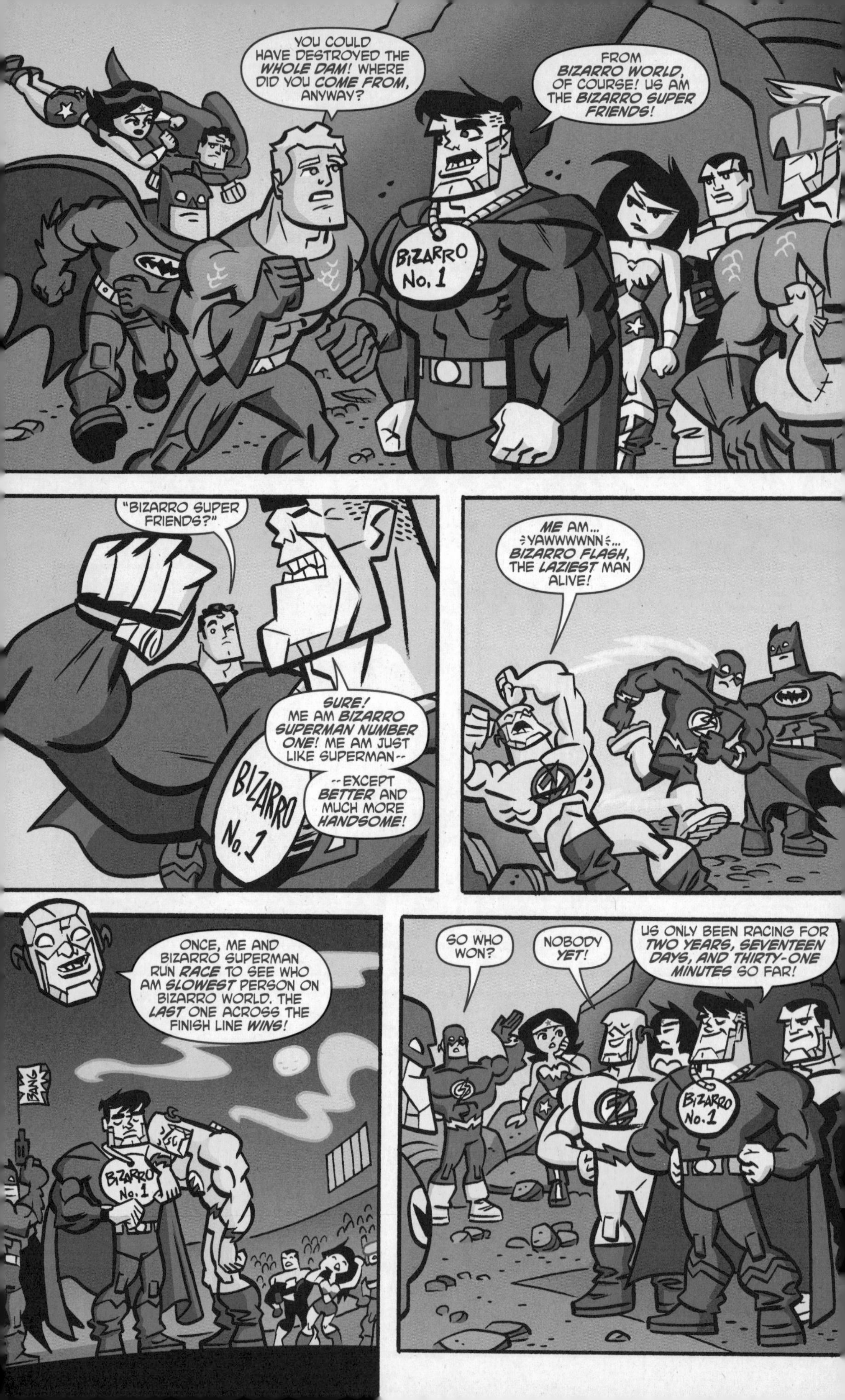
YOU COULD HAVE DESTROYED THE *WHOLE DAM*! WHERE DID YOU *COME FROM*, ANYWAY?
FROM *BIZARRO WORLD*, OF COURSE! US AM THE *BIZARRO SUPER FRIENDS*!
BIZARRO No. 1
"BIZARRO SUPER FRIENDS?"
*SURE!* ME AM *BIZARRO SUPERMAN NUMBER ONE!* ME AM JUST LIKE SUPERMAN--
--EXCEPT *BETTER* AND MUCH MORE *HANDSOME!*
BIZARRO No. 1
*ME* AM... YAWWWWNN... *BIZARRO FLASH*, THE *LAZIEST* MAN ALIVE!
ONCE, ME AND BIZARRO SUPERMAN RUN *RACE* TO SEE WHO AM *SLOWEST* PERSON ON BIZARRO WORLD. THE *LAST* ONE ACROSS THE FINISH LINE *WINS!*
BANG
BIZARRO No. 1
SO WHO WON?
NOBODY *YET!*
US ONLY BEEN RACING FOR *TWO YEARS, SEVENTEEN DAYS*, AND *THIRTY-ONE MINUTES* SO FAR!
BIZARRO No. 1

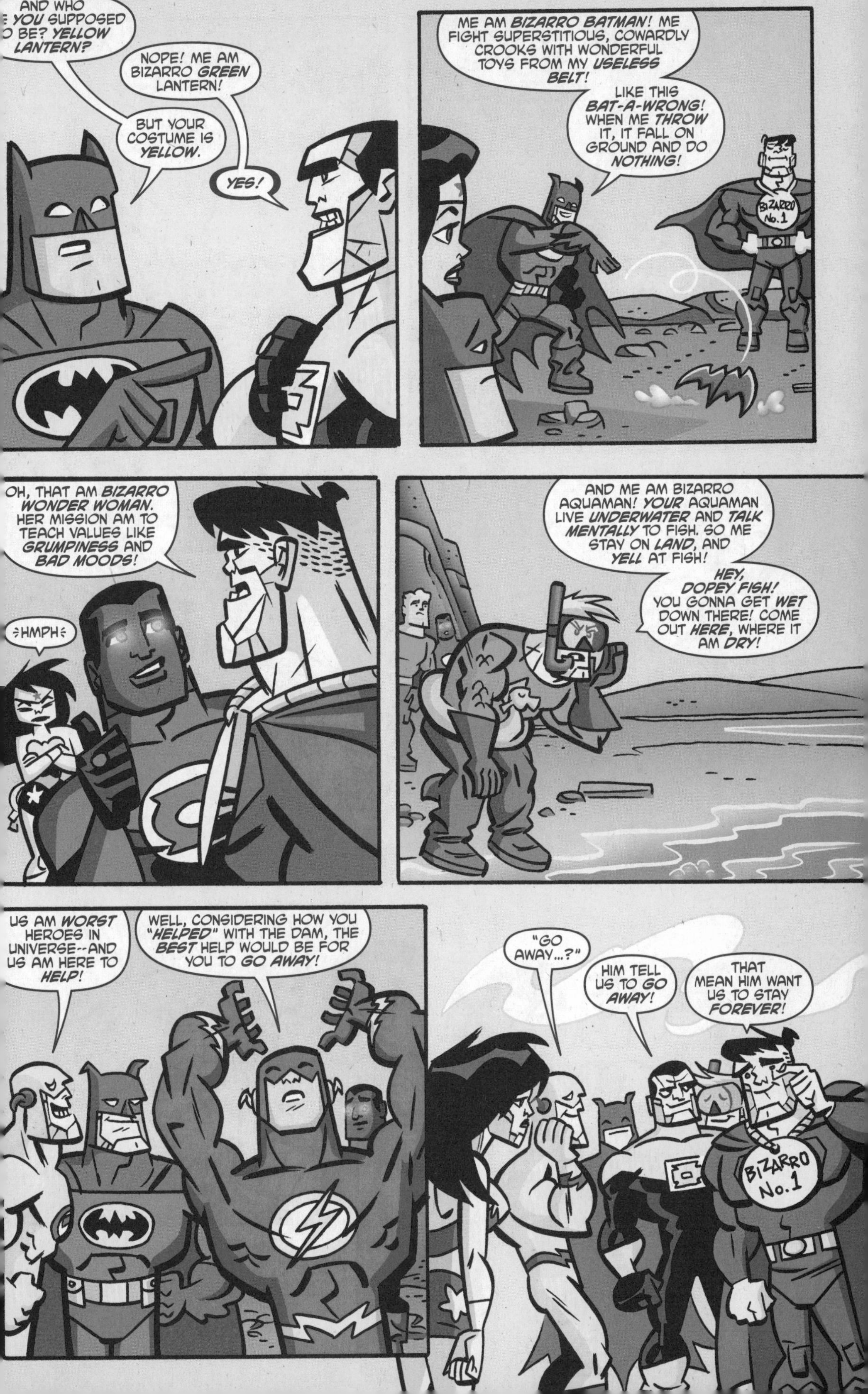
AND WHO E YOU SUPPOSED O BE? YELLOW LANTERN?
NOPE! ME AM BIZARRO GREEN LANTERN!
BUT YOUR COSTUME IS YELLOW.
YES!
ME AM BIZARRO BATMAN! ME FIGHT SUPERSTITIOUS, COWARDLY CROOKS WITH WONDERFUL TOYS FROM MY USELESS BELT!
LIKE THIS BAT-A-WRONG! WHEN ME THROW IT, IT FALL ON GROUND AND DO NOTHING!
BIZARRO No. 1
OH, THAT AM BIZARRO WONDER WOMAN. HER MISSION AM TO TEACH VALUES LIKE GRUMPINESS AND BAD MOODS!
HMPH
AND ME AM BIZARRO AQUAMAN! YOUR AQUAMAN LIVE UNDERWATER AND TALK MENTALLY TO FISH. SO ME STAY ON LAND, AND YELL AT FISH!
HEY, DOPEY FISH! YOU GONNA GET WET DOWN THERE! COME OUT HERE, WHERE IT AM DRY!
US AM WORST HEROES IN UNIVERSE--AND US AM HERE TO HELP!
WELL, CONSIDERING HOW YOU "HELPED" WITH THE DAM, THE BEST HELP WOULD BE FOR YOU TO GO AWAY!
"GO AWAY...?"
HIM TELL US TO GO AWAY!
THAT MEAN HIM WANT US TO STAY FOREVER!
BIZARRO No. 1

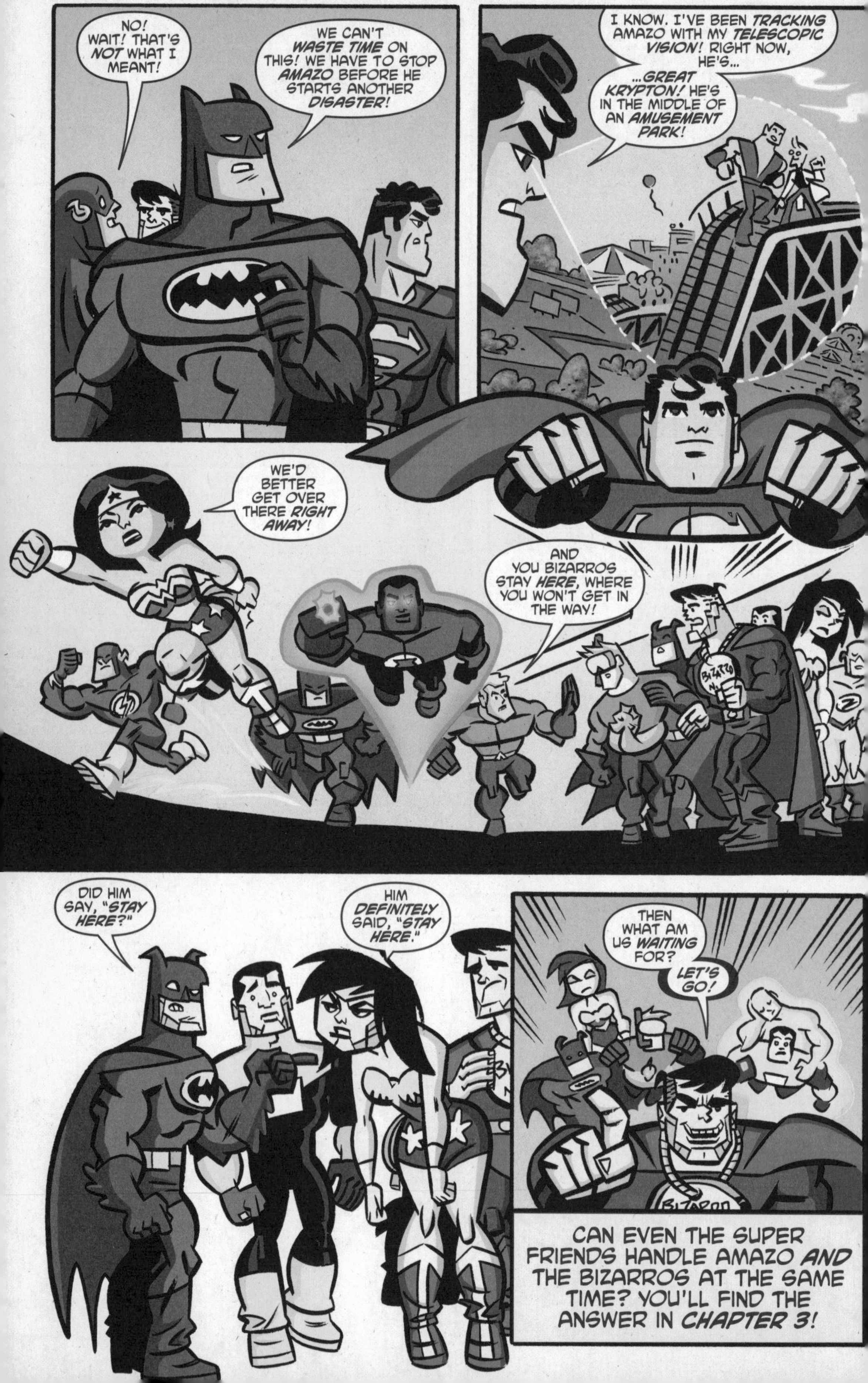
NO! WAIT! THAT'S NOT WHAT I MEANT!
WE CAN'T WASTE TIME ON THIS! WE HAVE TO STOP AMAZO BEFORE HE STARTS ANOTHER DISASTER!
I KNOW. I'VE BEEN TRACKING AMAZO WITH MY TELESCOPIC VISION! RIGHT NOW, HE'S...
...GREAT KRYPTON! HE'S IN THE MIDDLE OF AN AMUSEMENT PARK!
WE'D BETTER GET OVER THERE RIGHT AWAY!
AND YOU BIZARROS STAY HERE, WHERE YOU WON'T GET IN THE WAY!
DID HIM SAY, "STAY HERE?"
HIM DEFINITELY SAID, "STAY HERE."
THEN WHAT AM US WAITING FOR?
LET'S GO!
CAN EVEN THE SUPER FRIENDS HANDLE AMAZO AND THE BIZARROS AT THE SAME TIME? YOU'LL FIND THE ANSWER IN CHAPTER 3!

# THIS AM NOT THE TITLE! CHAPTER 3

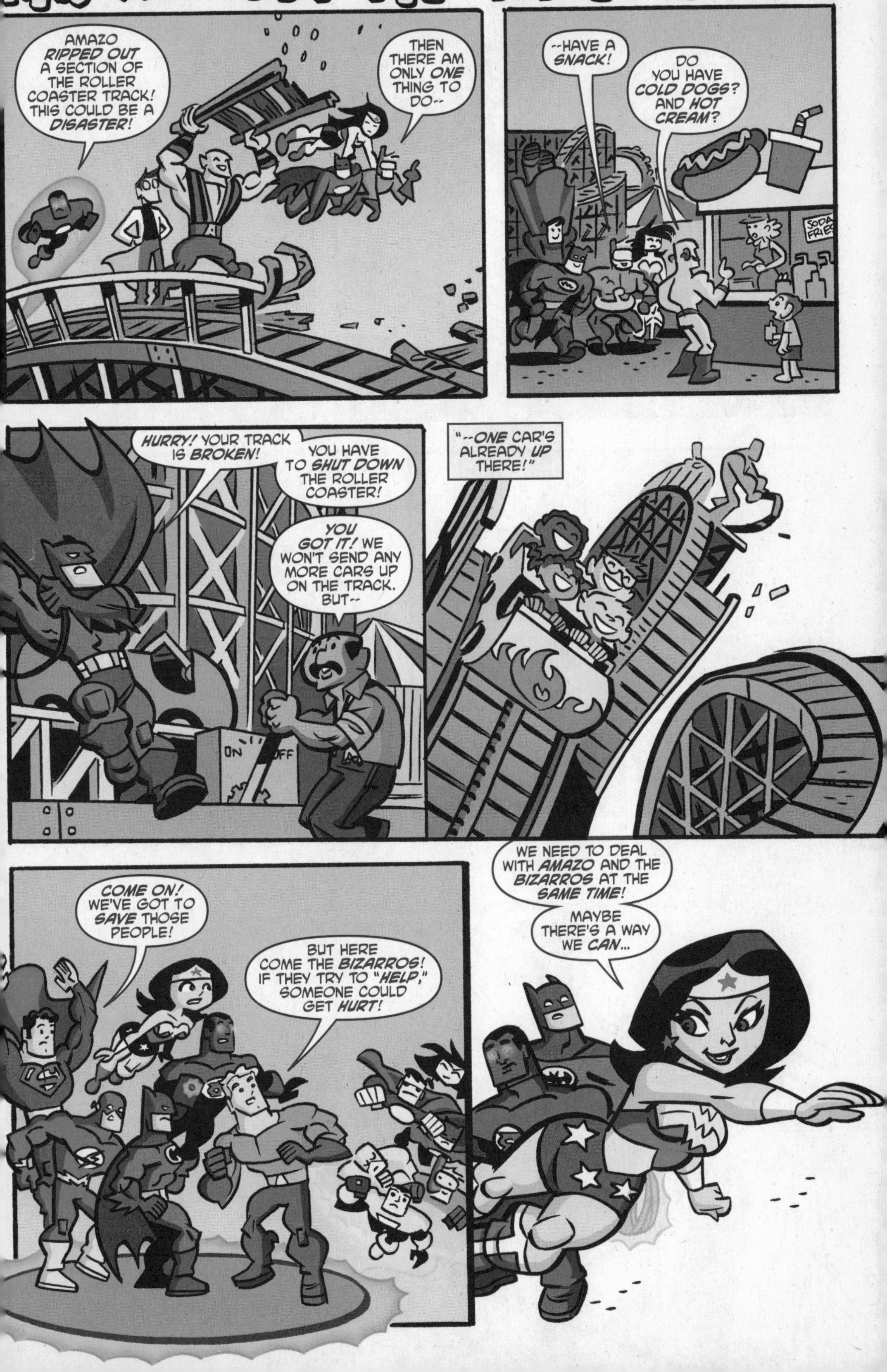
AMAZO RIPPED OUT A SECTION OF THE ROLLER COASTER TRACK! THIS COULD BE A DISASTER!
THEN THERE AM ONLY ONE THING TO DO--
--HAVE A SNACK!
DO YOU HAVE COLD DOGS? AND HOT CREAM?
SODA FRIES
HURRY! YOUR TRACK IS BROKEN!
YOU HAVE TO SHUT DOWN THE ROLLER COASTER!
YOU GOT IT! WE WON'T SEND ANY MORE CARS UP ON THE TRACK. BUT--
ON
OFF
"--ONE CAR'S ALREADY UP THERE!"
COME ON! WE'VE GOT TO SAVE THOSE PEOPLE!
BUT HERE COME THE BIZARROS! IF THEY TRY TO "HELP," SOMEONE COULD GET HURT!
WE NEED TO DEAL WITH AMAZO AND THE BIZARROS AT THE SAME TIME!
MAYBE THERE'S A WAY WE CAN...

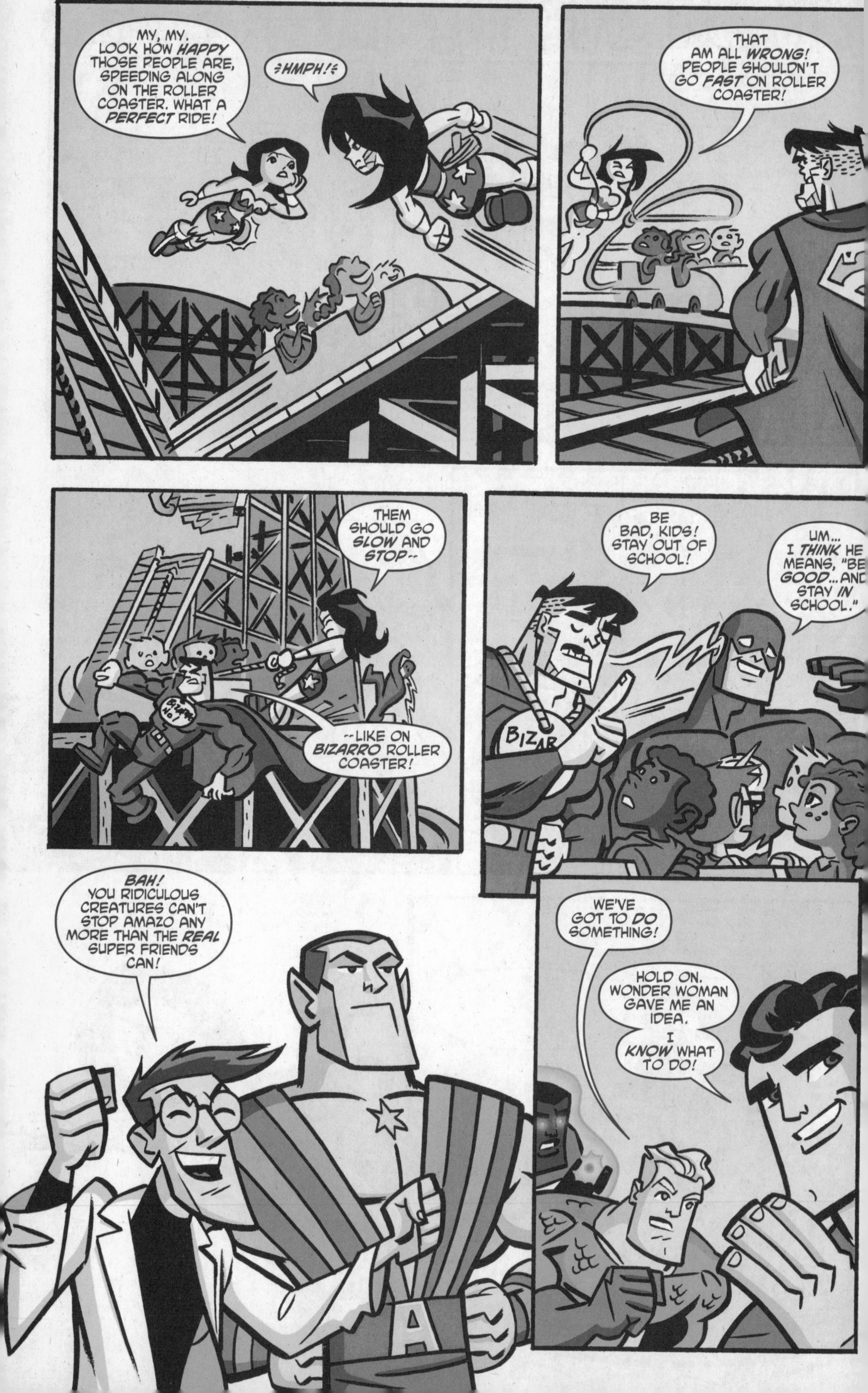

MY, MY. LOOK HOW HAPPY THOSE PEOPLE ARE, SPEEDING ALONG ON THE ROLLER COASTER. WHAT A PERFECT RIDE!
HMPH!
THAT AM ALL WRONG! PEOPLE SHOULDN'T GO FAST ON ROLLER COASTER!
THEM SHOULD GO SLOW AND STOP--
--LIKE ON BIZARRO ROLLER COASTER!
BE BAD, KIDS! STAY OUT OF SCHOOL!
UM... I THINK HE MEANS, "BE GOOD...AND STAY IN SCHOOL."
BAH! YOU RIDICULOUS CREATURES CAN'T STOP AMAZO ANY MORE THAN THE REAL SUPER FRIENDS CAN!
WE'VE GOT TO DO SOMETHING!
HOLD ON. WONDER WOMAN GAVE ME AN IDEA.
I KNOW WHAT TO DO!

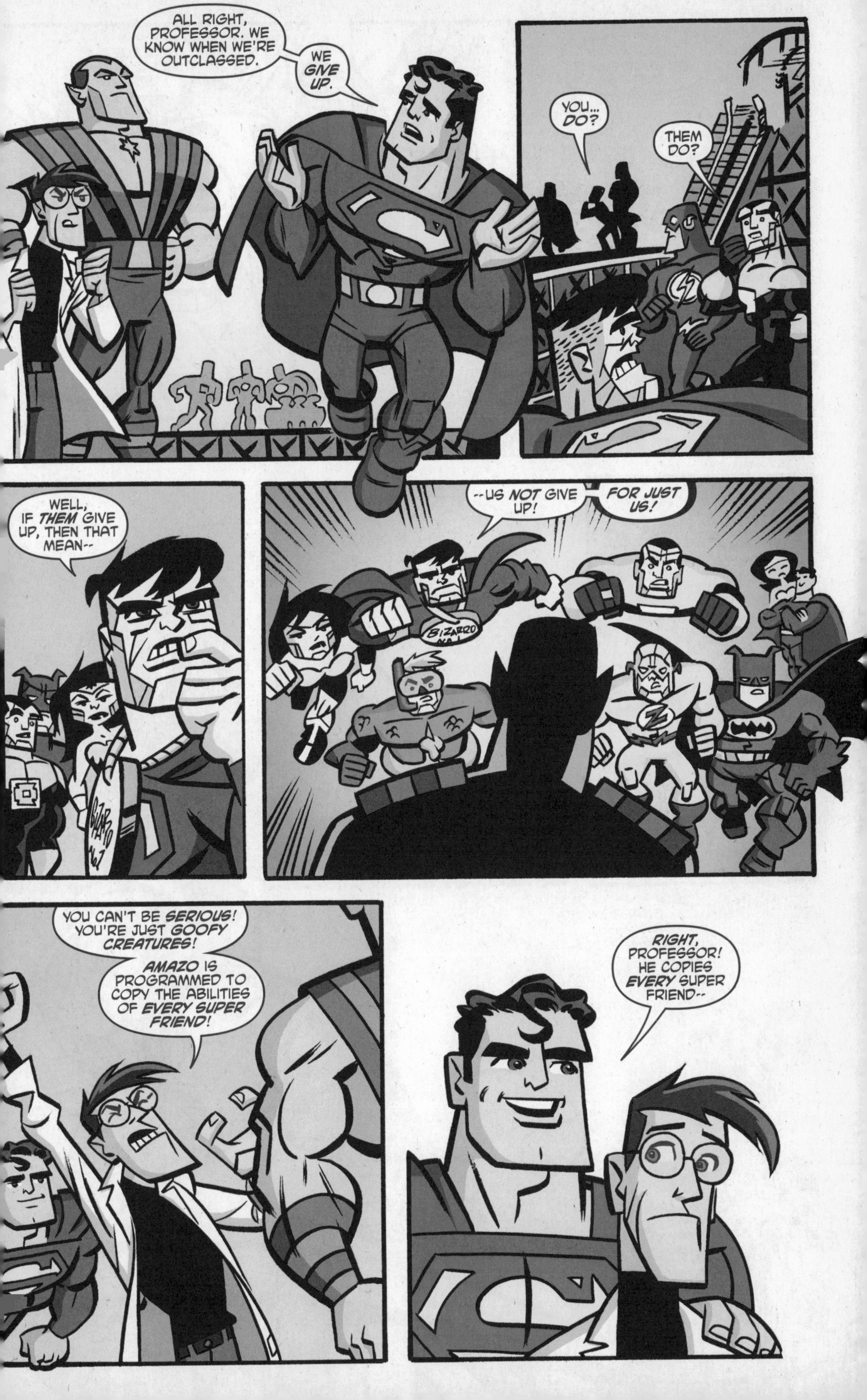

ALL RIGHT, PROFESSOR. WE KNOW WHEN WE'RE OUTCLASSED.
WE *GIVE UP*.
YOU... *DO*?
THEM DO?
WELL, IF *THEM* GIVE UP, THEN THAT MEAN--
--US *NOT* GIVE UP!
*FOR JUST US!*
YOU CAN'T BE *SERIOUS*! YOU'RE JUST *GOOFY CREATURES*!
*AMAZO* IS PROGRAMMED TO COPY THE ABILITIES OF *EVERY SUPER FRIEND*!
*RIGHT*, PROFESSOR! HE COPIES *EVERY* SUPER FRIEND--

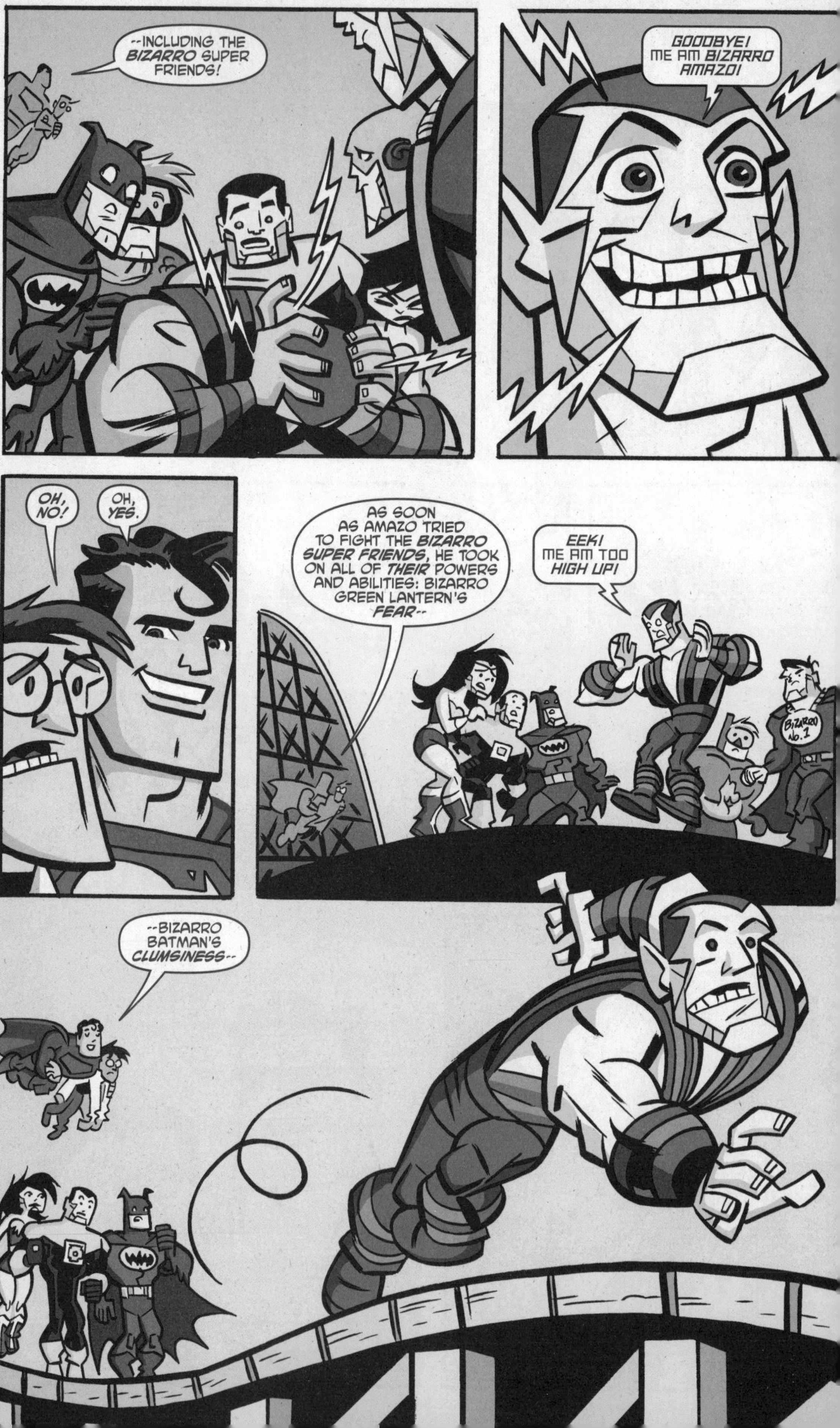
--INCLUDING THE BIZARRO SUPER FRIENDS!
GOODBYE! ME AM BIZARRO AMAZO!
OH, NO!
OH, YES.
AS SOON AS AMAZO TRIED TO FIGHT THE BIZARRO SUPER FRIENDS, HE TOOK ON ALL OF THEIR POWERS AND ABILITIES: BIZARRO GREEN LANTERN'S FEAR--
EEK! ME AM TOO HIGH UP!
BIZARRO NO. 1
--BIZARRO BATMAN'S CLUMSINESS--

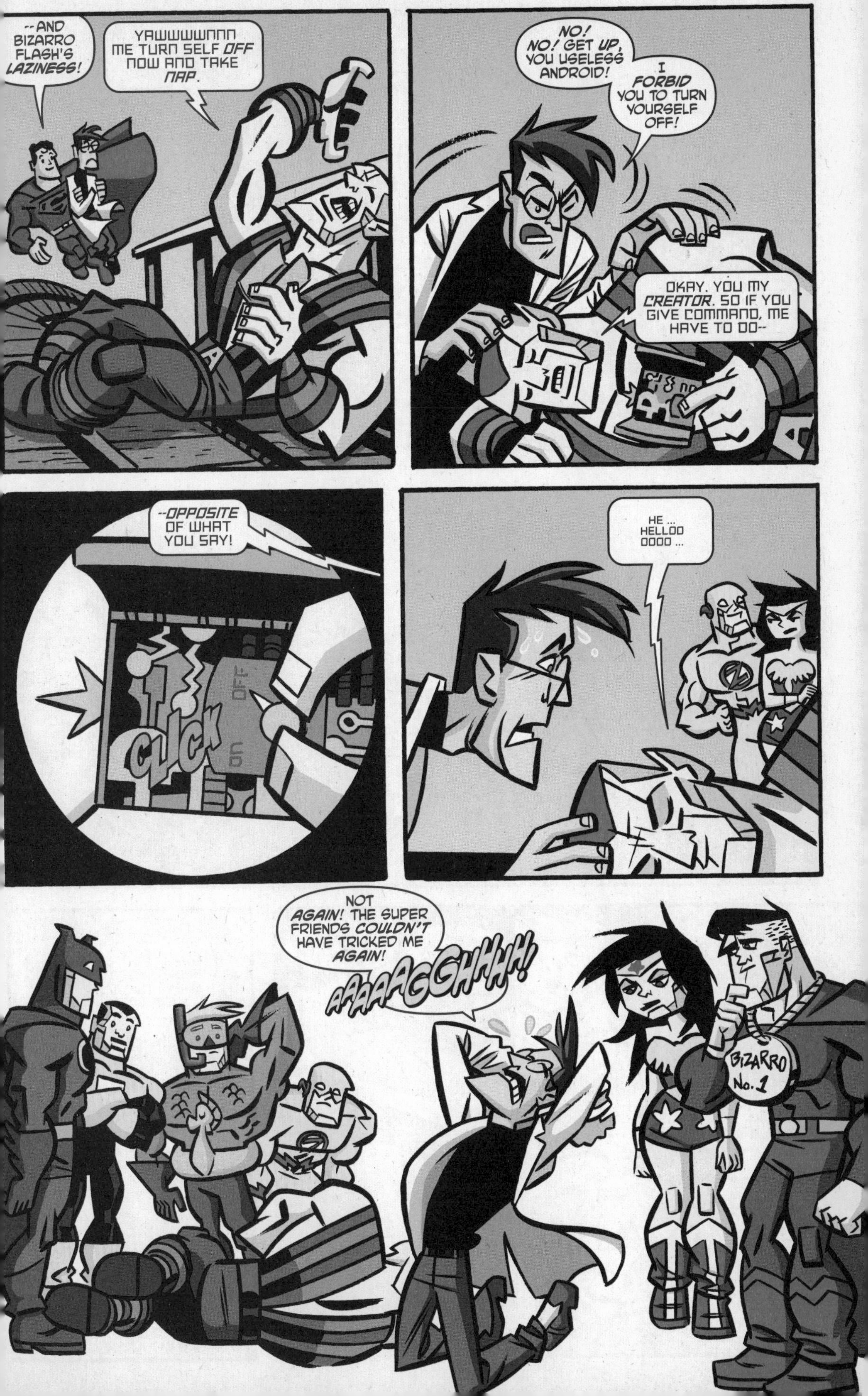
--AND BIZARRO FLASH'S LAZINESS!
YAWWWWNNN ME TURN SELF OFF NOW AND TAKE NAP.
NO! NO! GET UP, YOU USELESS ANDROID!
I FORBID YOU TO TURN YOURSELF OFF!
OKAY. YOU MY CREATOR. SO IF YOU GIVE COMMAND, ME HAVE TO DO--
--OPPOSITE OF WHAT YOU SAY!
OFF
ON
CLICK
HE ... HELLOO OOOO ...
NOT AGAIN! THE SUPER FRIENDS COULDN'T HAVE TRICKED ME AGAIN!
AAAAAGGHHHH!
BIZARRO No. 1

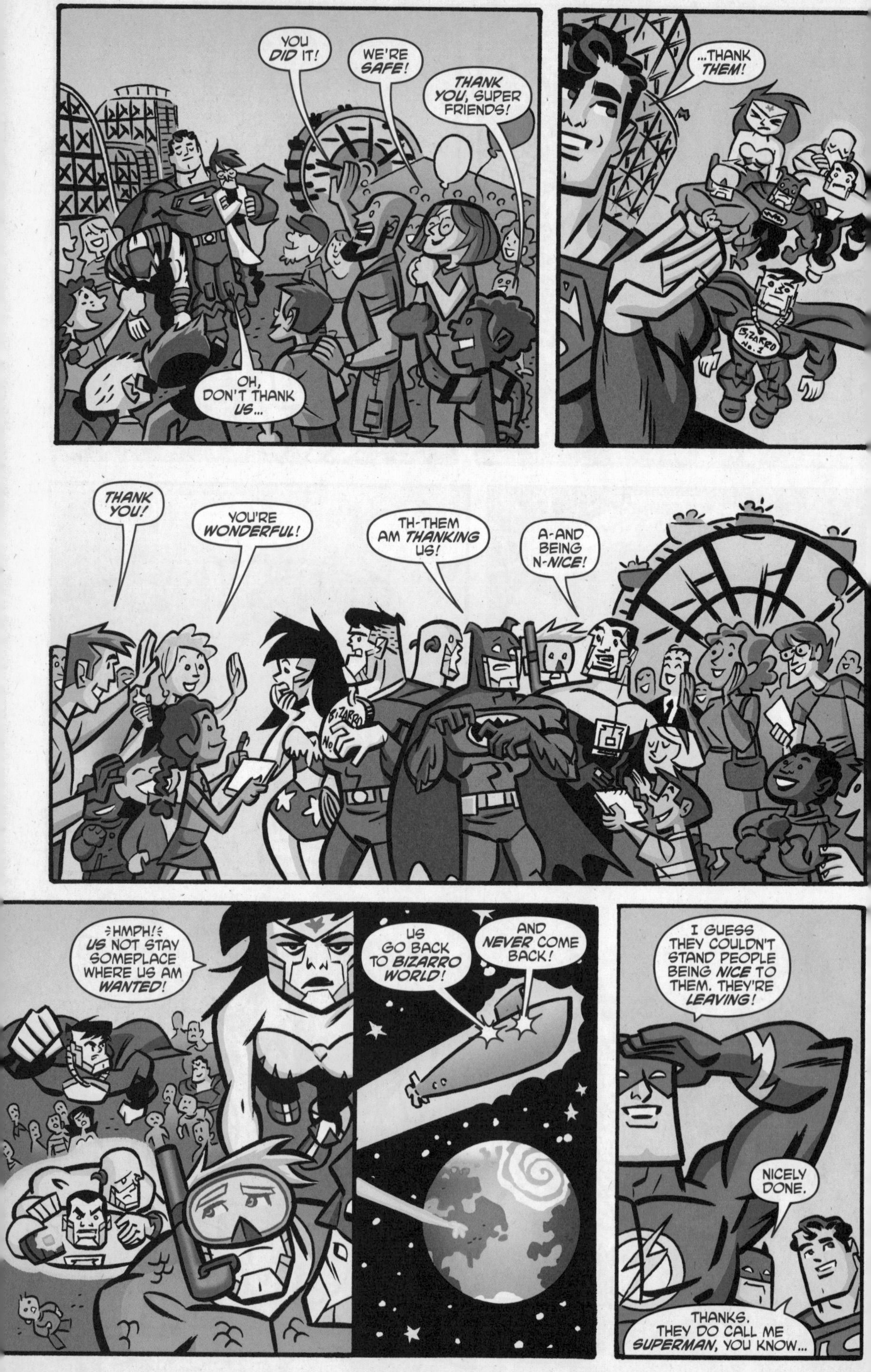
YOU DID IT!
WE'RE SAFE!
THANK YOU, SUPER FRIENDS!
OH, DON'T THANK US...
...THANK THEM!
BIZARRO NO. 1
THANK YOU!
YOU'RE WONDERFUL!
TH-THEM AM THANKING US!
A-AND BEING N-NICE!
BIZARRO NO. 1
HMPH! US NOT STAY SOMEPLACE WHERE US AM WANTED!
US GO BACK TO BIZARRO WORLD!
AND NEVER COME BACK!
I GUESS THEY COULDN'T STAND PEOPLE BEING NICE TO THEM. THEY'RE LEAVING!
NICELY DONE.
THANKS. THEY DO CALL ME SUPERMAN, YOU KNOW...

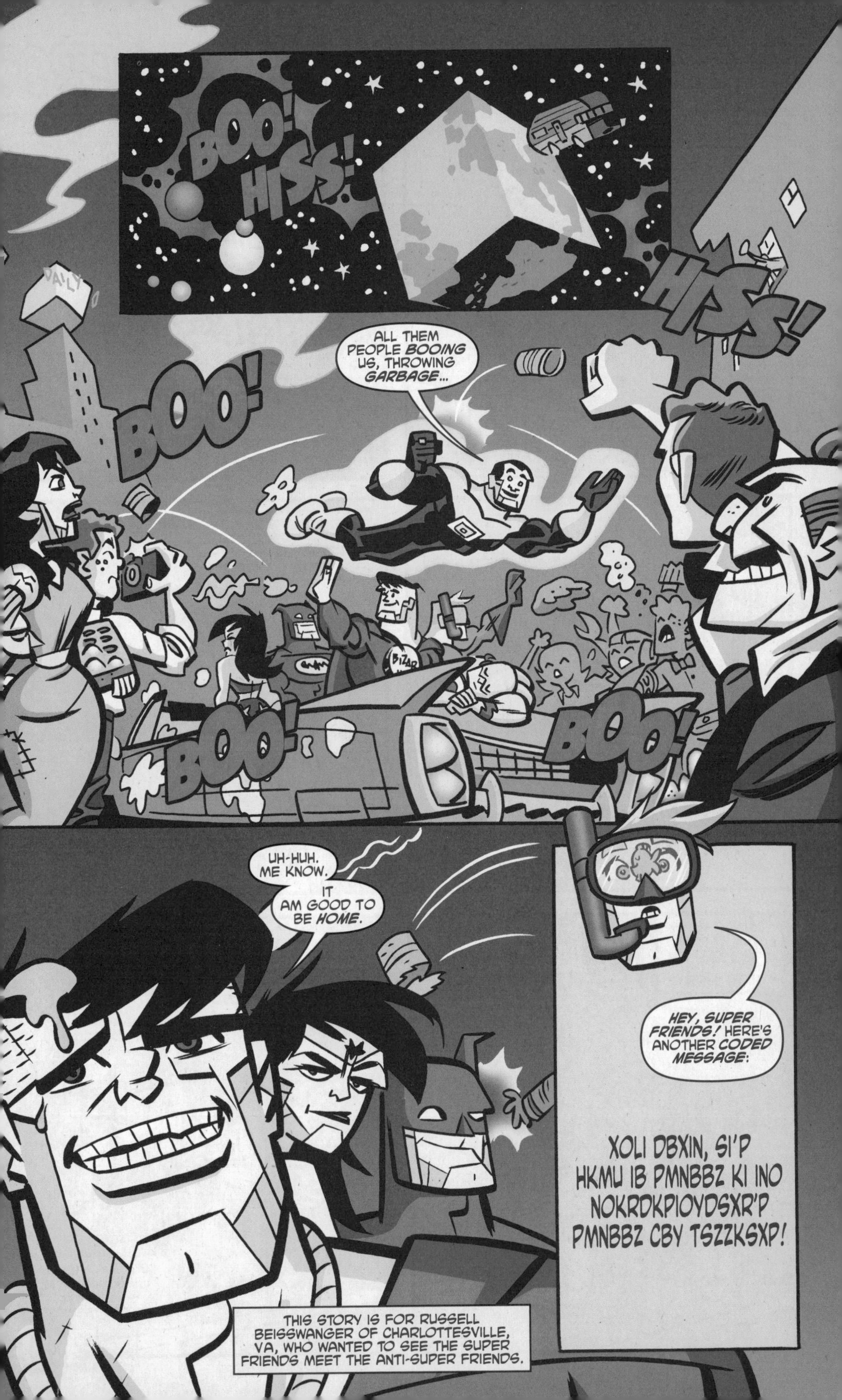
BOO!
HISS!
ALL THEM PEOPLE BOOING US, THROWING GARBAGE...
HISS!
BOO!
BOO!
BOO!
UH-HUH. ME KNOW.
IT AM GOOD TO BE HOME.
HEY, SUPER FRIENDS! HERE'S ANOTHER CODED MESSAGE:
XOLI DBXIN, SI'P HKMU IB PMNBBZ KI INO NOKRDKPIOYDSXR'P PMNBBZ CBY TSZZKSXP!
THIS STORY IS FOR RUSSELL BEISSWANGER OF CHARLOTTESVILLE, VA, WHO WANTED TO SEE THE SUPER FRIENDS MEET THE ANTI-SUPER FRIENDS.

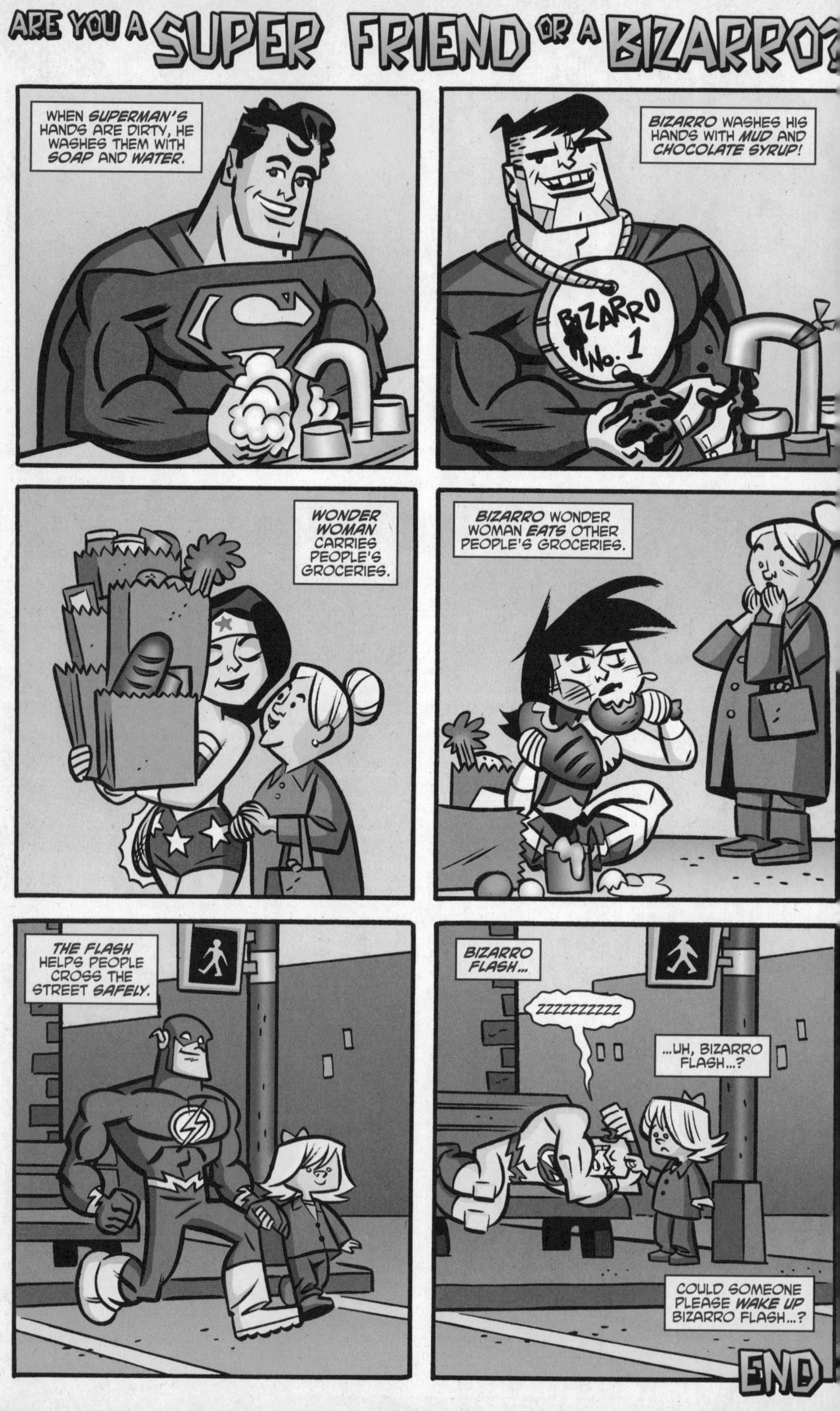
ARE YOU A SUPER FRIEND OR A BIZARRO?
WHEN SUPERMAN'S HANDS ARE DIRTY, HE WASHES THEM WITH SOAP AND WATER.
BIZARRO WASHES HIS HANDS WITH MUD AND CHOCOLATE SYRUP!
BIZARRO No. 1
WONDER WOMAN CARRIES PEOPLE'S GROCERIES.
BIZARRO WONDER WOMAN EATS OTHER PEOPLE'S GROCERIES.
THE FLASH HELPS PEOPLE CROSS THE STREET SAFELY.
BIZARRO FLASH...
ZZZZZZZZZZ
...UH, BIZARRO FLASH...?
COULD SOMEONE PLEASE WAKE UP BIZARRO FLASH...?
END

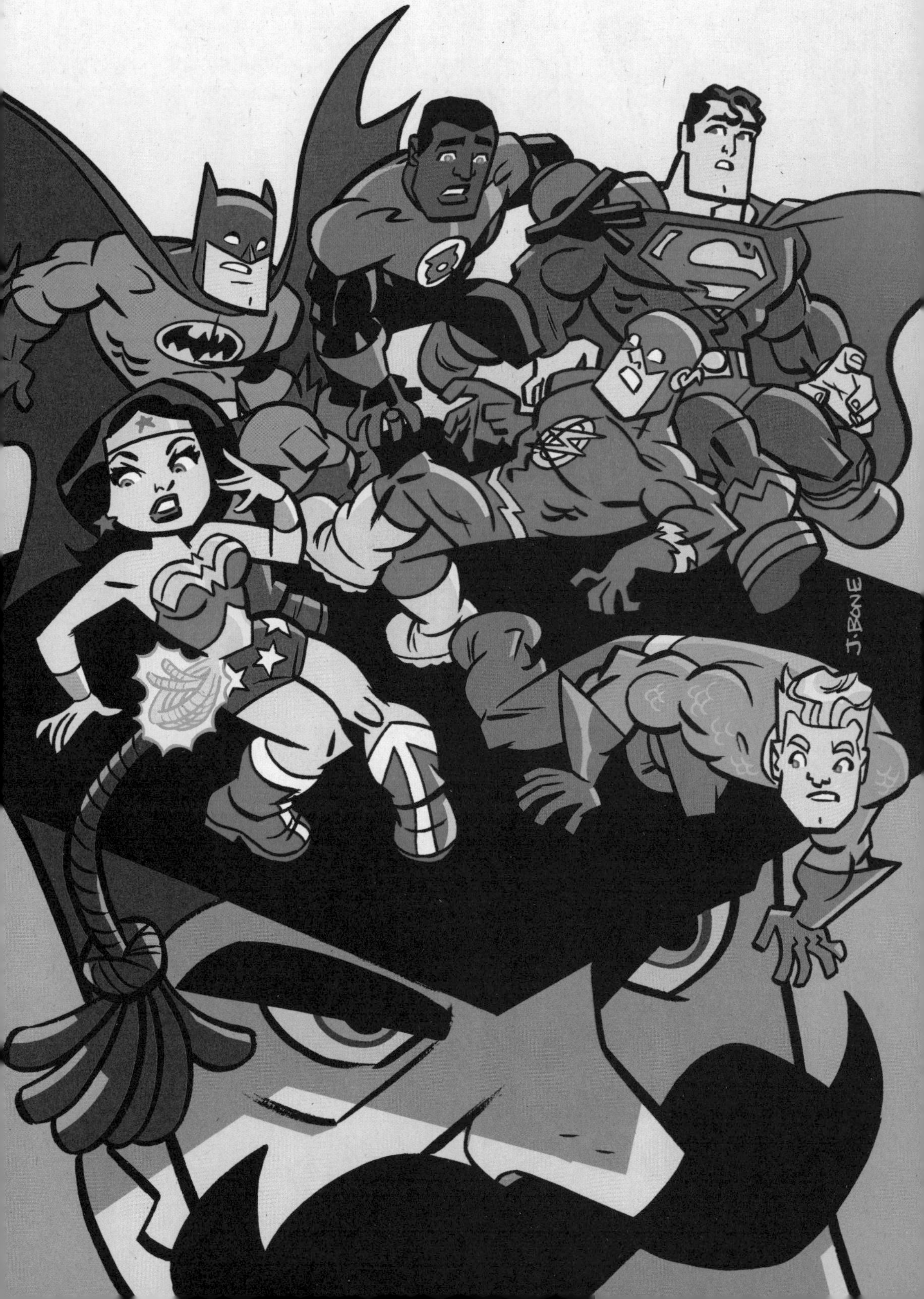
J. BONE

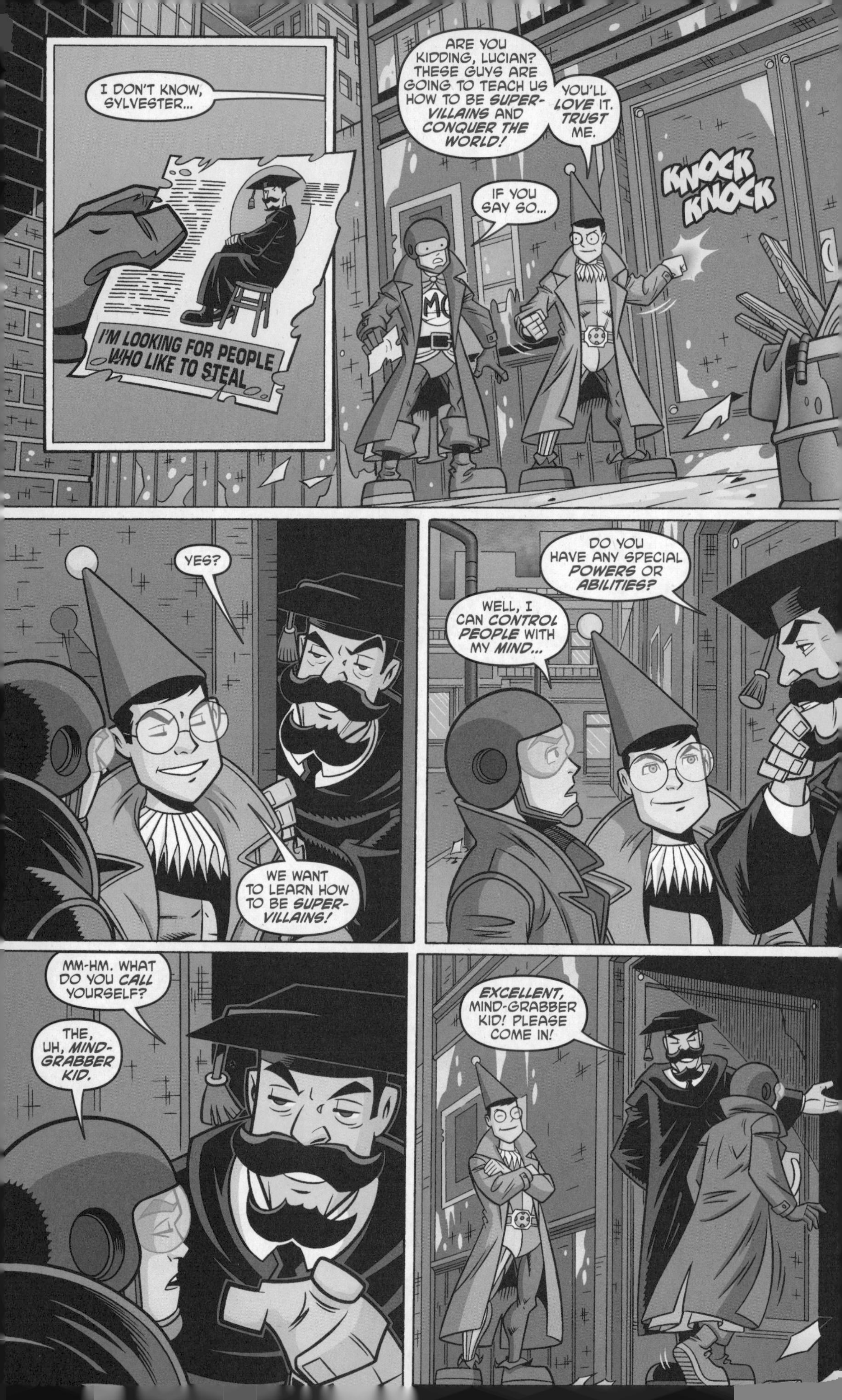
I DON'T KNOW, SYLVESTER...
I'M LOOKING FOR PEOPLE WHO LIKE TO STEAL
ARE YOU KIDDING, LUCIAN? THESE GUYS ARE GOING TO TEACH US HOW TO BE SUPER-VILLAINS AND CONQUER THE WORLD!
YOU'LL LOVE IT. TRUST ME.
IF YOU SAY SO...
KNOCK KNOCK
YES?
WE WANT TO LEARN HOW TO BE SUPER-VILLAINS!
DO YOU HAVE ANY SPECIAL POWERS OR ABILITIES?
WELL, I CAN CONTROL PEOPLE WITH MY MIND...
MM-HM. WHAT DO YOU CALL YOURSELF?
THE, UH, MIND-GRABBER KID.
EXCELLENT, MIND-GRABBER KID! PLEASE COME IN!

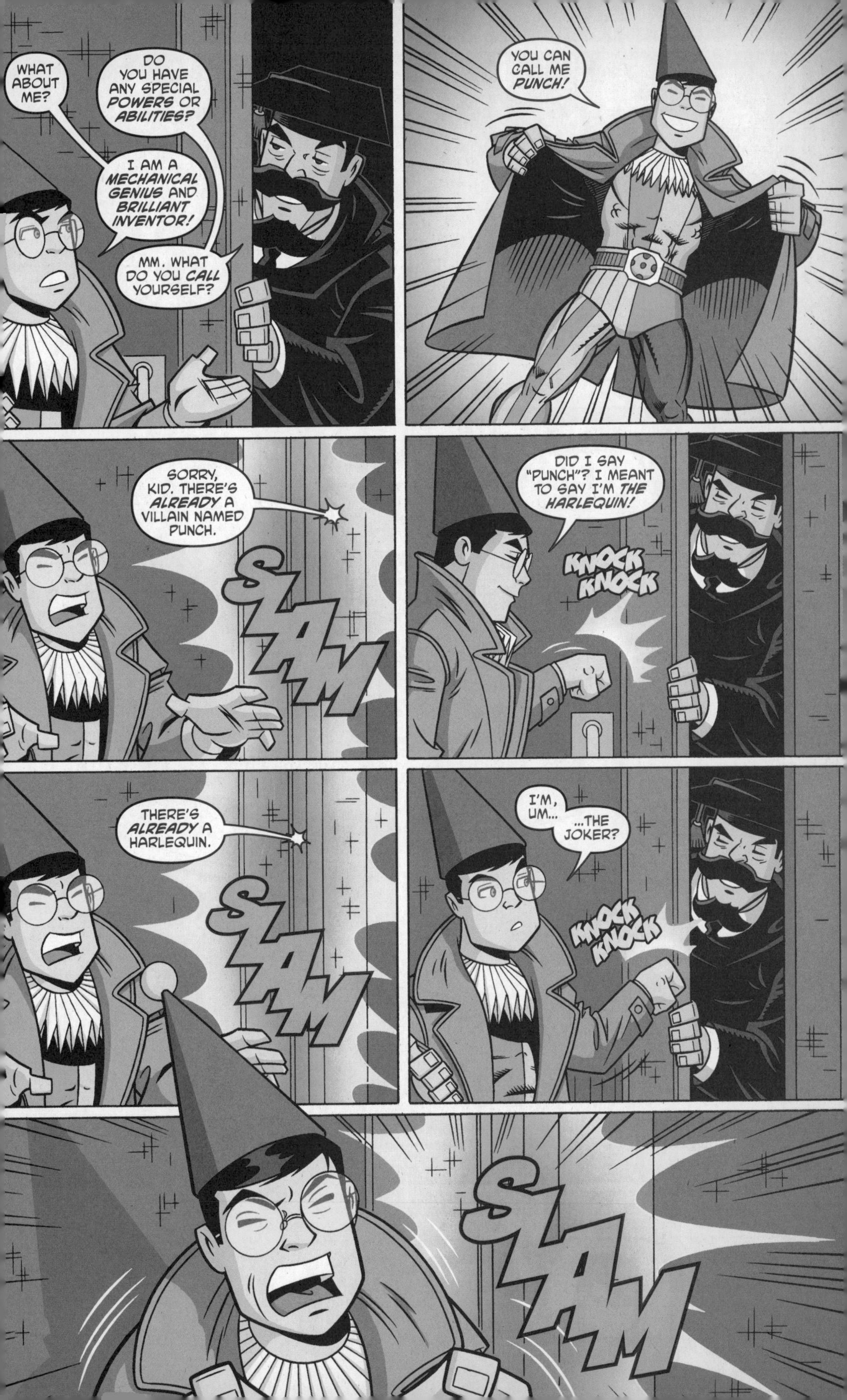
WHAT ABOUT ME?
DO YOU HAVE ANY SPECIAL POWERS OR ABILITIES?
I AM A MECHANICAL GENIUS AND BRILLIANT INVENTOR!
MM. WHAT DO YOU CALL YOURSELF?
YOU CAN CALL ME PUNCH!
SORRY, KID. THERE'S ALREADY A VILLAIN NAMED PUNCH.
SLAM
DID I SAY "PUNCH"? I MEANT TO SAY I'M THE HARLEQUIN!
KNOCK KNOCK
THERE'S ALREADY A HARLEQUIN.
SLAM
I'M, UM...
...THE JOKER?
KNOCK KNOCK
SLAM

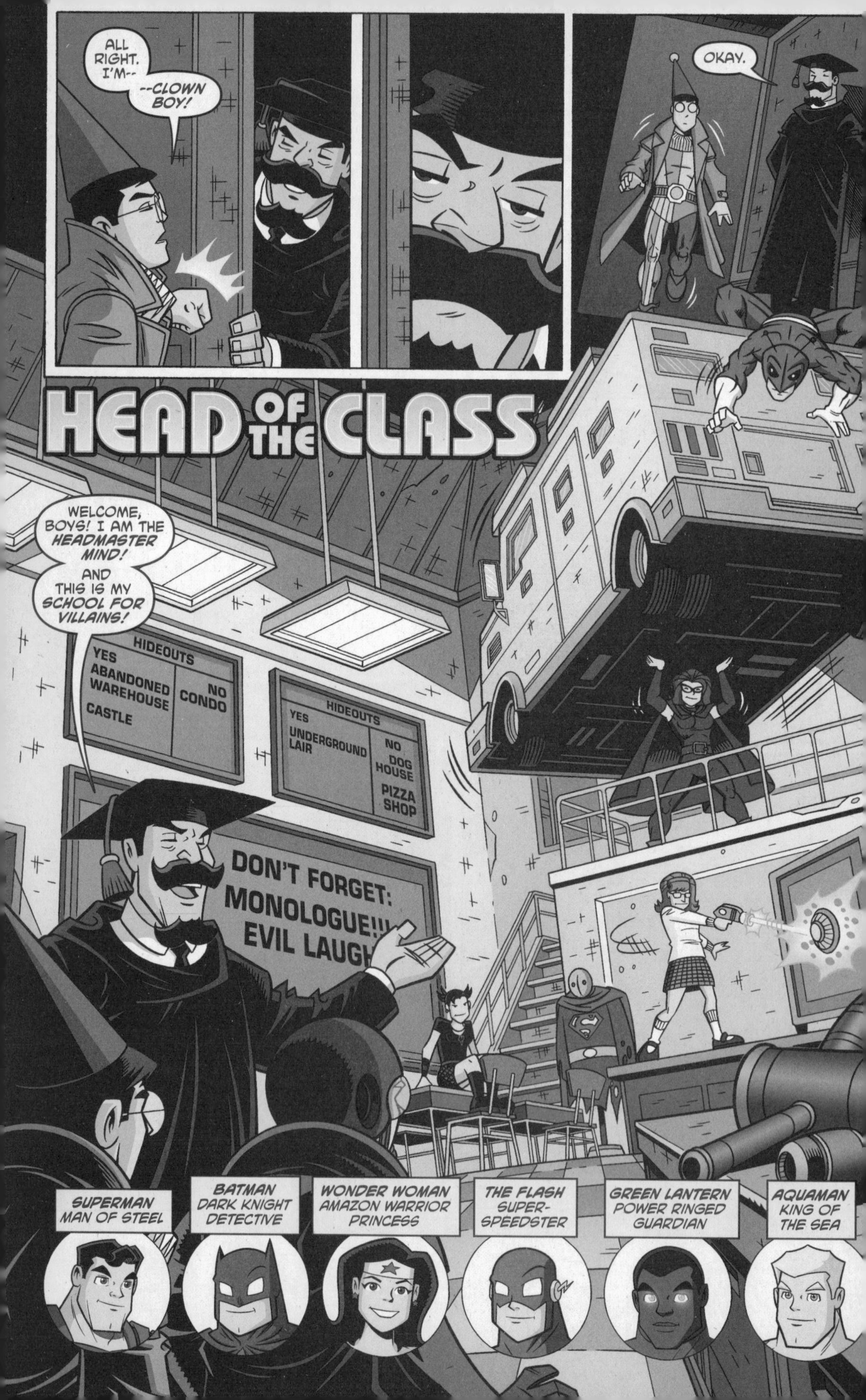

ALL RIGHT. I'M--
--CLOWN BOY!
OKAY.
HEAD OF THE CLASS
WELCOME, BOYS! I AM THE HEADMASTER MIND!
AND THIS IS MY SCHOOL FOR VILLAINS!
HIDEOUTS
YES
ABANDONED WAREHOUSE
CASTLE
NO
CONDO
HIDEOUTS
YES
UNDERGROUND LAIR
NO
DOG HOUSE
PIZZA SHOP
DON'T FORGET:
MONOLOGUE!!!
EVIL LAUGH
SUPERMAN MAN OF STEEL
BATMAN DARK KNIGHT DETECTIVE
WONDER WOMAN AMAZON WARRIOR PRINCESS
THE FLASH SUPER-SPEEDSTER
GREEN LANTERN POWER RINGED GUARDIAN
AQUAMAN KING OF THE SEA

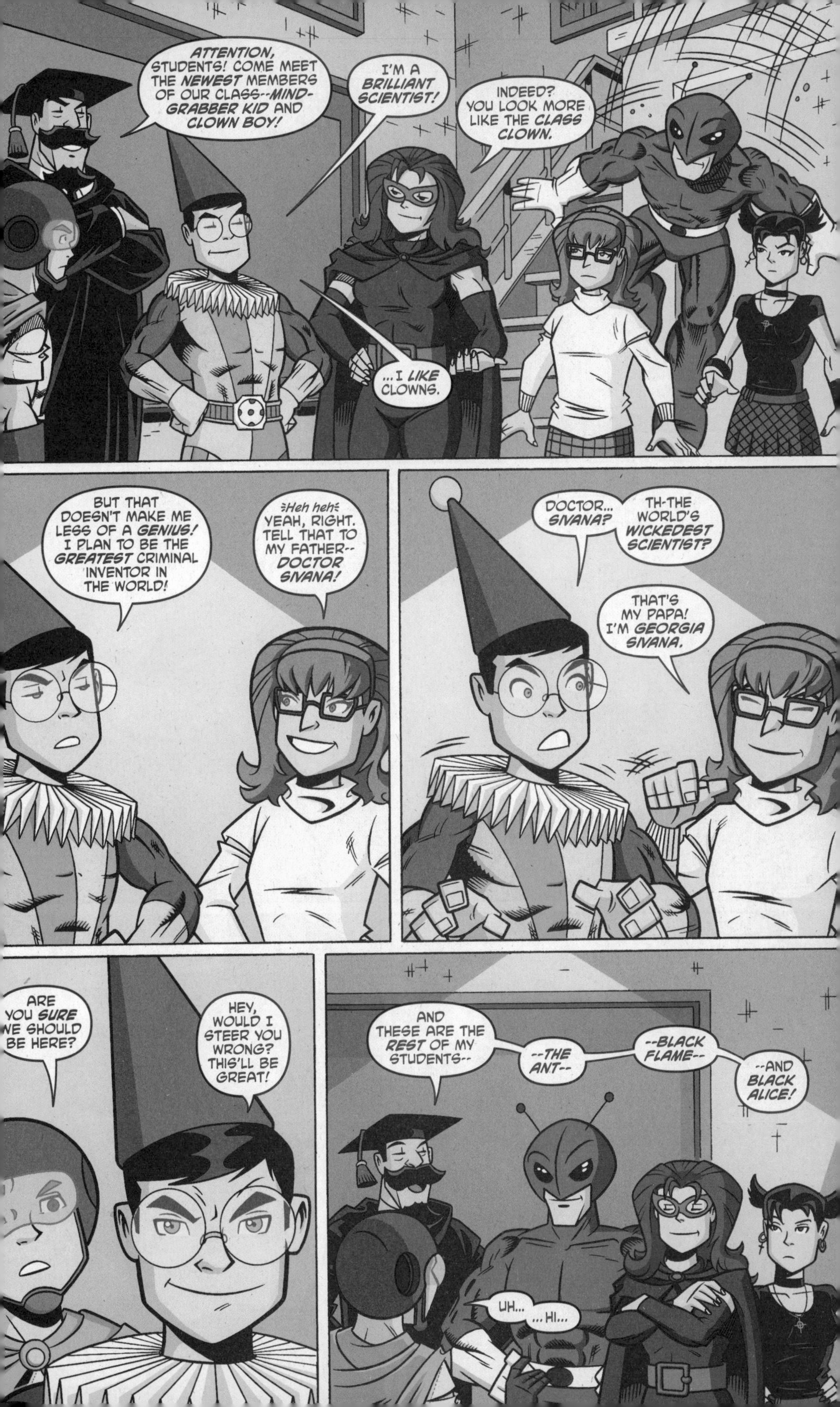
ATTENTION, STUDENTS! COME MEET THE NEWEST MEMBERS OF OUR CLASS--MIND-GRABBER KID AND CLOWN BOY!
I'M A BRILLIANT SCIENTIST!
INDEED? YOU LOOK MORE LIKE THE CLASS CLOWN.
...I LIKE CLOWNS.
BUT THAT DOESN'T MAKE ME LESS OF A GENIUS! I PLAN TO BE THE GREATEST CRIMINAL INVENTOR IN THE WORLD!
Heh heh YEAH, RIGHT. TELL THAT TO MY FATHER--DOCTOR SIVANA!
DOCTOR... SIVANA?
TH-THE WORLD'S WICKEDEST SCIENTIST?
THAT'S MY PAPA! I'M GEORGIA SIVANA.
ARE YOU SURE WE SHOULD BE HERE?
HEY, WOULD I STEER YOU WRONG? THIS'LL BE GREAT!
AND THESE ARE THE REST OF MY STUDENTS--
--THE ANT--
--BLACK FLAME--
--AND BLACK ALICE!
UH...
...HI...

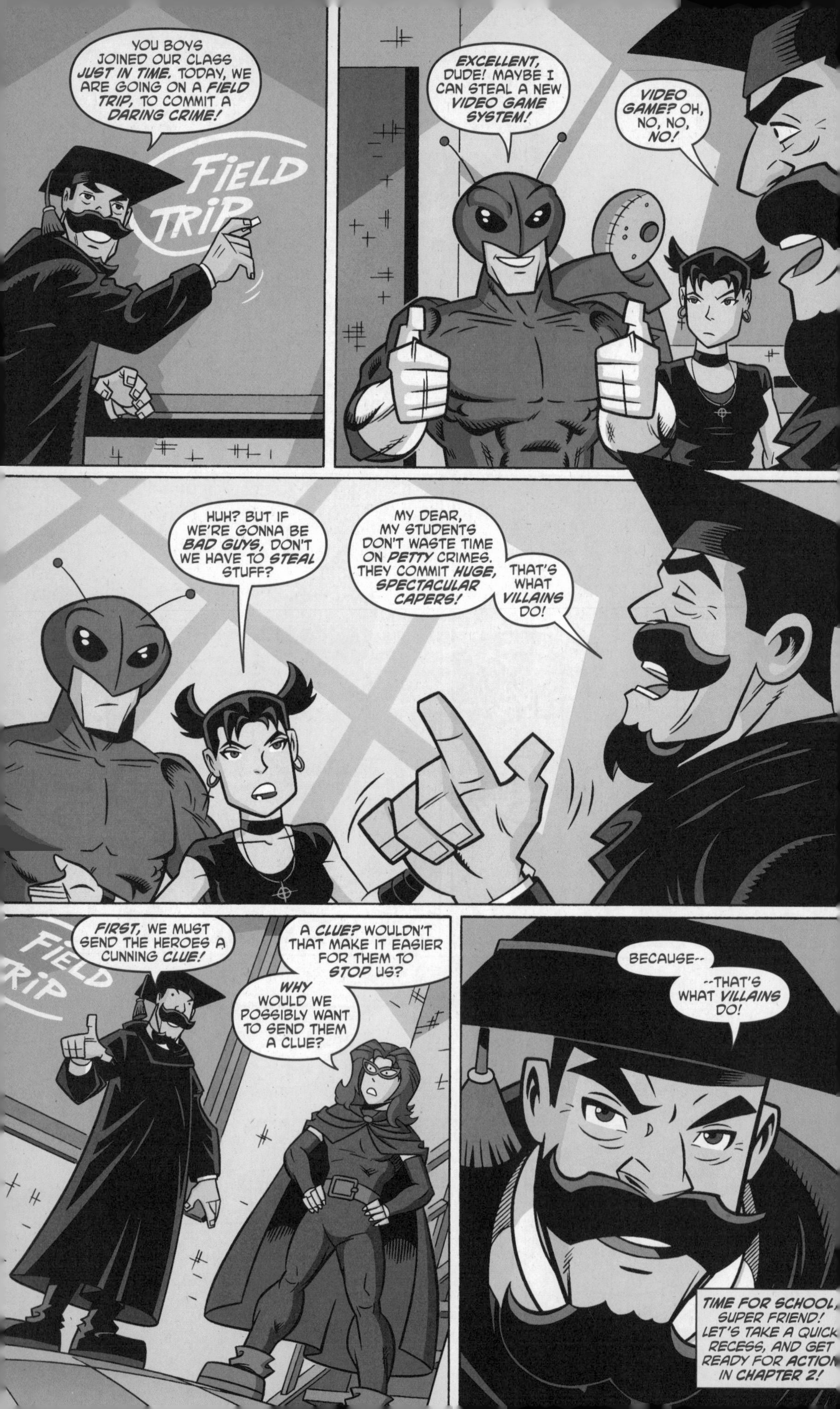
YOU BOYS JOINED OUR CLASS JUST IN TIME. TODAY, WE ARE GOING ON A FIELD TRIP, TO COMMIT A DARING CRIME!
FIELD TRIP
EXCELLENT, DUDE! MAYBE I CAN STEAL A NEW VIDEO GAME SYSTEM!
VIDEO GAME? OH, NO, NO, NO!
HUH? BUT IF WE'RE GONNA BE BAD GUYS, DON'T WE HAVE TO STEAL STUFF?
MY DEAR, MY STUDENTS DON'T WASTE TIME ON PETTY CRIMES. THEY COMMIT HUGE, SPECTACULAR CAPERS!
THAT'S WHAT VILLAINS DO!
FIRST, WE MUST SEND THE HEROES A CUNNING CLUE!
A CLUE? WOULDN'T THAT MAKE IT EASIER FOR THEM TO STOP US?
WHY WOULD WE POSSIBLY WANT TO SEND THEM A CLUE?
BECAUSE--
--THAT'S WHAT VILLAINS DO!
TIME FOR SCHOOL, SUPER FRIEND! LET'S TAKE A QUICK RECESS, AND GET READY FOR ACTION IN CHAPTER 2!

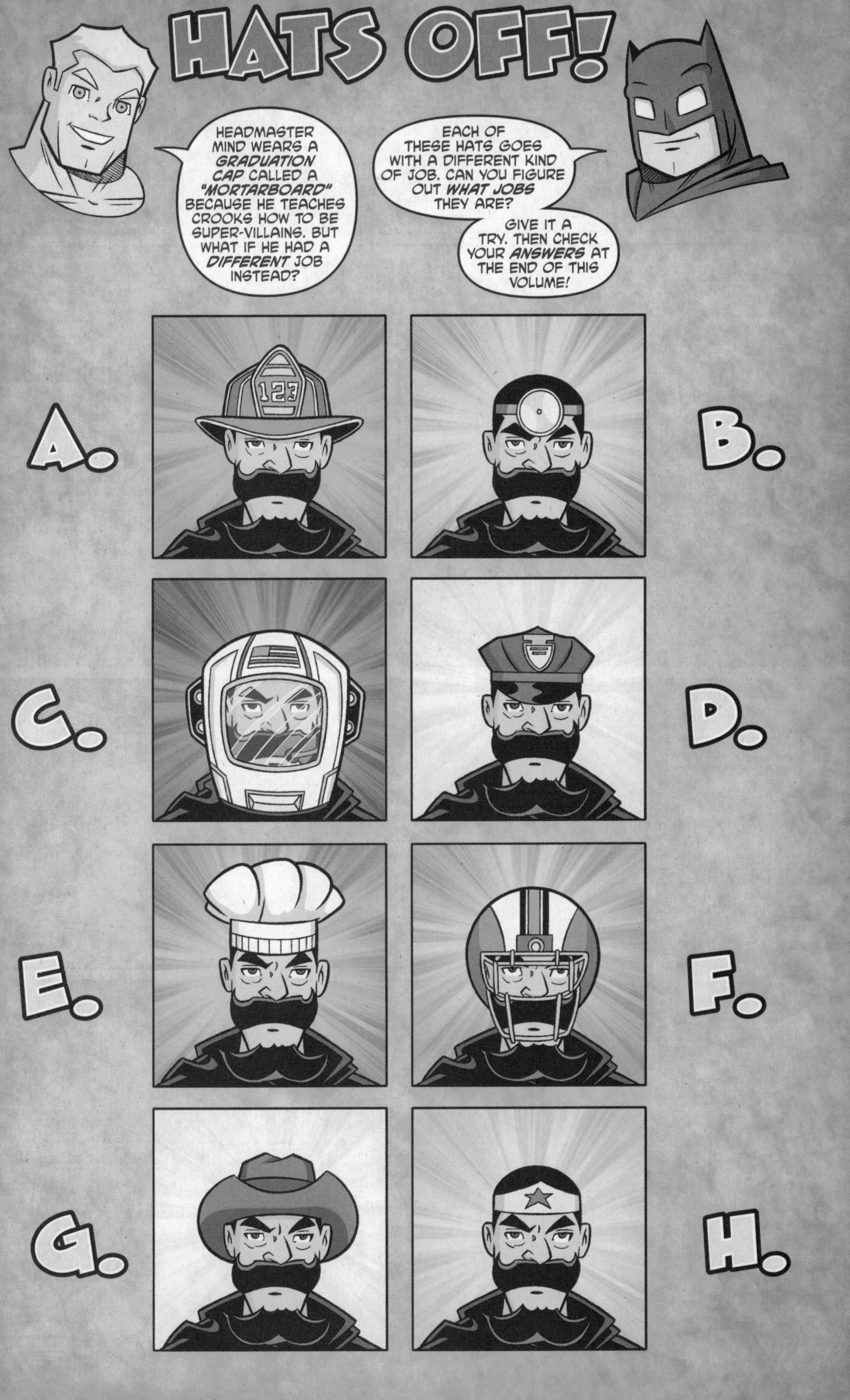
HATS OFF!
HEADMASTER MIND WEARS A GRADUATION CAP CALLED A "MORTARBOARD" BECAUSE HE TEACHES CROOKS HOW TO BE SUPER-VILLAINS. BUT WHAT IF HE HAD A DIFFERENT JOB INSTEAD?
EACH OF THESE HATS GOES WITH A DIFFERENT KIND OF JOB. CAN YOU FIGURE OUT WHAT JOBS THEY ARE?
GIVE IT A TRY. THEN CHECK YOUR ANSWERS AT THE END OF THIS VOLUME!
A.
123
B.
C.
D.
E.
F.
G.
H.

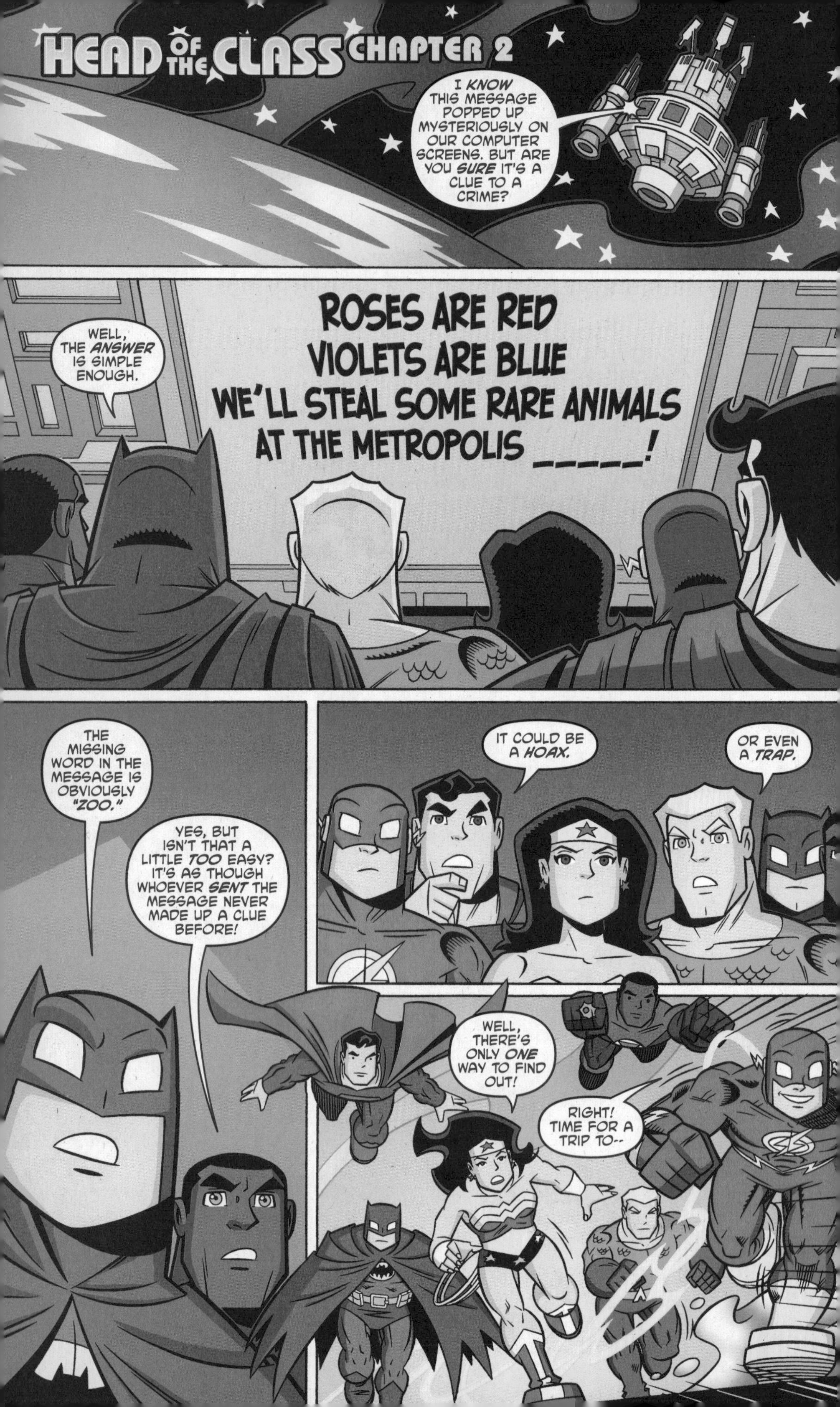
HEAD OF THE CLASS CHAPTER 2
I KNOW THIS MESSAGE POPPED UP MYSTERIOUSLY ON OUR COMPUTER SCREENS. BUT ARE YOU SURE IT'S A CLUE TO A CRIME?
ROSES ARE RED VIOLETS ARE BLUE WE'LL STEAL SOME RARE ANIMALS AT THE METROPOLIS _____!
WELL, THE ANSWER IS SIMPLE ENOUGH.
THE MISSING WORD IN THE MESSAGE IS OBVIOUSLY "ZOO."
YES, BUT ISN'T THAT A LITTLE TOO EASY? IT'S AS THOUGH WHOEVER SENT THE MESSAGE NEVER MADE UP A CLUE BEFORE!
IT COULD BE A HOAX.
OR EVEN A TRAP.
WELL, THERE'S ONLY ONE WAY TO FIND OUT!
RIGHT! TIME FOR A TRIP TO--

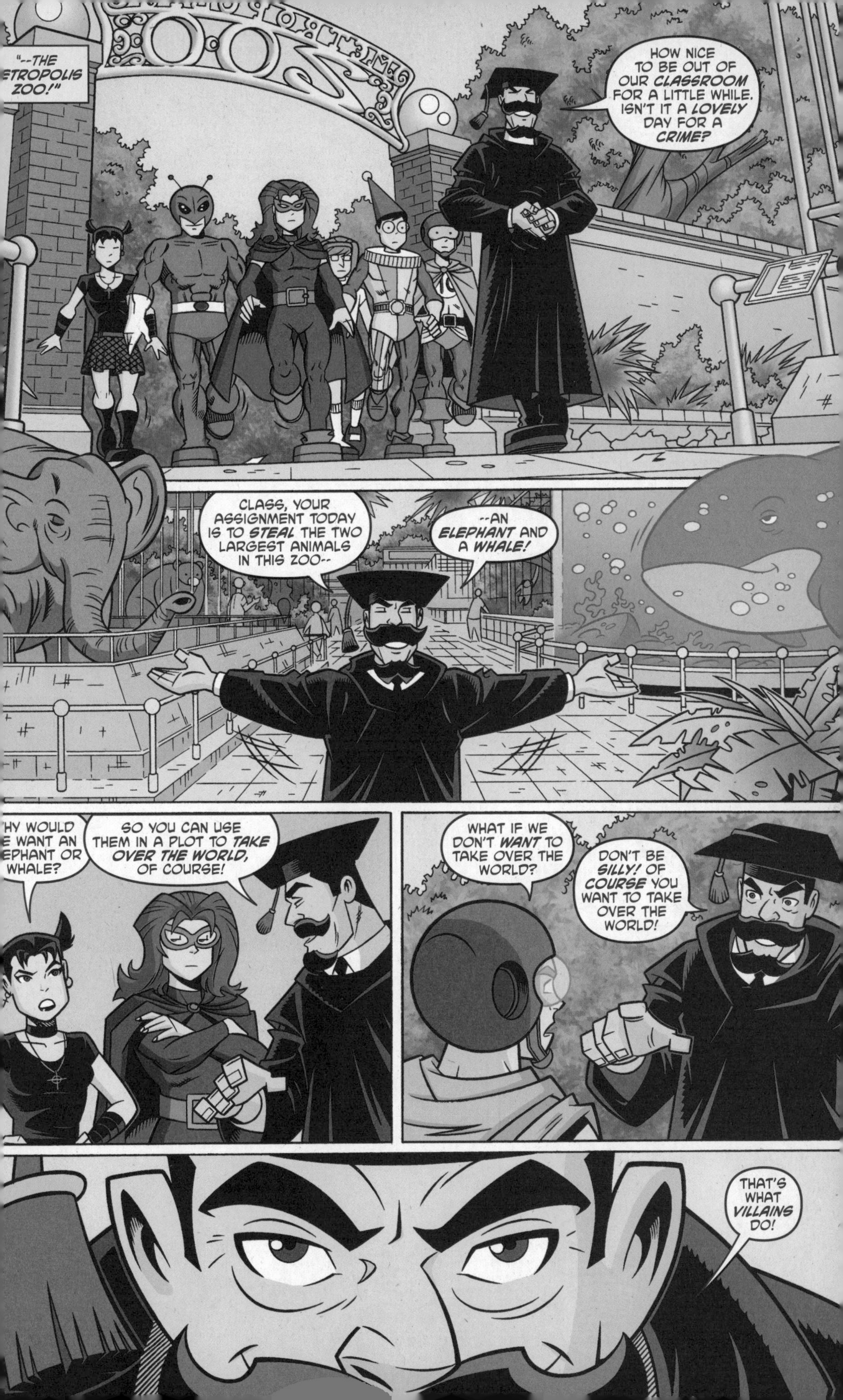
"--THE
ETROPOLIS
ZOO!"
HOW NICE TO BE OUT OF OUR *CLASSROOM* FOR A LITTLE WHILE. ISN'T IT A *LOVELY* DAY FOR A *CRIME?*
CLASS, YOUR ASSIGNMENT TODAY IS TO *STEAL* THE TWO LARGEST ANIMALS IN THIS ZOO--
--AN *ELEPHANT* AND A *WHALE!*
HY WOULD E WANT AN EPHANT OR WHALE?
SO YOU CAN USE THEM IN A PLOT TO *TAKE OVER THE WORLD,* OF COURSE!
WHAT IF WE DON'T *WANT* TO TAKE OVER THE WORLD?
DON'T BE *SILLY!* OF *COURSE* YOU WANT TO TAKE OVER THE WORLD!
THAT'S WHAT *VILLAINS* DO!

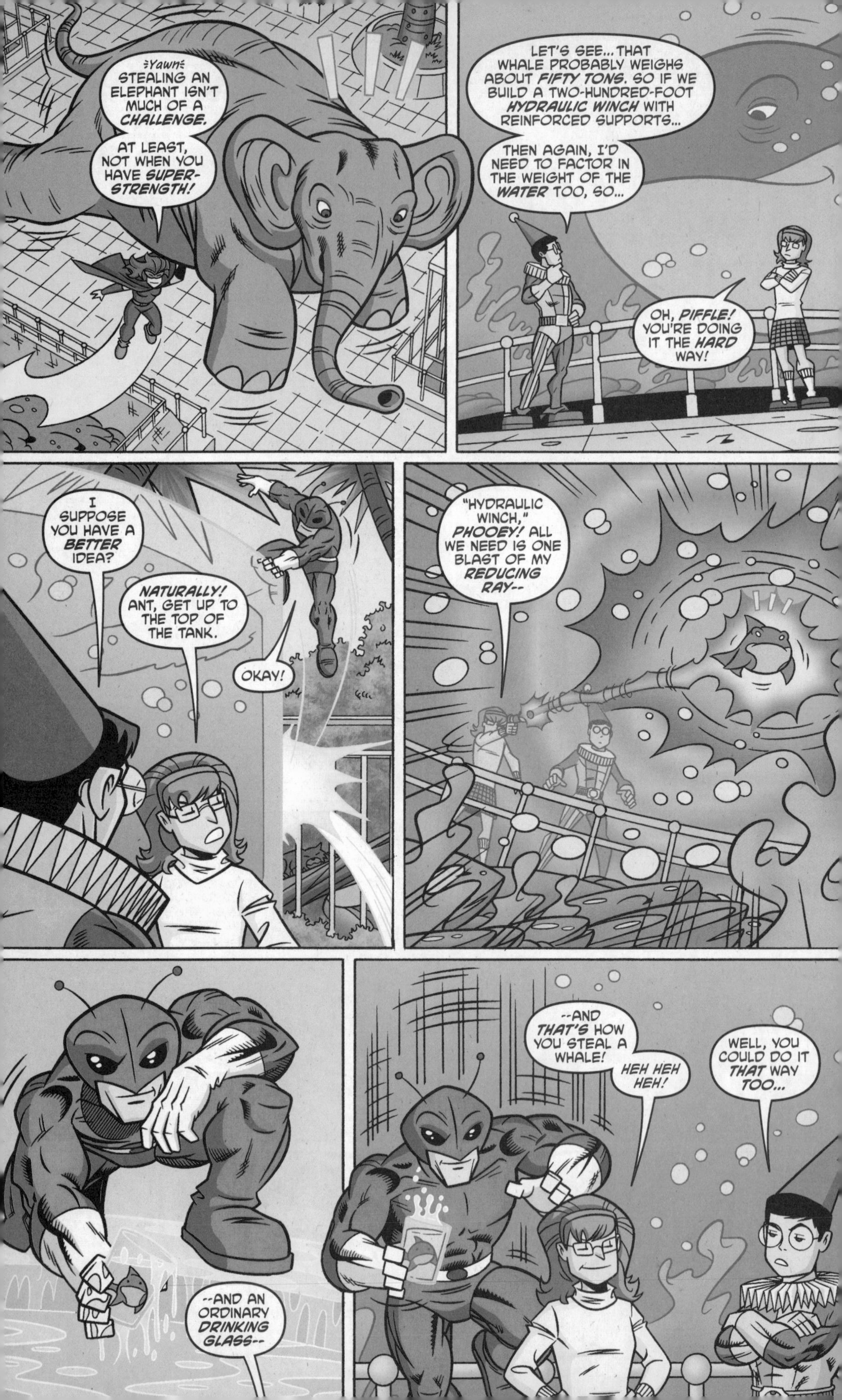

YAWN
STEALING AN ELEPHANT ISN'T MUCH OF A CHALLENGE.
AT LEAST, NOT WHEN YOU HAVE SUPER-STRENGTH!
LET'S SEE... THAT WHALE PROBABLY WEIGHS ABOUT FIFTY TONS. SO IF WE BUILD A TWO-HUNDRED-FOOT HYDRAULIC WINCH WITH REINFORCED SUPPORTS...
THEN AGAIN, I'D NEED TO FACTOR IN THE WEIGHT OF THE WATER TOO, SO...
OH, PIFFLE! YOU'RE DOING IT THE HARD WAY!
I SUPPOSE YOU HAVE A BETTER IDEA?
NATURALLY! ANT, GET UP TO THE TOP OF THE TANK.
OKAY!
"HYDRAULIC WINCH," PHOOEY! ALL WE NEED IS ONE BLAST OF MY REDUCING RAY--
--AND AN ORDINARY DRINKING GLASS--
--AND THAT'S HOW YOU STEAL A WHALE!
HEH HEH HEH!
WELL, YOU COULD DO IT THAT WAY TOO...

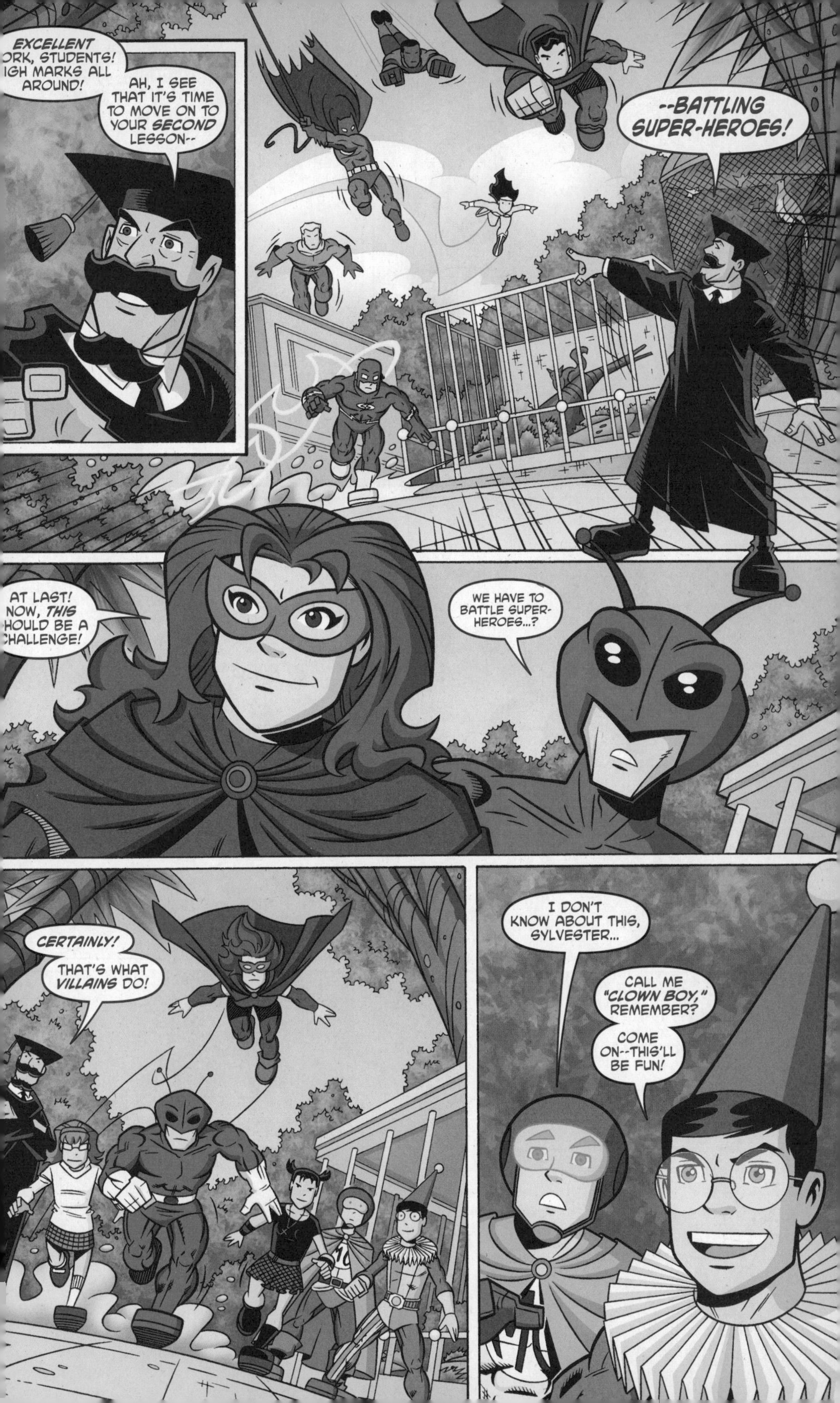
EXCELLENT
ORK, STUDENTS!
IGH MARKS ALL
AROUND!
AH, I SEE THAT IT'S TIME TO MOVE ON TO YOUR SECOND LESSON--
--BATTLING SUPER-HEROES!
AT LAST! NOW, THIS HOULD BE A HALLENGE!
WE HAVE TO BATTLE SUPER-HEROES...?
CERTAINLY!
THAT'S WHAT VILLAINS DO!
I DON'T KNOW ABOUT THIS, SYLVESTER...
CALL ME "CLOWN BOY," REMEMBER?
COME ON--THIS'LL BE FUN!

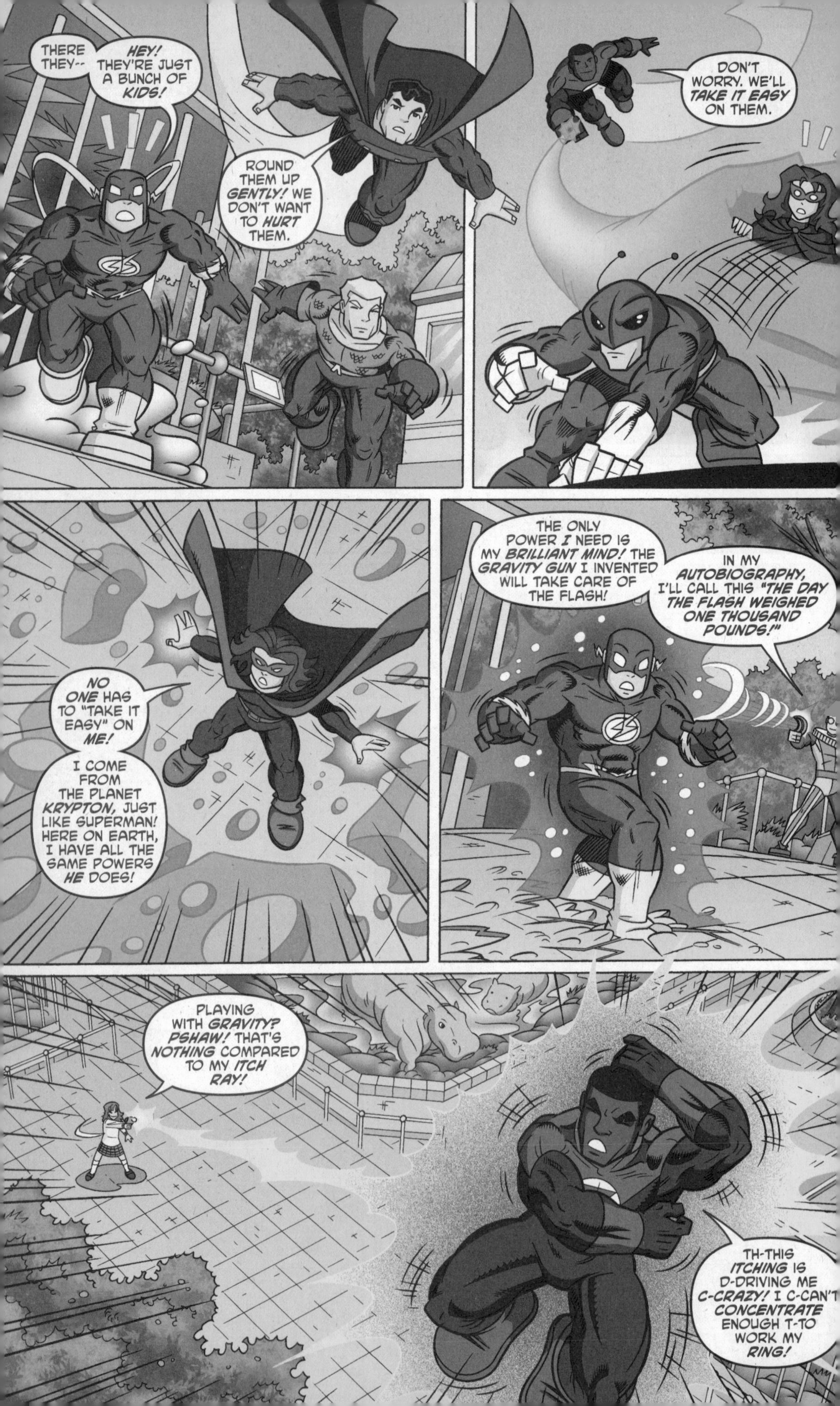
THERE THEY--
HEY! THEY'RE JUST A BUNCH OF KIDS!
ROUND THEM UP GENTLY! WE DON'T WANT TO HURT THEM.
DON'T WORRY. WE'LL TAKE IT EASY ON THEM.
NO ONE HAS TO "TAKE IT EASY" ON ME!
I COME FROM THE PLANET KRYPTON, JUST LIKE SUPERMAN! HERE ON EARTH, I HAVE ALL THE SAME POWERS HE DOES!
THE ONLY POWER I NEED IS MY BRILLIANT MIND! THE GRAVITY GUN I INVENTED WILL TAKE CARE OF THE FLASH!
IN MY AUTOBIOGRAPHY, I'LL CALL THIS "THE DAY THE FLASH WEIGHED ONE THOUSAND POUNDS!"
PLAYING WITH GRAVITY? PSHAW! THAT'S NOTHING COMPARED TO MY ITCH RAY!
TH-THIS ITCHING IS D-DRIVING ME C-CRAZY! I C-CAN'T CONCENTRATE ENOUGH T-TO WORK MY RING!

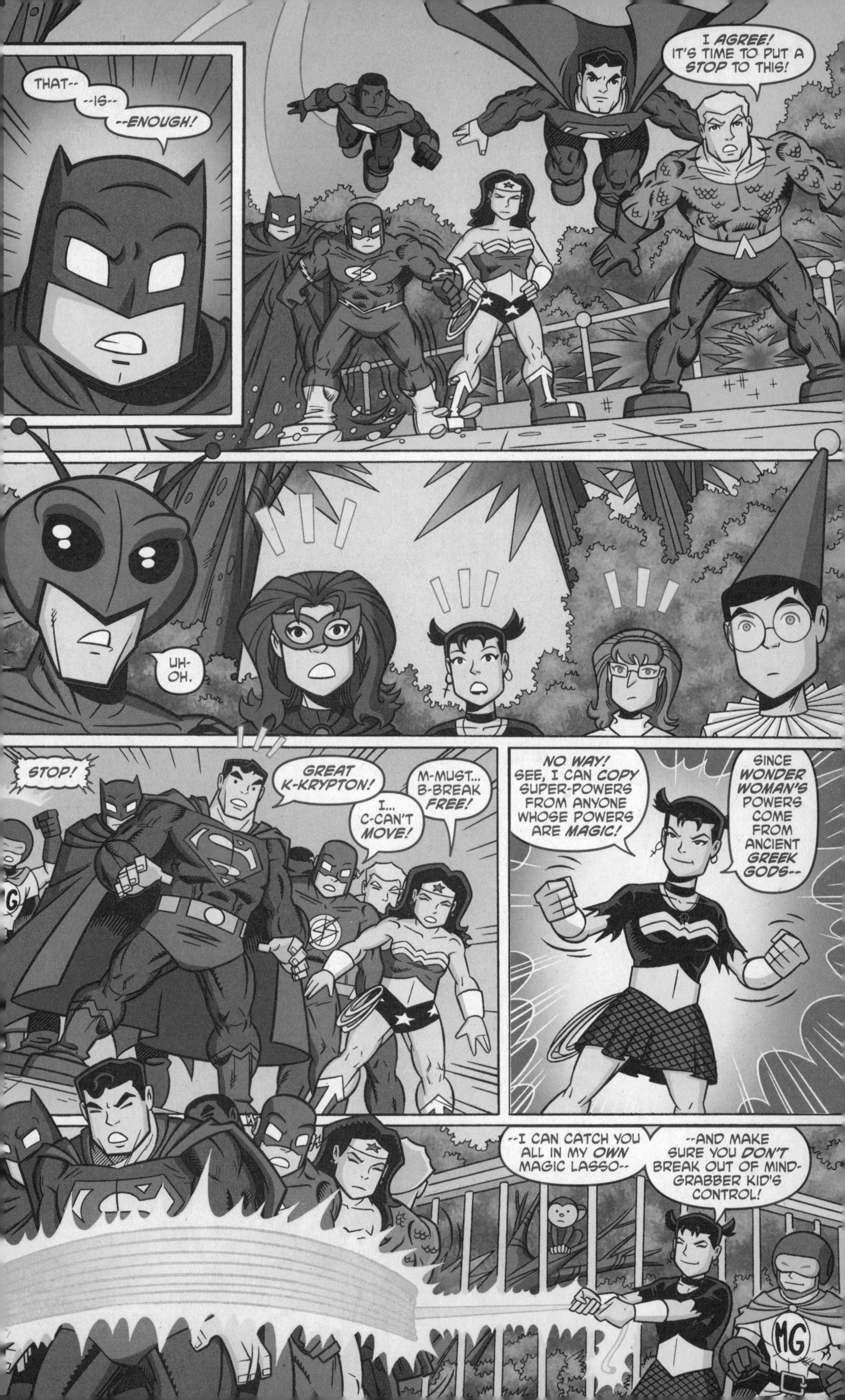
THAT--
--IS--
--ENOUGH!
I AGREE! IT'S TIME TO PUT A STOP TO THIS!
UH-OH.
STOP!
GREAT K-KRYPTON!
I... C-CAN'T MOVE!
M-MUST... B-BREAK FREE!
NO WAY! SEE, I CAN COPY SUPER-POWERS FROM ANYONE WHOSE POWERS ARE MAGIC!
SINCE WONDER WOMAN'S POWERS COME FROM ANCIENT GREEK GODS--
--I CAN CATCH YOU ALL IN MY OWN MAGIC LASSO--
--AND MAKE SURE YOU DON'T BREAK OUT OF MIND-GRABBER KID'S CONTROL!

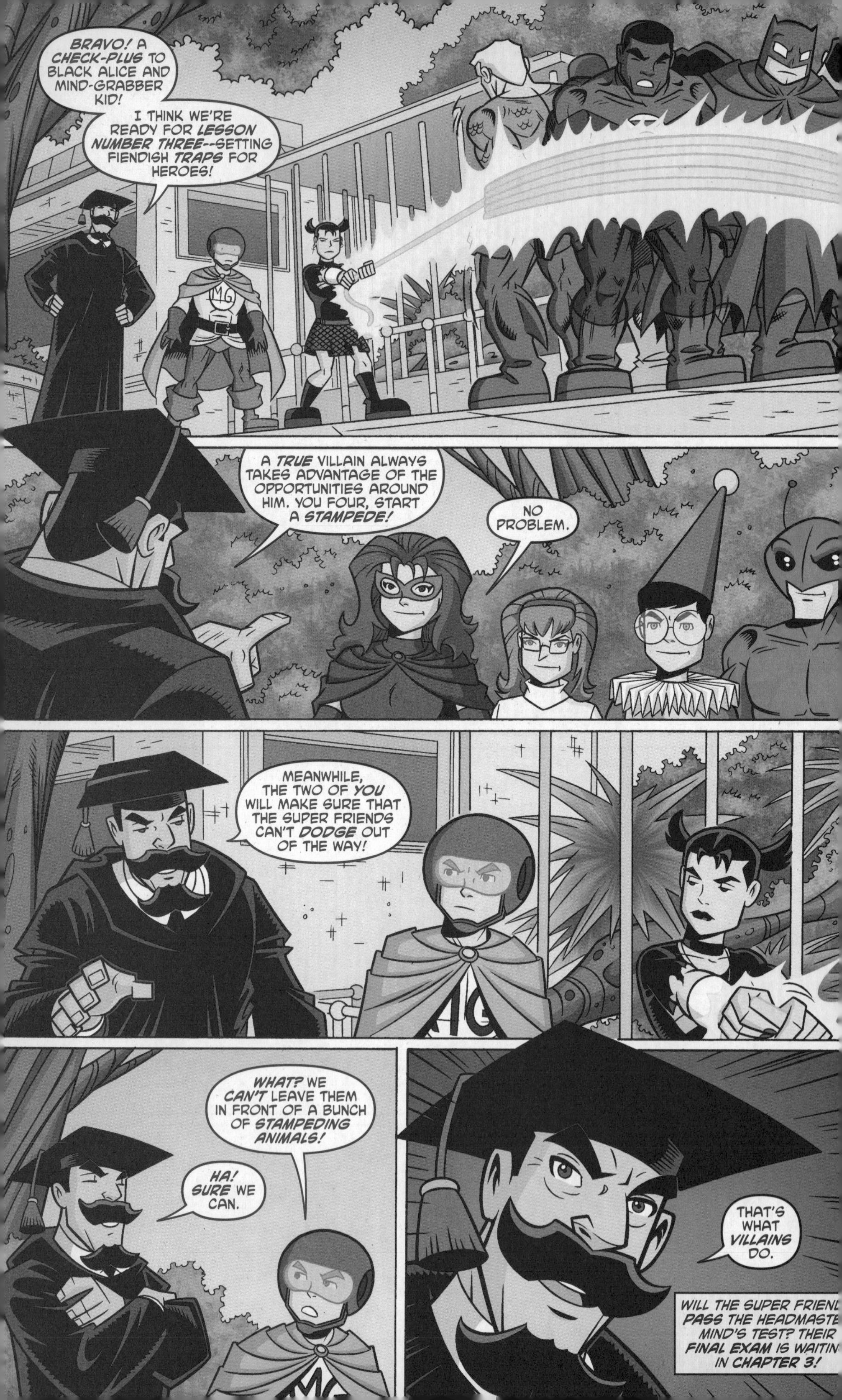

BRAVO! A CHECK-PLUS TO BLACK ALICE AND MIND-GRABBER KID!
I THINK WE'RE READY FOR LESSON NUMBER THREE--SETTING FIENDISH TRAPS FOR HEROES!
A TRUE VILLAIN ALWAYS TAKES ADVANTAGE OF THE OPPORTUNITIES AROUND HIM. YOU FOUR, START A STAMPEDE!
NO PROBLEM.
MEANWHILE, THE TWO OF YOU WILL MAKE SURE THAT THE SUPER FRIENDS CAN'T DODGE OUT OF THE WAY!
WHAT? WE CAN'T LEAVE THEM IN FRONT OF A BUNCH OF STAMPEDING ANIMALS!
HA! SURE WE CAN.
THAT'S WHAT VILLAINS DO.
WILL THE SUPER FRIEN PASS THE HEADMASTE MIND'S TEST? THEIR FINAL EXAM IS WAITIN IN CHAPTER 3!

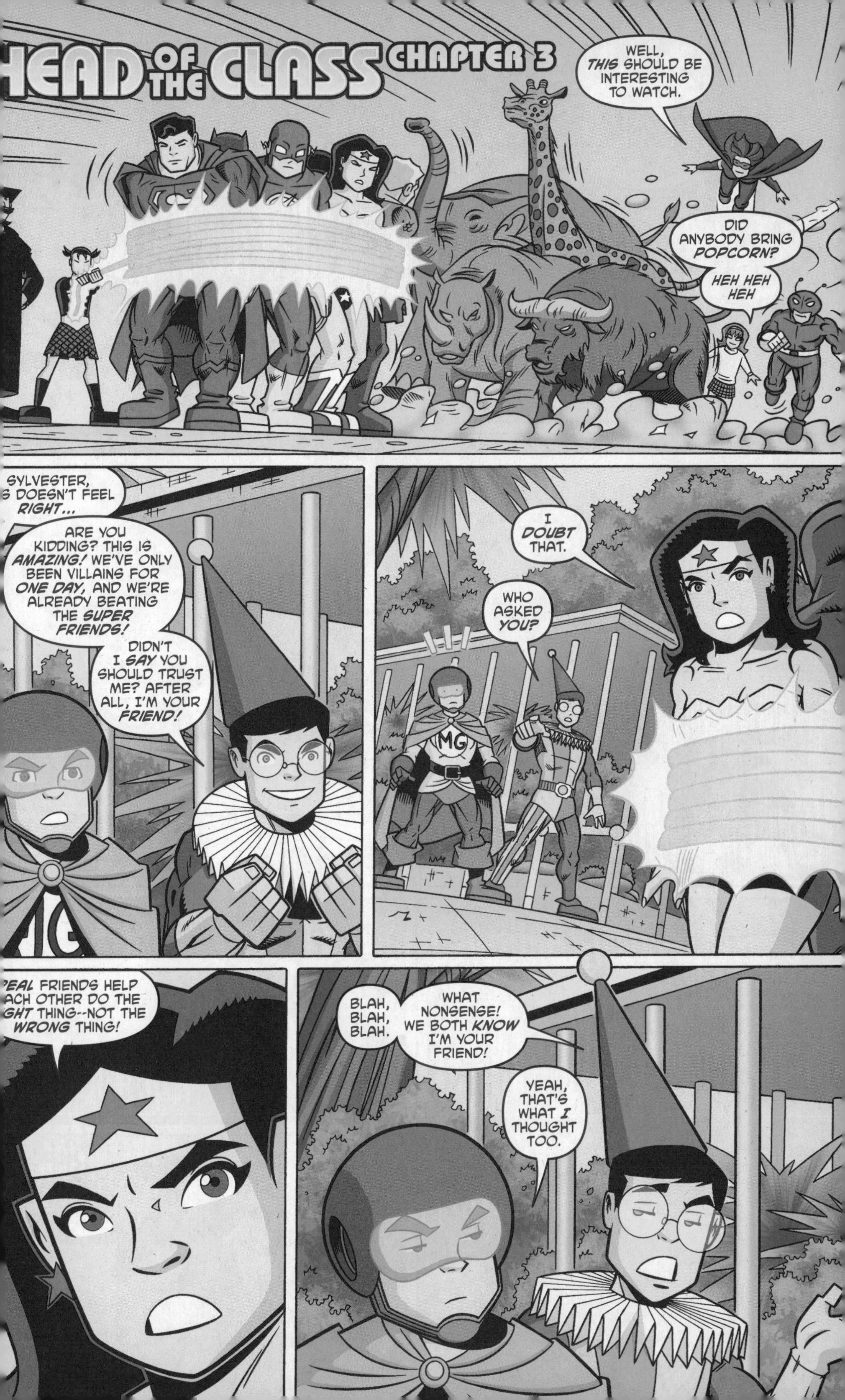
HEAD OF THE CLASS CHAPTER 3
WELL, THIS SHOULD BE INTERESTING TO WATCH.
DID ANYBODY BRING POPCORN?
HEH HEH HEH
SYLVESTER, S DOESN'T FEEL RIGHT...
ARE YOU KIDDING? THIS IS AMAZING! WE'VE ONLY BEEN VILLAINS FOR ONE DAY, AND WE'RE ALREADY BEATING THE SUPER FRIENDS!
DIDN'T I SAY YOU SHOULD TRUST ME? AFTER ALL, I'M YOUR FRIEND!
I DOUBT THAT.
WHO ASKED YOU?
EAL FRIENDS HELP ACH OTHER DO THE GHT THING--NOT THE WRONG THING!
BLAH, BLAH, BLAH.
WHAT NONSENSE! WE BOTH KNOW I'M YOUR FRIEND!
YEAH, THAT'S WHAT I THOUGHT TOO.

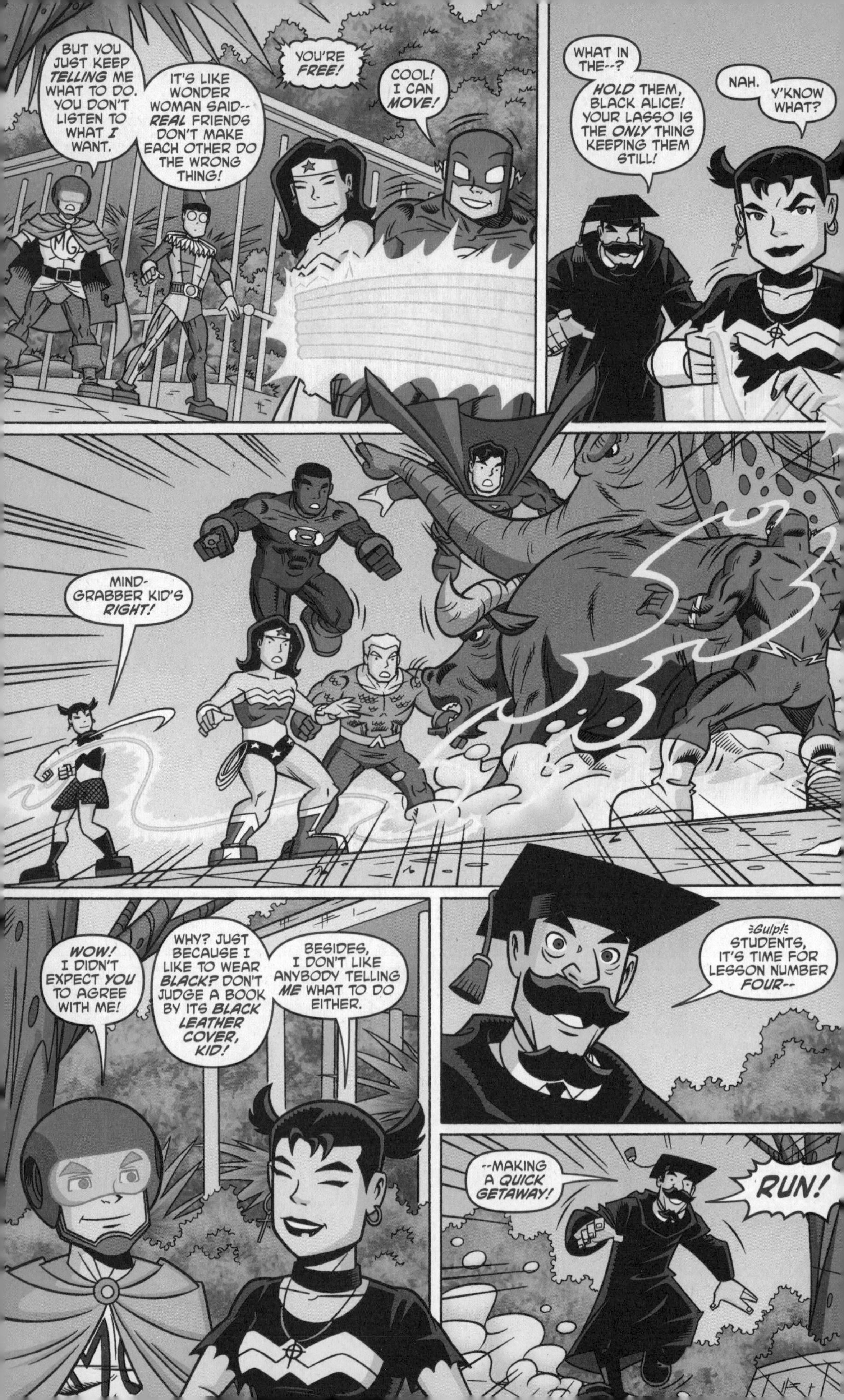
BUT YOU JUST KEEP TELLING ME WHAT TO DO. YOU DON'T LISTEN TO WHAT I WANT.
IT'S LIKE WONDER WOMAN SAID-- REAL FRIENDS DON'T MAKE EACH OTHER DO THE WRONG THING!
YOU'RE FREE!
COOL! I CAN MOVE!
WHAT IN THE--?
HOLD THEM, BLACK ALICE! YOUR LASSO IS THE ONLY THING KEEPING THEM STILL!
NAH.
Y'KNOW WHAT?
MIND-GRABBER KID'S RIGHT!
WOW! I DIDN'T EXPECT YOU TO AGREE WITH ME!
WHY? JUST BECAUSE I LIKE TO WEAR BLACK? DON'T JUDGE A BOOK BY ITS BLACK LEATHER COVER, KID!
BESIDES, I DON'T LIKE ANYBODY TELLING ME WHAT TO DO EITHER.
Gulp! STUDENTS, IT'S TIME FOR LESSON NUMBER FOUR--
--MAKING A QUICK GETAWAY!
RUN!

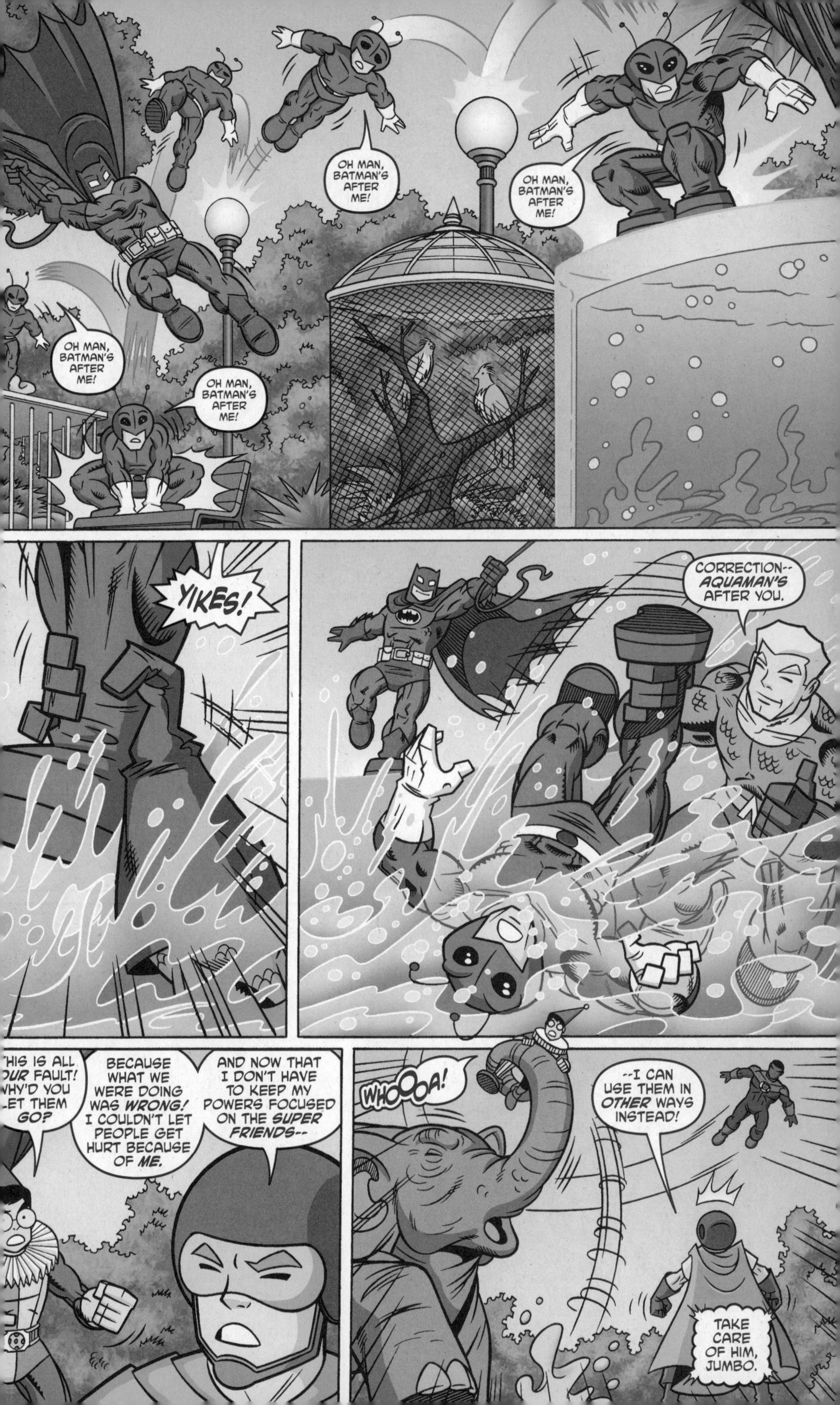
OH MAN, BATMAN'S AFTER ME!
OH MAN, BATMAN'S AFTER ME!
OH MAN, BATMAN'S AFTER ME!
OH MAN, BATMAN'S AFTER ME!
YIKES!
CORRECTION-- AQUAMAN'S AFTER YOU.
THIS IS ALL OUR FAULT! WHY'D YOU LET THEM GO?
BECAUSE WHAT WE WERE DOING WAS WRONG! I COULDN'T LET PEOPLE GET HURT BECAUSE OF ME.
AND NOW THAT I DON'T HAVE TO KEEP MY POWERS FOCUSED ON THE SUPER FRIENDS--
WHOOOOA!
--I CAN USE THEM IN OTHER WAYS INSTEAD!
TAKE CARE OF HIM, JUMBO.

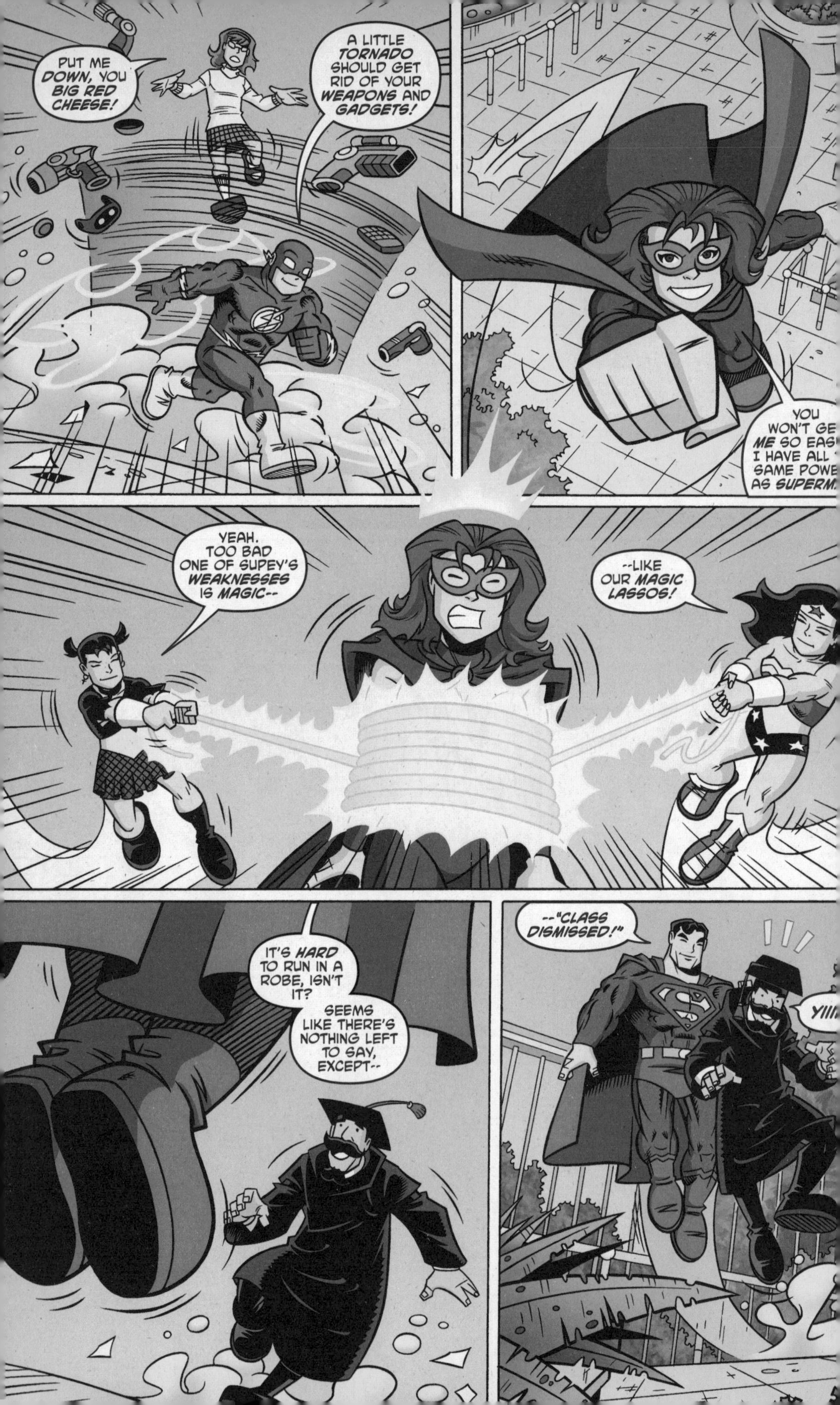

PUT ME DOWN, YOU BIG RED CHEESE!
A LITTLE TORNADO SHOULD GET RID OF YOUR WEAPONS AND GADGETS!
YOU WON'T GE ME SO EAS I HAVE ALL SAME POWE AS SUPERM
YEAH. TOO BAD ONE OF SUPEY'S WEAKNESSES IS MAGIC--
--LIKE OUR MAGIC LASSOS!
IT'S HARD TO RUN IN A ROBE, ISN'T IT?
SEEMS LIKE THERE'S NOTHING LEFT TO SAY, EXCEPT--
--"CLASS DISMISSED!"
YIII

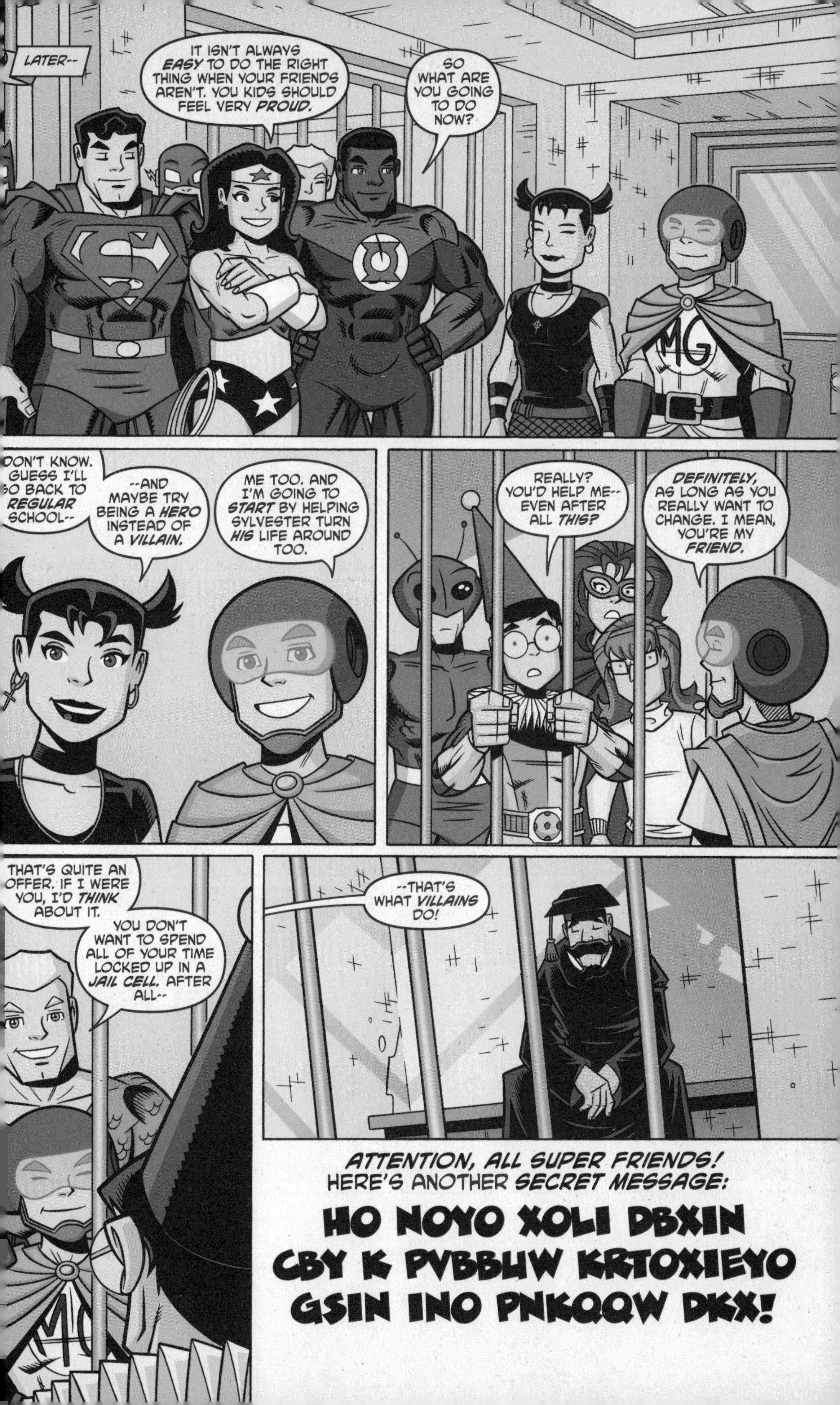
LATER--
IT ISN'T ALWAYS EASY TO DO THE RIGHT THING WHEN YOUR FRIENDS AREN'T. YOU KIDS SHOULD FEEL VERY PROUD.
SO WHAT ARE YOU GOING TO DO NOW?
DON'T KNOW. GUESS I'LL GO BACK TO REGULAR SCHOOL--
--AND MAYBE TRY BEING A HERO INSTEAD OF A VILLAIN.
ME TOO. AND I'M GOING TO START BY HELPING SYLVESTER TURN HIS LIFE AROUND TOO.
REALLY? YOU'D HELP ME--EVEN AFTER ALL THIS?
DEFINITELY, AS LONG AS YOU REALLY WANT TO CHANGE. I MEAN, YOU'RE MY FRIEND.
THAT'S QUITE AN OFFER. IF I WERE YOU, I'D THINK ABOUT IT.
YOU DON'T WANT TO SPEND ALL OF YOUR TIME LOCKED UP IN A JAIL CELL. AFTER ALL--
--THAT'S WHAT VILLAINS DO!
ATTENTION, ALL SUPER FRIENDS!
HERE'S ANOTHER SECRET MESSAGE:
HO NOYO XOLI DBXIN
CBY K PVBBUW KRTOXIEYO
GSIN INO PNKQQW DKX!

# DO THE WRITE THING!

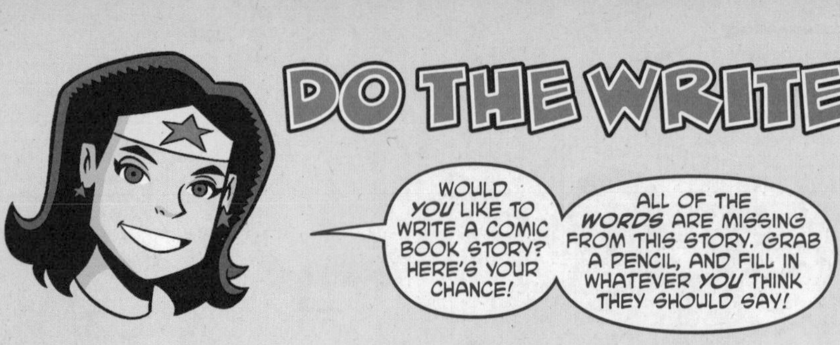
WOULD *YOU* LIKE TO WRITE A COMIC BOOK STORY? HERE'S YOUR CHANCE!
ALL OF THE *WORDS* ARE MISSING FROM THIS STORY. GRAB A PENCIL, AND FILL IN WHATEVER *YOU* THINK THEY SHOULD SAY!

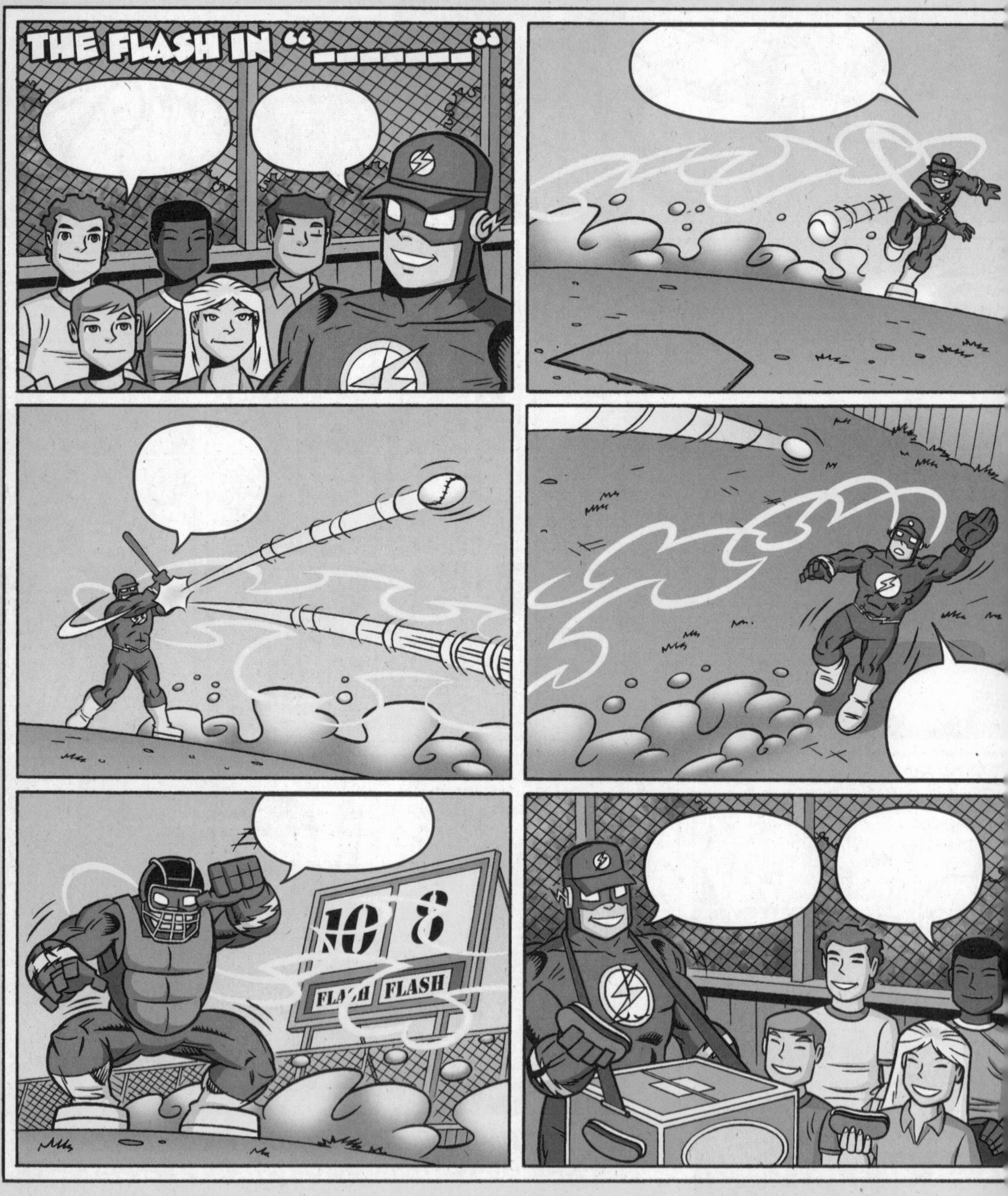
THE FLASH IN "_______"
10 8
FLASH

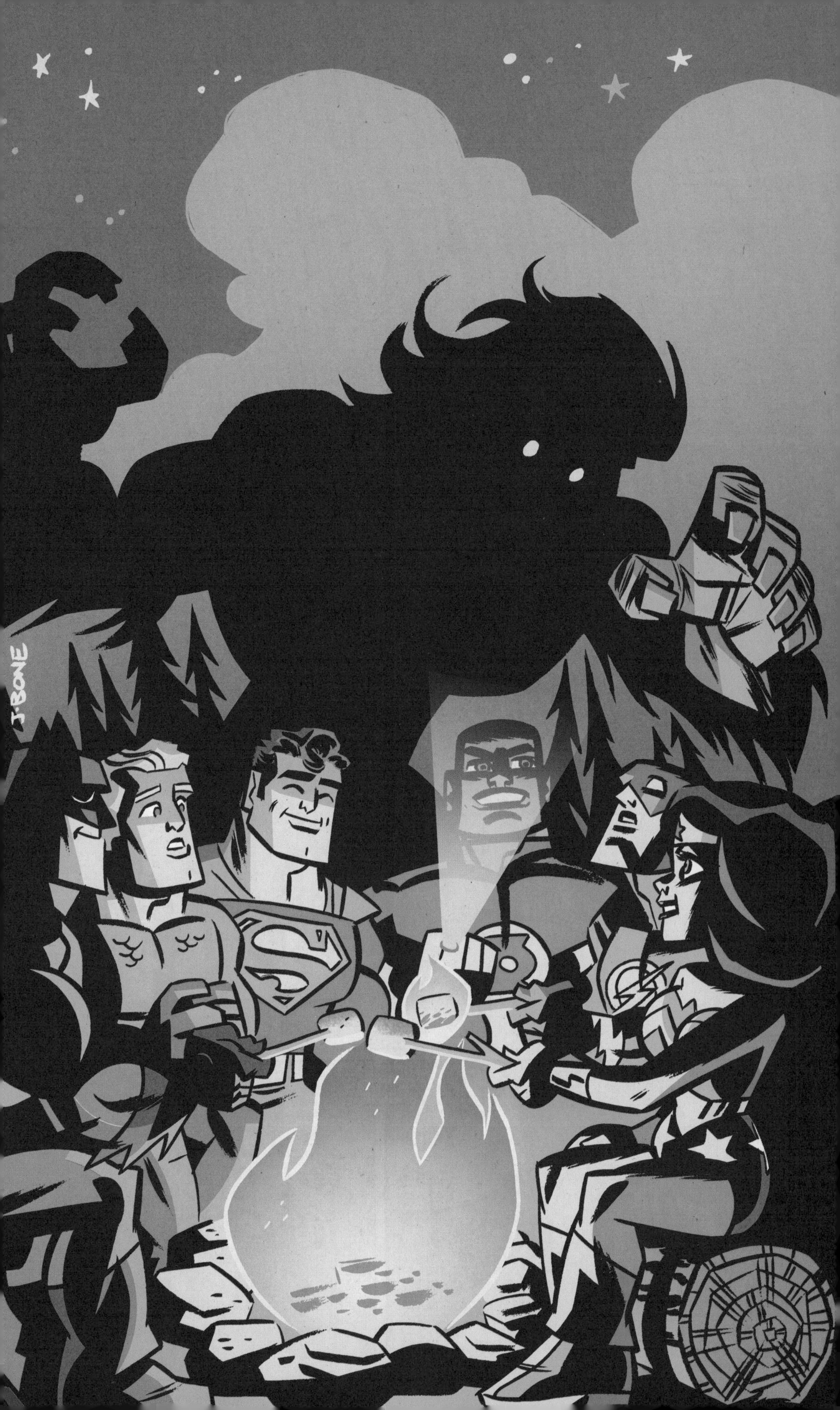
J·BONE

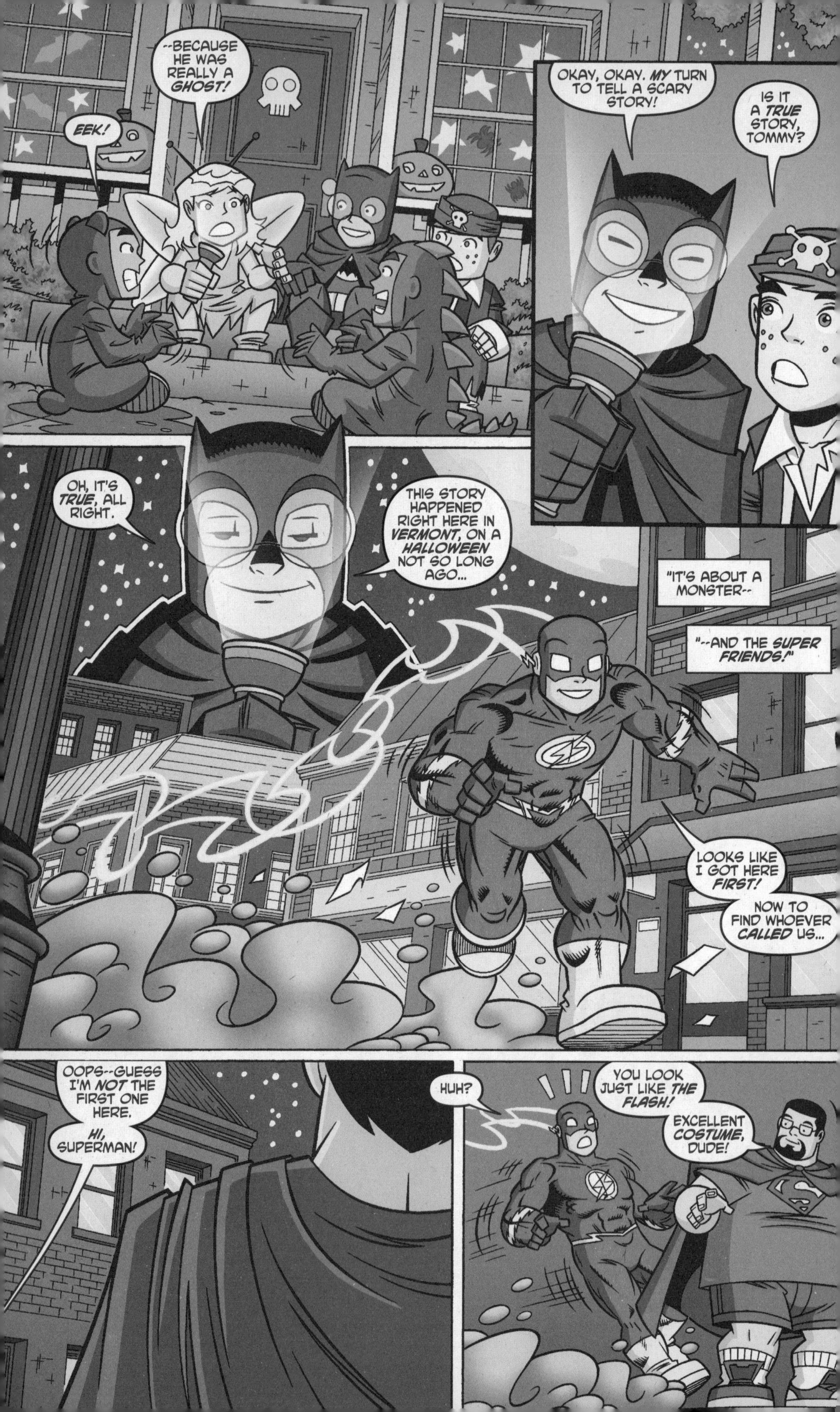
--BECAUSE HE WAS REALLY A *GHOST!*
*EEK!*
OKAY, OKAY. *MY* TURN TO TELL A SCARY STORY!
IS IT A *TRUE* STORY, TOMMY?
OH, IT'S *TRUE*, ALL RIGHT.
THIS STORY HAPPENED RIGHT HERE IN *VERMONT*, ON A *HALLOWEEN* NOT SO LONG AGO...
"IT'S ABOUT A MONSTER--
"--AND THE *SUPER FRIENDS!*"
LOOKS LIKE I GOT HERE *FIRST!*
NOW TO FIND WHOEVER *CALLED* US...
OOPS--GUESS I'M *NOT* THE FIRST ONE HERE.
*HI,* SUPERMAN!
HUH?
YOU LOOK JUST LIKE *THE FLASH!*
EXCELLENT *COSTUME,* DUDE!

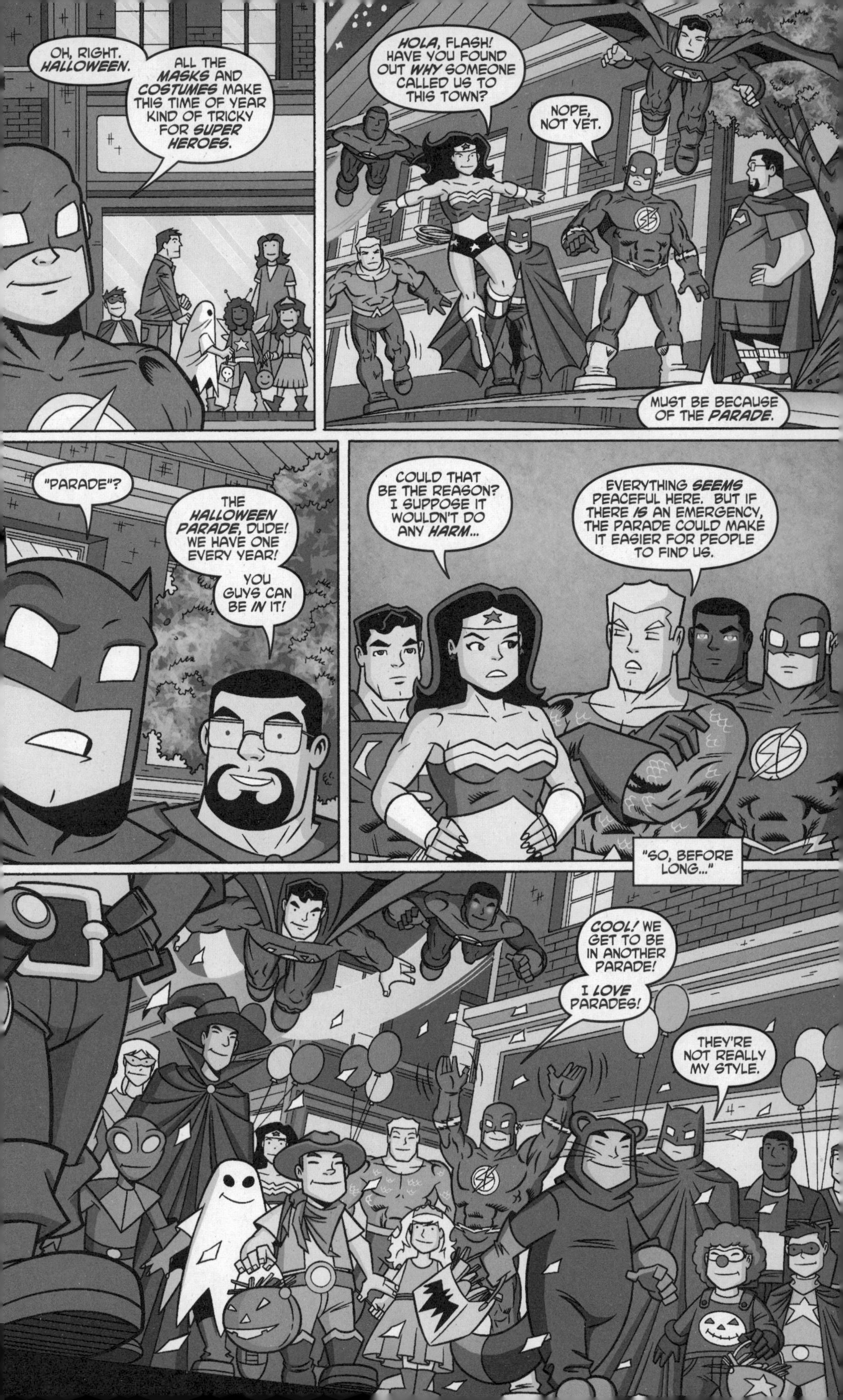
OH, RIGHT. HALLOWEEN.
ALL THE MASKS AND COSTUMES MAKE THIS TIME OF YEAR KIND OF TRICKY FOR SUPER HEROES.
HOLA, FLASH! HAVE YOU FOUND OUT WHY SOMEONE CALLED US TO THIS TOWN?
NOPE, NOT YET.
MUST BE BECAUSE OF THE PARADE.
"PARADE"?
THE HALLOWEEN PARADE, DUDE! WE HAVE ONE EVERY YEAR!
YOU GUYS CAN BE IN IT!
COULD THAT BE THE REASON? I SUPPOSE IT WOULDN'T DO ANY HARM...
EVERYTHING SEEMS PEACEFUL HERE. BUT IF THERE IS AN EMERGENCY, THE PARADE COULD MAKE IT EASIER FOR PEOPLE TO FIND US.
"SO, BEFORE LONG..."
COOL! WE GET TO BE IN ANOTHER PARADE!
I LOVE PARADES!
THEY'RE NOT REALLY MY STYLE.

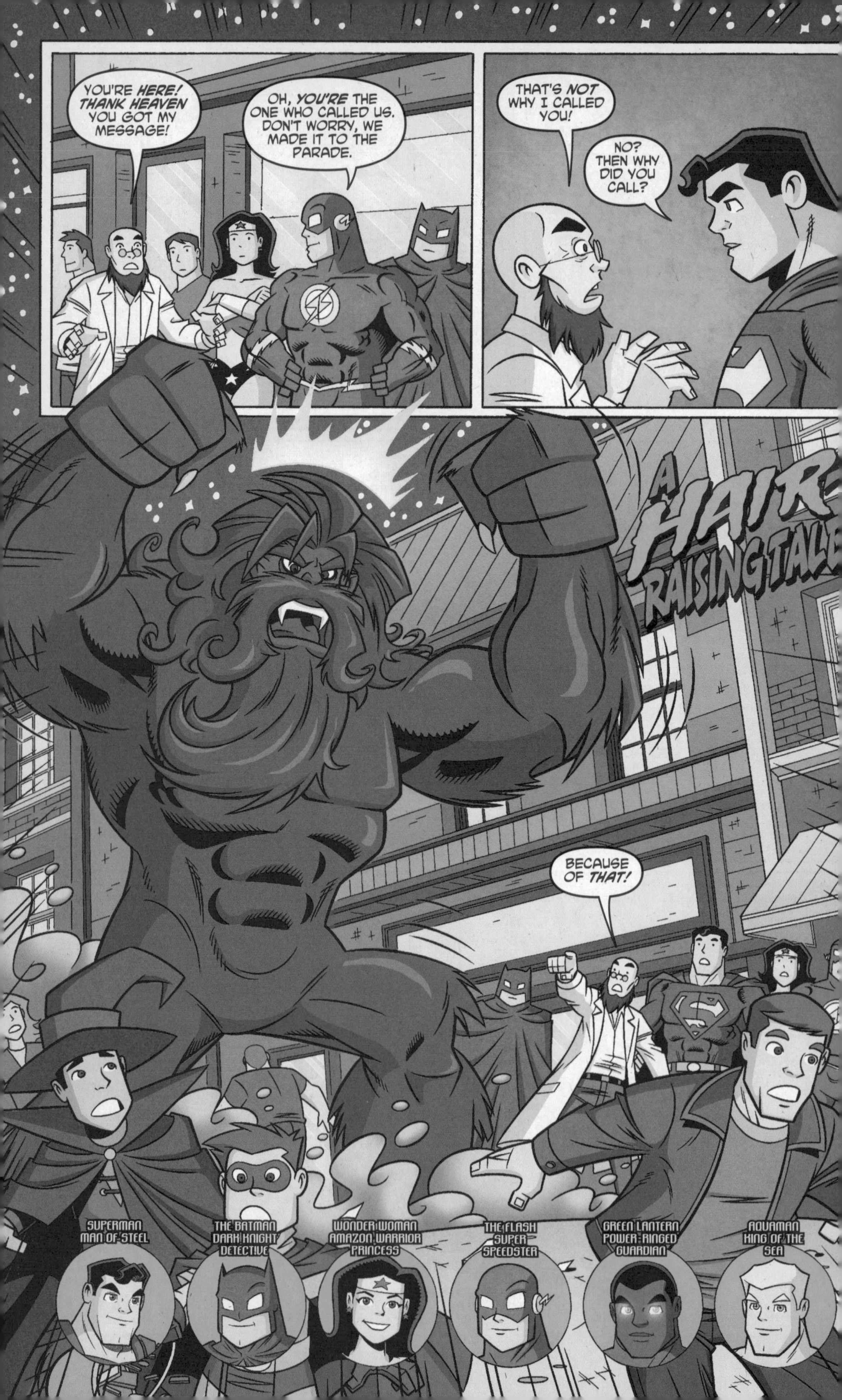

YOU'RE HERE! THANK HEAVEN YOU GOT MY MESSAGE!
OH, YOU'RE THE ONE WHO CALLED US. DON'T WORRY, WE MADE IT TO THE PARADE.
THAT'S NOT WHY I CALLED YOU!
NO? THEN WHY DID YOU CALL?
A HAIR RAISING TALE
BECAUSE OF THAT!
SUPERMAN MAN OF STEEL
THE BATMAN DARK KNIGHT DETECTIVE
WONDER WOMAN AMAZON WARRIOR PRINCESS
THE FLASH SUPER SPEEDSTER
GREEN LANTERN POWER-RINGED GUARDIAN
AQUAMAN KING OF THE SEA

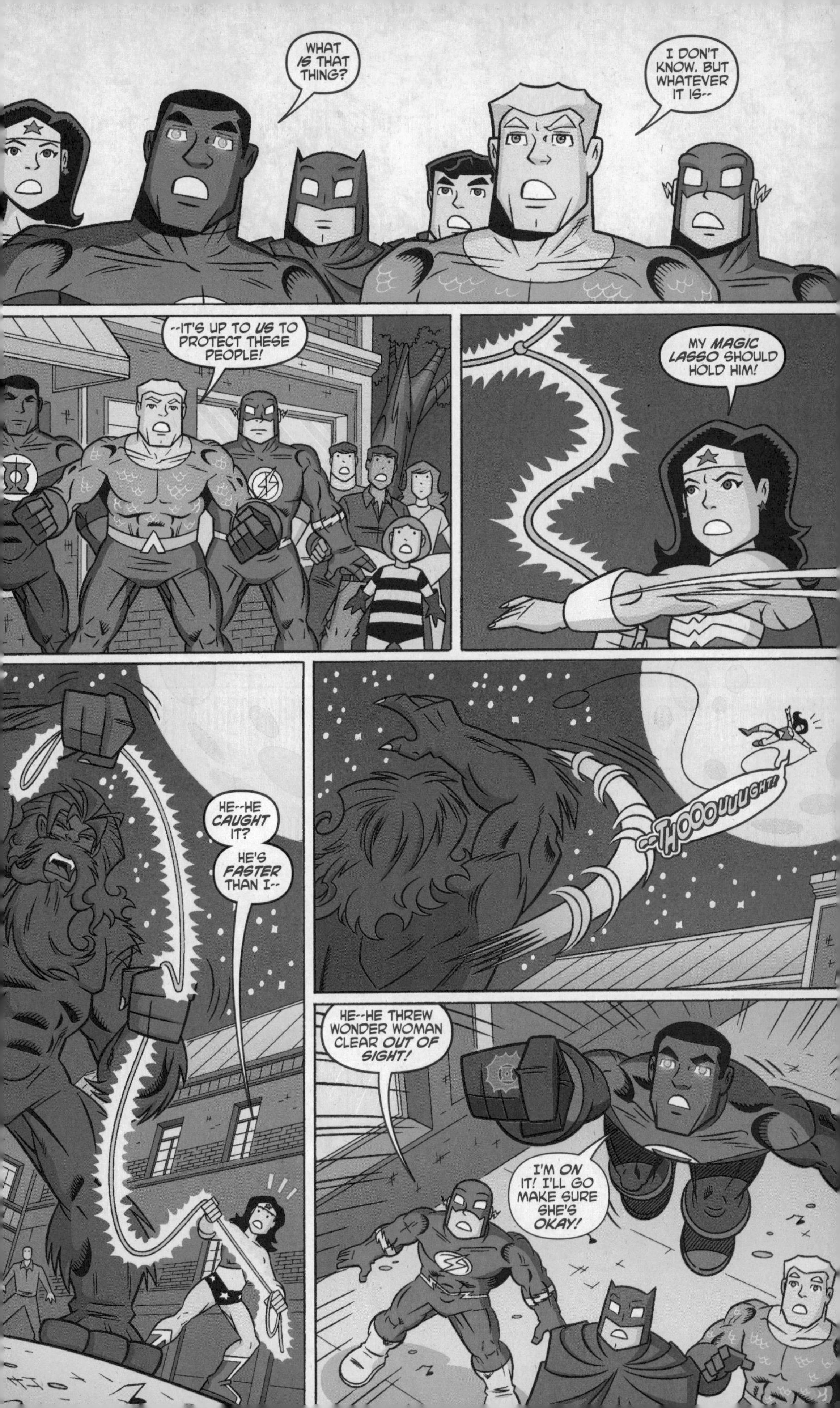

WHAT *IS* THAT THING?
I DON'T KNOW. BUT WHATEVER IT IS--
--IT'S UP TO *US* TO PROTECT THESE PEOPLE!
MY *MAGIC LASSO* SHOULD HOLD HIM!
HE--HE *CAUGHT* IT?
HE'S *FASTER* THAN I--
--THOOOUUUGHT!
HE--HE THREW WONDER WOMAN CLEAR *OUT OF SIGHT!*
I'M *ON* IT! I'LL GO MAKE SURE SHE'S *OKAY!*

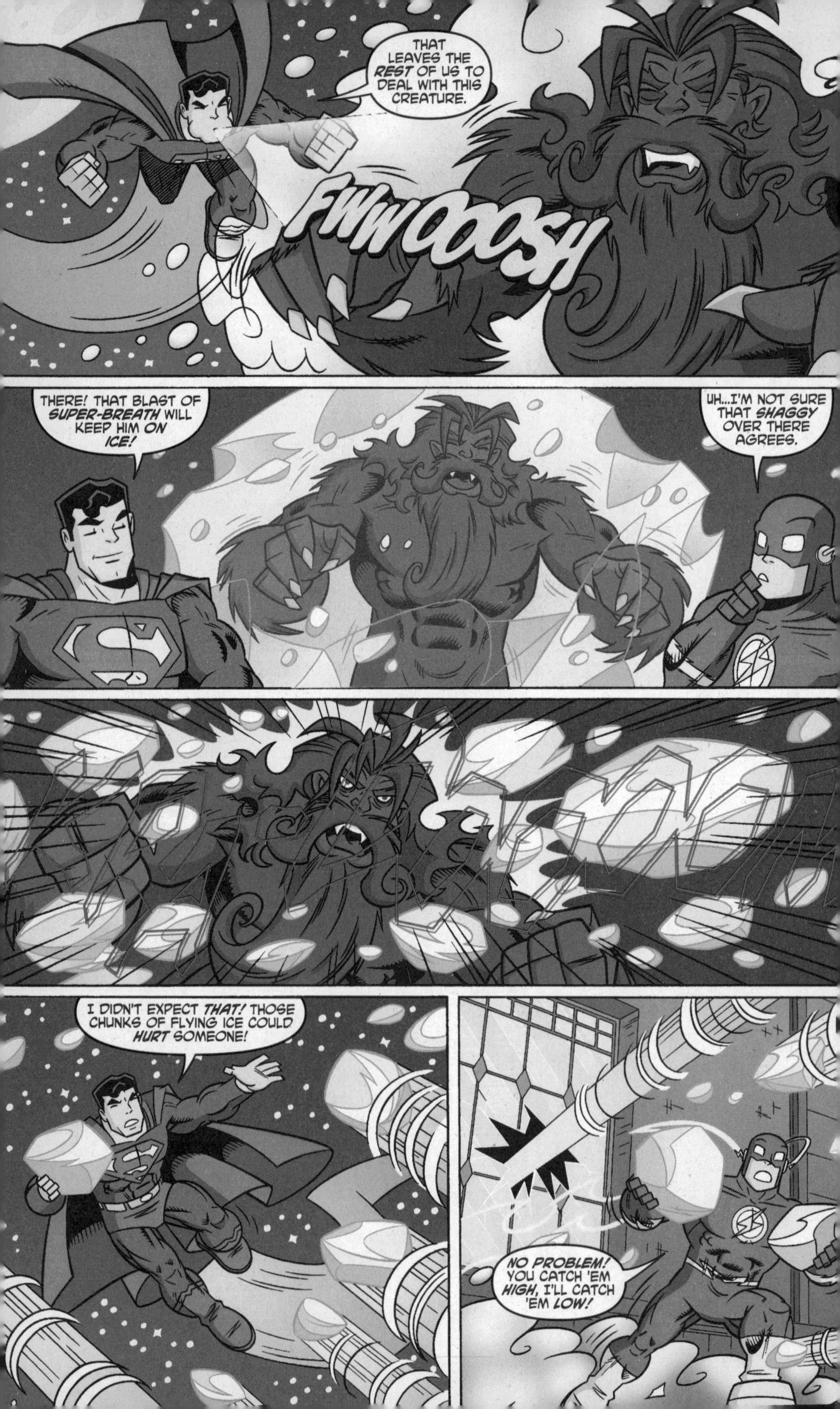
THAT LEAVES THE REST OF US TO DEAL WITH THIS CREATURE.
FWWOOOSH
THERE! THAT BLAST OF SUPER-BREATH WILL KEEP HIM ON ICE!
UH...I'M NOT SURE THAT SHAGGY OVER THERE AGREES.
I DIDN'T EXPECT THAT! THOSE CHUNKS OF FLYING ICE COULD HURT SOMEONE!
NO PROBLEM! YOU CATCH 'EM HIGH, I'LL CATCH 'EM LOW!

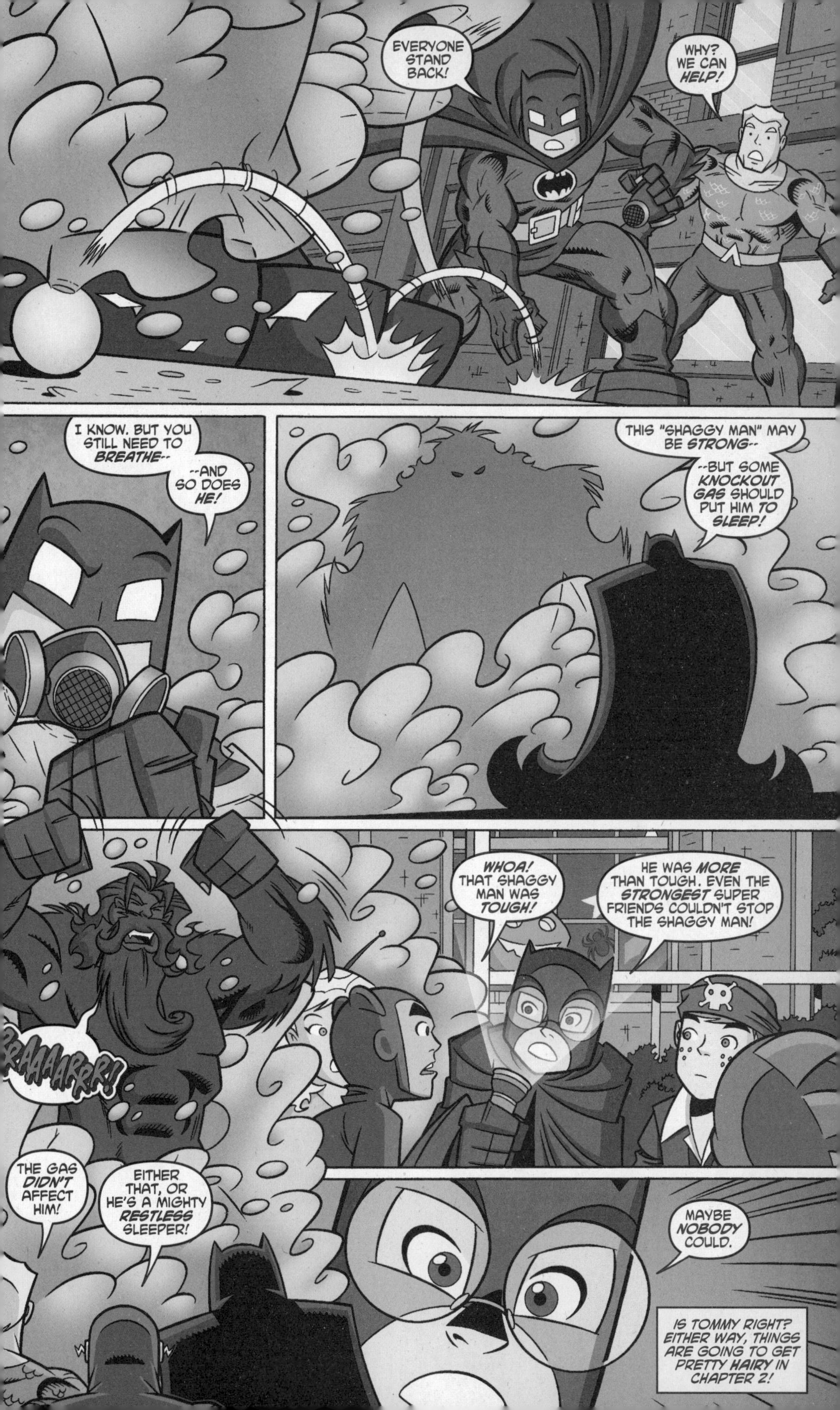
EVERYONE STAND BACK!
WHY? WE CAN HELP!
I KNOW. BUT YOU STILL NEED TO BREATHE--
--AND SO DOES HE!
THIS "SHAGGY MAN" MAY BE STRONG--
--BUT SOME KNOCKOUT GAS SHOULD PUT HIM TO SLEEP!
RRAAAAARRR!
WHOA! THAT SHAGGY MAN WAS TOUGH!
HE WAS MORE THAN TOUGH. EVEN THE STRONGEST SUPER FRIENDS COULDN'T STOP THE SHAGGY MAN!
THE GAS DIDN'T AFFECT HIM!
EITHER THAT, OR HE'S A MIGHTY RESTLESS SLEEPER!
MAYBE NOBODY COULD.
IS TOMMY RIGHT? EITHER WAY, THINGS ARE GOING TO GET PRETTY HAIRY IN CHAPTER 2!

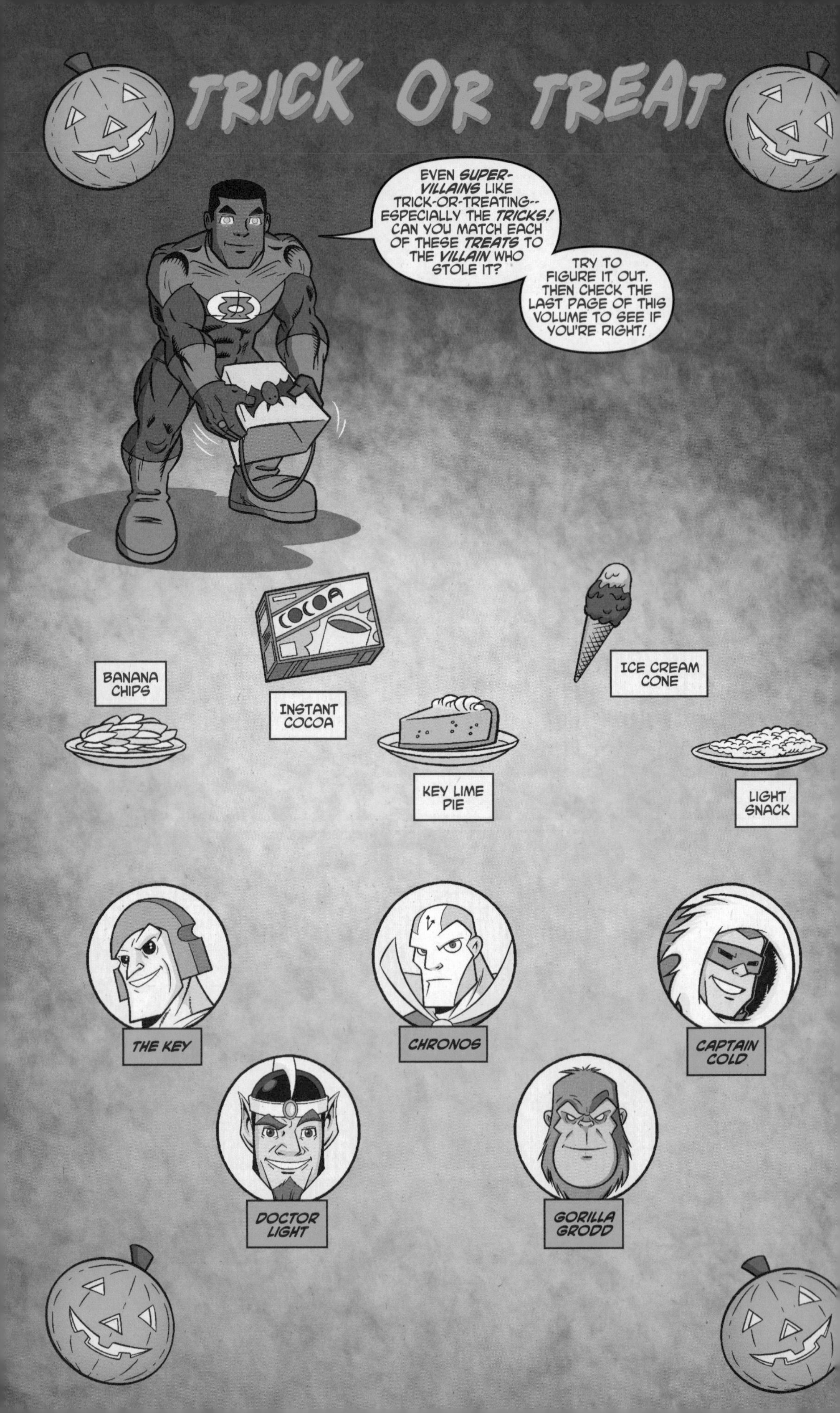
TRICK OR TREAT
EVEN SUPER-VILLAINS LIKE TRICK-OR-TREATING-- ESPECIALLY THE TRICKS! CAN YOU MATCH EACH OF THESE TREATS TO THE VILLAIN WHO STOLE IT?
TRY TO FIGURE IT OUT. THEN CHECK THE LAST PAGE OF THIS VOLUME TO SEE IF YOU'RE RIGHT!
COCOA
BANANA CHIPS
INSTANT COCOA
KEY LIME PIE
ICE CREAM CONE
LIGHT SNACK
THE KEY
CHRONOS
CAPTAIN COLD
DOCTOR LIGHT
GORILLA GRODD

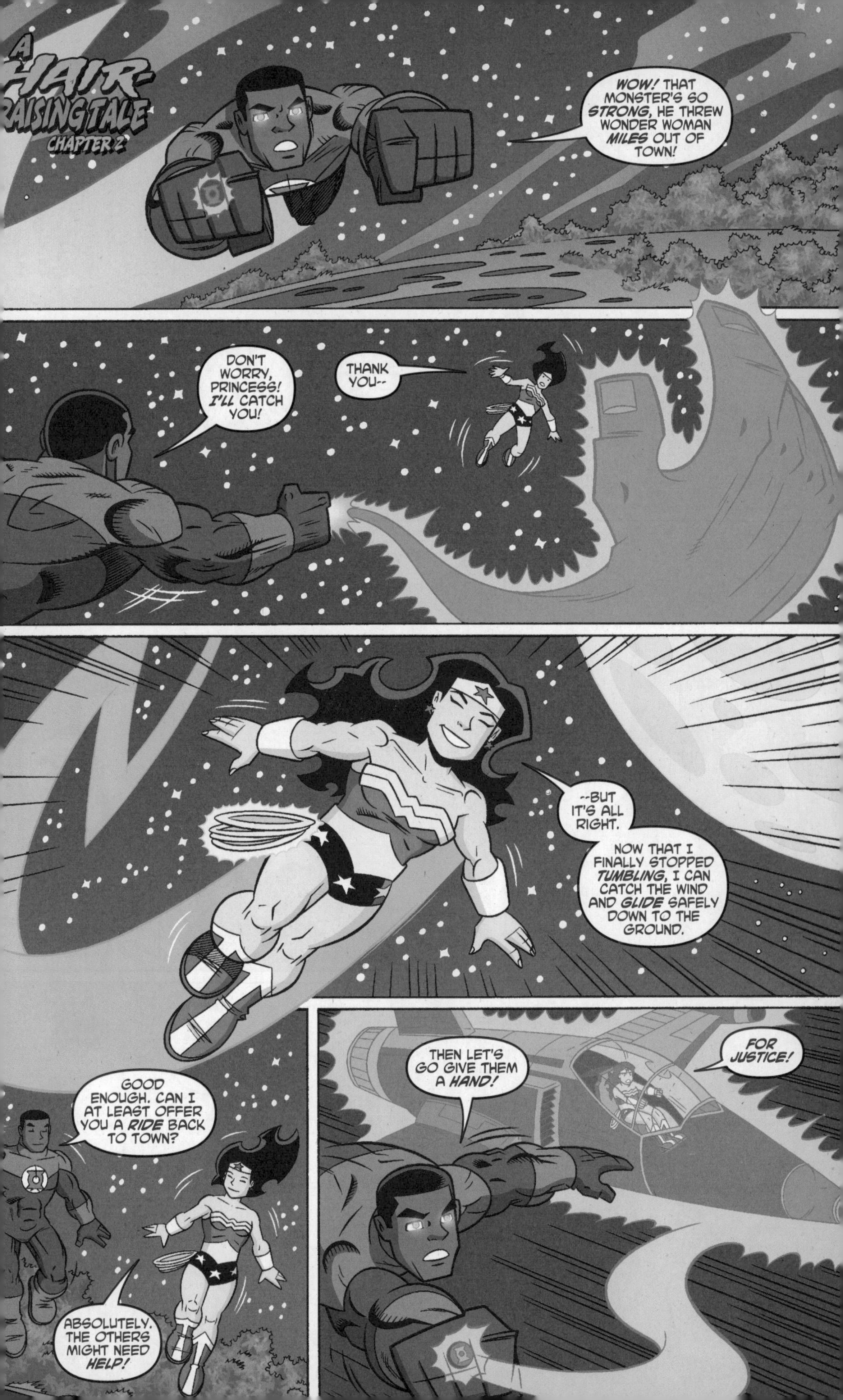
A HAIR-RAISING TALE
CHAPTER 2
WOW! THAT MONSTER'S SO STRONG, HE THREW WONDER WOMAN MILES OUT OF TOWN!
DON'T WORRY, PRINCESS! I'LL CATCH YOU!
THANK YOU--
--BUT IT'S ALL RIGHT.
NOW THAT I FINALLY STOPPED TUMBLING, I CAN CATCH THE WIND AND GLIDE SAFELY DOWN TO THE GROUND.
GOOD ENOUGH. CAN I AT LEAST OFFER YOU A RIDE BACK TO TOWN?
ABSOLUTELY. THE OTHERS MIGHT NEED HELP!
THEN LET'S GO GIVE THEM A HAND!
FOR JUSTICE!

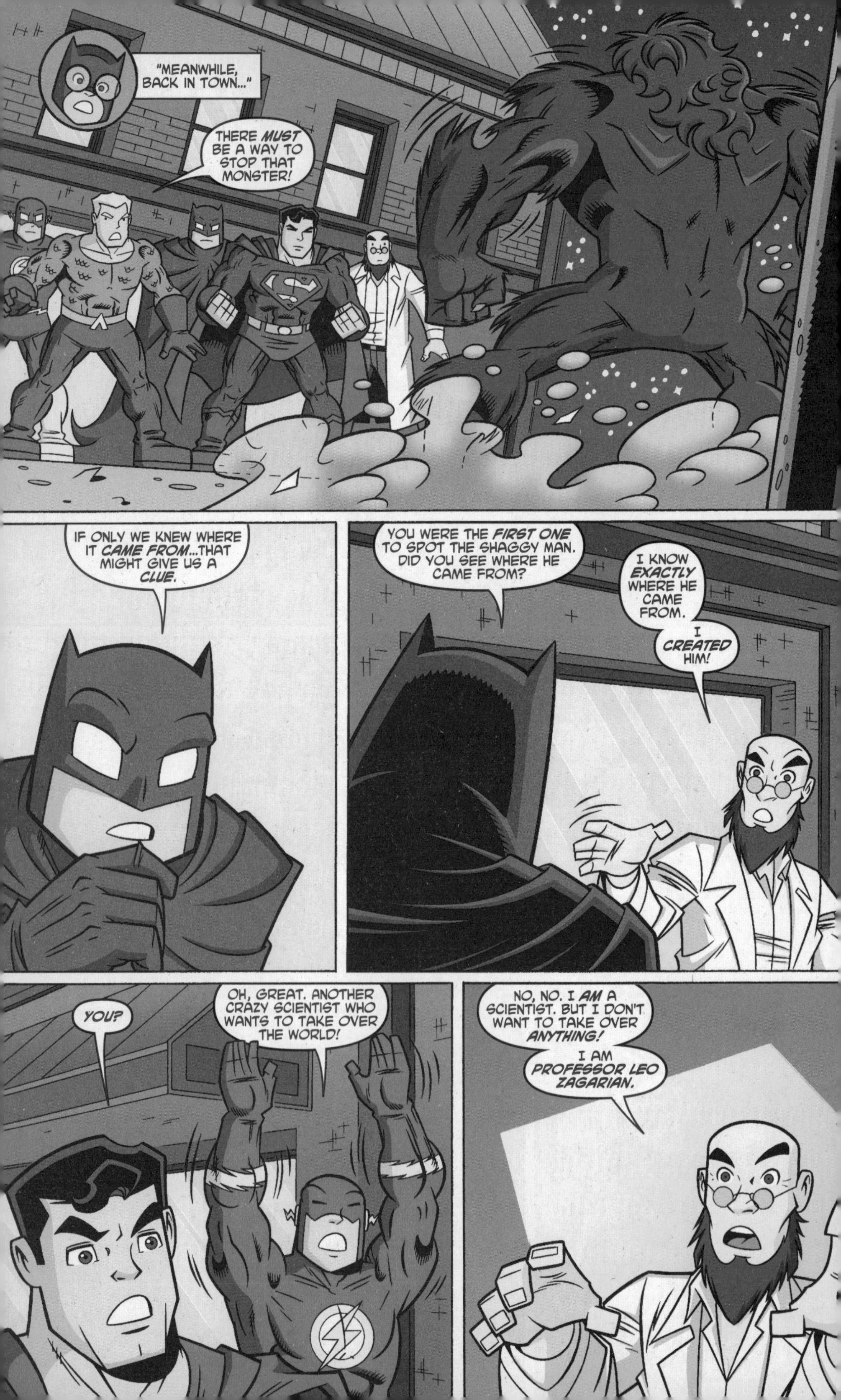
"MEANWHILE, BACK IN TOWN..."
THERE MUST BE A WAY TO STOP THAT MONSTER!
IF ONLY WE KNEW WHERE IT CAME FROM...THAT MIGHT GIVE US A CLUE.
YOU WERE THE FIRST ONE TO SPOT THE SHAGGY MAN. DID YOU SEE WHERE HE CAME FROM?
I KNOW EXACTLY WHERE HE CAME FROM.
I CREATED HIM!
YOU?
OH, GREAT. ANOTHER CRAZY SCIENTIST WHO WANTS TO TAKE OVER THE WORLD!
NO, NO. I AM A SCIENTIST. BUT I DON'T WANT TO TAKE OVER ANYTHING!
I AM PROFESSOR LEO ZAGARIAN.

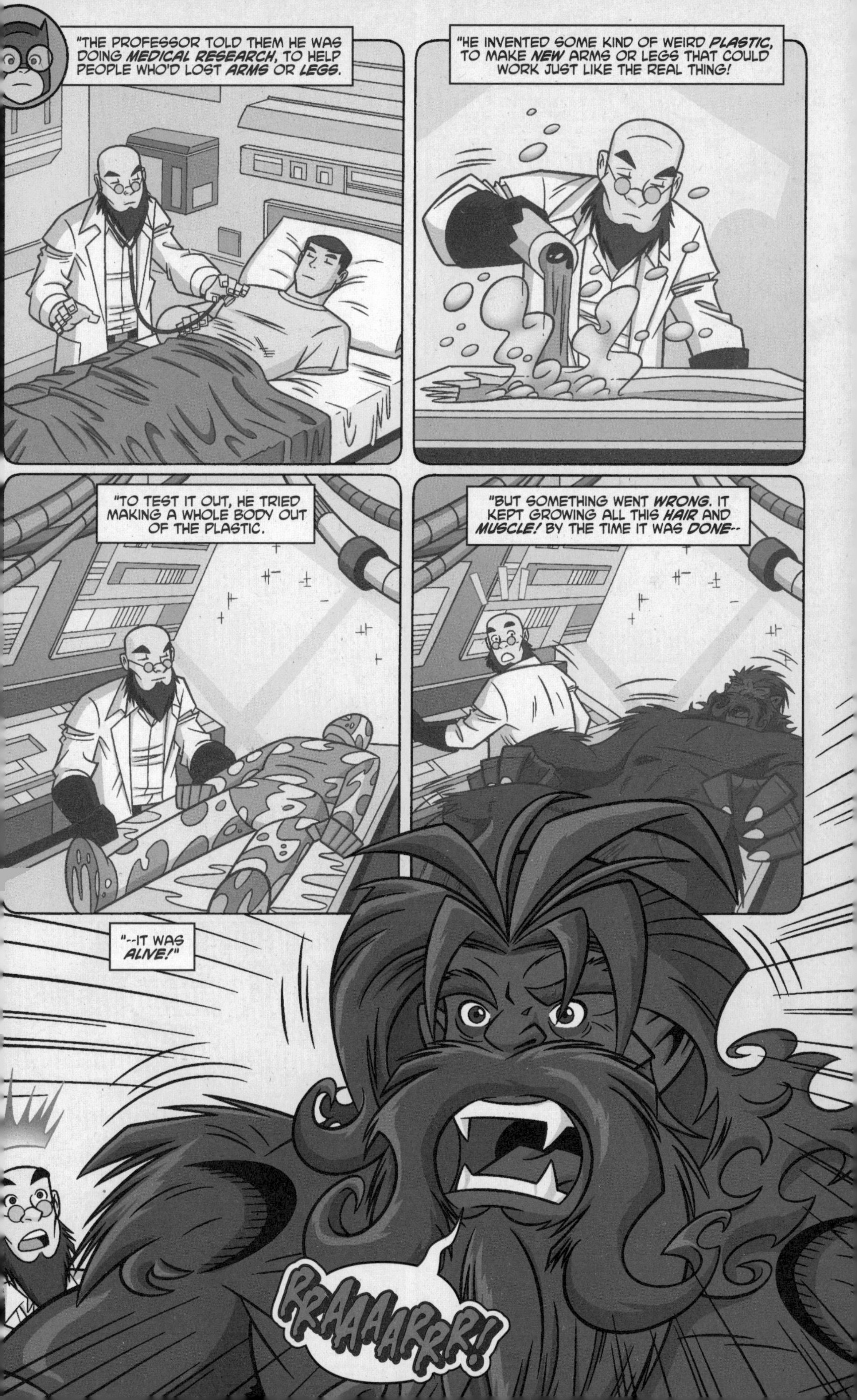
"THE PROFESSOR TOLD THEM HE WAS DOING MEDICAL RESEARCH, TO HELP PEOPLE WHO'D LOST ARMS OR LEGS.
"HE INVENTED SOME KIND OF WEIRD PLASTIC, TO MAKE NEW ARMS OR LEGS THAT COULD WORK JUST LIKE THE REAL THING!
"TO TEST IT OUT, HE TRIED MAKING A WHOLE BODY OUT OF THE PLASTIC.
"BUT SOMETHING WENT WRONG. IT KEPT GROWING ALL THIS HAIR AND MUSCLE! BY THE TIME IT WAS DONE--
"--IT WAS ALIVE!"
RRAAAAARRR!

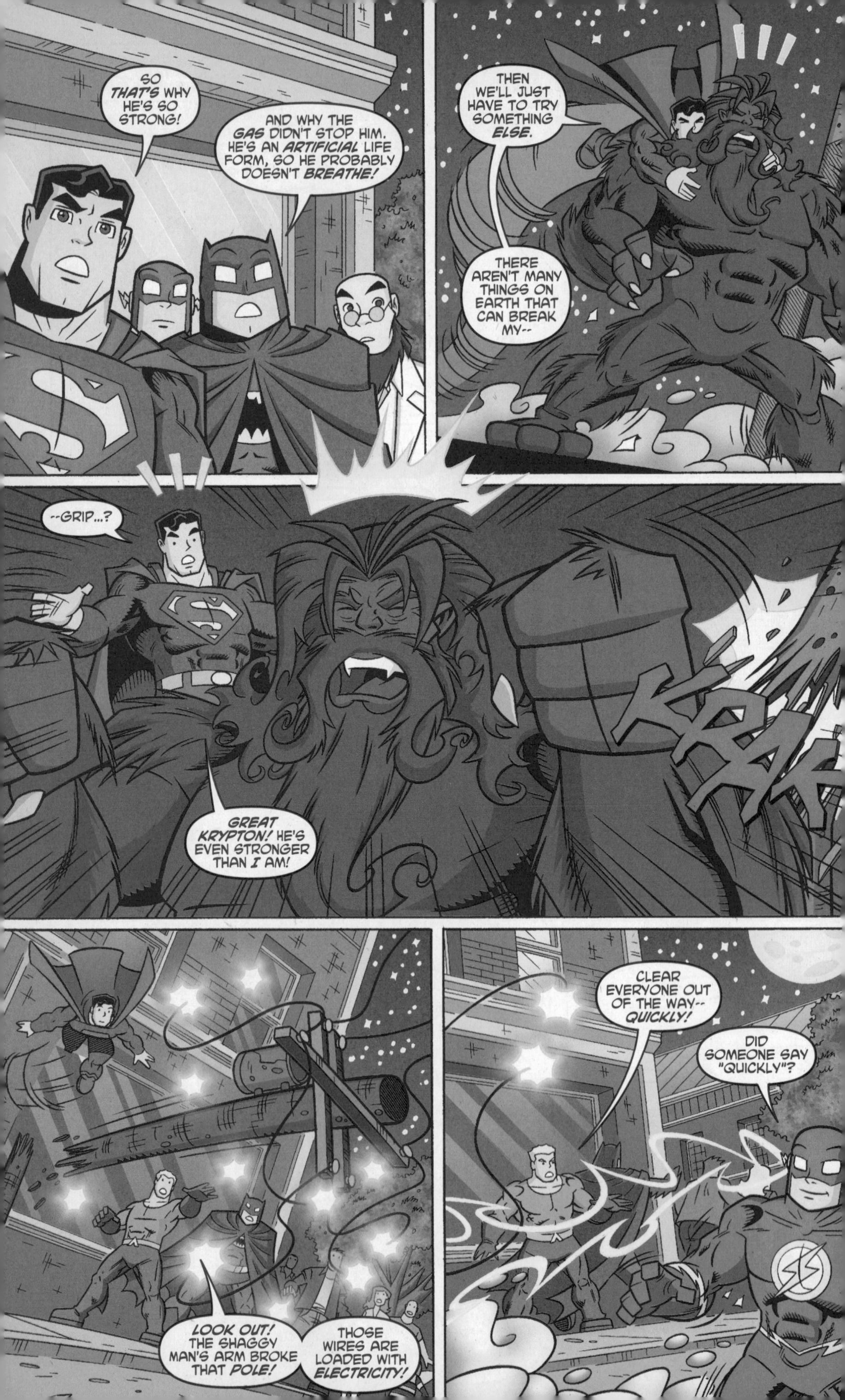
SO THAT'S WHY HE'S SO STRONG!
AND WHY THE GAS DIDN'T STOP HIM. HE'S AN ARTIFICIAL LIFE FORM, SO HE PROBABLY DOESN'T BREATHE!
THEN WE'LL JUST HAVE TO TRY SOMETHING ELSE.
THERE AREN'T MANY THINGS ON EARTH THAT CAN BREAK MY--
--GRIP...?
GREAT KRYPTON! HE'S EVEN STRONGER THAN I AM!
KRAK
LOOK OUT! THE SHAGGY MAN'S ARM BROKE THAT POLE!
THOSE WIRES ARE LOADED WITH ELECTRICITY!
CLEAR EVERYONE OUT OF THE WAY-- QUICKLY!
DID SOMEONE SAY "QUICKLY"?

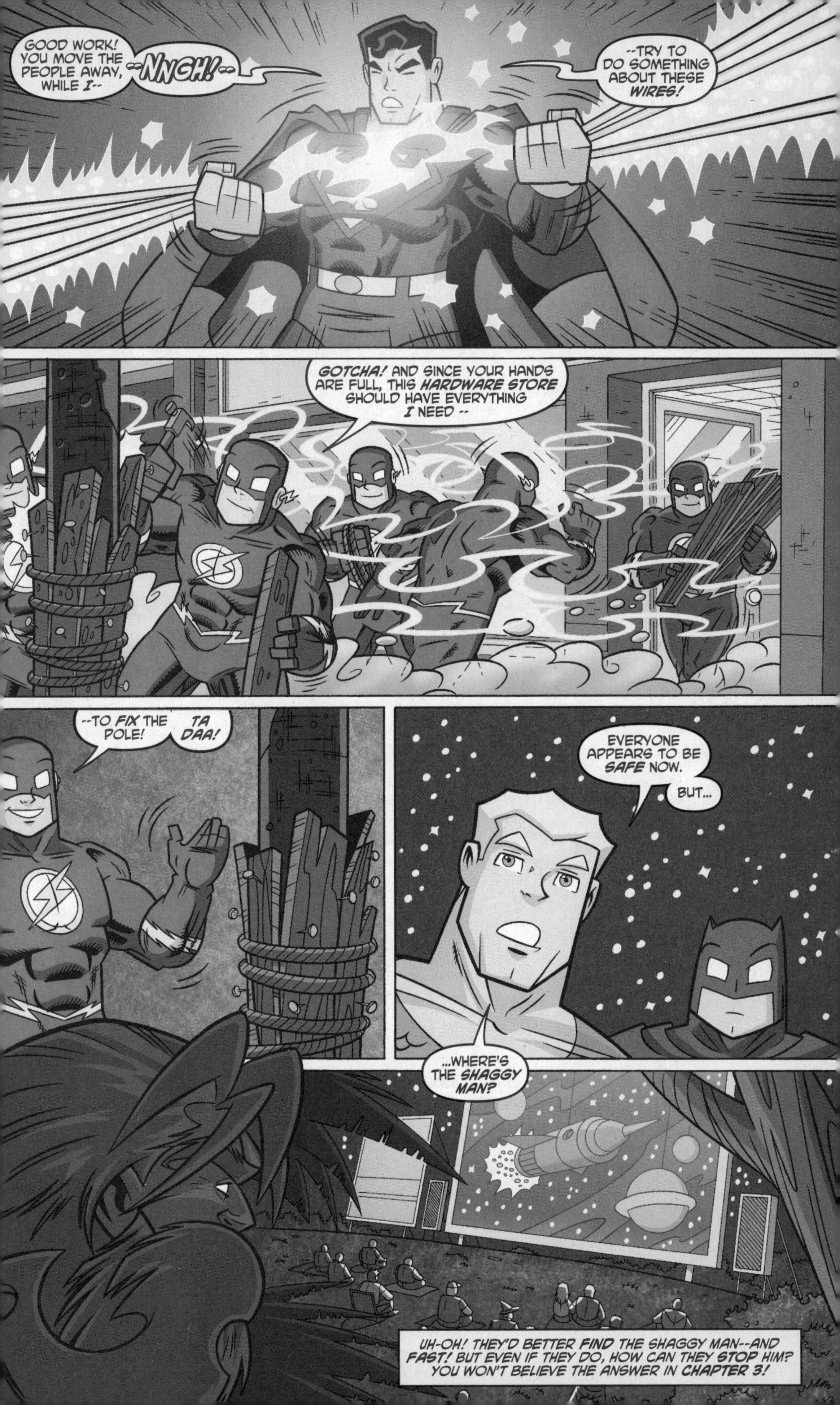
GOOD WORK! YOU MOVE THE PEOPLE AWAY, WHILE I--
--NNGH!--
--TRY TO DO SOMETHING ABOUT THESE WIRES!
GOTCHA! AND SINCE YOUR HANDS ARE FULL, THIS HARDWARE STORE SHOULD HAVE EVERYTHING I NEED --
--TO FIX THE POLE!
TA DAA!
EVERYONE APPEARS TO BE SAFE NOW.
BUT...
...WHERE'S THE SHAGGY MAN?
UH-OH! THEY'D BETTER FIND THE SHAGGY MAN--AND FAST! BUT EVEN IF THEY DO, HOW CAN THEY STOP HIM? YOU WON'T BELIEVE THE ANSWER IN CHAPTER 3!

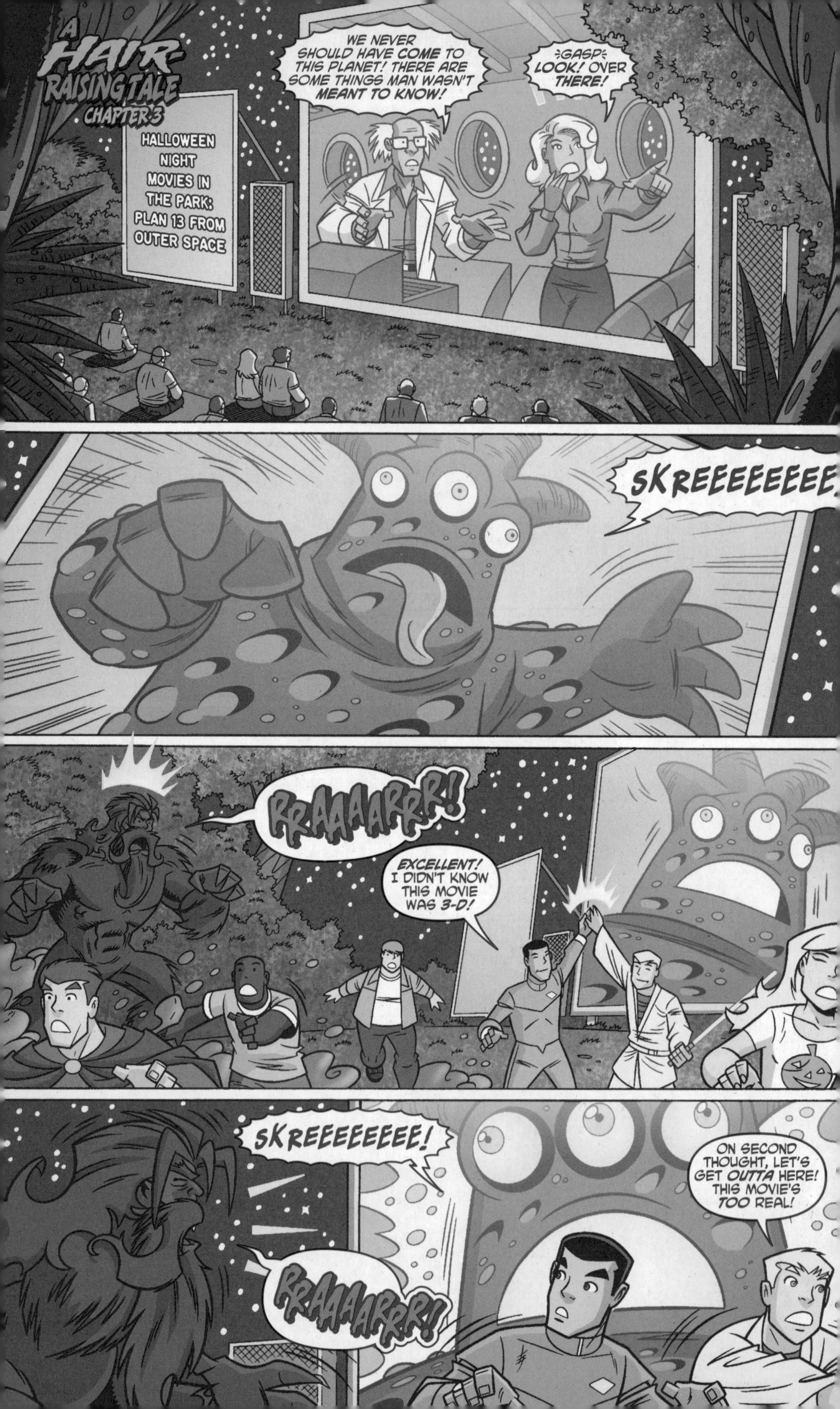
A HAIR-RAISING TALE
CHAPTER 3
HALLOWEEN NIGHT MOVIES IN THE PARK: PLAN 13 FROM OUTER SPACE
WE NEVER SHOULD HAVE COME TO THIS PLANET! THERE ARE SOME THINGS MAN WASN'T MEANT TO KNOW!
GASP LOOK! OVER THERE!
SKREEEEEEEEE
RRAAAAARRR!
EXCELLENT! I DIDN'T KNOW THIS MOVIE WAS 3-D!
SKREEEEEEEEE!
RRAAAAARRR!
ON SECOND THOUGHT, LET'S GET OUTTA HERE! THIS MOVIE'S TOO REAL!

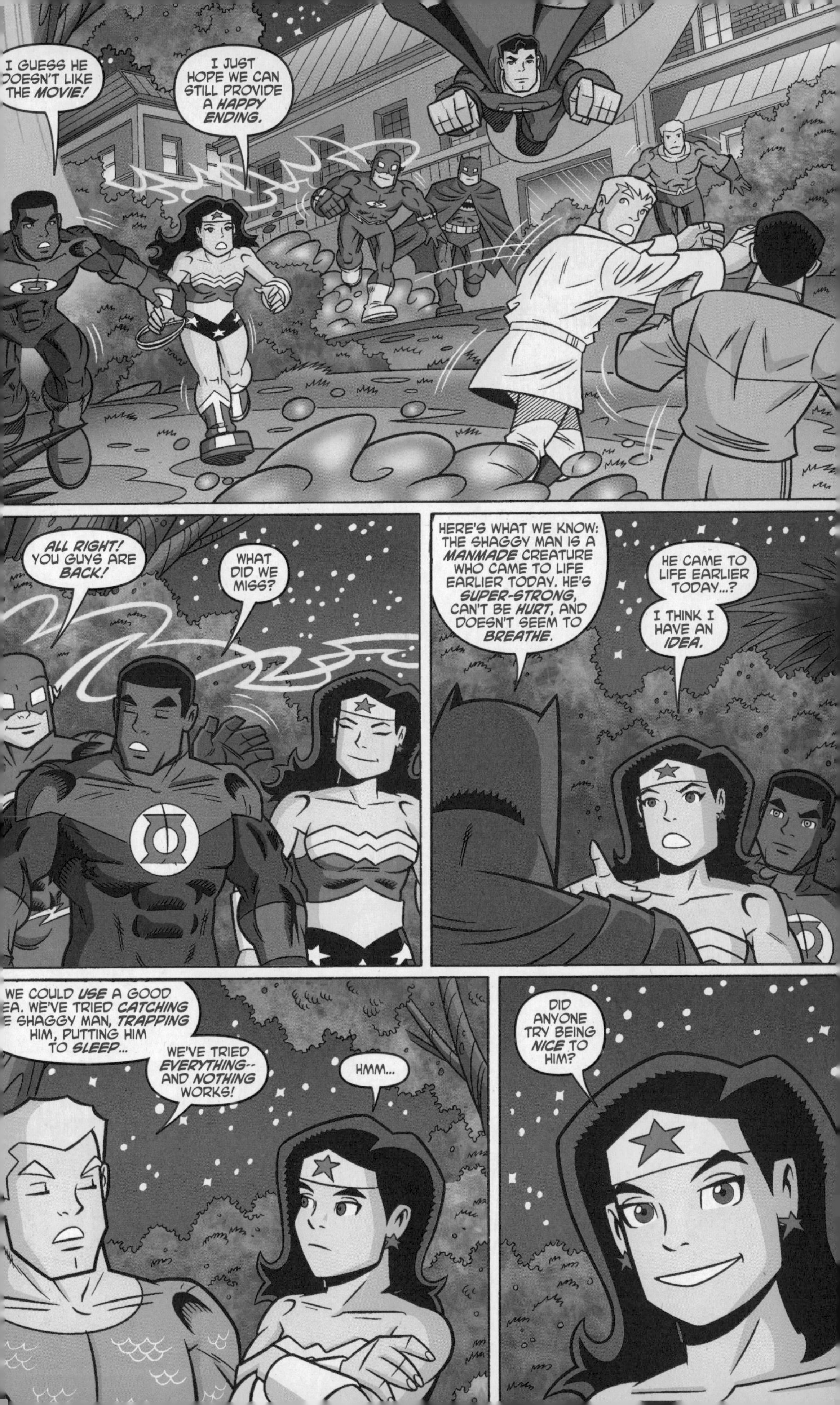

I GUESS HE DOESN'T LIKE THE MOVIE!
I JUST HOPE WE CAN STILL PROVIDE A HAPPY ENDING.
ALL RIGHT! YOU GUYS ARE BACK!
WHAT DID WE MISS?
HERE'S WHAT WE KNOW: THE SHAGGY MAN IS A MANMADE CREATURE WHO CAME TO LIFE EARLIER TODAY. HE'S SUPER-STRONG, CAN'T BE HURT, AND DOESN'T SEEM TO BREATHE.
HE CAME TO LIFE EARLIER TODAY...?
I THINK I HAVE AN IDEA.
WE COULD USE A GOOD IDEA. WE'VE TRIED CATCHING THE SHAGGY MAN, TRAPPING HIM, PUTTING HIM TO SLEEP...
WE'VE TRIED EVERYTHING-- AND NOTHING WORKS!
HMM...
DID ANYONE TRY BEING NICE TO HIM?

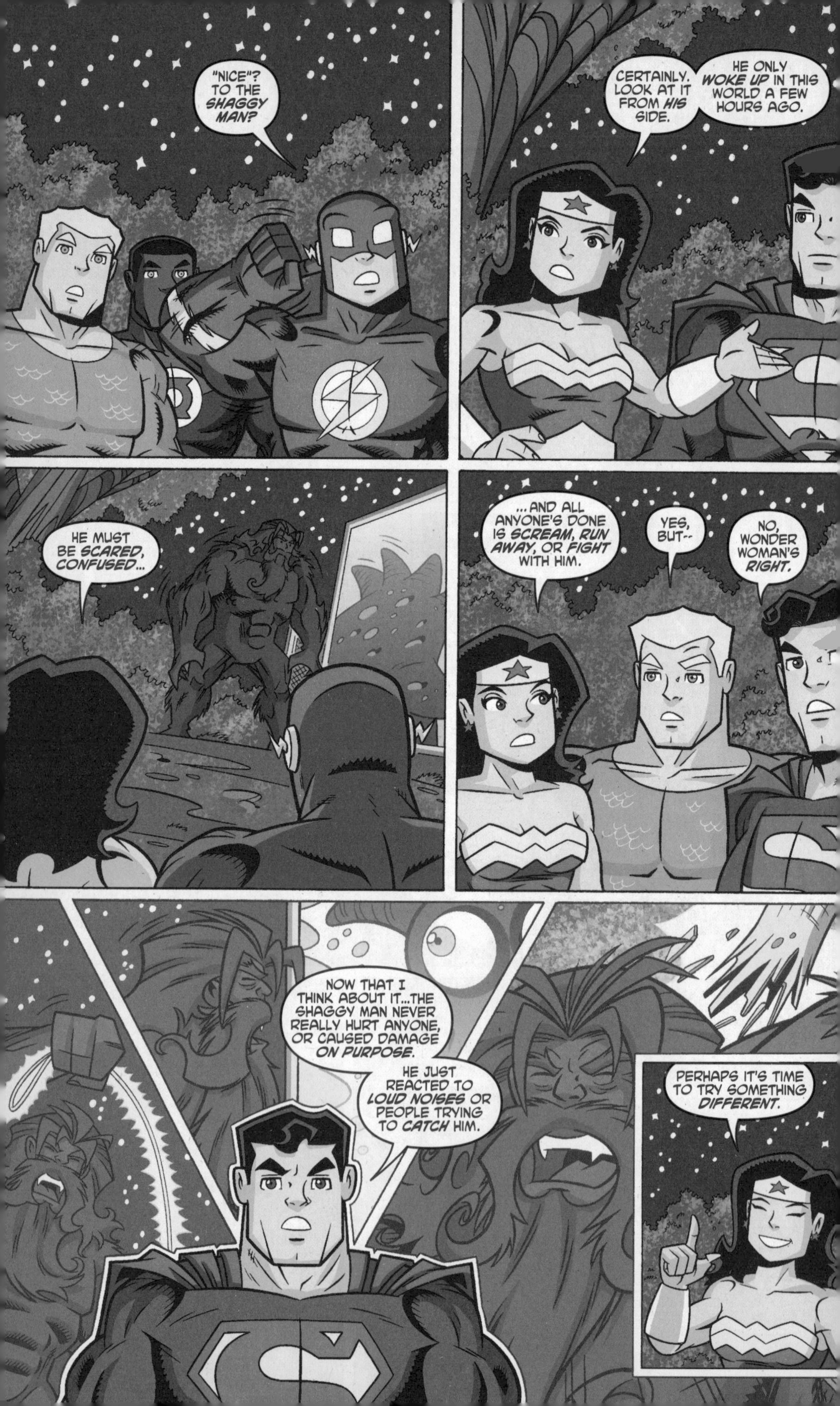
"NICE"? TO THE SHAGGY MAN?
CERTAINLY. LOOK AT IT FROM HIS SIDE.
HE ONLY WOKE UP IN THIS WORLD A FEW HOURS AGO.
HE MUST BE SCARED, CONFUSED...
...AND ALL ANYONE'S DONE IS SCREAM, RUN AWAY, OR FIGHT WITH HIM.
YES, BUT--
NO, WONDER WOMAN'S RIGHT.
NOW THAT I THINK ABOUT IT...THE SHAGGY MAN NEVER REALLY HURT ANYONE, OR CAUSED DAMAGE ON PURPOSE.
HE JUST REACTED TO LOUD NOISES OR PEOPLE TRYING TO CATCH HIM.
PERHAPS IT'S TIME TO TRY SOMETHING DIFFERENT.

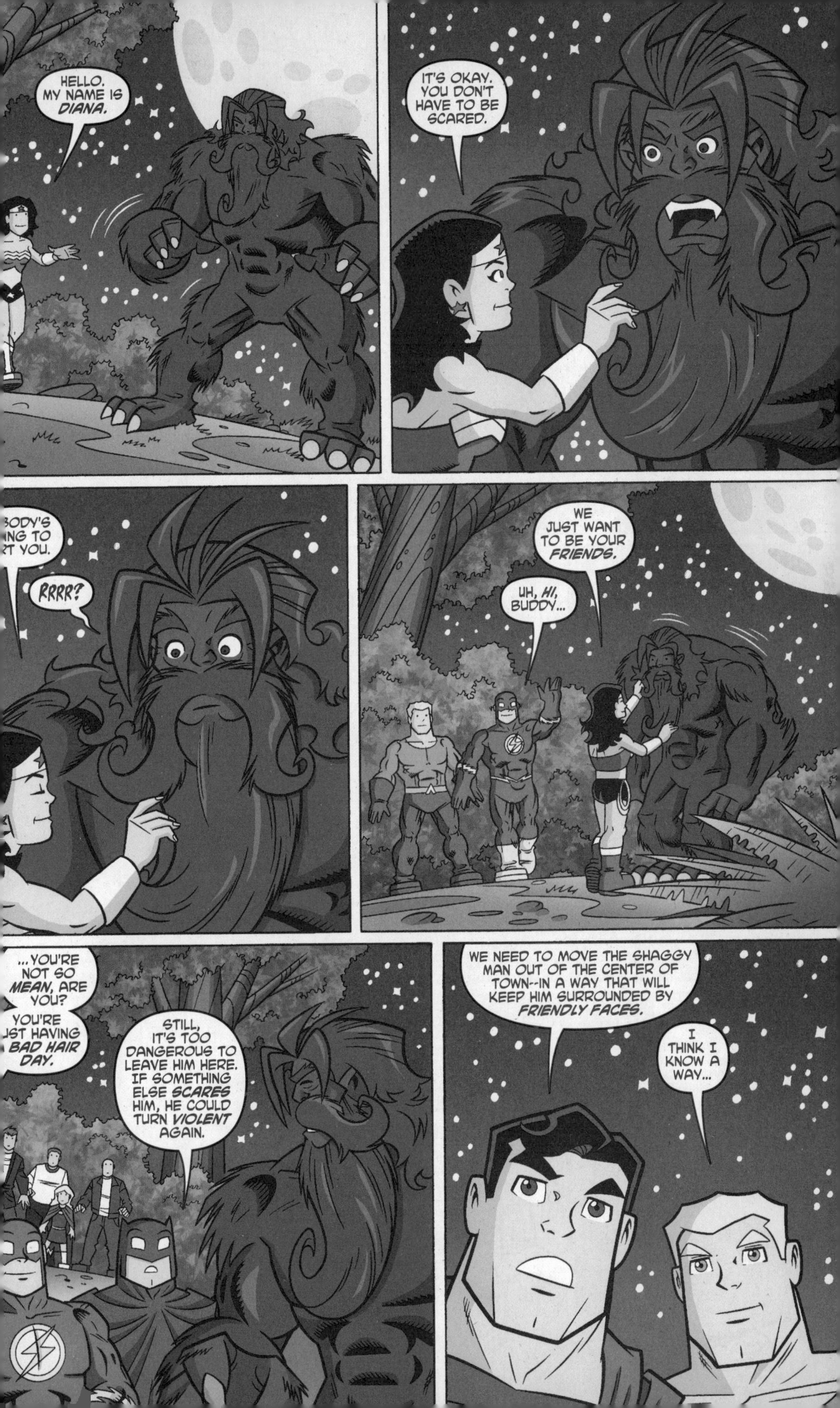
HELLO. MY NAME IS DIANA.
IT'S OKAY. YOU DON'T HAVE TO BE SCARED.
BODY'S ING TO RT YOU.
RRRR?
WE JUST WANT TO BE YOUR FRIENDS.
UH, HI, BUDDY...
...YOU'RE NOT SO MEAN, ARE YOU? YOU'RE ST HAVING BAD HAIR DAY.
STILL, IT'S TOO DANGEROUS TO LEAVE HIM HERE. IF SOMETHING ELSE SCARES HIM, HE COULD TURN VIOLENT AGAIN.
WE NEED TO MOVE THE SHAGGY MAN OUT OF THE CENTER OF TOWN--IN A WAY THAT WILL KEEP HIM SURROUNDED BY FRIENDLY FACES.
I THINK I KNOW A WAY...

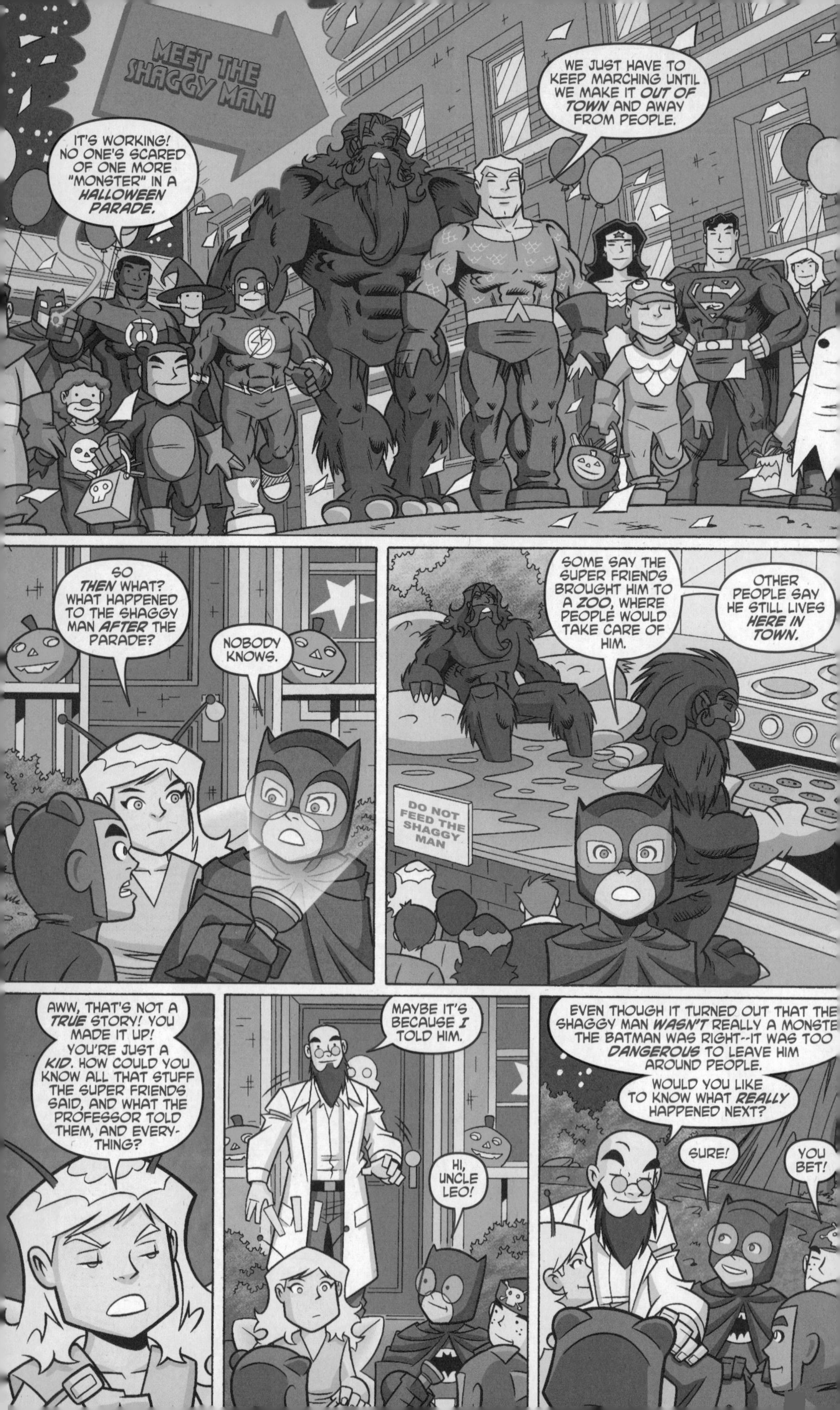

MEET THE SHAGGY MAN!
IT'S WORKING! NO ONE'S SCARED OF ONE MORE "MONSTER" IN A HALLOWEEN PARADE.
WE JUST HAVE TO KEEP MARCHING UNTIL WE MAKE IT OUT OF TOWN AND AWAY FROM PEOPLE.
SO THEN WHAT? WHAT HAPPENED TO THE SHAGGY MAN AFTER THE PARADE?
NOBODY KNOWS.
SOME SAY THE SUPER FRIENDS BROUGHT HIM TO A ZOO, WHERE PEOPLE WOULD TAKE CARE OF HIM.
DO NOT FEED THE SHAGGY MAN
OTHER PEOPLE SAY HE STILL LIVES HERE IN TOWN.
AWW, THAT'S NOT A TRUE STORY! YOU MADE IT UP! YOU'RE JUST A KID. HOW COULD YOU KNOW ALL THAT STUFF THE SUPER FRIENDS SAID, AND WHAT THE PROFESSOR TOLD THEM, AND EVERY-THING?
MAYBE IT'S BECAUSE I TOLD HIM.
HI, UNCLE LEO!
EVEN THOUGH IT TURNED OUT THAT THE SHAGGY MAN WASN'T REALLY A MONSTE THE BATMAN WAS RIGHT--IT WAS TOO DANGEROUS TO LEAVE HIM AROUND PEOPLE.
WOULD YOU LIKE TO KNOW WHAT REALLY HAPPENED NEXT?
SURE!
YOU BET!

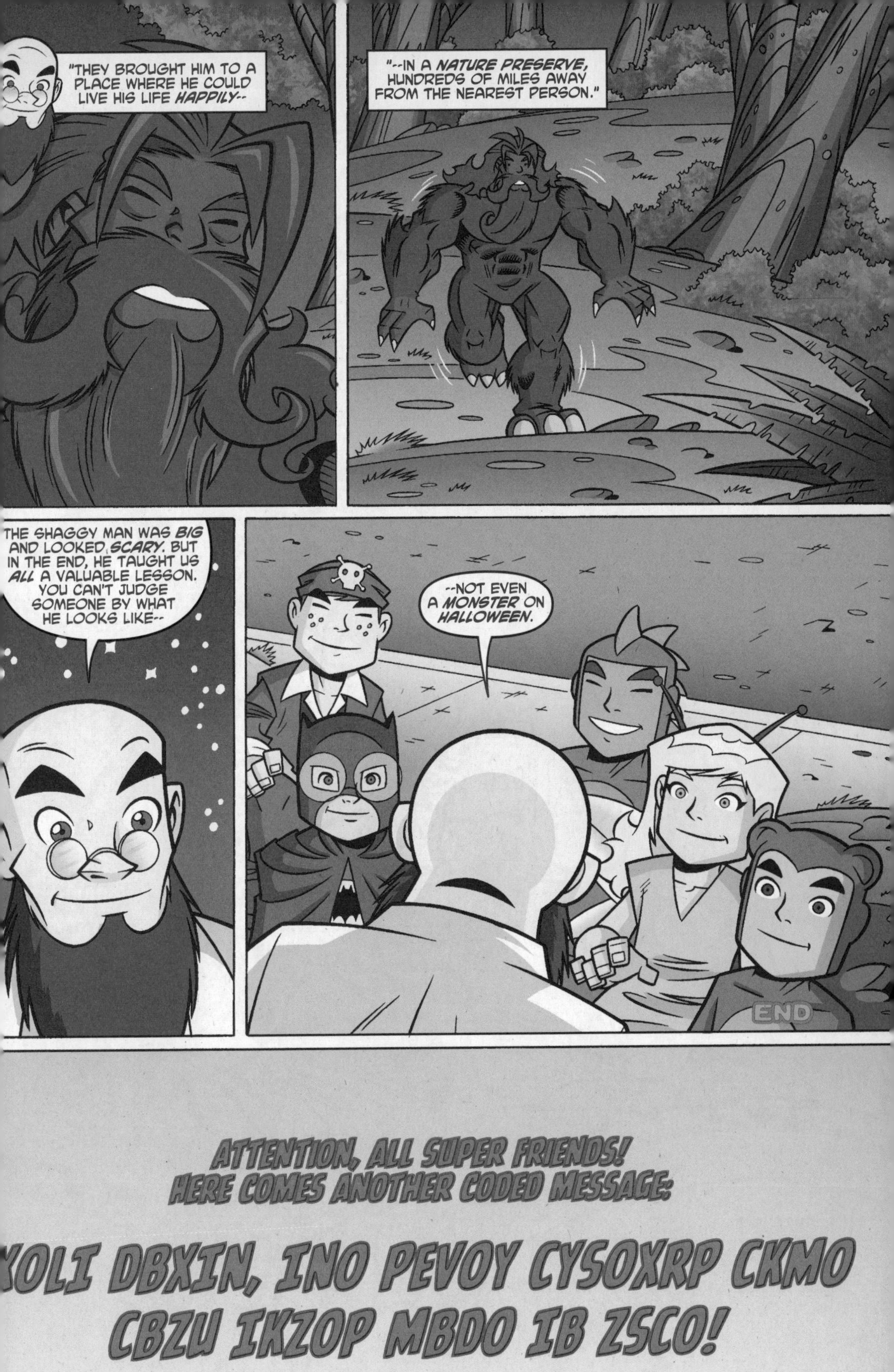
"THEY BROUGHT HIM TO A PLACE WHERE HE COULD LIVE HIS LIFE *HAPPILY*--
"--IN A *NATURE PRESERVE*, HUNDREDS OF MILES AWAY FROM THE NEAREST PERSON."
THE SHAGGY MAN WAS *BIG* AND LOOKED *SCARY*. BUT IN THE END, HE TAUGHT US *ALL* A VALUABLE LESSON. YOU CAN'T JUDGE SOMEONE BY WHAT HE LOOKS LIKE--
--NOT EVEN A *MONSTER* ON *HALLOWEEN*.
END

ATTENTION, ALL SUPER FRIENDS!
HERE COMES ANOTHER CODED MESSAGE:

XOLI DBXIN, INO PEVOY CYSOXRP CKMO
CBZU IKZOP MBDO IB ZSCO!

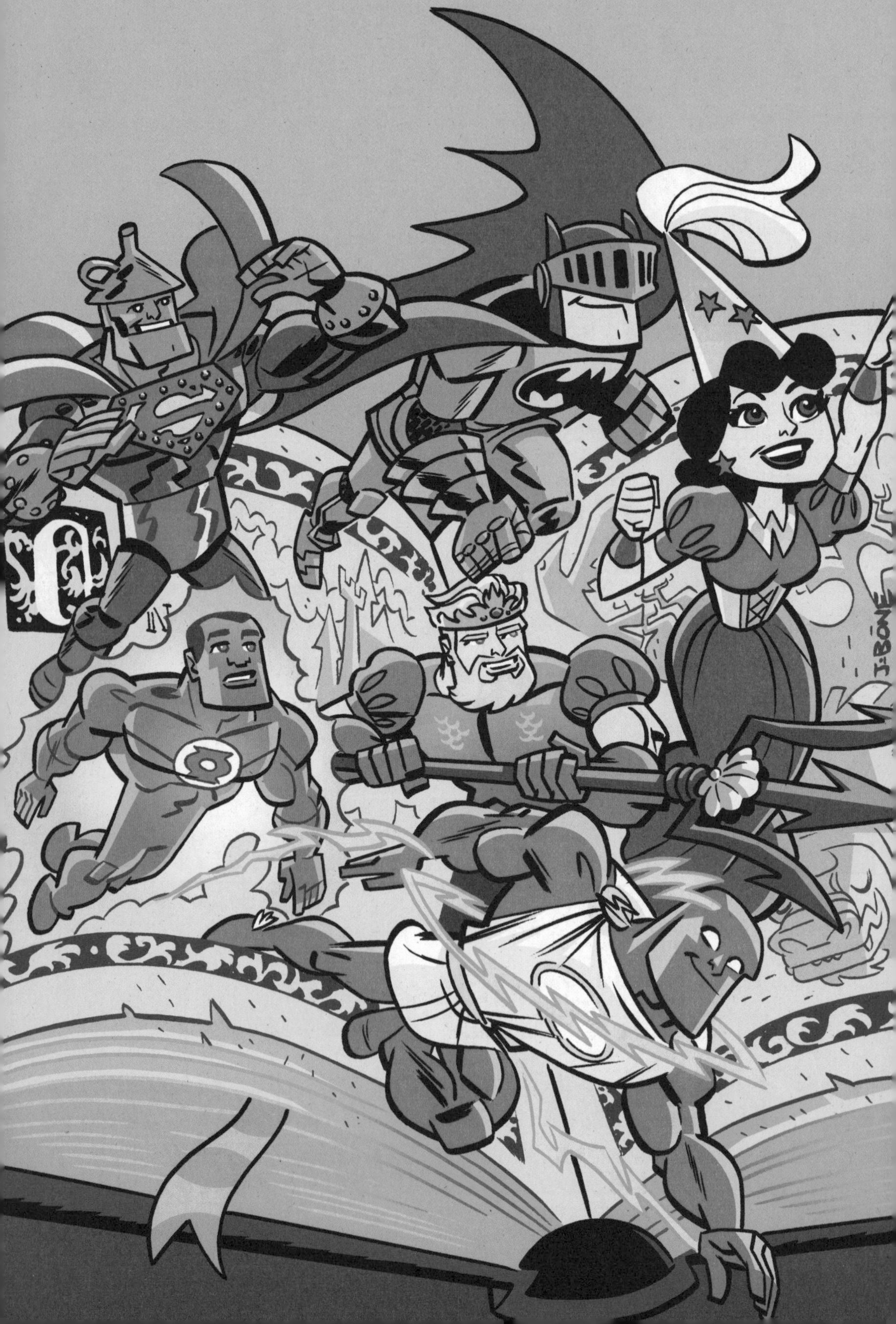
J-BONE

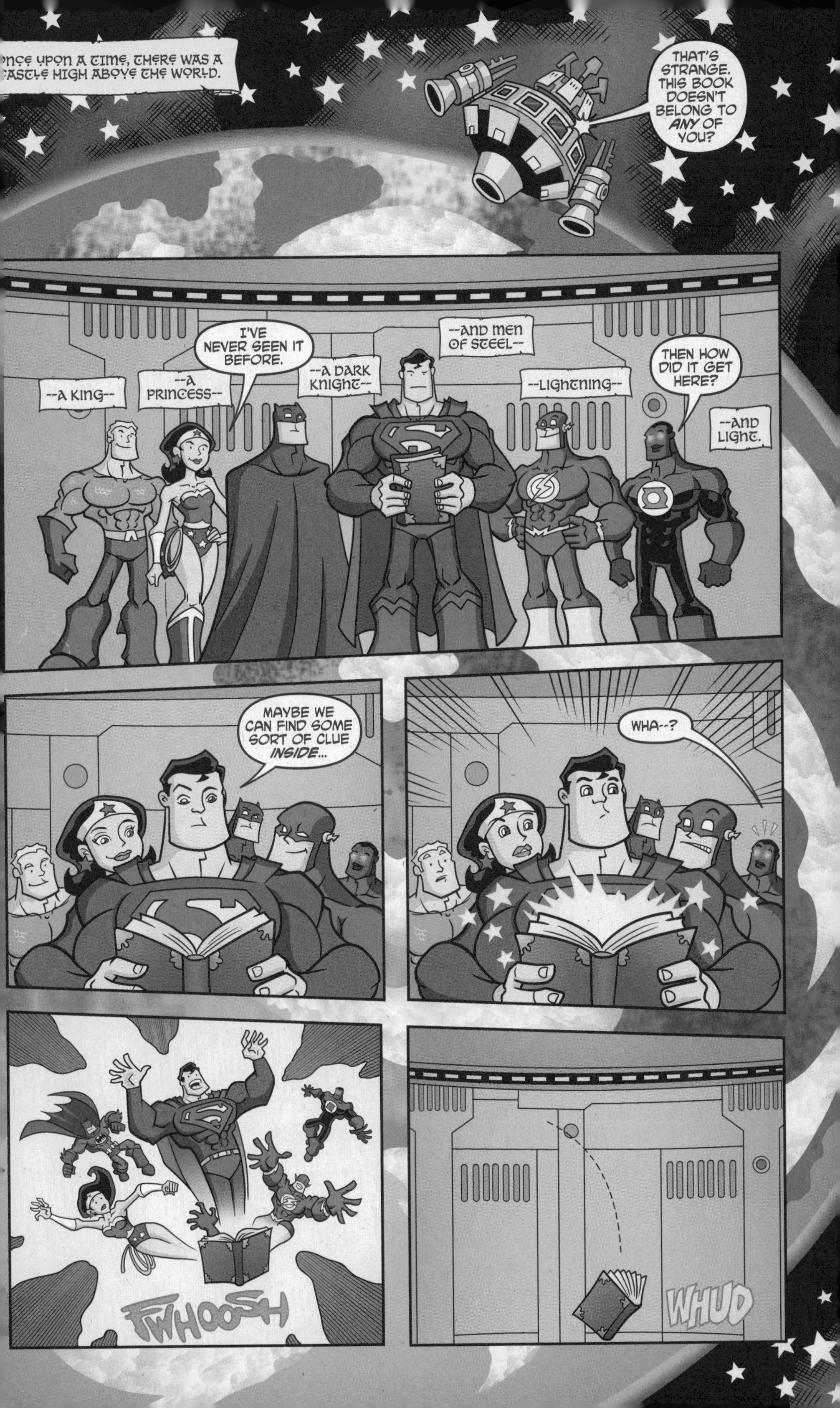

ONCE UPON A TIME, THERE WAS A CASTLE HIGH ABOVE THE WORLD.
THAT'S STRANGE. THIS BOOK DOESN'T BELONG TO ANY OF YOU?
--A KING--
--A PRINCESS--
I'VE NEVER SEEN IT BEFORE.
--A DARK KNIGHT--
--AND MEN OF STEEL--
--LIGHTNING--
THEN HOW DID IT GET HERE?
--AND LIGHT.
MAYBE WE CAN FIND SOME SORT OF CLUE INSIDE...
WHA--?
FWHOOSH
WHUD

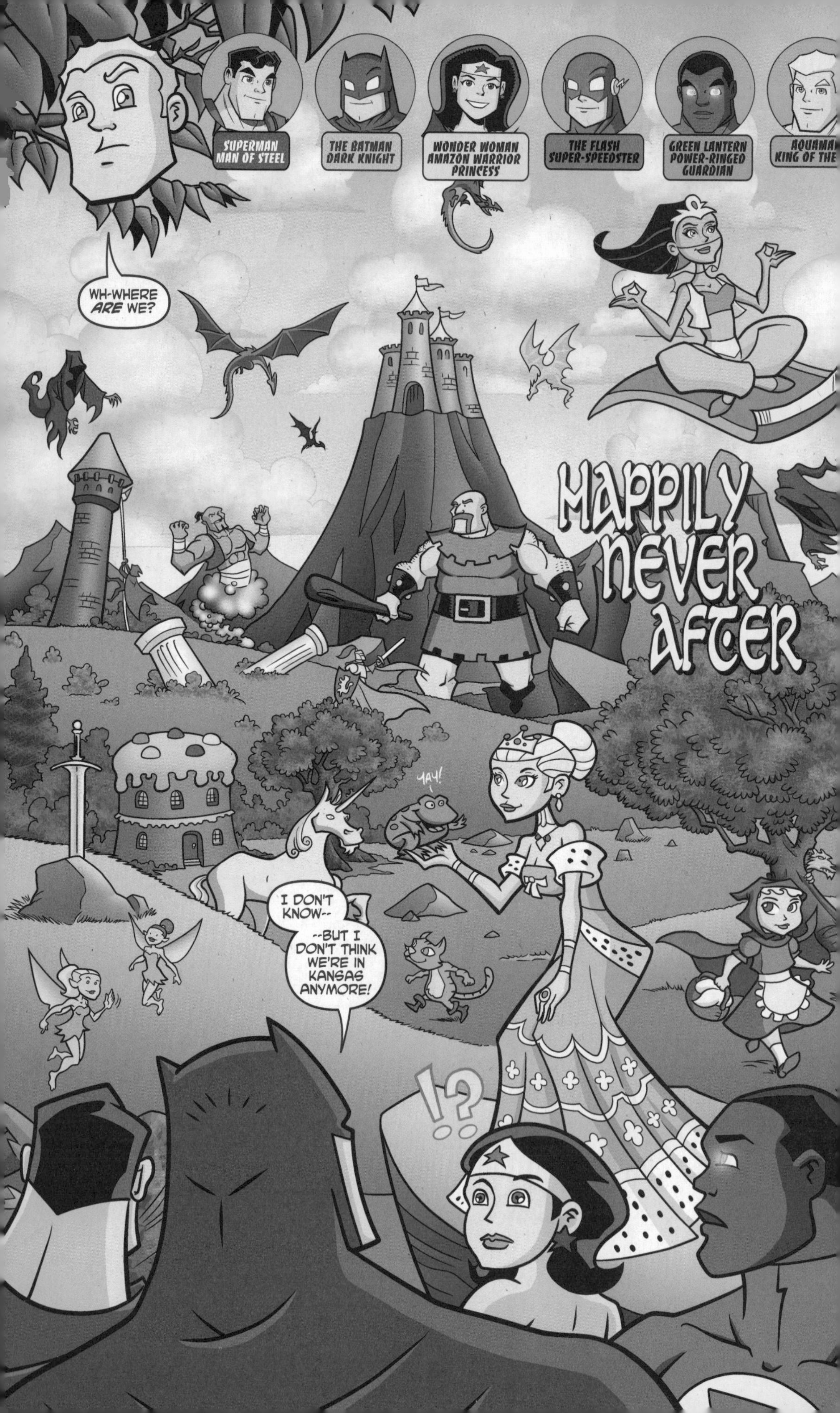
SUPERMAN MAN OF STEEL
THE BATMAN DARK KNIGHT
WONDER WOMAN AMAZON WARRIOR PRINCESS
THE FLASH SUPER-SPEEDSTER
GREEN LANTERN POWER-RINGED GUARDIAN
AQUAMAN KING OF THE
WH-WHERE *ARE* WE?
HAPPILY NEVER AFTER
YAY!
I DON'T KNOW--
--BUT I DON'T THINK WE'RE IN KANSAS ANYMORE!
!?

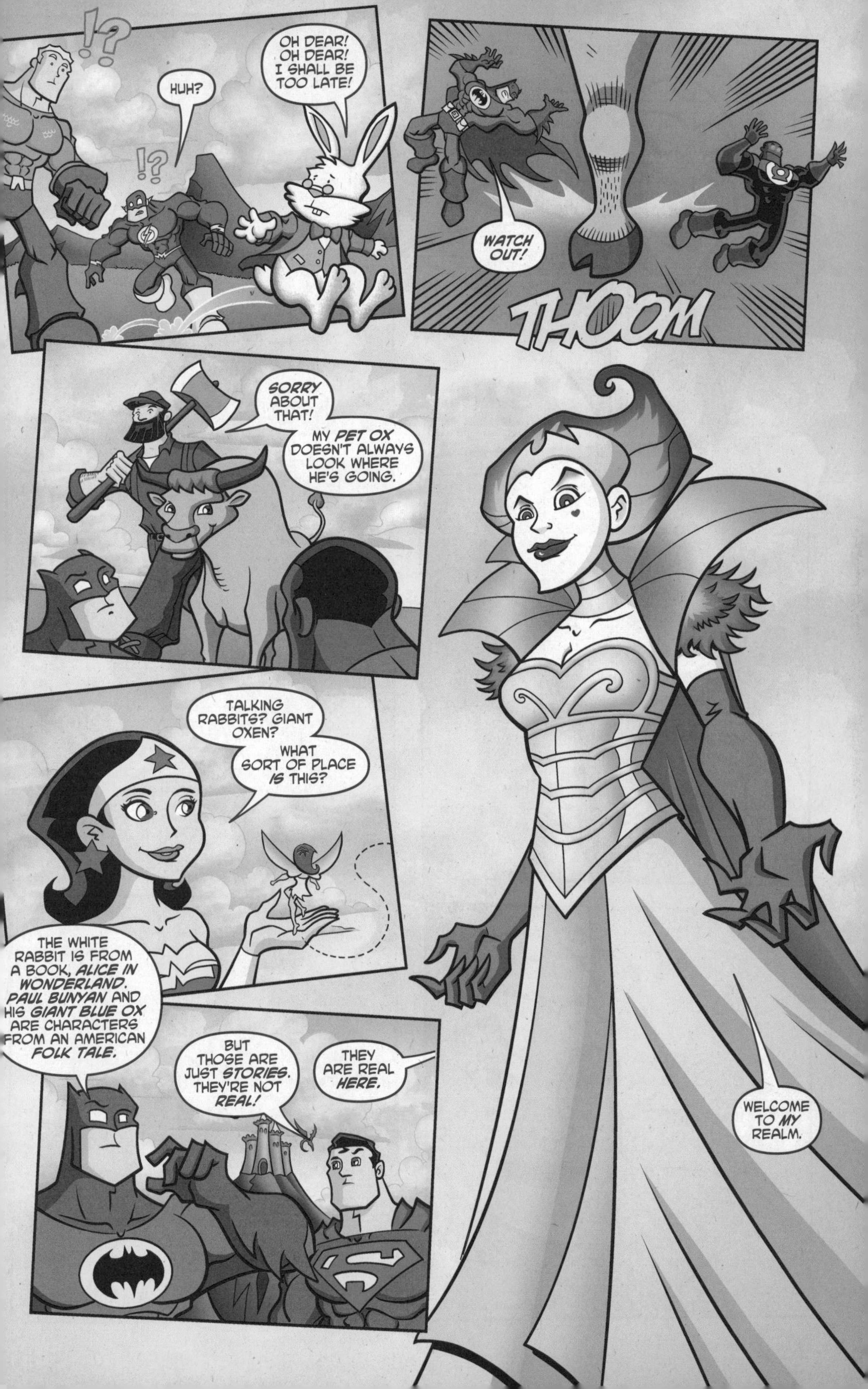
HUH?
OH DEAR! OH DEAR! I SHALL BE TOO LATE!
WATCH OUT!
THOOM
SORRY ABOUT THAT!
MY PET OX DOESN'T ALWAYS LOOK WHERE HE'S GOING.
TALKING RABBITS? GIANT OXEN?
WHAT SORT OF PLACE IS THIS?
THE WHITE RABBIT IS FROM A BOOK, ALICE IN WONDERLAND. PAUL BUNYAN AND HIS GIANT BLUE OX ARE CHARACTERS FROM AN AMERICAN FOLK TALE.
BUT THOSE ARE JUST STORIES. THEY'RE NOT REAL!
THEY ARE REAL HERE.
WELCOME TO MY REALM.

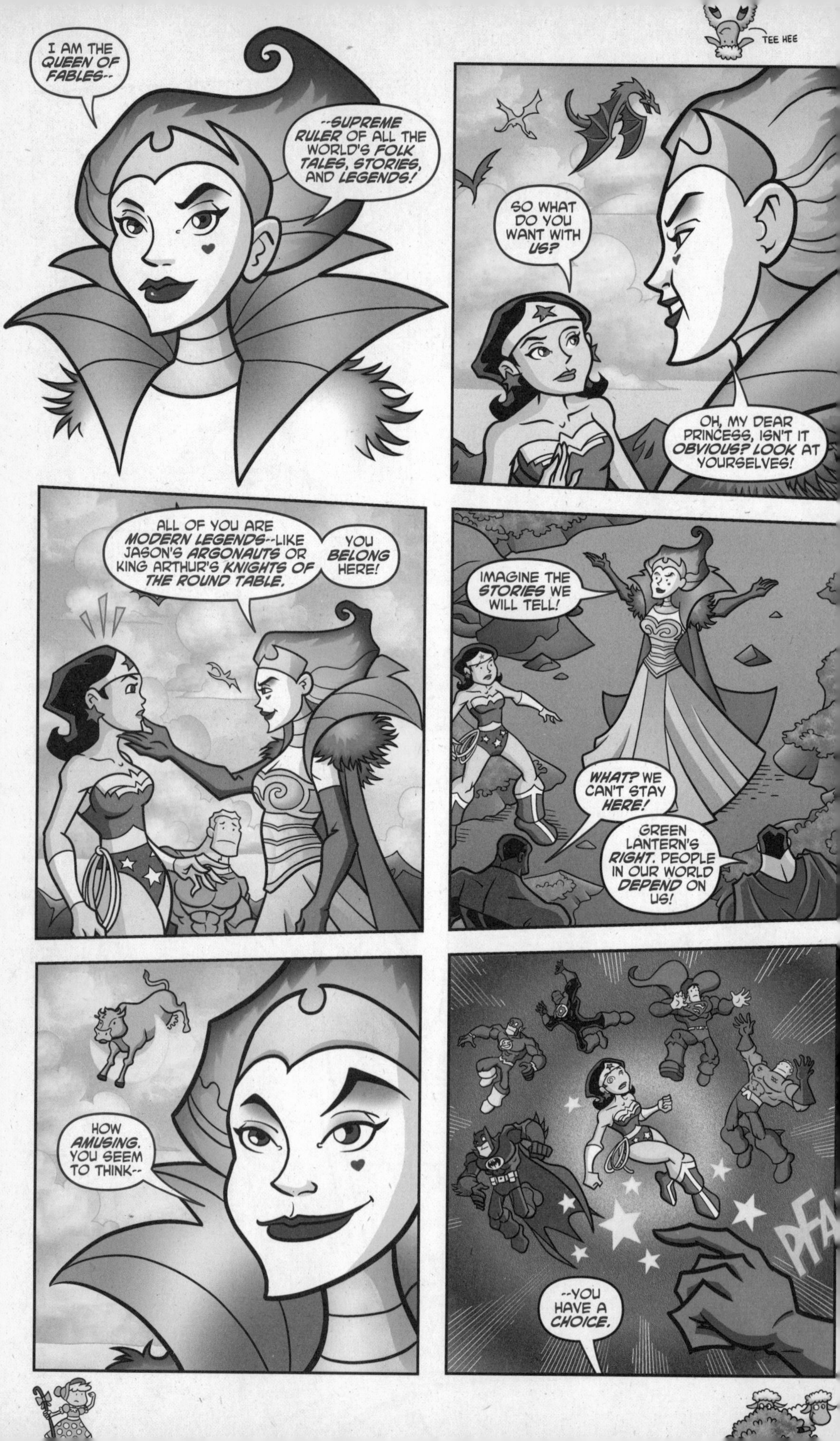
TEE HEE
I AM THE QUEEN OF FABLES--
--SUPREME RULER OF ALL THE WORLD'S FOLK TALES, STORIES, AND LEGENDS!
SO WHAT DO YOU WANT WITH US?
OH, MY DEAR PRINCESS, ISN'T IT OBVIOUS? LOOK AT YOURSELVES!
ALL OF YOU ARE MODERN LEGENDS--LIKE JASON'S ARGONAUTS OR KING ARTHUR'S KNIGHTS OF THE ROUND TABLE.
YOU BELONG HERE!
IMAGINE THE STORIES WE WILL TELL!
WHAT? WE CAN'T STAY HERE!
GREEN LANTERN'S RIGHT. PEOPLE IN OUR WORLD DEPEND ON US!
HOW AMUSING. YOU SEEM TO THINK--
--YOU HAVE A CHOICE.

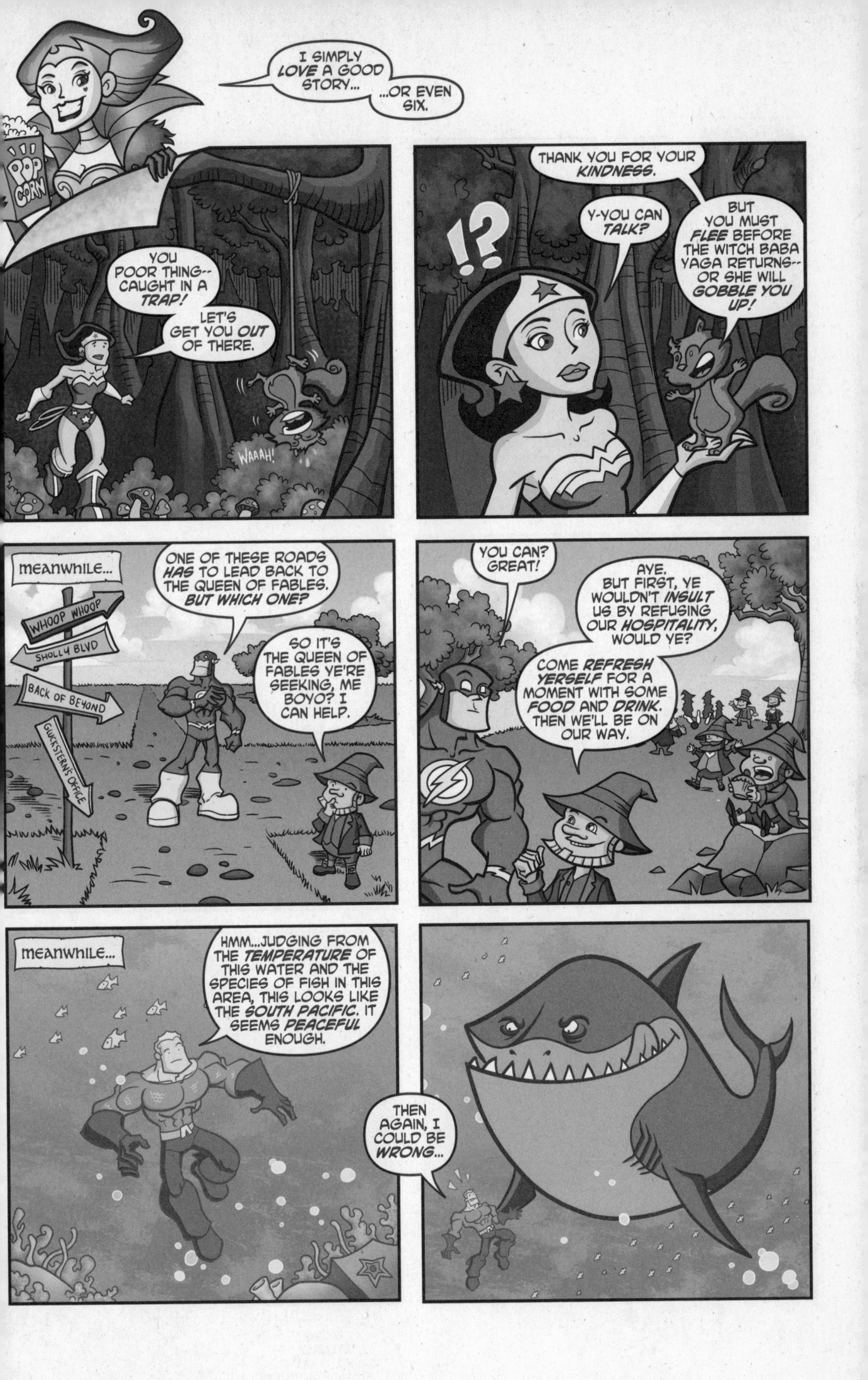
I SIMPLY LOVE A GOOD STORY...
...OR EVEN SIX.
YOU POOR THING--CAUGHT IN A TRAP!
LET'S GET YOU OUT OF THERE.
WAAAH!
THANK YOU FOR YOUR KINDNESS.
!?
Y-YOU CAN TALK?
BUT YOU MUST FLEE BEFORE THE WITCH BABA YAGA RETURNS--OR SHE WILL GOBBLE YOU UP!
MEANWHILE...
ONE OF THESE ROADS HAS TO LEAD BACK TO THE QUEEN OF FABLES. BUT WHICH ONE?
WHOOP WHOOP
SHOLLY BLVD
BACK OF BEYOND
GUCKSTERN'S OFFICE
SO IT'S THE QUEEN OF FABLES YE'RE SEEKING, ME BOYO? I CAN HELP.
YOU CAN? GREAT!
AYE. BUT FIRST, YE WOULDN'T INSULT US BY REFUSING OUR HOSPITALITY, WOULD YE?
COME REFRESH YERSELF FOR A MOMENT WITH SOME FOOD AND DRINK. THEN WE'LL BE ON OUR WAY.
MEANWHILE...
HMM...JUDGING FROM THE TEMPERATURE OF THIS WATER AND THE SPECIES OF FISH IN THIS AREA, THIS LOOKS LIKE THE SOUTH PACIFIC. IT SEEMS PEACEFUL ENOUGH.
THEN AGAIN, I COULD BE WRONG...

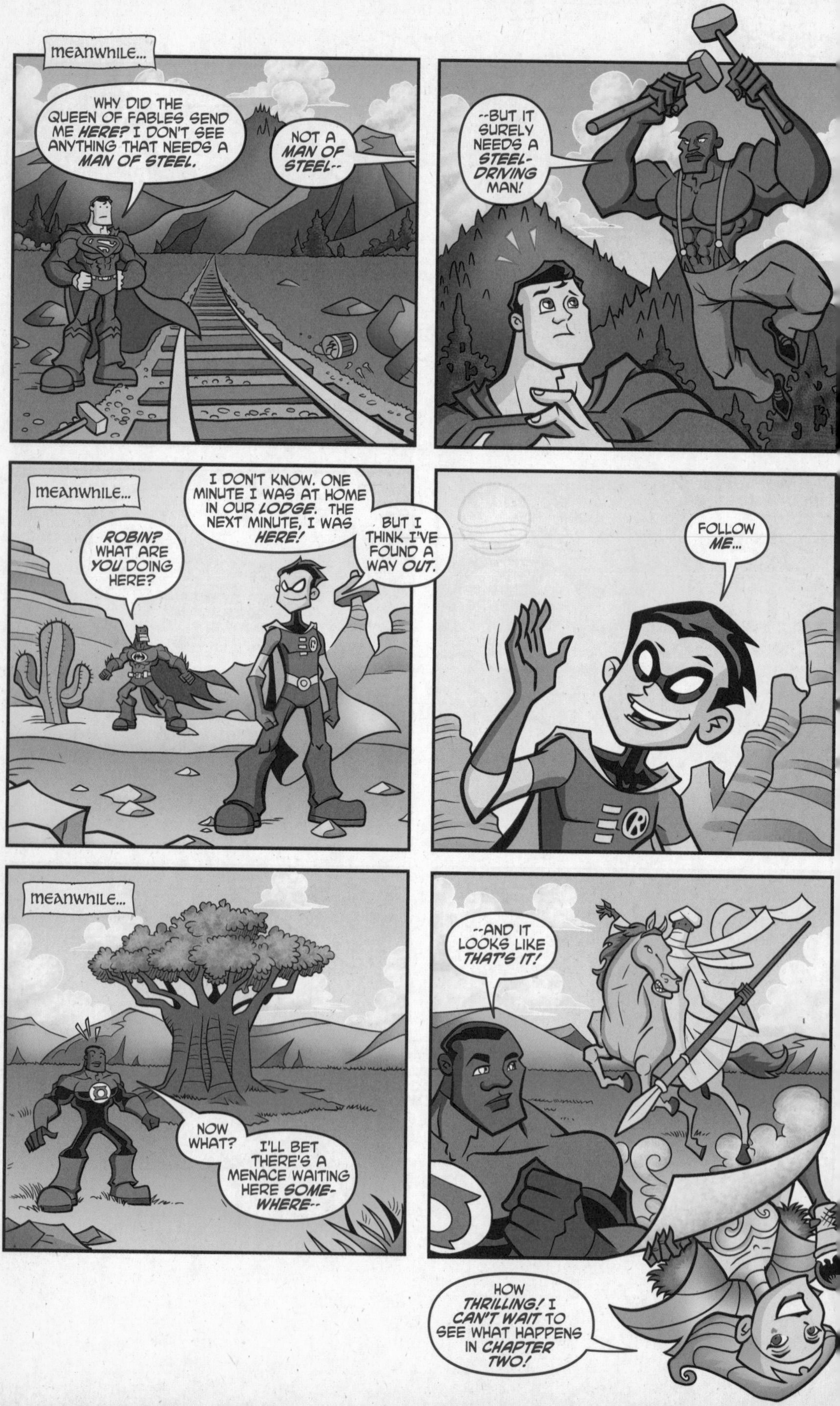
MEANWHILE...
WHY DID THE QUEEN OF FABLES SEND ME HERE? I DON'T SEE ANYTHING THAT NEEDS A MAN OF STEEL.
NOT A MAN OF STEEL--
--BUT IT SURELY NEEDS A STEEL-DRIVING MAN!
MEANWHILE...
ROBIN? WHAT ARE YOU DOING HERE?
I DON'T KNOW. ONE MINUTE I WAS AT HOME IN OUR LODGE. THE NEXT MINUTE, I WAS HERE!
BUT I THINK I'VE FOUND A WAY OUT.
FOLLOW ME...
MEANWHILE...
NOW WHAT?
I'LL BET THERE'S A MENACE WAITING HERE SOME-WHERE--
--AND IT LOOKS LIKE THAT'S IT!
HOW THRILLING! I CAN'T WAIT TO SEE WHAT HAPPENS IN CHAPTER TWO!

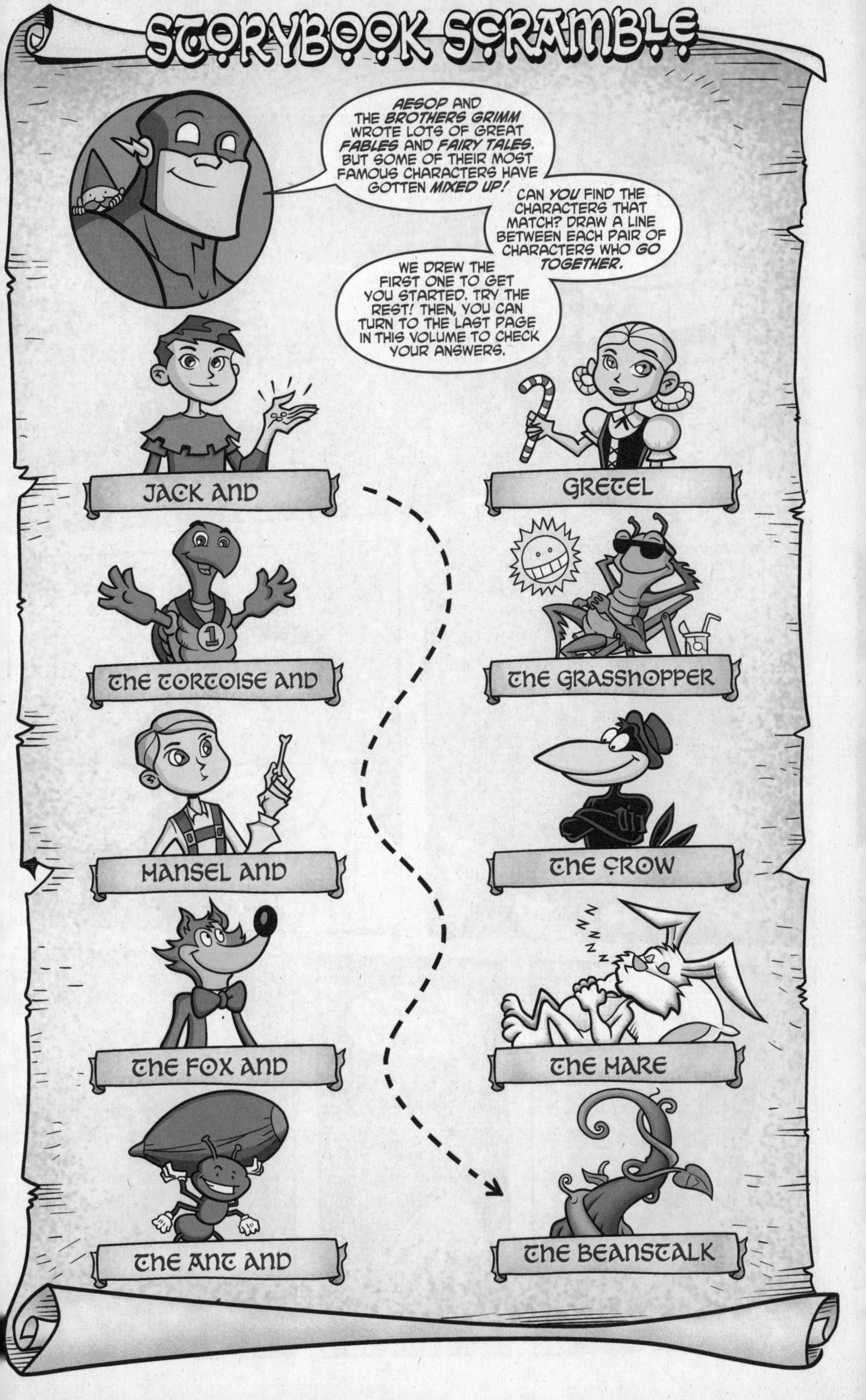

STORYBOOK SCRAMBLE
AESOP AND THE BROTHERS GRIMM WROTE LOTS OF GREAT FABLES AND FAIRY TALES. BUT SOME OF THEIR MOST FAMOUS CHARACTERS HAVE GOTTEN MIXED UP!
CAN YOU FIND THE CHARACTERS THAT MATCH? DRAW A LINE BETWEEN EACH PAIR OF CHARACTERS WHO GO TOGETHER.
WE DREW THE FIRST ONE TO GET YOU STARTED. TRY THE REST! THEN, YOU CAN TURN TO THE LAST PAGE IN THIS VOLUME TO CHECK YOUR ANSWERS.
JACK AND
GRETEL
THE TORTOISE AND
THE GRASSHOPPER
HANSEL AND
THE CROW
THE FOX AND
THE HARE
THE ANT AND
THE BEANSTALK

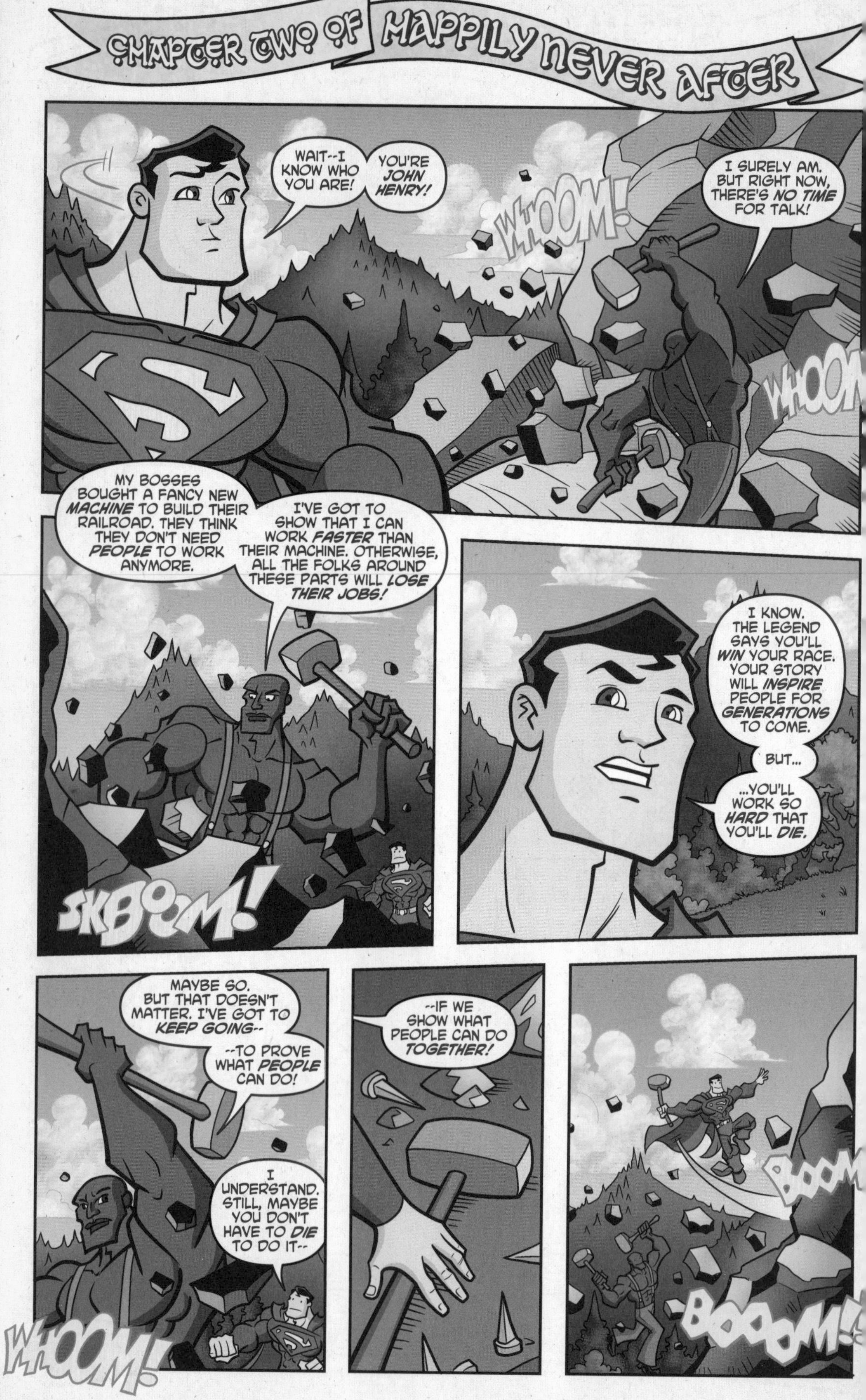
CHAPTER TWO OF HAPPILY NEVER AFTER
WAIT--I KNOW WHO YOU ARE!
YOU'RE JOHN HENRY!
WHOOM!
I SURELY AM. BUT RIGHT NOW, THERE'S NO TIME FOR TALK!
WHOOM
MY BOSSES BOUGHT A FANCY NEW MACHINE TO BUILD THEIR RAILROAD. THEY THINK THEY DON'T NEED PEOPLE TO WORK ANYMORE.
I'VE GOT TO SHOW THAT I CAN WORK FASTER THAN THEIR MACHINE. OTHERWISE, ALL THE FOLKS AROUND THESE PARTS WILL LOSE THEIR JOBS!
SKBOOM!
I KNOW. THE LEGEND SAYS YOU'LL WIN YOUR RACE. YOUR STORY WILL INSPIRE PEOPLE FOR GENERATIONS TO COME.
BUT...
...YOU'LL WORK SO HARD THAT YOU'LL DIE.
MAYBE SO. BUT THAT DOESN'T MATTER. I'VE GOT TO KEEP GOING--
--TO PROVE WHAT PEOPLE CAN DO!
I UNDERSTAND. STILL, MAYBE YOU DON'T HAVE TO DIE TO DO IT--
WHOOM!
--IF WE SHOW WHAT PEOPLE CAN DO TOGETHER!
BOOOM
BOOOOM!!

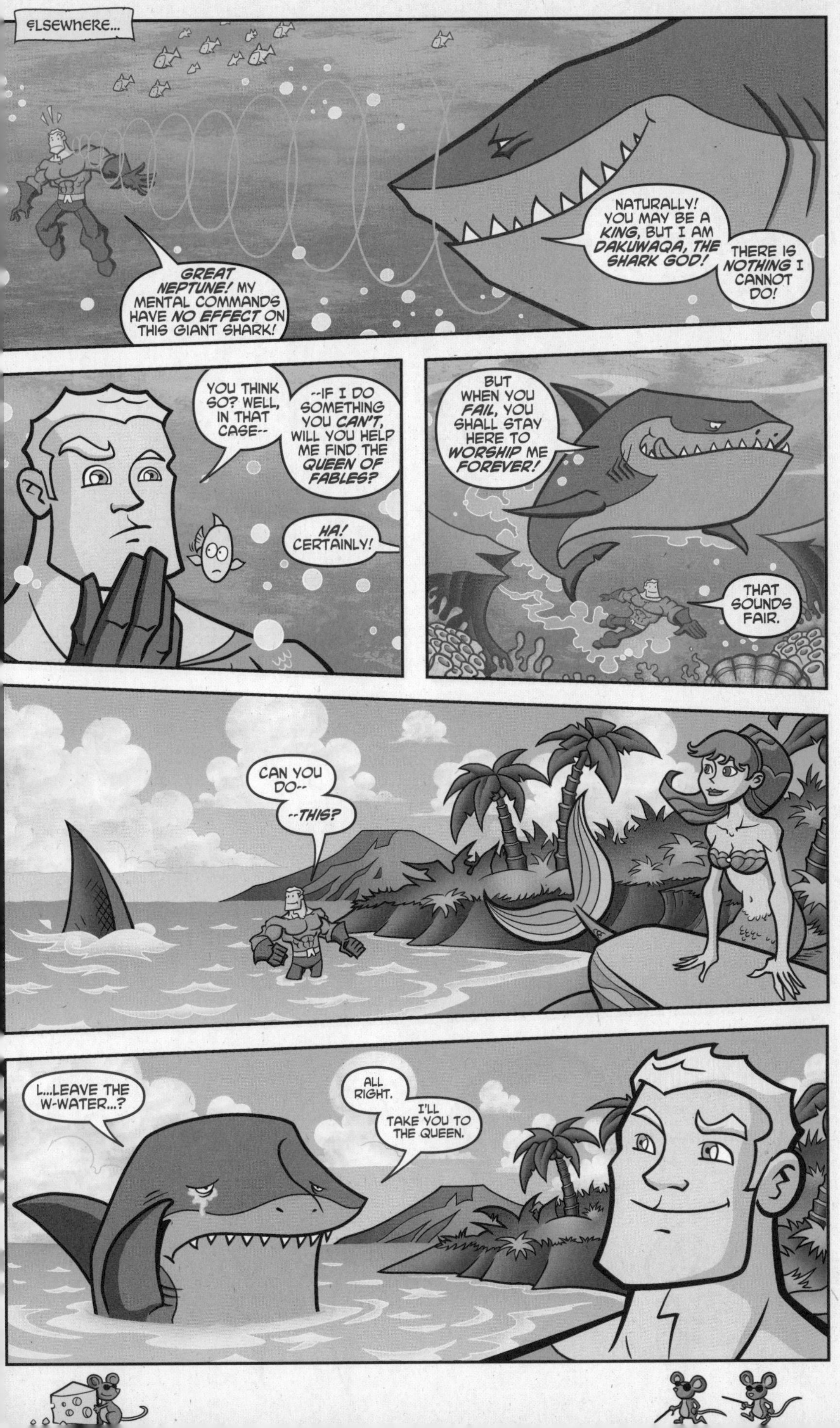
ELSEWHERE...
GREAT NEPTUNE! MY MENTAL COMMANDS HAVE NO EFFECT ON THIS GIANT SHARK!
NATURALLY! YOU MAY BE A KING, BUT I AM DAKUWAQA, THE SHARK GOD!
THERE IS NOTHING I CANNOT DO!
YOU THINK SO? WELL, IN THAT CASE--
--IF I DO SOMETHING YOU CAN'T, WILL YOU HELP ME FIND THE QUEEN OF FABLES?
HA! CERTAINLY!
BUT WHEN YOU FAIL, YOU SHALL STAY HERE TO WORSHIP ME FOREVER!
THAT SOUNDS FAIR.
CAN YOU DO--
--THIS?
L...LEAVE THE W-WATER...?
ALL RIGHT.
I'LL TAKE YOU TO THE QUEEN.

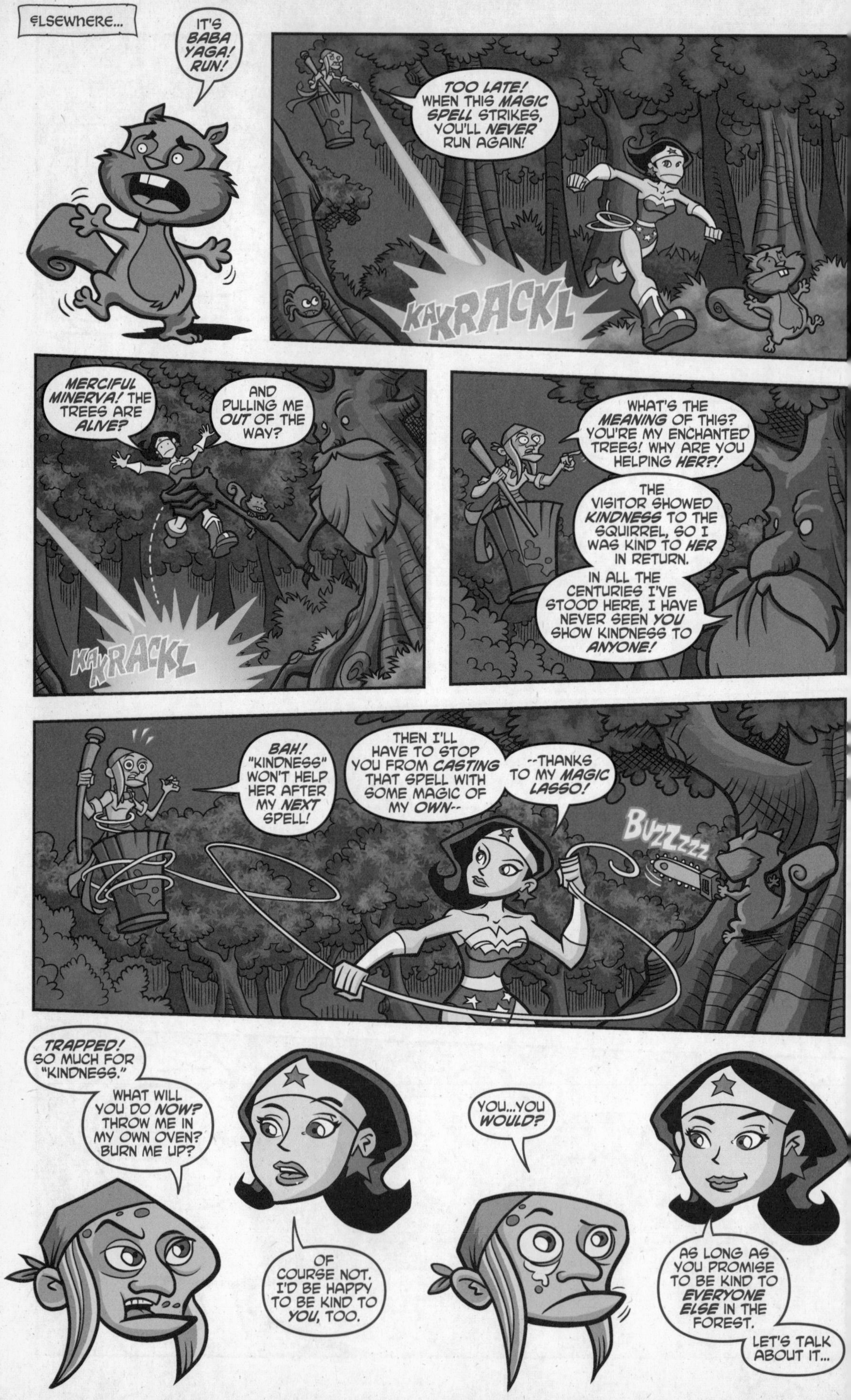
ELSEWHERE...
IT'S BABA YAGA! RUN!
TOO LATE! WHEN THIS MAGIC SPELL STRIKES, YOU'LL NEVER RUN AGAIN!
KAKRACKL
MERCIFUL MINERVA! THE TREES ARE ALIVE?
AND PULLING ME OUT OF THE WAY?
KAKRACKL
WHAT'S THE MEANING OF THIS? YOU'RE MY ENCHANTED TREES! WHY ARE YOU HELPING HER?!
THE VISITOR SHOWED KINDNESS TO THE SQUIRREL, SO I WAS KIND TO HER IN RETURN.
IN ALL THE CENTURIES I'VE STOOD HERE, I HAVE NEVER SEEN YOU SHOW KINDNESS TO ANYONE!
BAH! "KINDNESS" WON'T HELP HER AFTER MY NEXT SPELL!
THEN I'LL HAVE TO STOP YOU FROM CASTING THAT SPELL WITH SOME MAGIC OF MY OWN--
--THANKS TO MY MAGIC LASSO!
BUZZZZZ
TRAPPED! SO MUCH FOR "KINDNESS."
WHAT WILL YOU DO NOW? THROW ME IN MY OWN OVEN? BURN ME UP?
OF COURSE NOT. I'D BE HAPPY TO BE KIND TO YOU, TOO.
YOU...YOU WOULD?
AS LONG AS YOU PROMISE TO BE KIND TO EVERYONE ELSE IN THE FOREST.
LET'S TALK ABOUT IT...

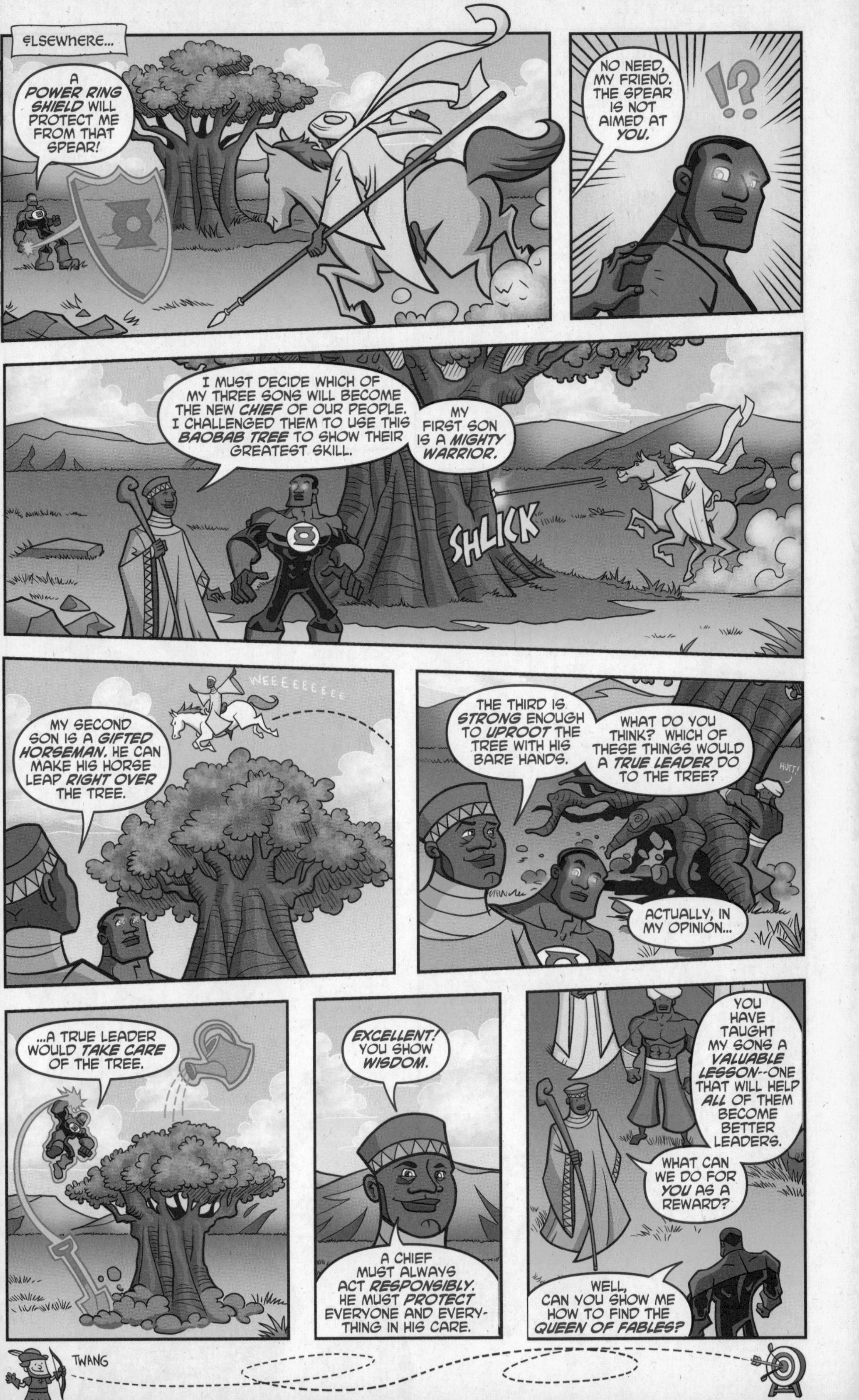
ELSEWHERE...
A POWER RING SHIELD WILL PROTECT ME FROM THAT SPEAR!
NO NEED, MY FRIEND. THE SPEAR IS NOT AIMED AT YOU.
!?
I MUST DECIDE WHICH OF MY THREE SONS WILL BECOME THE NEW CHIEF OF OUR PEOPLE. I CHALLENGED THEM TO USE THIS BAOBAB TREE TO SHOW THEIR GREATEST SKILL.
MY FIRST SON IS A MIGHTY WARRIOR.
SHLICK
WEEEEEEEEE
MY SECOND SON IS A GIFTED HORSEMAN. HE CAN MAKE HIS HORSE LEAP RIGHT OVER THE TREE.
THE THIRD IS STRONG ENOUGH TO UPROOT THE TREE WITH HIS BARE HANDS.
WHAT DO YOU THINK? WHICH OF THESE THINGS WOULD A TRUE LEADER DO TO THE TREE?
HUTT!
ACTUALLY, IN MY OPINION...
...A TRUE LEADER WOULD TAKE CARE OF THE TREE.
EXCELLENT! YOU SHOW WISDOM.
A CHIEF MUST ALWAYS ACT RESPONSIBLY. HE MUST PROTECT EVERYONE AND EVERY-THING IN HIS CARE.
YOU HAVE TAUGHT MY SONS A VALUABLE LESSON--ONE THAT WILL HELP ALL OF THEM BECOME BETTER LEADERS.
WHAT CAN WE DO FOR YOU AS A REWARD?
WELL, CAN YOU SHOW ME HOW TO FIND THE QUEEN OF FABLES?
TWANG

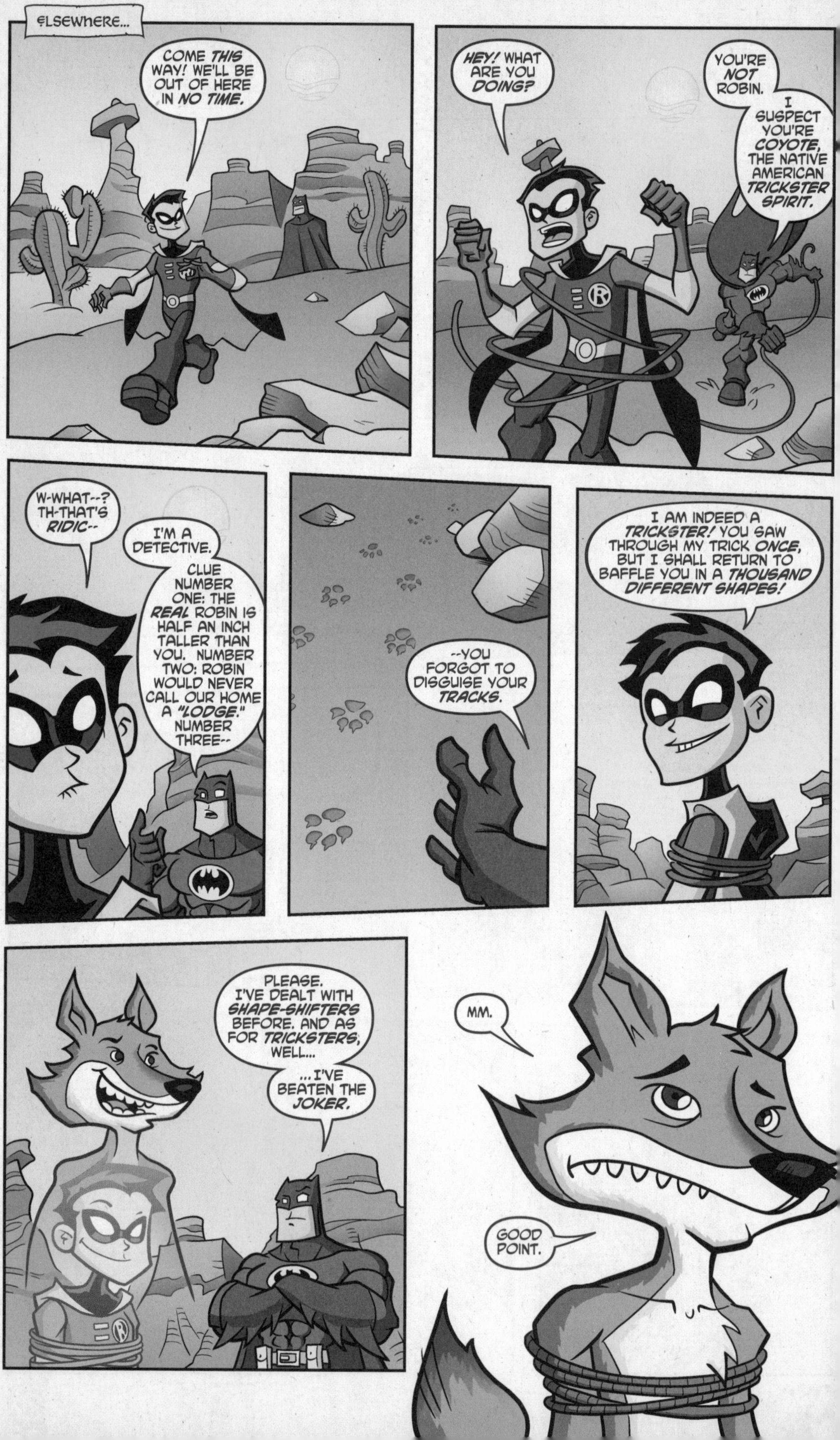
ELSEWHERE...
COME THIS WAY! WE'LL BE OUT OF HERE IN NO TIME.
HEY! WHAT ARE YOU DOING?
YOU'RE NOT ROBIN.
I SUSPECT YOU'RE COYOTE, THE NATIVE AMERICAN TRICKSTER SPIRIT.
W-WHAT--? TH-THAT'S RIDIC--
I'M A DETECTIVE.
CLUE NUMBER ONE: THE REAL ROBIN IS HALF AN INCH TALLER THAN YOU. NUMBER TWO: ROBIN WOULD NEVER CALL OUR HOME A "LODGE." NUMBER THREE--
--YOU FORGOT TO DISGUISE YOUR TRACKS.
I AM INDEED A TRICKSTER! YOU SAW THROUGH MY TRICK ONCE, BUT I SHALL RETURN TO BAFFLE YOU IN A THOUSAND DIFFERENT SHAPES!
PLEASE. I'VE DEALT WITH SHAPE-SHIFTERS BEFORE. AND AS FOR TRICKSTERS, WELL...
...I'VE BEATEN THE JOKER.
MM.
GOOD POINT.

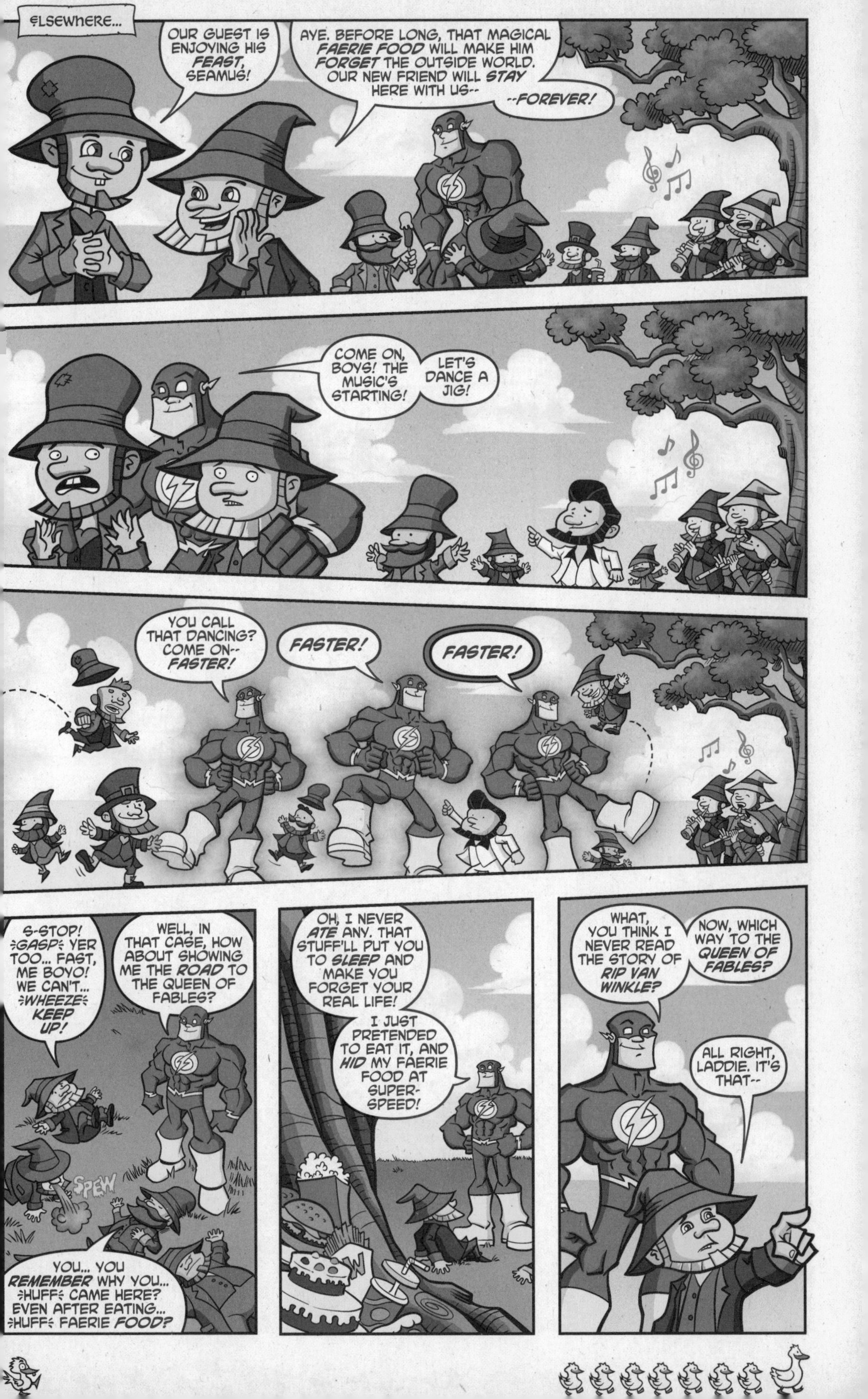
ELSEWHERE...
OUR GUEST IS ENJOYING HIS FEAST, SEAMUS!
AYE. BEFORE LONG, THAT MAGICAL FAERIE FOOD WILL MAKE HIM FORGET THE OUTSIDE WORLD. OUR NEW FRIEND WILL STAY HERE WITH US--
--FOREVER!
COME ON, BOYS! THE MUSIC'S STARTING!
LET'S DANCE A JIG!
YOU CALL THAT DANCING? COME ON-- FASTER!
FASTER!
FASTER!
S-STOP! ≑GASP≑ YER TOO... FAST, ME BOYO! WE CAN'T... ≑WHEEZE≑ KEEP UP!
WELL, IN THAT CASE, HOW ABOUT SHOWING ME THE ROAD TO THE QUEEN OF FABLES?
SPEW
YOU... YOU REMEMBER WHY YOU... ≑HUFF≑ CAME HERE? EVEN AFTER EATING... ≑HUFF≑ FAERIE FOOD?
OH, I NEVER ATE ANY. THAT STUFF'LL PUT YOU TO SLEEP AND MAKE YOU FORGET YOUR REAL LIFE!
I JUST PRETENDED TO EAT IT, AND HID MY FAERIE FOOD AT SUPER-SPEED!
WHAT, YOU THINK I NEVER READ THE STORY OF RIP VAN WINKLE?
NOW, WHICH WAY TO THE QUEEN OF FABLES?
ALL RIGHT, LADDIE. IT'S THAT--

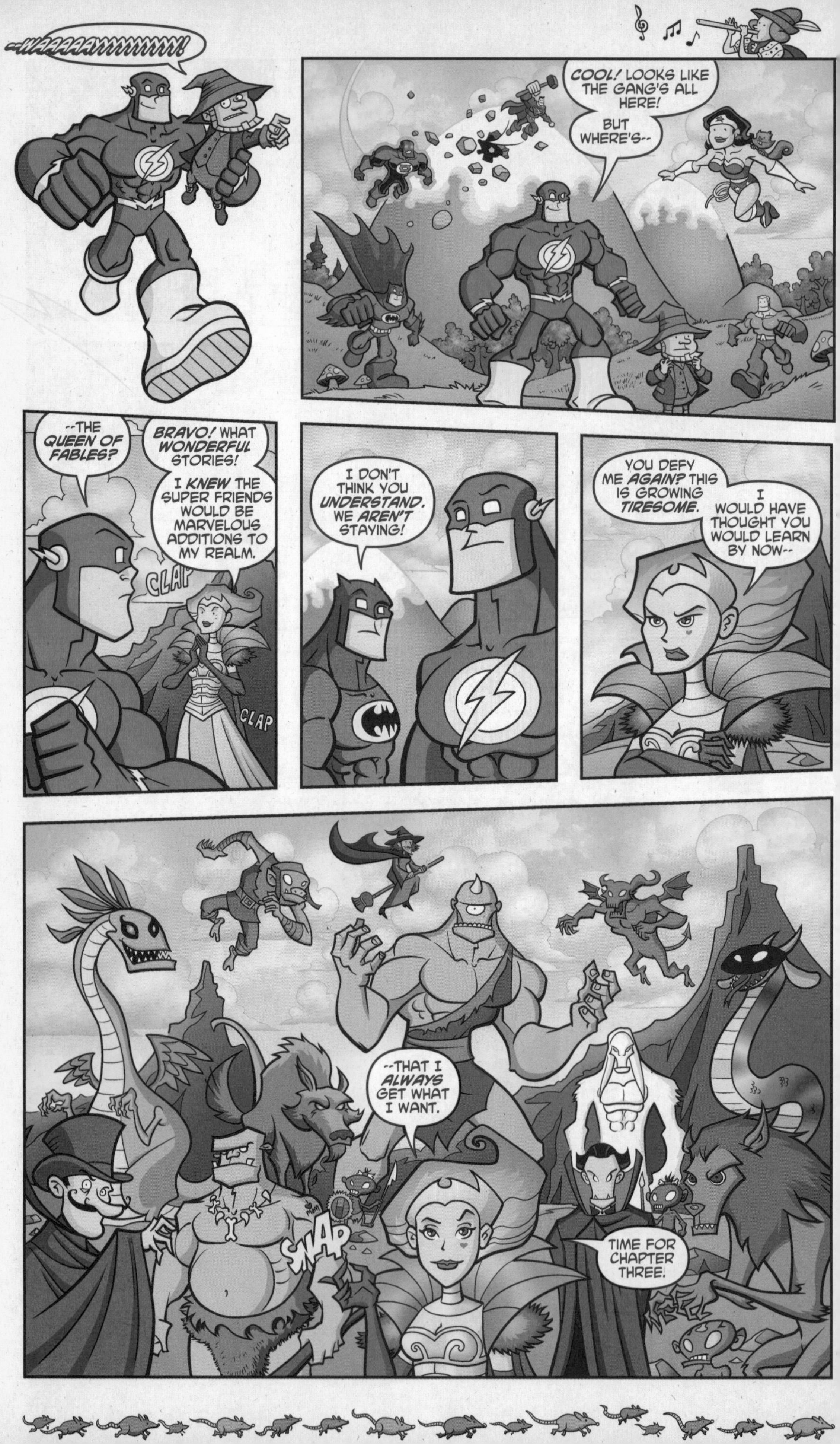
--WAAAAAYYYYYYYYY!
COOL! LOOKS LIKE THE GANG'S ALL HERE!
BUT WHERE'S--
--THE QUEEN OF FABLES?
BRAVO! WHAT WONDERFUL STORIES!
I KNEW THE SUPER FRIENDS WOULD BE MARVELOUS ADDITIONS TO MY REALM.
CLAP
CLAP
I DON'T THINK YOU UNDERSTAND. WE AREN'T STAYING!
YOU DEFY ME AGAIN? THIS IS GROWING TIRESOME.
I WOULD HAVE THOUGHT YOU WOULD LEARN BY NOW--
--THAT I ALWAYS GET WHAT I WANT.
SNAP
TIME FOR CHAPTER THREE.

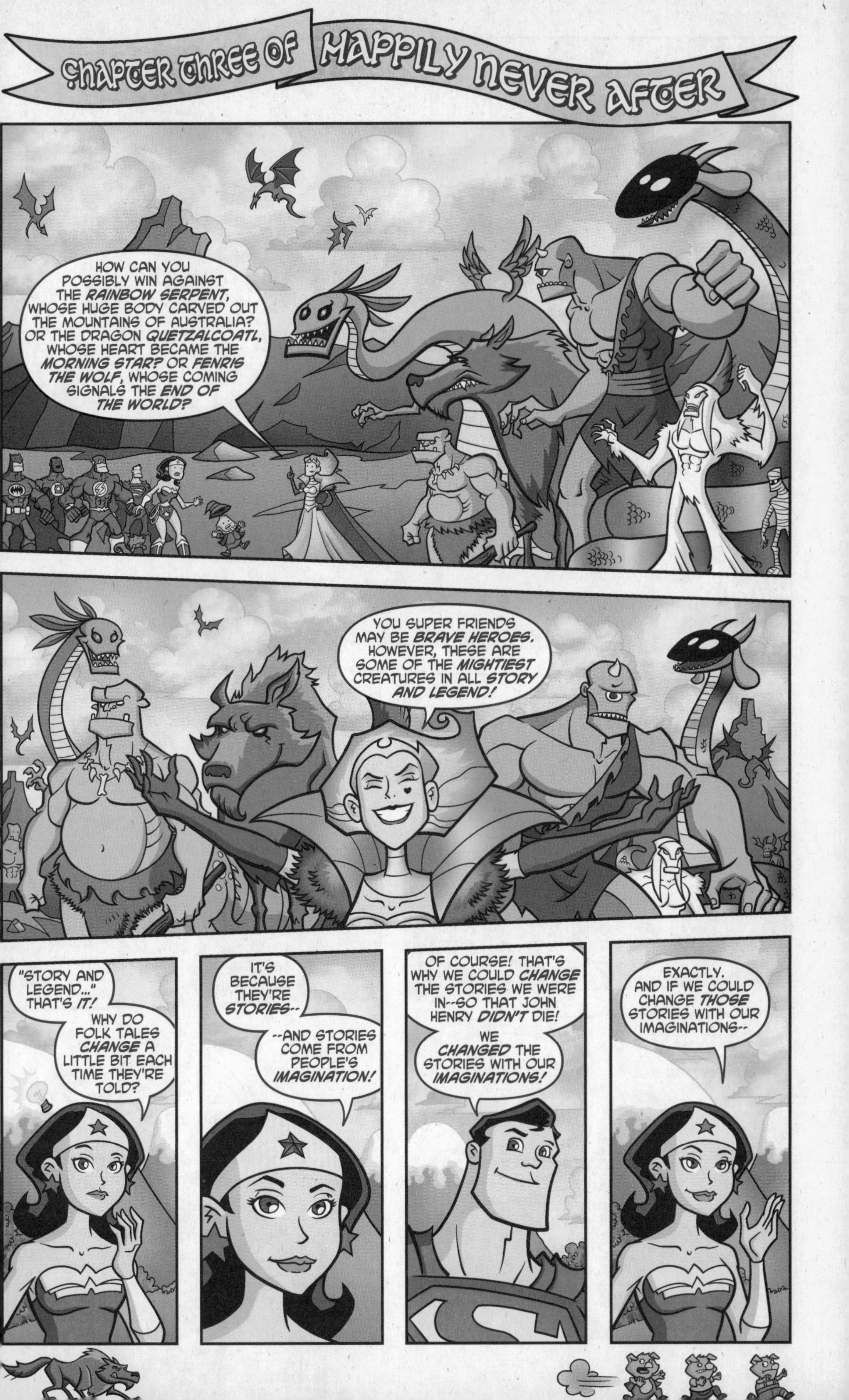
CHAPTER THREE OF HAPPILY NEVER AFTER
HOW CAN YOU POSSIBLY WIN AGAINST THE RAINBOW SERPENT, WHOSE HUGE BODY CARVED OUT THE MOUNTAINS OF AUSTRALIA? OR THE DRAGON QUETZALCOATL, WHOSE HEART BECAME THE MORNING STAR? OR FENRIS THE WOLF, WHOSE COMING SIGNALS THE END OF THE WORLD?
YOU SUPER FRIENDS MAY BE BRAVE HEROES. HOWEVER, THESE ARE SOME OF THE MIGHTIEST CREATURES IN ALL STORY AND LEGEND!
"STORY AND LEGEND..." THAT'S IT!
WHY DO FOLK TALES CHANGE A LITTLE BIT EACH TIME THEY'RE TOLD?
IT'S BECAUSE THEY'RE STORIES--
--AND STORIES COME FROM PEOPLE'S IMAGINATION!
OF COURSE! THAT'S WHY WE COULD CHANGE THE STORIES WE WERE IN--SO THAT JOHN HENRY DIDN'T DIE!
WE CHANGED THE STORIES WITH OUR IMAGINATIONS!
EXACTLY. AND IF WE COULD CHANGE THOSE STORIES WITH OUR IMAGINATIONS--

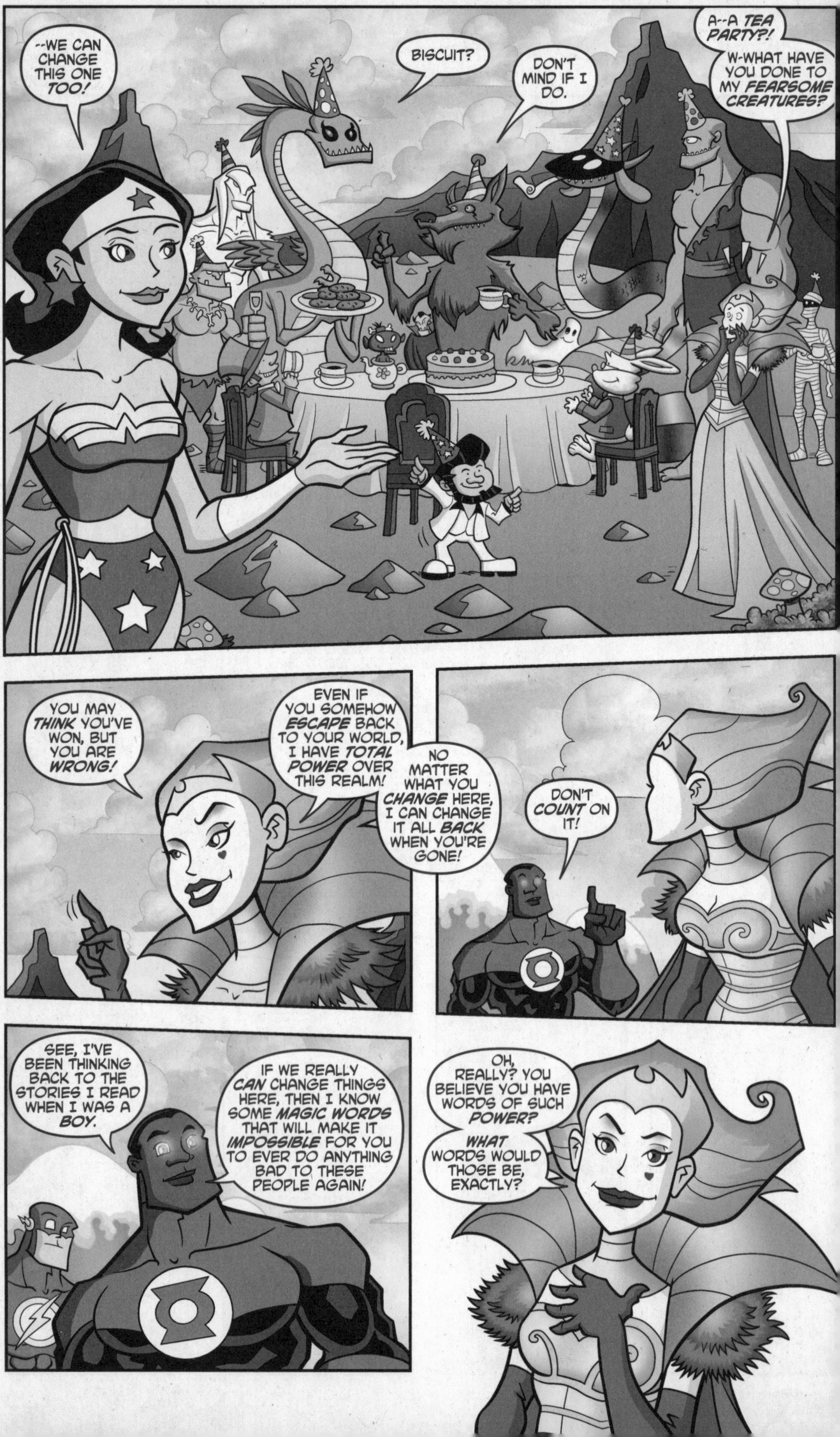
--WE CAN CHANGE THIS ONE TOO!
BISCUIT?
DON'T MIND IF I DO.
A--A TEA PARTY?!
W-WHAT HAVE YOU DONE TO MY FEARSOME CREATURES?
YOU MAY THINK YOU'VE WON, BUT YOU ARE WRONG!
EVEN IF YOU SOMEHOW ESCAPE BACK TO YOUR WORLD, I HAVE TOTAL POWER OVER THIS REALM!
NO MATTER WHAT YOU CHANGE HERE, I CAN CHANGE IT ALL BACK WHEN YOU'RE GONE!
DON'T COUNT ON IT!
SEE, I'VE BEEN THINKING BACK TO THE STORIES I READ WHEN I WAS A BOY.
IF WE REALLY CAN CHANGE THINGS HERE, THEN I KNOW SOME MAGIC WORDS THAT WILL MAKE IT IMPOSSIBLE FOR YOU TO EVER DO ANYTHING BAD TO THESE PEOPLE AGAIN!
OH, REALLY? YOU BELIEVE YOU HAVE WORDS OF SUCH POWER?
WHAT WORDS WOULD THOSE BE, EXACTLY?

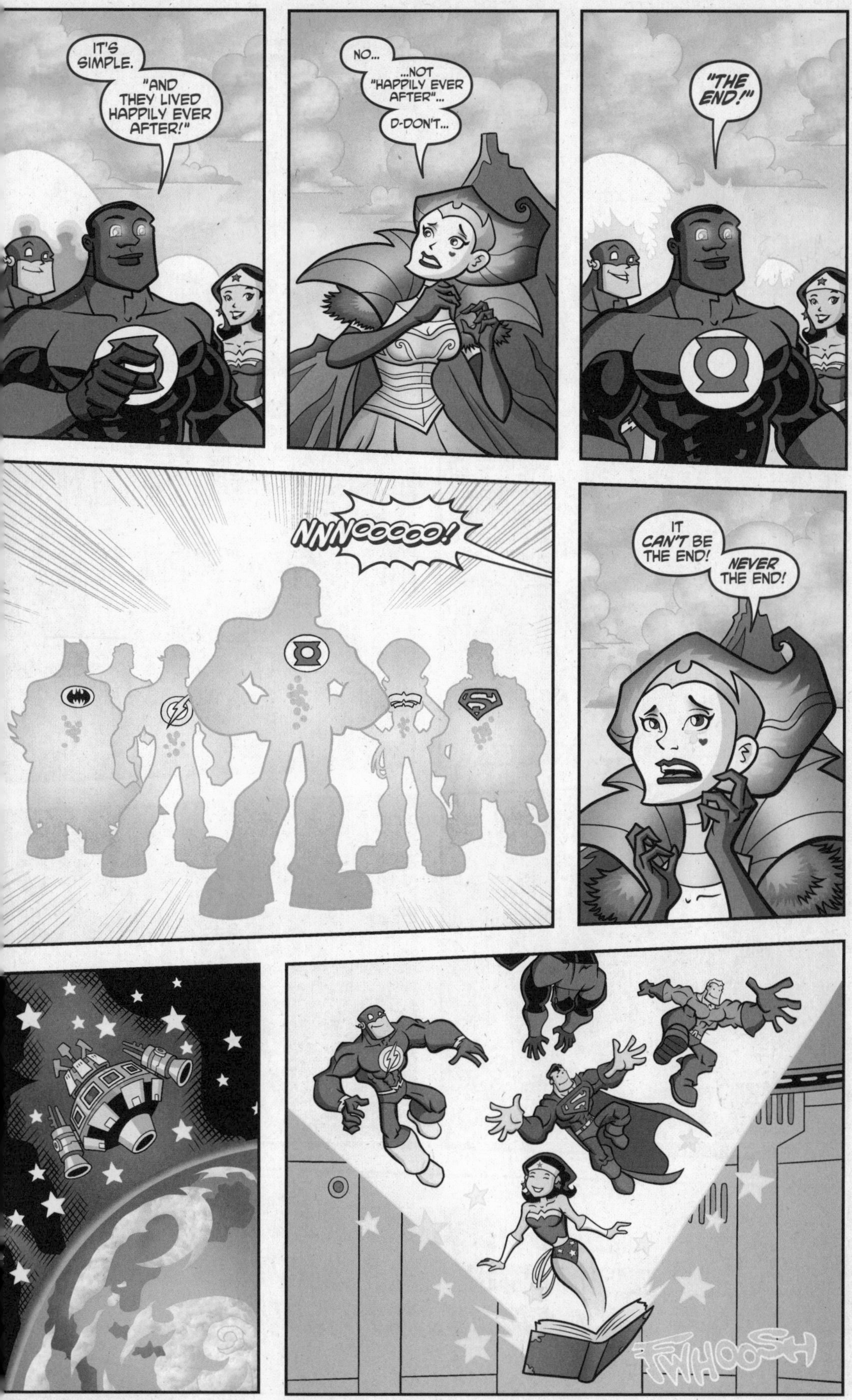
IT'S SIMPLE.
"AND THEY LIVED HAPPILY EVER AFTER!"
NO...
...NOT "HAPPILY EVER AFTER"...
D-DON'T...
"THE END!"
NNNOOOOOO!
IT CAN'T BE THE END!
NEVER THE END!
FWHOOSH

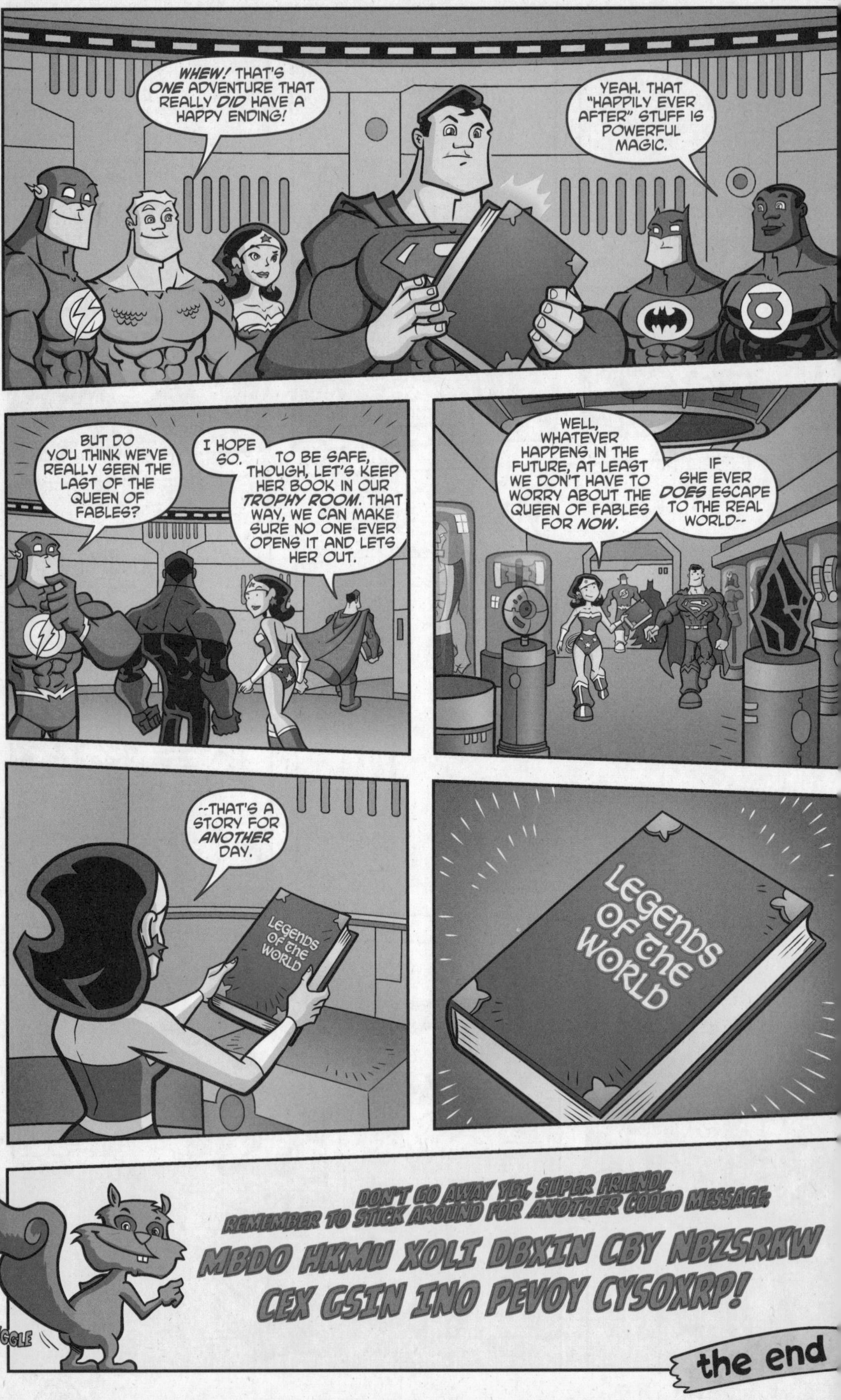
WHEW! THAT'S ONE ADVENTURE THAT REALLY DID HAVE A HAPPY ENDING!
YEAH. THAT "HAPPILY EVER AFTER" STUFF IS POWERFUL MAGIC.
BUT DO YOU THINK WE'VE REALLY SEEN THE LAST OF THE QUEEN OF FABLES?
I HOPE SO.
TO BE SAFE, THOUGH, LET'S KEEP HER BOOK IN OUR TROPHY ROOM. THAT WAY, WE CAN MAKE SURE NO ONE EVER OPENS IT AND LETS HER OUT.
WELL, WHATEVER HAPPENS IN THE FUTURE, AT LEAST WE DON'T HAVE TO WORRY ABOUT THE QUEEN OF FABLES FOR NOW.
IF SHE EVER DOES ESCAPE TO THE REAL WORLD--
--THAT'S A STORY FOR ANOTHER DAY.
LEGENDS OF THE WORLD
LEGENDS OF THE WORLD
DON'T GO AWAY YET, SUPER FRIEND!
REMEMBER TO STICK AROUND FOR ANOTHER CODED MESSAGE:
MBDO HKMU XOLI DBXIN CBY NBZSRKW
CEX GSIN INO PEVOY CYSOXRP!
WIGGLE
the end

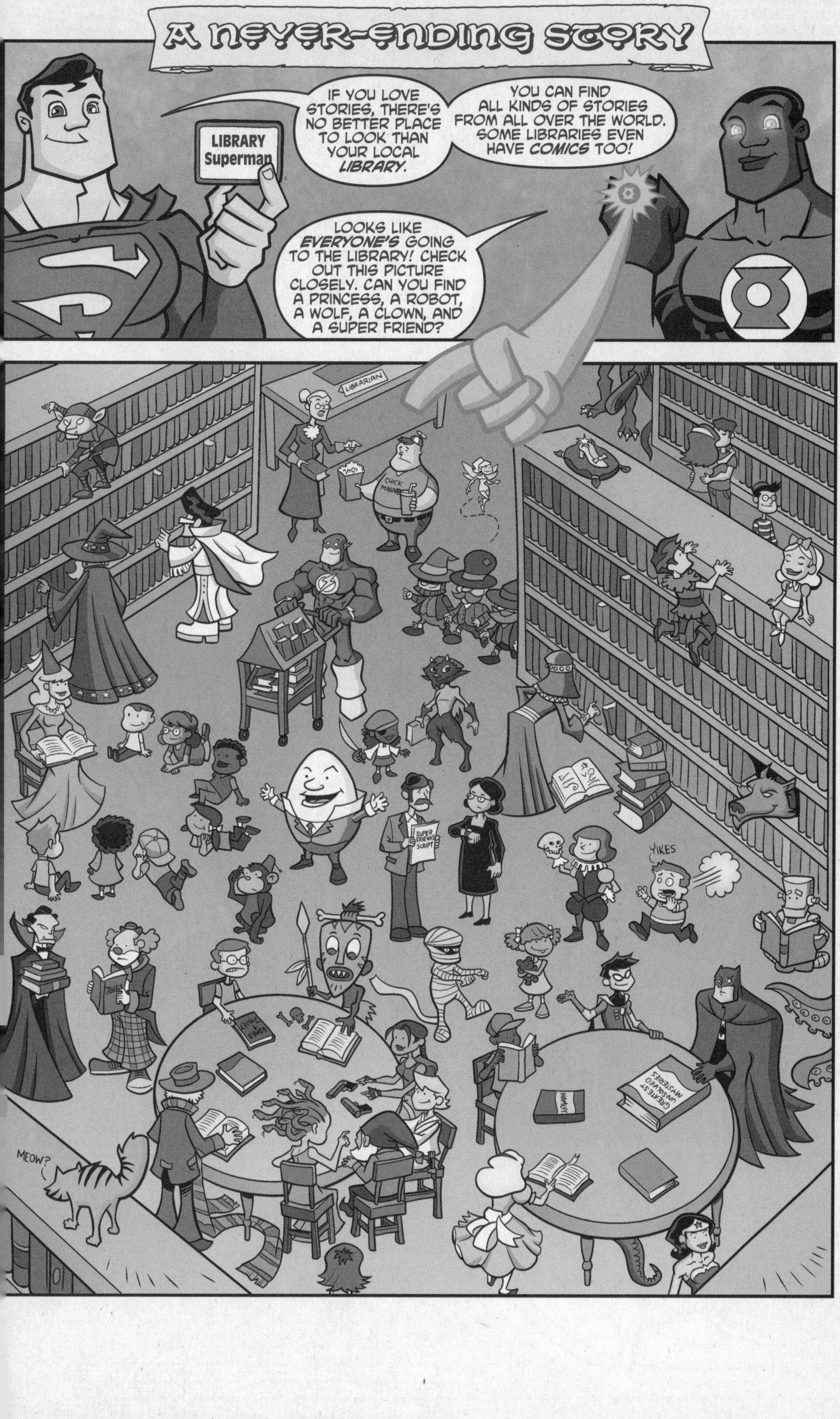
A NEVER-ENDING STORY
IF YOU LOVE STORIES, THERE'S NO BETTER PLACE TO LOOK THAN YOUR LOCAL LIBRARY.
LIBRARY Superman
YOU CAN FIND ALL KINDS OF STORIES FROM ALL OVER THE WORLD. SOME LIBRARIES EVEN HAVE COMICS TOO!
LOOKS LIKE EVERYONE'S GOING TO THE LIBRARY! CHECK OUT THIS PICTURE CLOSELY. CAN YOU FIND A PRINCESS, A ROBOT, A WOLF, A CLOWN, AND A SUPER FRIEND?
LIBRARIAN
SUPER FRIENDS SCRIPT
YIKES
JOKES
HAMLET
GREATEST UNSOLVED MYSTERIES
MEOW?

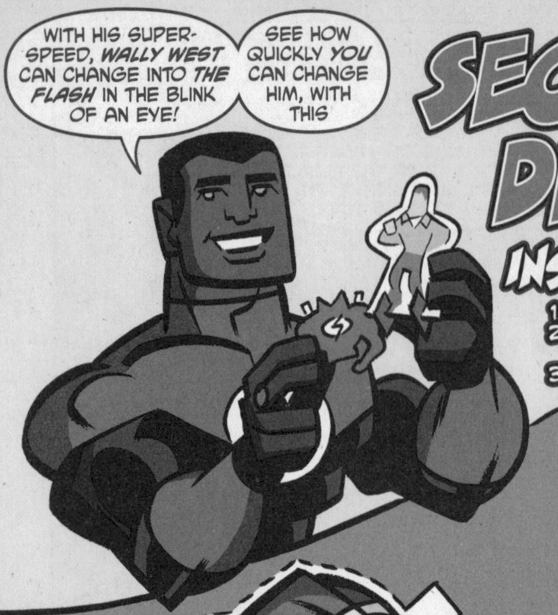
WITH HIS SUPER-SPEED, *WALLY WEST* CAN CHANGE INTO *THE FLASH* IN THE BLINK OF AN EYE!
SEE HOW QUICKLY *YOU* CAN CHANGE HIM, WITH THIS

# SECRET IDENTITY DRESS-UP KIT

## INSTRUCTIONS:

1. CUT OUT FIGURE AND STAND.
2. PASTE THE FIGURE AND STAND ONTO CARDBOARD. TRIM THE CARDBOARD TO FIT.
3. CUT THE DOTTED SLOTS IN THE BOTTOM OF THE FIGURE AND THE BASE. SLIDE ONE SLOT INTO THE OTHER, TO ATTACH THE FIGURE TO THE BASE.

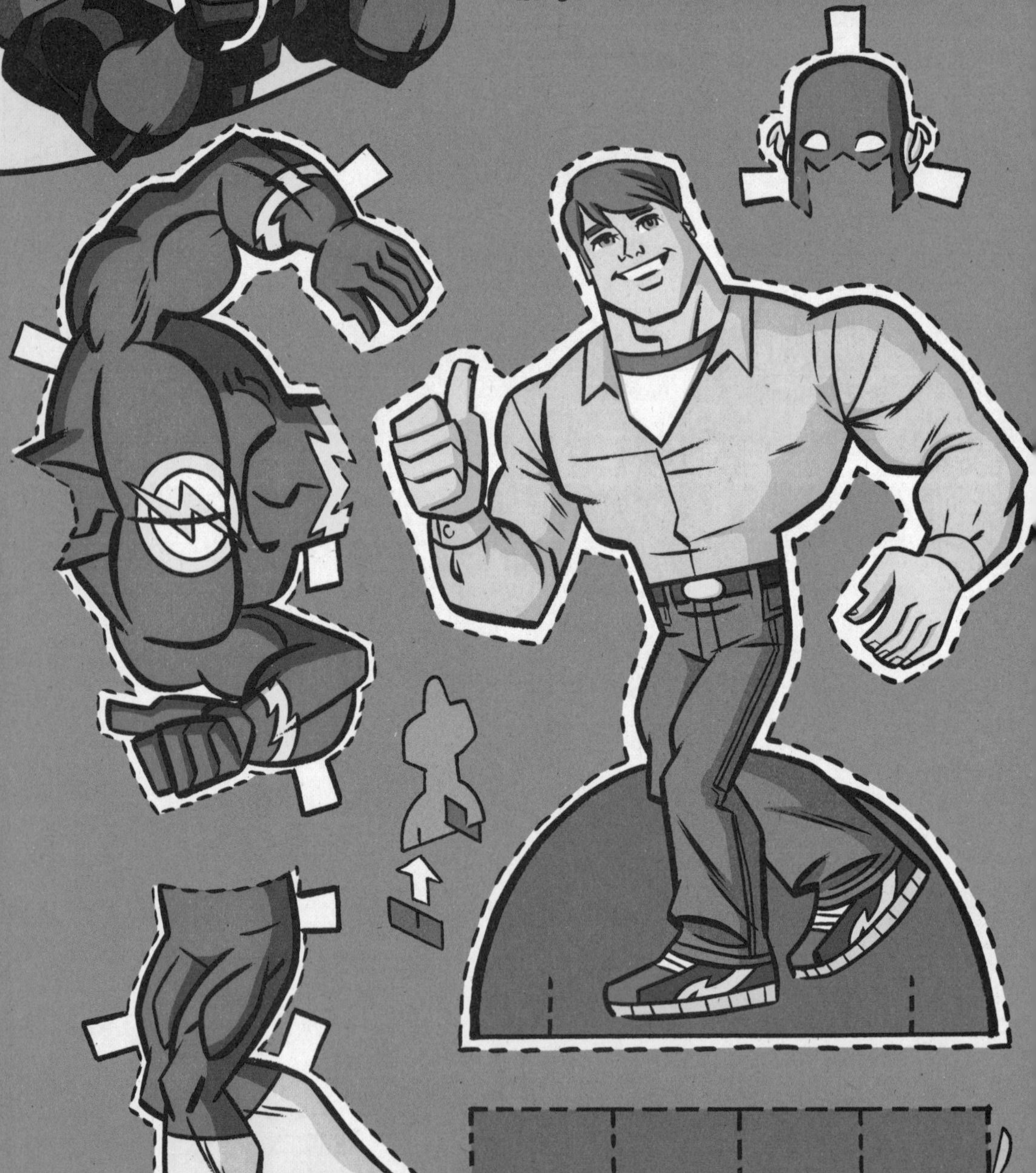

4. CUT OUT THE PIECES OF CLOTHING. KEEP THE TABS ATTACHED TO THE CLOTHES.
5. FOLD OVER THE TABS ON THE CLOTHES. USE THEM TO ATTACH THE PIECES TO THE FIGURE.
6. GET READY TO RUN!

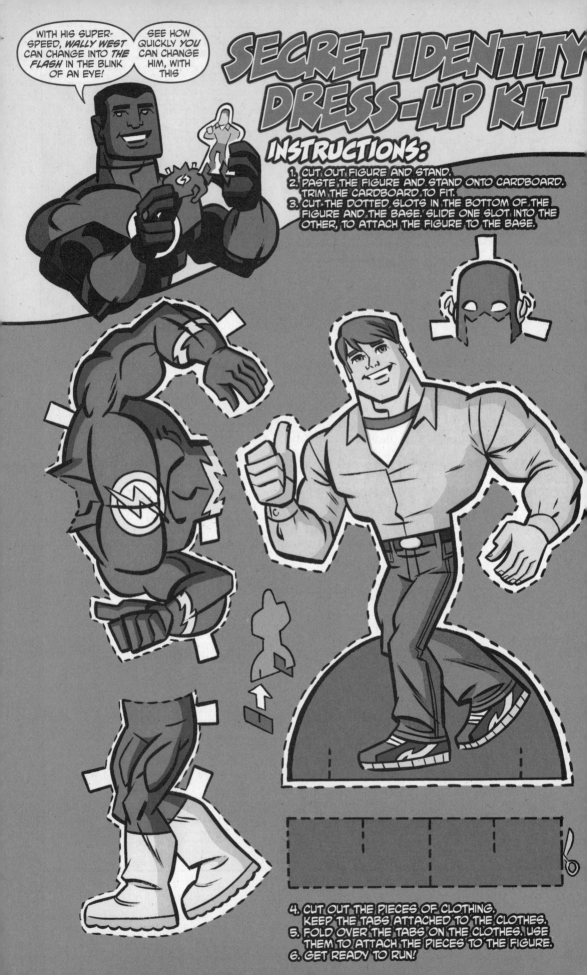

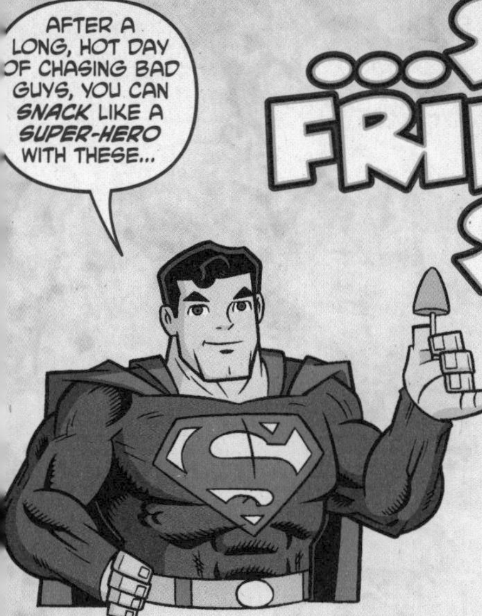
AFTER A LONG, HOT DAY OF CHASING BAD GUYS, YOU CAN SNACK LIKE A SUPER-HERO WITH THESE...

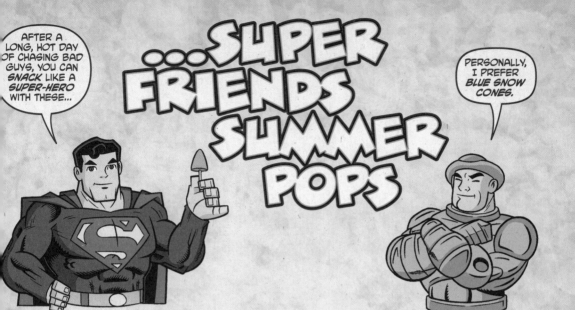

# ...SUPER FRIENDS SUMMER POPS

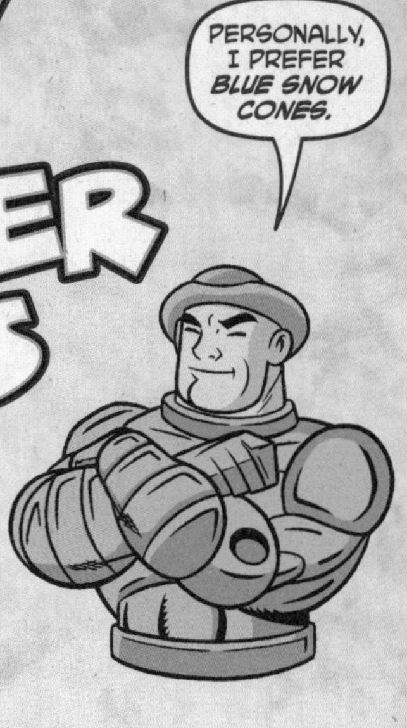
PERSONALLY, I PREFER BLUE SNOW CONES.

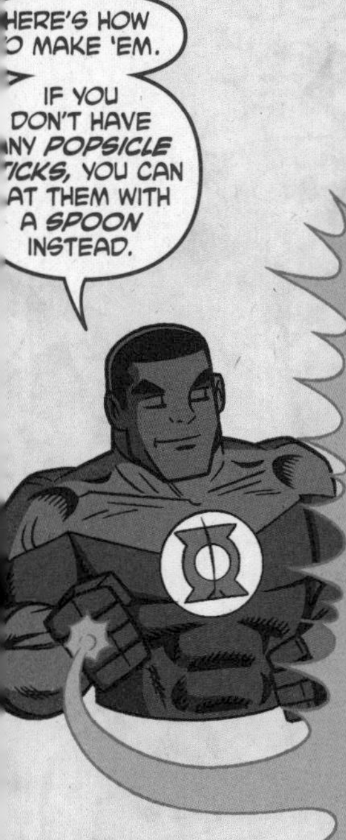
HERE'S HOW
O MAKE 'EM.
IF YOU DON'T HAVE
NY POPSICLE
ICKS, YOU CAN
AT THEM WITH
A SPOON INSTEAD.

**INGREDIENTS:**

- 1 EIGHT-OUNCE CONTAINER OF PLAIN YOGURT
- 3 TABLESPOONS OF YOUR FAVORITE JAM
- 2 PAPER CUPS
- 2 WOODEN POPSICLE STICKS

**WHAT TO DO:**

1.) MIX THE YOGURT AND JAM TOGETHER IN A BOWL.
2.) POUR THE MIXTURE INTO THE TWO CUPS.
3.) PLACE ONE STICK IN THE MIDDLE OF EACH CUP.
4.) LEAVE THE CUPS IN THE FREEZER OVERNIGHT.
5.) WHEN THE POPS ARE FROZEN, TEAR OFF THE PAPER CUPS AND ENJOY!

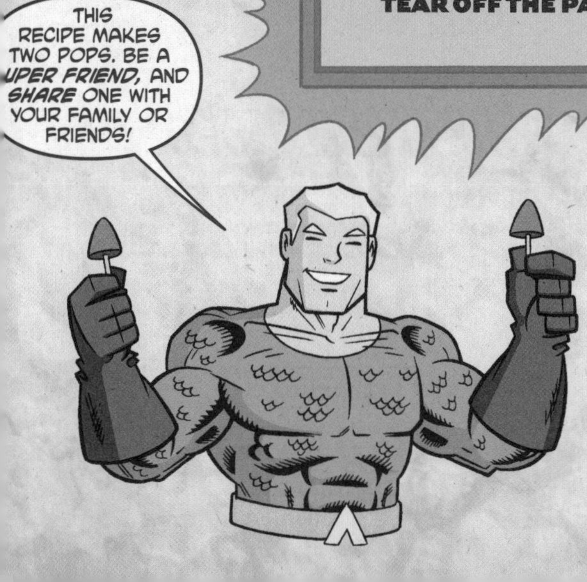
THIS RECIPE MAKES TWO POPS. BE A
UPER FRIEND, AND SHARE ONE WITH YOUR FAMILY OR FRIENDS!

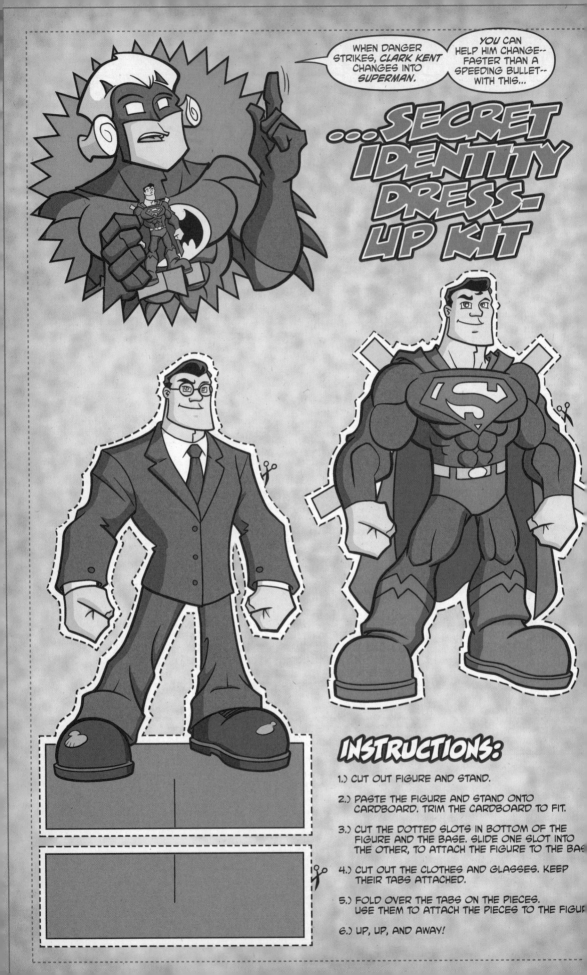

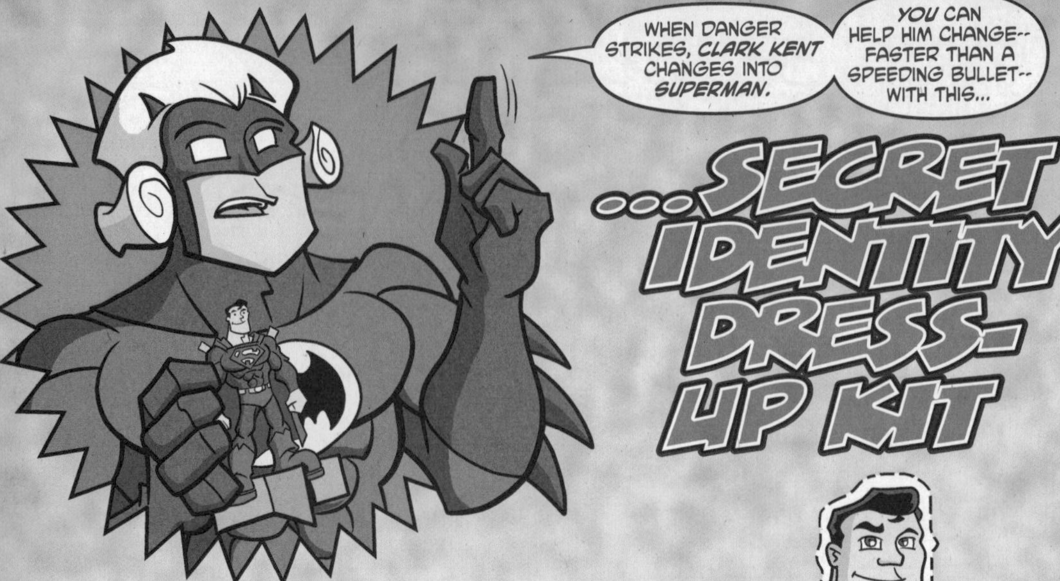
WHEN DANGER STRIKES, *CLARK KENT* CHANGES INTO *SUPERMAN.*
*YOU* CAN HELP HIM CHANGE-- FASTER THAN A SPEEDING BULLET-- WITH THIS...

# ...SECRET IDENTITY DRESS-UP KIT

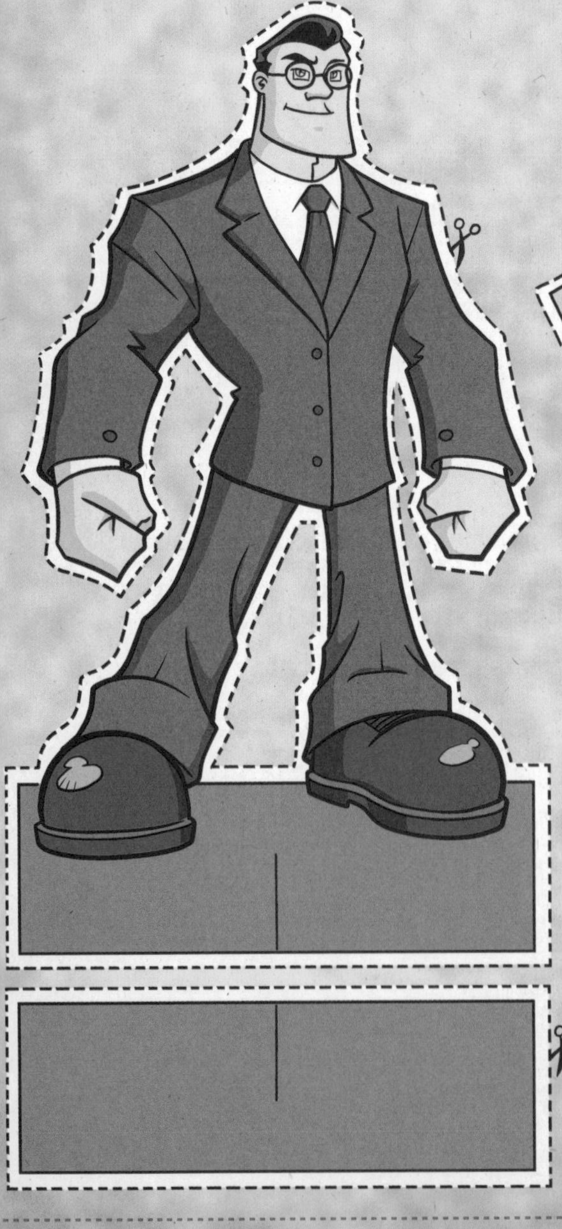

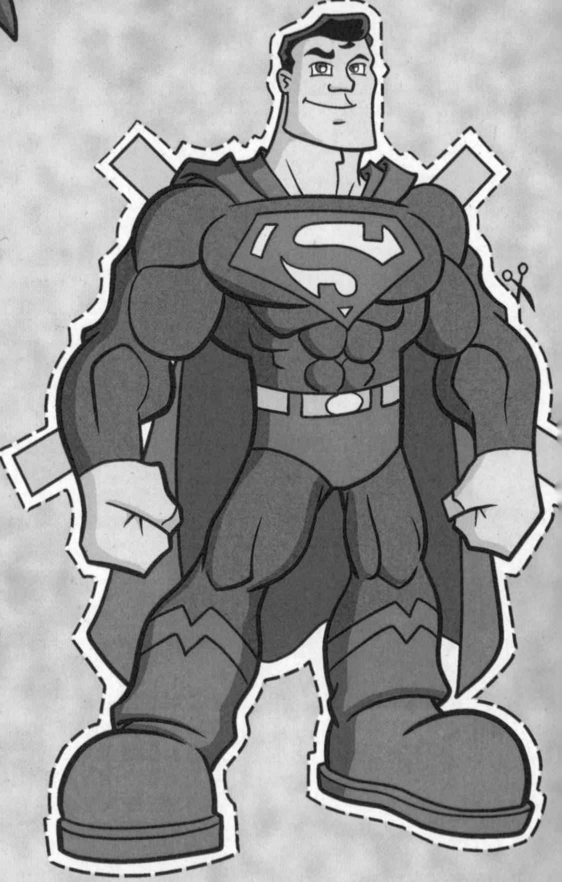

## INSTRUCTIONS:

1.) CUT OUT FIGURE AND STAND.

2.) PASTE THE FIGURE AND STAND ONTO CARDBOARD. TRIM THE CARDBOARD TO FIT.

3.) CUT THE DOTTED SLOTS IN BOTTOM OF THE FIGURE AND THE BASE. SLIDE ONE SLOT INTO THE OTHER, TO ATTACH THE FIGURE TO THE BAS

4.) CUT OUT THE CLOTHES AND GLASSES. KEEP THEIR TABS ATTACHED.

5.) FOLD OVER THE TABS ON THE PIECES. USE THEM TO ATTACH THE PIECES TO THE FIGUR

6.) UP, UP, AND AWAY!

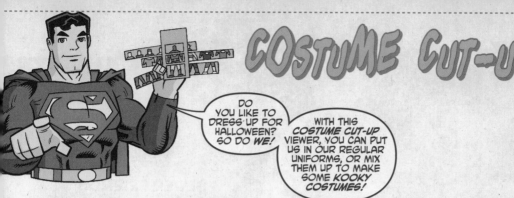

# COSTUME CUT-UPS

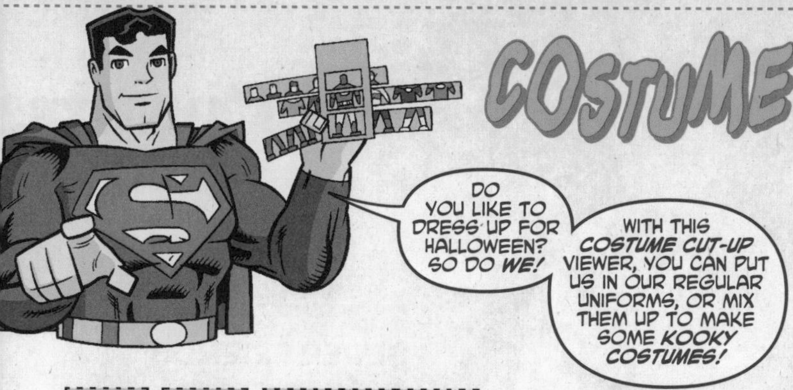
DO YOU LIKE TO DRESS UP FOR HALLOWEEN? SO DO *WE!*
WITH THIS *COSTUME CUT-UP* VIEWER, YOU CAN PUT US IN OUR REGULAR UNIFORMS, OR MIX THEM UP TO MAKE SOME *KOOKY COSTUMES!*

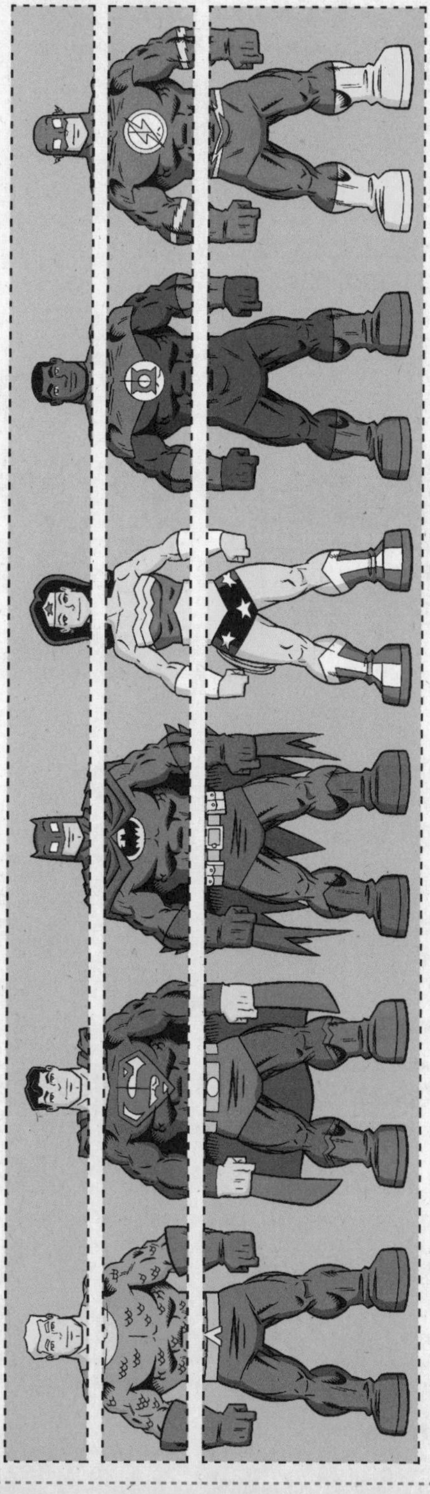

INSTRUCTIONS:

1. CUT OUT THE VIEWER AND THREE STRIPS.

2. CUT THE DOTTED LINES IN THE VIEWER TO MAKE SIX SLOTS.

3. SLIP THE STRIPS THROUGH THE SLOTS, JUST LIKE SUPERMAN'S VIEWER.

4. SLIDE THE STRIPS BACK AND FORTH TO MAKE YOUR OWN MIX-AND-MATCH SUPER FRIENDS!

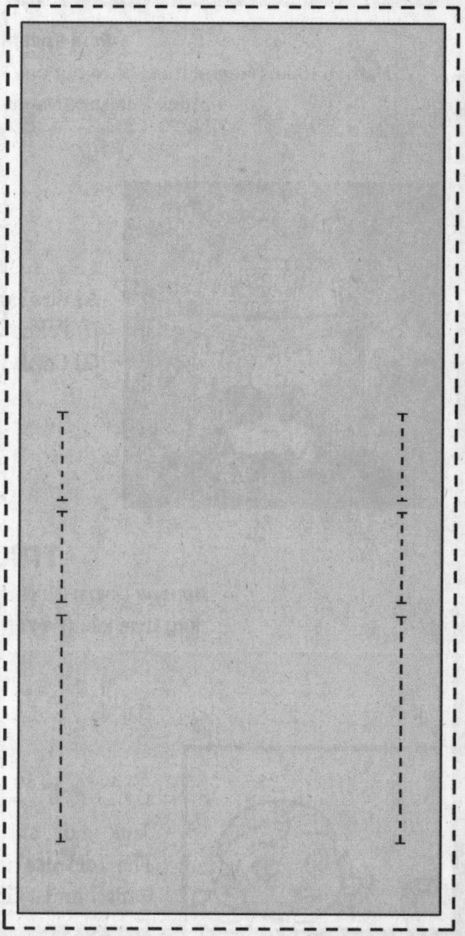

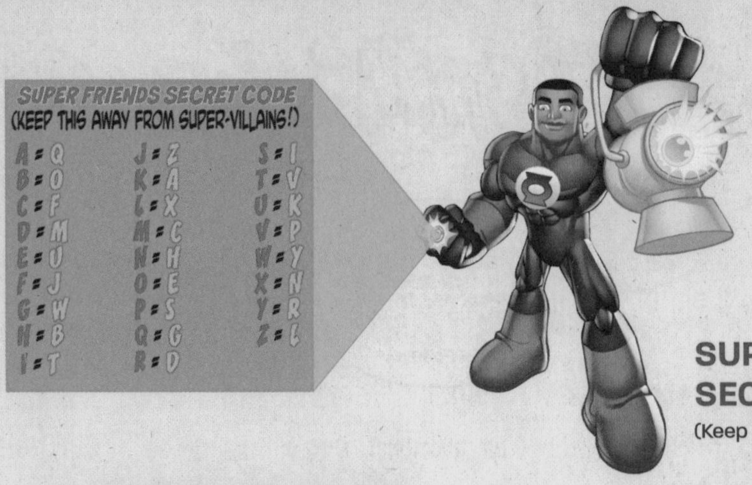
SUPER FRIENDS SECRET CODE
(KEEP THIS AWAY FROM SUPER-VILLAINS!)
A = Q
B = O
C = F
D = M
E = U
F = J
G = W
H = B
I = T
J = Z
K = A
L = X
M = C
N = H
O = E
P = S
Q = G
R = D
S = I
T = V
U = K
V = P
W = Y
X = N
Y = R
Z = L

# THE ANSWERS PAGE!

## SUPER FRIENDS SECRET CODE

(Keep this away from super-villains!)

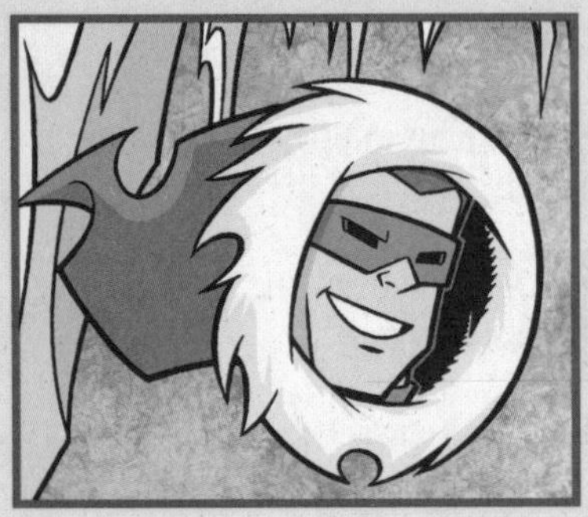

## CAPTAIN COLD'S CHILLY CHALLENGE (page 29)

Answers: TWICE, POLICE, RICE, NIECE, NICELY

Answer to riddle: "FROZEN CORN-Y"

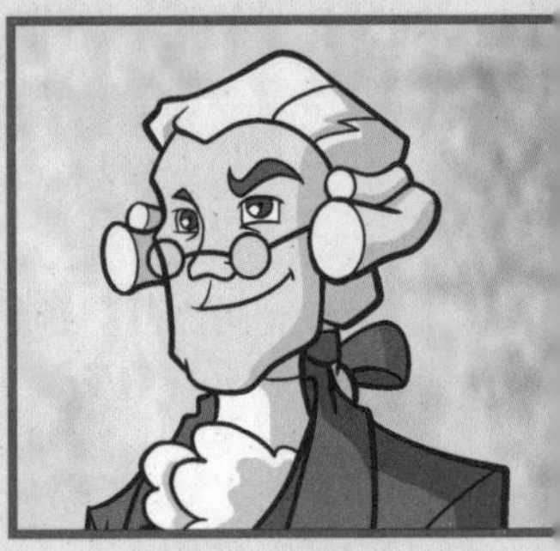

## WHAT DID HE SAY? (page 48)

**Paul Revere:** "The BRITISH are coming"

**Nathan Hale:** "I regret that I have but one LIFE to give for my country"

**Patrick Henry:** "Give me liberty, or give me DEATH!"

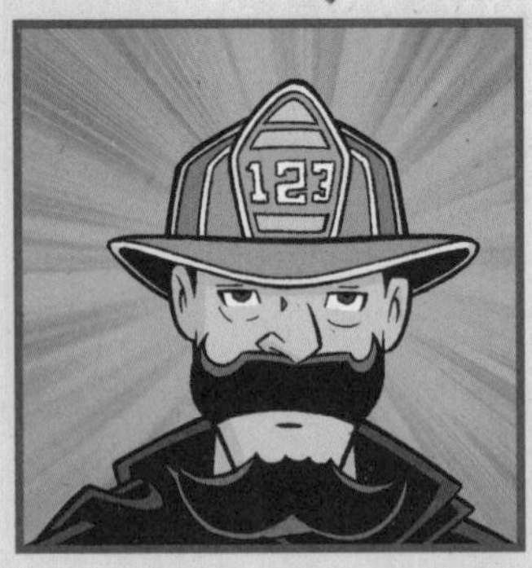
123

## HATS OFF! (page 87)

A) Firefighter B) Doctor C) Astronaut
D) Police Officer E) Chef F) Football Player
G) Cowboy H) Wonder Woman

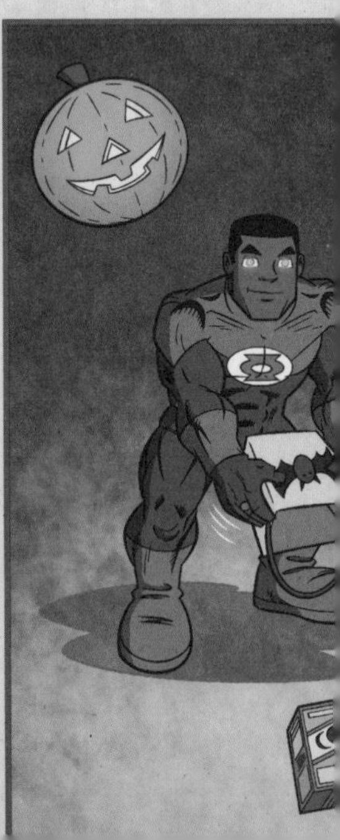

## TRICK OR TREAT (page 108)

**Banana** Chips: Gorilla Grodd **Instant** Cocoa: Chronos
**Key** Lime Pie: The Key **Ice** Cream Cone: Captain Cold
**Light** Snack: Doctor Light

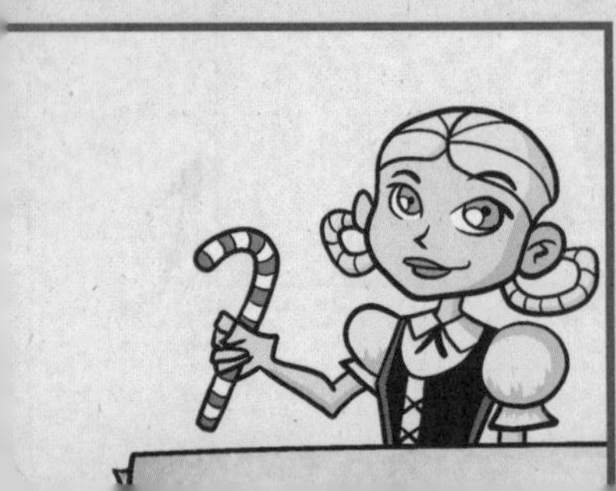

## STORYBOOK SCRAMBLE (page 127)

Jack and... the Beanstalk
The Tortoise and... the Hare
Hansel and... Gretel
The Fox and... the Crow
The Ant and... the Grasshopper